DJ

CW01021826

Advance praise for *The Handbook of Credit Portfolio Management*

"On the heels of the recent subprime mortgage crisis in the U.S. and the resulting credit market fallout, this book represents a timely response to groundswell concerns about the valuation models of credit-sensitive investments. A superb exposition of practical models for any credit risk manager!"

—**Andreas A. Jobst,** International Monetary Fund (IMF)

"In a context of greater uncertainty regarding the relevance of the practices of credit risk measurement and management, this Handbook greatly contributes to our understanding of the real place of credit risky securities in the portfolio allocation and the risk management processes."

—**Georges Hübner, PhD,** HEC-University of Liège, Maastricht University, and The Luxembourg School of Finance

"Handbook of Credit Portfolio Management addresses the critical issues faced by professionals in today's challenging investment world. It not only reviews mainstream topics such as managing credit portfolio risk and exposure, but also addresses the more exotic credit risks embedded in default swaps and collateralized debt obligations. Of particular interest is the focus on credit trading strategies covering arbitrage, synthetic replication, and other hedge fund applications."

—**R. McFall Lamm Jr., PhD,** Chief Investment Strategist, Global Investment Management, Deutsche Bank, London

"An important compendium for all of us who spend our days thinking about debt and issues of financial distress. This handy volume covers the full range of issues that both academics and practitioners face on a daily basis and will surely be a frequent reference."

—**Stephen J. Lubben**, Daniel J. Moore Professor of Law, Seton Hall University School of Law

"The discovery of credit derivatives is a milestone in the history of the financial markets, similar to the arrival of the interest rate swap in the early 1980s. Today credit derivatives have surpassed the bond markets in volume, and even in volatile markets, their importance continues to grow. Gregoriou and Hoppe are commended for bringing together experts from various disciplines in this book. The handbook of credit portfolio management is an indispensable tool for financial markets practitioners."

—**Jan Job de Vries Robbé,** Senior Counsel Structured Finance, Netherlands Development Finance Company

"Risk Management is the most important challenge in banking in times driven by market turbulences and uncertainness. Due to this fact measuring the inherent risk and optimizing the portfolio has to become a key competence of successful market players."

—**Wolfgang Hartmann,** Member of the Board of Managing Directors and Chief Risk Officer, Commerzbank, AG

THE HANDBOOK OF CREDIT PORTFOLIO MANAGEMENT

THE HANDBOOK OF CREDIT PORTFOLIO MANAGEMENT

GREG N. GREGORIOU
CHRISTIAN HOPPE

EDITORS

New York   Chicago   San Francisco
Lisbon   London   Madrid   Mexico City
Milan   New Delhi   San Juan   Seoul
Singapore   Sydney   Toronto

Copyright © 2009 by The McGraw-Hill Companies, Inc. All rights reserved.
Printed in the United States of America. Except as permitted under the United States Copyright Act
of 1976, no part of this publication may be reproduced or distributed in any form or by any means, or
stored in a database or retrieval system, without the prior written permission of the publisher.

1 2 3 4 5 6 7 8 9 0   DOC/DOC   0 9 8

ISBN: 978-0-07159-834-7
MHID: 0-07159-834-0

This publication is designed to provide accurate and authoritative information in regard to the subject
matter covered. It is sold with the understanding that neither the author nor the publisher is engaged in
rendering legal, accounting, futures/securities trading, or other professional service. If legal advice or
other expert assistance is required, the services of a competent professional person should be sought.

—From a Declaration of Principles jointly adopted by a Committee
of the American Bar Association and a Committee of Publishers

Neither the editors nor the publisher can guarantee the accuracy of individual chapters. All authors are
responsible for their own written material.

McGraw-Hill books are available at special quantity discounts to use as premiums and sales promo-
tions, or for use in corporate training programs. For more information, please write to the Director of
Special Sales, Professional Publishing, McGraw-Hill, Two Penn Plaza, New York, NY 10121–2298.
Or contact your local bookstore.

This book is printed on acid-free paper.

Library of Congress Cataloging-in-Publication Data

Gregoriou, Greg N., 1956-
The handbook of credit portfolio management / by Greg N. Gregoriou and Christian Hoppe.
    p. cm.
 ISBN-13: 978-0-07-159834-7
 ISBN-10: 0-07-159834-0
  1. Credit—Management—Handbooks, manuals, etc. 2. Risk management—Handbooks, manuals,
etc. 3. Portfolio management—Handbooks, manuals, etc. I. Hoppe, Christian. II. Title.

HG3751.G74 2009

332.7—dc22   2008018182

C O N T E N T S

Chapter 4

Basel II Expected Loss as a Control Parameter   67

Bernd Appasamy and Uwe Dörr

Chapter 5

Credit Risk Capital Allocation and Performance Measurement in Banking Institutions   79

Valerio Potì

PART TWO

EVALUATION OF CREDIT RISK

Chapter 6

Characteristics of Credit Assets and Their Relevance for Credit Asset Management   99

Stephan Bucher and Jochen von Frowein

Chapter 13

What Drives the Arrangement Timetable of Bank Loan Syndication?   223

Christophe J. Godlewski

Chapter 14

Credit Default Swap and Other Credit Derivatives: Valuation and Application   247

Ralph Karels

Chapter 15

Loan-Only Credit Default Swaps   271

Moorad Choudhry

In times such as these, when credit markets are experiencing unprecedented volatility and a turn in the credit cycle seems imminent, credit portfolio managers across the world are exceptionally challenged. Steering clear of large-scale credit losses is an ingenious art; a skill that is literally dividing the banking industry to "winners" and "losers," creating a new ranking order of profitability and competitive position in the sector. Banks always faced the risk of losing substantial amounts of capital due to default risk; what is new is that some banks run colossal losses stemming from devaluation of their secondary markets credit investments, whereas others record vast mark-to-market (MTM) profits generated by their sizable hedge books.

The development of alternative credit products in recent years instigated a rising number of credit exposures in various industries and regions. The Credit Markets brought up a variety of structured solutions, which leaves almost no gaps for end users to be able to create their own custom made investment and hedging strategy. Most transactions are driven by diversification and concentration motives as made transparent by quantitative credit models. This new climate offers greater liquidity but also introduces added complexities and risks.

Now portfolio managers (and other banking officials) have to work even harder at firstly understanding all aspects of the credit assets, both those originated in the primary market and those purchased or sold on the secondary market. Secondly, portfolio managers have to be very clear about economic, accounting and regulatory implications resulting from their originated credit asset and when buying protection for their underlying instrument. Finally, it is vital all portfolio effects of combinations of origination, investments and hedges in single-name assets and pool transactions are fully recognized.

The Handbook of Credit Portfolio Management will help portfolio managers around the world to master this challenge. The book endeavors to give honest guidance for portfolio managers actively running a wide range of asset classes. Its focus on credit assets also reflects the fact that most credit portfolio management (CPM) functions have now been established, and going forward, the main attention of CPM is transaction driven. The book provides an extensive collection of articles drafted by practitioners and academics engaged in this topic.

However, the handbook is not just intended for credit portfolio managers. It is also a recommended read for senior management and risk managers in financial institutions so as to master the crises the industry has seen since July 2007. Further, and as the convergence between products and markets continues, the handbook will be similarly appreciated by relationship managers, hedge fund managers, and asset managers. It will also help finance officers and regulators to understand many of the aspects a CPM function can have, and as such *The Handbook of Credit Portfolio Management* could not come at a more appropriate time.

Portfolio management had almost 15 years to develop and establish itself as a profit-enhancing function. Credit portfolio management often fundamentally changed the way banks were run. One of its major achievements is the change in origination behavior due to new economic transparency introduced by modern quantitative methods and the tools helping to assess risk-adjusted client profitability. Basel II was kicked off by leading banks developing their own risk-adjusted measures and eventually the regulators followed suit. Building on these fundamentals it is now time to refine and integrate areas of negligence.

The book points out the issues around asymmetric accounting introduced in 2005 by U.S. GAAP and International Financial Reporting Standards (IFRS). Whereas the election to "fair value" the underlying loan is economically honorable, it throws up a variety of administrational and transactional difficulties that makes this option less attractive. Many institutions prefer the more flexible solution and "hedge the credit hedge," i.e., engage in offsetting derivative transactions with the intention of avoiding MTM volatility. As a result, CPM units enter proprietary trading desks and hedge fund territory. The integration of counterparty risk into CPM units is another area where the benefit can be significant due to the netting of long and short derivative positions, but it can become a minefield if this initiative is not carefully aligned with the strategy of the bank. The handbook evaluates some choices to be considered when fair valuing illiquid instruments and managing credit risk from trading activities. Further, the book also touches on points brought up in recent subprime crises such as the insufficient rating process for structured transactions and the inability to find appropriate marks to market for tranches of collateralized debt obligations. As such, *The Handbook of Credit Portfolio Management* can be seen as a current inventory of relevant topics in the credit arena.

Rainer Rettinger
Director
Global Corporate Banking—Portfolio Management
HSBC
London

EDITORS

Greg N. Gregoriou is Professor of Finance in the School of Business and Economics at State University of New York (Plattsburgh). He obtained his joint PhD (Finance) from the University of Quebec at Montreal, which pools its resources with Montreal's three other major universities (McGill, HEC, and Concordia). He is coeditor and editorial board member for the peer-reviewed scientific *Journal of Derivatives and Hedge Funds*. He is also an editorial board member for the *Journal of Wealth Management, Journal of Risk Management in Financial Institutions*, and *Brazilian Business Review*. He has authored over 50 articles on hedge funds, and managed futures in various U.S. and UK peer-reviewed publications, including the *Journal of Portfolio Management, Journal of Futures Markets, European Journal of Operational Research,* and *Annals of Operations Research*. He has published 26 books with John Wiley & Sons, Elsevier-Butterworth-Heinemann, McGraw-Hill, Palgrave-MacMillan, and Risk Books.

Christian Hoppe works as senior specialist for securitization and credit derivatives in credit portfolio management in the corporate banking of Commerzbank AG Frankfurt. His main focus is on structured credit transactions to actively manage the corporate credit portfolio. Prior to this, he was credit portfolio manager at Dresdner Kleinwort, the Investment Bank arm of Dresdner Bank AG in Frankfurt. He started his career as a Business and Financial Controller for Dresdner Bank in Frankfurt, responsible for the corporate client business in Germany. He completed his economics degree at the University of Essen-Duisburg in 2003. While writing his master's thesis, Christian worked in the Institutional Research Department of Benchmark Alternative Strategies GmbH in Frankfurt. Christian is the coauthor of several articles and books as well as the author of the German book *Derivate auf Alternative Investments—Konstruktion und Bewertungsmöglichkeiten,* published by Gabler.

CONTRIBUTORS

Bernd Appasamy is Managing Director of d-fine GmbH. At d-fine, he is responsible for the area of credit risk and for the expansion of d-fine's services in Asia and Pacific. Doctor Appasamy manages several projects in credit risk, credit portfolio models, Basel II compliance, economic capital, commercial real estate, shipping, and aviation. Apart from quantitative and strategic advisory projects in these areas, the development and application of pricing methods or bank operations is also of importance. Further projects examine the development of aggregation methods for different key risk figures as well as quantifying business or reputation risk.

Sabine Bank works as a project manager in the securitization department of KfW Bankengruppe. She is responsible for quantitative structuring and modeling of ABS transactions, especially small- and medium-sized enterprise (SME) collateralized debt obligations (CDOs) and commercial mortgage-backed securities (CMBS). Sabine Bank joined KfW Bankengruppe in March 2005 after graduating in economics from Rheinische Friedrich-Wilhelms-Universität, Bonn.

Antonella Basso is professor of Financial Mathematics and Mathematical Finance at the University Ca' Foscari of Venice and is currently Chairman of the Department of Applied Mathematics. She has a degree in economics and commerce and a PhD in mathematics applied to economic problems. She was visiting fellow at the University of Warwick and its Financial Options Research Centre, at the University of Toronto, and at the Imperial College of London. She is also a member of the faculty of the Consorzio MIB—School of Management of Trieste, in the finance area. Her main areas of expertise include financial mathematics, mathematical finance, and operations research. In particular, her research activities concern mainly the following subjects: models for the credit risk for portfolios of bank loans, theory of financial options (option pricing bounds, exotic options, computational methods for option pricing, lattice models, Monte

Carlo simulation, American-style options, discrete monitoring, and optimal exercise boundary), stochastic dominance and financial applications, evaluation criteria for the performance of mutual funds, and efficiency evaluation of decision-making units with data envelopment analysis.

Claas Becker works as a director for the Loan Exposure Management Group of Deutsche Bank AG in Frankfurt. He is responsible for the development and implementation of loan pricing methodology. Claas studied mathematics and physics at the University of Bochum and has a PhD in mathematics. Following a postdoctoral position at the Institute of Applied Mathematics in Bonn, he started his professional career in the Risk Controlling department of Commerzbank. Since 1998, he has been working for Deutsche Bank AG in the areas of credit risk modeling, loan pricing, and securitization.

Michael Blatz is a partner and head of the Corporate Performance Competence Centers of Roland Berger Strategy Consultants, Berlin. He is responsible for the industrywide development and implementation of restructuring concepts as well as for corporate finance transactions. Mr. Blatz holds a degree in engineering from the Technical University of Magdeburg and joined Roland Berger Strategy Consultants in 1990.

Stephan Bucher is a Client Relationship Manager at Dresdner Kleinwort, the Investment Bank arm of Dresdner Bank AG. He covers financial institutions on the Indian subcontinent. Prior to this, he was working in Global Markets business units of Dresdner Bank in Frankfurt, London, and Dubai. He then joined the Risk Management department where he held the position of a Senior Credit Analyst for Banks and Financial Institutions. Stephan graduated with a degree in economics at the Frankfurt School of Finance and Management.

Christian Burmester, PhD has been General Manager of the London Branch of Landesbank Berlin AG since 2004. The branch is an integral part of the capital markets business of the group, specializing in proprietary trading with and investment in structured products. Prior to this, he was based in Berlin, holding the position of Managing Director of Group Risk Control and Exposure Management for over four years. He was responsible for the successful design and implementation of a global credit risk reporting system covering the group's retail, property finance, and capital markets business. He also developed the internal Basel II compliant rating methodology. His banking career started in 1995 in the asset liability management and later in the risk control division. His PhD focused on risk issues and Monte Carlo simulation in agricultural economics.

Moorad Choudhry is Group Head of Treasury at Europe Arab Bank plc in London, and Visiting Professor at the Department of Economics, London Metropolitan University. He is author of *Structured Credit Products: Credit Derivatives and Synthetic Securitisation* (John Wiley 2004) and *Bank Asset and Liability Management* (John Wiley 2007). Moorad led the structuring team at KBC Financial Products that arranged Picaros Funding plc, the world's first synthetic ABCP conduit and winner of the *Euromoney* "Structured Finance Deal of the Year" award for 2005.

Uwe Dörr, PhD is Manager at d-fine GmbH. He currently works in the area of credit risk and manages several projects ranging from modeling of credit risk parameters to full Basel II implementation for international clients. He works on modeling the residual value risk of lease contracts. In former projects he was engaged in interest rate and energy risk.

Roland Füss is lecturer at the department of Empirical Research and Econometrics and assistant professor at the department of Finance and Banking at the University of Freiburg, Germany. He holds an MBA from the University of Applied Science in Lörrach and MEc and PhD degrees in Economics from the University of Freiburg. His research interests are in the field of applied econometrics, alternative investments as well as international and real estate finance. Roland Füss has authored numerous articles in finance journals as well as book chapters and a coeditor of a book on commodity investments published Wiley (2008).

Jean-Luc Gardère has a Master in Financial Engineering from HEC Montreal in 2005 where he worked on copulas in the pricing of credit derivatives. He is currently working at CIBC World Markets as a marketer in their Derivatives Sales & Trading Department.

Christophe J. Godlewski is assistant professor of finance at the Faculty of Business and Economics of the Université Louis Pasteur in Strasbourg (France) where he teaches corporate finance, financial analysis, and risk management. He holds a PhD in Finance from the Université Robert Schuman and a Master of Sciences in Banking and Finance from the Université Louis Pasteur. His research interests include credit risk management, bank loan syndication, organization and governance in banks, bank efficiency and regulation, and emerging markets finance. He has presented his work at numerous international finance conferences and has published in several refereed finance journals. He is a member of the French and the German Finance Associations. Prior to his PhD, he worked as a junior credit risk analyst at the Deutsche Bank AG in Strasbourg.

J. Kingsley Greenland II, PhD is the President and Chief Executive Officer of DebtX and is responsible for setting strategy at DebtX and leading its growth as a premier service provider to the secondary debt markets. Prior to joining DebtX, he was President of Boston Capital Mortgage Company, where he established the company as an originator of commercial real estate debt for securitization. Prior to Boston Capital, Mr. Greenland served as Executive Vice President and Chief Operating Officer of Fleet Real Estate Capital, a subsidiary of Fleet Financial Group. Mr. Greenland received his Bachelor degree in Business Administration from the College of William and Mary and Juris Doctor from the University of Miami, School of Law. He previously rose to the rank of Captain in the United States Army Reserve and is currently a member of the Florida bar. He is Series 24 and 7 licensed by the NASD.

Riccardo Gusso is contract professor at the Faculty of Economics of the University "Ca' Foscari" of Venice. He has a degree in Economics, a Master in Advanced Studies in Finance, and a PhD in Mathematics applied to economic problems. He is working as part of the research project entitled "Models for credit risk in a portfolio of bank loans" at University of Venice. His main areas of expertise include mathematical finance and risk management. His research focuses mainly models for credit risk estimations in portfolios of credit instruments.

Michael Hampden-Turner is a director in Citi's Credit Products Strategy Group in London. Within this global research and strategy group he focuses on European cash CDOs, CLOs, and synthetic structured products. He has worked in similar research roles in structured credit at the Royal Bank of Scotland, interest rate derivatives at WestLB, and equities Smith New Court Merrill Lynch. Michael studied economics and history at Trinity College Cambridge and Harvard University.

Dieter G. Kaiser is a Director of Alternative Investments at FERI Institutional Advisors GmbH in Bad Homburg, Germany where he is responsible for portfolio management and the selection of event-driven and commodity hedge funds. From 2003 to 2007 he was responsible for institutional research and business development at Benchmark Alternative Strategies GmbH in Frankfurt. He has written numerous articles on alternative investments that have been published in both academic and professional journals and is the author and editor of seven books. Dieter G. Kaiser holds a BA in Business Administration from the University of Applied Sciences Offenburg, an MA in Banking and Finance from the Frankfurt School of Finance and Management, and a PhD in Finance from the University of Technology Chemnitz.

Ralph Karels is with Deka Investment as a portfolio and product manager for special funds focusing on quantitative fixed income and equity strategies since 2005. From 2003 to 2005 he was a portfolio manager for quantitative structured equity products at Invesco of Germany. He obtained a Master of Arts degree in Banking & Finance at the Frankfurt School of Finance and Management in 2003, specializing in investment banking. Ralph Karels was born in Munich, Germany in May 1971 and studied mathematics and economics at the technical university (TU) of Munich, specializing in stochastic processes and martingale theory.

Christian Kasten holds an LL.M.Eur. and started at HSH Nordbank in 2003 as structure and documentation specialist after passing his bar exam. He was member of the securitization team structuring Ocean Star 2004 and 2005 and was involved in all shipping securitization activities of the bank. Today he works as a structurer at HSH Nordbank London Branch and is also responsible for CMBS transactions.

Matt King is Managing Director and global head of Credit Products Strategy at Citi. His team aims to provide clients on any aspect of credit portfolio management, from the latest views on $, Ä, and £ and cash markets through valuation and risk management techniques, and spanning the whole range of credit instruments including cash, CDS, CDOs, and other forms of structured credit. His team was ranked #1 in 2004, 2005, and 2006 for Credit Strategy and #1 for Credit Derivatives in 2006 by Euromoney. Prior to joining Citi, Matt was head of European Credit Strategy at JPMorgan, where his group was also ranked #1 (Euromoney, 2003). Before shifting into credit strategy, he spent three years as a government bond strategist. Mr King is British and a graduate of Emmanuel College, Cambridge, where he read Social & Political Sciences.

Thomas C. Knecht, PhD is academic director of the Center for Corporate Restructuring and Investment Management at the European Business School in Oestrich-Winkel and Principal of the Competence Center Restructuring & Corporate Finance at Roland Berger Strategy Consultants, Berlin. His research and teaching focus on corporate finance, corporate restructuring, and investment management. In numerous mandates he advised corporations and financial investors in the design and implementation of organizational restructurings and accompanied these in national and international M&A transactions. Professor Knecht has published extensively in these areas.

Martin Knocinski is employed at Bayerische Hypo- und Vereinsbank AG (HVB) where he provides solutions and performs research in the field of regulatory and accounting issues within the Markets & Investment banking division of the UniCredit Group. Prior to joining HVB in 2007, he was with KPMG's Regulatory Services Group where he worked as a specialist for regulatory questions within the context of different audit and advisory project for large German banks. He studied at the J. Mack Robinson College of Business at Georgia State University and University of Duisburg-Essen, where he holds a degree in business administration. He is author of publications on different aspects of accounting and auditing.

William F. Looney is Executive Vice President, US Loan Sales and manages the company's sales team and handles direct sales for select financial institutions. Prior to joining DebtX, he was a founding partner in the Boston law firm of Looney, Cohen, Reagan & Aisenberg LLP, which specializes in representing banks and investment banks in commercial loan sales and other commercial transactions. Prior to becoming a lawyer, Mr. Looney was Vice President at a Boston commercial bank in commercial real estate and commercial lending. Mr. Looney received his Bachelor of Arts degree from Harvard College and received his law degree from Suffolk University Law School.

Marcus R. W. Martin heads the risk model examination group in the banking examination department of Deutsche Bundesbank, regional office Frankfurt. He is responsible for conducting and preparing regulatory examinations of all kinds of quantitative internal risk models (including internal rating-based approaches, market risk, advanced measurement approaches for operational risk, and liquidity risk as well as credit portfolio and economic capital modeling approaches). Furthermore, Dr. Martin is reviewer for the American Mathematical Society (Providence, RI) and holds a PhD degree in mathematics.

Nicolas Papageorgiou is Associate Professor of Finance at HEC Montreal and Director of Research at Desjardins Global Asset Management. He also serves as the codirector of the DGAM-HEC Alternative Investment Research Center. Professor Papageorgiou has published articles in leading academic and practitioner journals and has been invited to present his research at numerous conferences in North America and Europe. He obtained his PhD at the ISMA Center, University of Reading in 2002.

Kai Pohl heads up the pricing and hedging function for liquid credits within Counterparty Exposure Management at ABN Amro Bank NV in London. Forming part of the Credit and Alternatives Trading, the group owns the credit exposure resulting from the fixed-income derivatives transactions the bank executes with external clients. He joined ABN Amro in 2002. Before that, he worked as a quantitative risk analyst in credit risk management at Deutsche Bank in both London and Frankfurt for seven years. Kai holds a MS in computer science awarded at University of Karlsruhe in 1998. He majored in financial engineering, neural networks, and genetic algorithms. His thesis is on the application of neural networks in forecasting the USD-DEM exchange rate.

Valerio Potì is a finance lecturer at Dublin City University and a consultant with Ambrosetti Stern Stewart in Milan. In Dublin City University, he teaches courses on investments and financial theory, and he is the coordinator of the French–Irish stream of the European Business programme. In Ambrosetti Stern Stewart he specializes in projects on risk and performance attribution and on issues related to the usage of derivatives. He graduated in Banking and Finance from Bocconi University Milan, gained a PhD in Finance from Trinity College Dublin, and subsequently conducted postdoctoral research in the Finance department of New York University Stern Business School as an International Visiting Research Scholar. His research interests include asset pricing, performance attribution, market efficiency, behavioral finance, and financial econometrics. His papers have been published or are forthcoming in international peer-reviewed journals, such as *European Financial Management* and *Applied Financial Economics* letters, and as chapters in practitioner-oriented books on portfolio and risk management. He also taught international finance at Queen's University Belfast, and before moving to academia, he worked for many years as an equity option market maker on the Milan derivatives exchange and as the head of the Financial Engineering desk of the Dublin subsidiary of Banca Monte dei Paschi di Siena.

Nandita Reisinger-Chowdhury is Head of Department for Country Risk and Portfolio Management at RZB AG (Raiffeisenzentralbank AG). She heads the department responsible for analysis of country risk, country risk ratings, and managing country risk for the RZB Group of banks. She has been with RZB AG since 1996 and was previously Deputy Head of Department for Country and Bank Risk Management. Prior to joining RZB AG, she held positions at other banks and in academia and has been an independent consultant. Nandita Reisinger-Chowdhury holds a Masters degree from the Vienna University of Economics and Business Administration where she studied economics. She has a postgraduate diploma in international economics from the Institute of Advanced Studies in Vienna, where she specialized in international trade.

Stefan Reitz holds a PhD degree in mathematics and is professor for financial mathematics at the University of Applied Sciences in Stuttgart, Germany. He also works as a consultant in the financial industry in various projects (risk controlling, risk management, and pricing of derivatives). Prior to his current position, he was an auditor and audit supervisor within the banking examination department, Deutsche Bundesbank, regional office Frankfurt. He conducted international audits at major and regional banks in the areas portfolio risk models, pricing of derivatives, risk management, minimum requirements for trading activities, and Basel II implementation.

Bruno Rémillard is Professor of Financial Engineering at HEC Montréal since 2001. After his PhD in probability at Carleton University, he was a NSERC postdoctoral fellow at Cornell University before joining Université du Québec à Trois-Rivières. He is the author or coauthor of more than 40 research articles on probability, statistics, and financial engineering.

Thomas Ridder, PhD is Head of Credit Portfolio Consulting Services at DZ BANK AG, Frankfurt. He has been with DZ BANK since 1994 when he joined the Capital Markets Research Team. From 2003 to 2007 he was Head of the Credit Portfolio Management team. Thomas holds a diploma degree in quantitative economics and a PhD in statistics from Mannheim University. He is lecturer at Goethe Business School, Frankfurt and author of several articles regarding topics in financial risk management.

Michael Sandigursky, CFA is a Vice President in the Credit Derivative Structuring team of Citigroup, based in London. Before moving to structuring, he specialised in quantitative elements of credit derivatives and structured credit in his role within Credit Strategy. Previously, Michael worked for a number of years in Citigroup Corporate Bank in London and Russia. Michael holds an MBA from London Business School, and degrees from the University of Economics and Finance and the University of Electronics in St. Petersburg, Russia.

Mathias Schwarz, PhD is currently employed as a quantitative analyst in the securitization department of KfW Bankengruppe, after having worked for several years as a senior economist for the same company. He studied economics at the University of Mainz, where he received his doctoral degree in 2003.

Torsten Seil started his career as financial engineer in the securitization team of HSH Nordbank in 2003. During his time in the Global Market Department, he worked on the Ocean Star 2004 and 2005 transactions. In 2006 he joined HSH Nordbank's Shipping Department, where he builds up further know how of modeling shipping portfolio risk. He holds a degree in business administration of Christian-Albrechts-University of Kiel, Germany, with focus on statistics and econometrics.

Michael Stein is a doctoral candidate at the Department of Statistics at the University of Karlsruhe, Germany. He holds a M.Ec. from the University of Freiburg, Germany, where he taught courses in Microeconomics and Financial Data Analysis. After graduating, Michael Stein joined Credit Suisse Asset Management Immobilien KAG in Frankfurt, Germany, where he is responsible for quantitative portfolio management solutions.

Panayiotis Teklos is a senior structured credit strategist in the Credit Products Strategy team at Citigroup. He is responsible for standard and bespoke synthetic CDOs, other exotic Credit Derivatives, as well as European CLOs and Leveraged Loans. Prior to joining Citigroup, Panikos was a senior quant in the Global Loan Portfolio Management group at Barclays Capital, where he was responsible for developing credit portfolio models and models for profitability assessment and performance measurement. Before Barclays Capital, he was a member of the Fixed Income Capital Management Quant team at BNP Paribas, where he worked on advancements of the team's pioneering "saddlepoint" method of modeling portfolio loss distributions analytically. Panikos holds an MS in finance and economics from the London School of Economics.

Jochen von Frowein works as a Client Relationship Manager at Dresdner Kleinwort, covering financial institutions in Mexico and several Central American countries. Before joining Dresdner Kleinwort, Jochen held positions in risk management and client relationship management at BHF-BANK AG, Frankfurt. He graduated with a degree in business administration from Frankfurt School of Finance and Management and holds an MA from the University of London (SOAS).

Carsten S. Wehn works as a market risk specialist at DekaBank, Frankfurt. At DekaBank he currently heads the project for the implementation of a market risk model and is also involved in the further development of the bank's economic capital model. Before joining DekaBank, he worked at Deutsche Bundesbank as an auditor and audit supervisor for regulatory examinations of banks' quantitative models for risk measurement and management. He holds a PhD in applied mathematics and gives lectures at universities. He regularly publishes in well-known industrial magazines as well as in books, mainly about quantitative aspects of risk modeling.

PART ONE

Performance
Measurement

CHAPTER 1

Implementing Credit Portfolio Management

Thomas Ridder

ABSTRACT

As more credit markets have become liquid in recent years and new financial instruments have been developed, an increasing number of institutions became capable of active portfolio-based credit management. Thus, implementing a dedicated credit portfolio management function has evolved as a major project in many financial institutions. This chapter discusses fundamental issues in setting up this function.

INTRODUCTION

The management of credit portfolios in financial institutions has undergone material changes in the last decade. Due to essentially illiquid credit markets, until the mid–1990s, relationship banking dominated credit business and lead to positions that were mainly buy and hold. Accordingly, financial institutions understood credit management mainly as a part of their client management. The focus of credit management was set on the analysis, monitoring, and risk–return measurement of individual clients. The rationale behind this was the cognition that "at the end of the day," it is always individual obligors that default. Accordingly, a single-client-based design of business processes and risk measurement was regarded as adequate to ensure a sufficient quality of credit management. If used at all, the phrase *credit portfolio management* was mainly understood as consecutively monitoring and processing the positions of a given credit portfolio.

Today's credit portfolio management (CPM) practice does not consider a portfolio just a collection of financial positions any more, put together mainly for administrative purposes. Rather, CPM understands a portfolio as a set of interdependent credit positions with related risk–return profiles. The focus on understanding and profitably shaping these relationships constitutes the difference from traditional credit management. Credit portfolio management delivers additional value by creating higher transparency with respect to the portfolio's key characteristics, which by itself usually helps to make more efficient management decisions. Advances from modern statistical portfolio analysis are picked up and deliver a toolbox comparable to the well-known quantitative instruments that tackle market risk. However, CPM also opens up new sources of additional income for financial institutions. Immediate cash flows are generated by driving origination to accomplish more risk adequate prices, by freeing capital tied up to less profitable assets to foster profitable growth or by fees from trading, structuring, or repackaging credit risk. Felsenheimer et al. (2006) and De Servigny and Renault (2004) provide a detailed introduction to strategies, methods, and instruments of modern CPM.

This chapter surveys major issues when implementing a CPM function in financial institutions. It addresses the change management necessary to transform an essential buy-and-hold credit strategy to a more active approach of shaping the performance of credit portfolios. The second section of this chapter discusses the potential levers of CPM, and the third section highlights questions of the organizational implementation of CPM functions. Recent experience with the so-called subprime crisis has heavily challenged the use of quantitative methods in CPM. As such, the fourth section of this chapter will pick up some of the arguments. The chapter concludes with some evidence from a market survey.

THE LEVERS OF CREDIT PORTFOLIO MANAGEMENT

In general, the outline of credit portfolio management in financial institution encompasses a great variety of potential activities and responsibilities. This can easily be recognized by discussing a stylized credit process (Figure 1.1) from a CPM point of view.

Step 1: Individual Risk Analysis

The first step is the classical credit risk management responsibility, which is focused on analyzing the credit risk linked to individual obligors or projects before granting new loans and other defaultable contracts. The creditworthiness of the individual risk positions is to be revealed and is transformed into the probability of future obligor or project default, ultimately. Elaborate analysis is usually necessary to minimize asymmetric information between obligors and creditors and, thus, to reduce implications of moral hazard and adverse selection. This is achieved by analyzing business plans, balance sheets, income statements, and additional information from the customer relationship management typically to be attached to credit applications. Most financial institutions today apply internal rating systems for individual credit analysis. These were developed not just for reasonable and consistent economic risk assessment but in many institutions to also determine regulatory capital requirements. Thus, obligor and project risk analysis delivers the basic input of managing the quality of inflow to the credit portfolio. By definition, this analysis does not refer to comprehensive portfolio-based reasoning.

FIGURE   1.1

Generic credit process

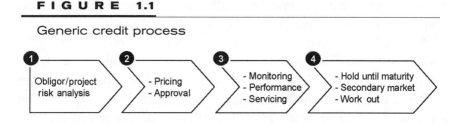

Step 2: Pricing and Credit Approval

The second step of the credit process might introduce specific portfolio-based activities. First, to ensure sustained profitability of the credit business risk adequate prices have to be accomplished. It is important to recognize that a requirement of sufficient high profitability is reasonable ex-ante and on a mean portfolio level, only. Due to the binary character of default events, any credit position that suffers a default will typically result in a net loss. Margins received up to the credit event rarely cover subsequent losses of principal and interest. Otherwise, in the case of no default a certain profit can be earned from the position. As there always will be some residual risk in credit analysis, ex post wrong decisions will continue to be derived in some cases, and this will possibly lead to losses with respect to some individual credit positions. The goal of risk adequate pricing is, thus, to generate enough aggregated earnings on the portfolio to provide an adequate net return on capital with a high degree of confidence. Therefore, typical loan pricing systems require that loan prices have to cover the following four different building blocks: (1) funding cost, (2) administrative and operational cost, (3) expected loss, and (4) a given target profitability above cost constituents (1) to (3).

Funding cost, administrative cost, and expected loss can be allocated to single risk positions in a straightforward way. The breakdown of the target portfolio profitability to required individual profit margins affords a little reflection. In general, a simple, flat profit margin will not be accepted since more risky positions ought to contribute more earnings to the portfolio than less risky ones. *Portfolio profitability* is usually defined as the economic performance of the capital required to cover total portfolio risk. A natural way to determine individual profit margins would then be to break down total capital to individual risk positions and determine the required pro rata profitability. Expressed as a margin on nominal exposure, this price component is usually called *cost of economic capital*.

The breakdown of total capital may be achieved according to regulatory rules or according to the institution's internal portfolio model. While being basically simple, the regulatory approach has several shortcomings when applied to pricing. For example, even the new Basel II rules do not account for diversification within the portfolio, and the regulatory acceptance of risk mitigation instruments is strictly constrained. A comprehensive assessment of the capital needed to cover the credit risk of a given portfolio is thus better based on internal portfolio analysis representing the financial institution's own understanding of material economic risks. In doing so, economic relationships between the individual return distributions can consistently be allowed for in the loan pricing system.

Even if the rating is above the required minimum threshold and adequate prices can be accomplished, the credit approval process might take into account additional criteria like the region, the sector, the product type, or other structural characteristics of the application. The reason for this is the experience that credit positions with similar structural characteristics are usually exposed to common risk factors. This leads to a higher degree of credit quality dynamics within a portfolio. Especially when credit positions are determined to be held to maturity, for strategic reasons or because there are no liquid secondary markets, credit quality management should include structural portfolio limits for new risks to be taken. Structural limits may address the distribution of nominal exposure, expected loss, or economic capital along material systematic risk factors. The goal of these limits is to reduce risk volatility by ensuring a sufficiently diversified portfolio allocation with respect to material structural risk factors. Structural portfolio limits can be derived by comparing results from scenario simulations to a given risk appetite and/or allocated risk capital, for example.

Step 3: Monitoring

Credit portfolio management contributes to monitoring and reporting by regular analysis of the portfolio structure, evaluation of its aggregated return distribution and the conduction of stress tests. This enables senior bank management to check whether the portfolio is in line with given structural limits and whether required aggregated economic capital needs conform to the institution's risk appetite. Additionally, detailed capital analysis contributes to the risk-adjusted performance measurement of the business lines.

Monitoring and reporting data may reveal the need for corrective management action to bring back the credit portfolio to the intended risk–return profile. As the rationale for these actions is usually grounded on a formal and rather abstract understanding of the dynamic relationships within the portfolio, a particular confidence regarding the applied quantitative methods is essential throughout the financial institution. The section

Quantitative Methods in Credit Portfolio Management of this chapter will address this point.

Step 4: Secondary Market Activities

Recent years have seen considerable progress regarding the evolution of liquid credit markets. More institutions find themselves in a position where secondary market activities may extend their scope of credit portfolio management. Instruments are no longer confined to syndication or other true sale activities. Today, a variety of single-risk and portfolio-specific derivative and securitization instruments are available for hedging and investing purposes. Derivative instruments and securitization products may be used for managing a classical loan portfolio originated from client business, or they may be understood as an asset class of its own. Meanwhile, the traditional credit business paradigm of "buy and hold" has been replaced with "buy, structure, and sell" by many institutions. Earning fees by structuring, repackaging, and trading credit risk has evolved as a new business for many of today's banks and often defines the credit portfolio management function as a profit center within the investment banking division.

As discussed above, CPM touches nearly all steps of the credit process. To complete the discussion, we can illustrate the CPM approaches

F I G U R E   1.2

Portfolio return distribution

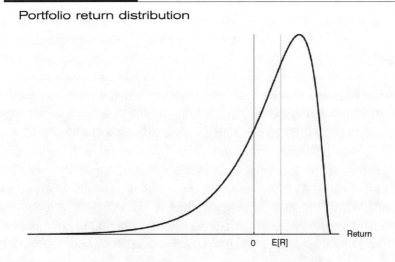

with the help of the statistical credit portfolio return distribution. Figure 1.2 displays the typical shape of such a distribution and depicts portfolio return at the horizontal axis with positive return to the right of zero. The bold black line shows a stylized return probability distribution allocating a large probability to positive returns and a small probability to extreme losses (negative returns). Usually, expected return E[R] should be positive to ensure sustained profitability of the portfolio. However, as the plot displays, upside is limited by some amount, and downside risk can be fierce.

All CPM efforts can now be characterized as means of shifting or reshaping the return distribution. A rise of margins of originated loans or, in general, a more efficient use of available capital will shift the distribution to the right giving more probability to positive returns. Decreasing concentration by structural limits or hedging activities will narrow the distribution with a large cut of the left tail of the distribution. In general, the laws of financial markets admit higher (expected) returns at the cost of higher risk, only. This implies a heavier left tail of the return distribution. The challenge of the CPM function can then best be described as striving for more probability at the right-hand side of the graph while keeping the left tail in compliance with the institution's risk appetite.

ORGANIZATION OF CREDIT PORTFOLIO MANAGEMENT

Until now, a general best practice design of the CPM function in financial institution has not been established. Further, it probably never will as strategic and operative objectives differ widely between institutions. Subsequently, a variety of organizational implementations can be found in today's financial firms. The implementation of CPM usually takes place in living organizations with more or less well-established management processes. A new CPM function might then be regarded as a hostile invader claiming responsibilities and earnings at the expense of established units. Therefore, to achieve a successful implementation, a careful design of responsibilities and interfaces between the different organizational units involved is required. A set of key questions has been established that an institution might work through to ensure a consistent implementation of CPM activities. The questions are discussed in the following paragraphs.

The answers should result in an explicit mandate of the CPM unit describing the goals to be achieved, the tasks and responsibilities of the CPM unit as well as performance measurement topics.

Which are the Goals of the Credit Portfolio Management Function?

Without a precise understanding of which goals the CPM function has to accomplish, a consistent division of labor within the institute is probably impossible. Most financial institutions use a stepwise implementation of the CPM function. The typical start of CPM is to complement the traditional single-client risk management. At this stage, the task of the CPM function is mainly to build up a risk-focused view on the credit portfolio structure. Setting up information technology (IT) and databases, ensuring data quality, and developing of methods and reports to assess aggregated risk dominate the activities. The CPM function then usually moves into an advisory function. Based on sound analytics and the institution's given risk appetite, specific opinions on the optimal portfolio structure, the current risk–return profile, and appropriate management actions are developed by the CPM. These should be obligatory inputs to the internal decision and credit approval processes. The goal of the CPM function at this stage is mainly to contribute to the alignment of the comprehensive credit portfolio's profile with the institute's business and risk strategy.

Of course, if the CPM function is explicitly expected to generate profit, the general advisory function can no longer be sustained. Instead, CPM is to be dealt with as a true profit center—responsible for the profit and loss of a precisely defined portfolio under management. Then, acting as credit treasury, CPM should be sited in the investment banking division.

What Assets Are Addressed by the Credit Portfolio Management Function? What Is the Definition of the Portfolio under Management?

Credit-risk-bearing transactions can be found in nearly every business line of a financial institution. Consequently, any reference to an institution's "actively managed credit portfolio" needs to be stated more precisely to be operationally useful. A narrow definition of the portfolio to be managed conforms to business-line-specific CPM units that can be integrated without severe frictions into existing profit centers. A wide and comprehensive definition of the portfolio, covering several business lines, moves the CPM function more toward general bank or risk management and may afford the separation of origination, individual risk management, and portfolio management. The scope of the portfolio managed by the CPM function should be set with respect to the degree of exposure to common structural risk factors of the subportfolios.

Who Is Responsible for Quantitative Credit Portfolio Analysis and Regular Portfolio Reporting?

For reasons of sound corporate governance portfolio monitoring and reporting are typical responsibilities of "non-profit-driven" risk management units or risk control units. Accordingly, these activities should only be attributed to the CPM function if it is not located within profit-generating business lines.

Is an Internal Transfer Pricing System Required?

Internal transfer prices form the economic interface between origination and CPM units. They deliver the price at which a CPM unit takes over credit positions from originating units. Originating units can take into account these transfer prices in their pricing considerations and have to take any shortfall resulting from failure to accomplish adequate returns. Transfer price systems are required if CPM is established as a profit center, acting mainly on secondary markets but without direct access to primary markets.

There are currently two fundamental approaches for the design of transfer price systems. The traditional approach uses the four building blocks discussed in Step 2: Pricing and Credit Approval. If complete internal *asset transfer* is to be achieved, a calculated transfer price can be derived as present value of the assets cash flows, its funding cost, administrative cost, expected loss, and capital cost. If just *risk transfer* to the CPM unit has to be achieved, adequate "insurance premiums" for each credit position can be derived from expected loss and capital cost.

More advanced transfer price systems are based on market quotes. In this case, the CPM unit acts as a credit treasurer that buys credit positions from the origination at prices that cover current hedge cost at secondary markets. The decision whether to hedge or leave the position open (always within given risk limits) is then left to the credit treasurer and depends on his view on changes in future credit spreads. Although appealing from an economic point of view, mark-to-market–based transfer prices are difficult to establish if liquid secondary markets are not available for the assets originated at primary markets. In some of theses cases, a grid of approximate prices (mark-to-matrix) can be derived from more liquid securitization markets.

What Significance Will Credit Portfolio Management Have in Formal Credit Approval Decision Processes?

If CPM is not understood just as informal portfolio analytics but intended to contribute seriously to the improvement of the portfolio's quality and efficiency of capital allocation, it has to be fit into the internal credit approval process. Even if CPM does not take part in the actual credit decision, a CPM opinion should be obligatory at least for "large" or "risky" applications that possibly could stress portfolio quality, e.g., by increasing concentration risk.

Who Is Responsible for the Portfolio Strategy or Asset Allocation within the Credit Portfolio?

This question is strongly linked to a following paragraph where profit and loss will be strongly implied by the strategic asset allocation. Establishing a CPM function that is responsible for portfolio P&L but not willing to decide on its strategic credit asset allocation within given limits is somewhat difficult.

How Are Decisions about (Corrective) Portfolio Management Actions Reached? Who Is the Owner of the Assets?

Most banks charge a risk committee with deciding about the target credit portfolio structure and initiating appropriate hedge or investment activities. The members of the committee are usually senior delegates from the asset-generating business lines, from risk management, as well as from the financial controlling and accounting departments. An advisory CPM unit typically supports the committee by coordinating the agenda (regarding the portfolio specific topics), preparing data and information for the meetings, reporting on significant changes of the portfolio structure and its risk–return profile, giving advice on appropriate management activities, and following up decisions of the committee. The committee solution calls for an agreement about the treatment of CPM activities in the internal performance measurement system. (1) Since there is a committee and not a specific unit acting as the "owner of the assets" and (2) since management activities, like portfolio hedges or securitization, may pertain to assets originated by several units, no single unit will accept to take the cost of such management activities. Usually, special accounts have to be operated to collect cost and return of operative CPM activities.

If the CPM unit is expected to generate profit by trading, structuring, or repackaging credit risk, it should be established as a profit center within the investment banking units. The assets that will be under management by the CPM unit have to be defined exactly and must be passed into sole return responsibility of the CPM function. If the portfolio encompasses loans and other credit positions originated by the corporate banking units, then this calls for some internal transfer price system to separate performance of the origination and CPM units.

Which Unit Is in Charge of the Operative Portfolio Management Activities?

There has to be a clear-cut arrangement identifying which units account for management activities like loan sales, syndication, hedging, investing, or securitization if applied by CPM. Typically, the specific trading desks or credit structuring departments take over these activities on behalf of the CPM unit or the relevant risk committee.

Who Takes the Profit and Loss Resulting from Portfolio Management Activities?

As argued, profit and loss resulting from CPM activities should basically be linked to the unit acting as the owner of the assets — if it exists. If a committee accounts for CPM decisions, then resulting profit and loss usually must be allocated to "neutral" accounts.

Is It Appropriate to Establish
a Dedicated CPM Unit?

As soon as the CPM function is expected to give specific management recommendations, a dedicated unit becomes helpful. This supports the development of the specific core competence of the CPM team and visibly assigns responsibility within the organization. This is true even if a committee formally decides about actual portfolio management activities. If an institution implements the CPM function as an operative profit center, a dedicated CPM unit is inescapably required, of course.

International surveys have shown that answers to the above question are typically clustered among institutions. This indicates a range of prototype CPM implementations. Wolcott (2006) gives an informative overview over current developments in major banks. McKinsey & Company, for example, has found three different CPM business models in financial institutions called *reactive controller, active advisors,* and *credit treasury*. See Beitel et al. (2006) for details. These models comply with the three stages of CPM evolution discussed in the first question above. Table 1.1 displays a summary of the above discussion along the three business models mentioned.

Additionally, the International Association of Credit Portfolio Managers (IACPM) has published a list of "sound practices of credit portfolio management" that discusses further topics regarding an efficient and effective implementation of the CPM function in financial institutions [see IACPM (2005)].

QUANTITATIVE METHODS IN CREDIT
PORTFOLIO MANAGEMENT

The development of modern CPM would not have been possible if quantitative methods for analyzing and pricing credit portfolios had not advanced as they did in the last 10 years. Even though the banking industry has, among all possible sources of risk, the longest experience with lending, it took until the late 1990s to have adequate statistical models available for credit portfolio analysis. Until then, quite comfortable margins in the business and a restraint evolution of liquid credit markets just had not created sufficient demand for advanced pricing and risk measurement methods. Likewise, at that time, international regulators started negotiations about the

T A B L E   1.1

Typical designs of CPM business models

	Reactive Controller	Active Advisor	Credit Treasury
Value added	Higher transparency, limiting return volatility, risk focus	Optimization of risk–return profile of the credit portfolio, optimization of capital allocation	Higher profitability of credit business line
Portfolio definition	Comprehensive, with monitoring and/or reporting view	Comprehensive, with strategic view	Clear-cut definition of portfolio under management by CPM unit
Quantitative portfolio analysis	Responsible for methods, monitoring, and reporting	CPM as essential part of model validation process. Commenting regular reports.	Not responsible for methods, monitoring, and reporting
Transfer pricing	Not required	Not required	Required to separate performance of CPM and origination
Formal approval of new business	CPM opinion where appropriate, focus on utilization of (structural) limits	CPM opinion mandatory	Fully integrated with respect to defined CPM portfolio
Portfolio strategy and/or asset allocation	CPM opinion based on quantitative portfolio analysis, scenario evaluation	CPM opinion mandatory, joint responsibility with origination and/or risk committee	CPM responsible for asset allocation within given limits
Decision about corrective portfolio management actions	Origination units and/or risk management and/or committee	Origination units or risk committee, CPM opinion	CPM within given limits
Operative management activity, secondary market access	Investment banking units on behalf of origination or committee decision	Investment banking units on behalf of committee decision	CPM unit or other investment banking units on behalf of CPM
P&L responsibility of CPM unit	CPM as part of risk control cost center	CPM as cost center, if separate unit	CPM as profit center
Organizational structure of CPM	Separate unit not necessary, may be integrated as part of risk control or risk management	Separate unit beneficial if understood as effective support of risk committee	Separate unit within investment banking division

new capital accord, or about "Basel II," for short. This regulatory framework was finalized in 2004 and became effective in most countries in 2007 or 2008.

From the beginning of the negotiations, the new capital accord was aimed at a more economic way to determine required regulatory capital for the credit portfolio of financial institutions. Thus, a comprehensive discussion about adequate credit portfolio risk measurement methods was initiated among regulators, practitioners and academics. This interchange generated, for example, material insight about how to define, model, and calibrate return dependencies within a credit portfolio. As a result, today there are several reasonable and pragmatic methods to aggregate individual risks as to generate the statistical portfolio loss distribution, even for large portfolios (see Figure 1.2). McNeil et al. (2005) and Lando (2004) provide basics and applications of current quantitative risk modeling. For an example of the current methodological discussions regarding the use of credit portfolio models in banks, see Jeffrey (2006).

Despite the fact that rather advanced mathematical and statistical reasoning, as a result, usually derives it, the portfolio return distribution is not an abstract, artificial looking, and mere academic object. It represents, from a risk point of view, all available information about uncertain future portfolio performance. Thus, it is the essential input for any reasonable and consistent portfolio-pricing algorithm used in today's credit markets and, thus, one of the important ingredients of any CPM activity. Nevertheless, the heavy use of quantitative methods in credit portfolio management has been blamed as one of the major reasons for the credit crisis, triggered by the breakdown of the market for so-called subprime instruments in mid–2007. As the argument roughly goes, it was mainly greed and a naive confidence of rating agencies, banks, and institutional investors in their quantitative portfolio models that prevented them from realizing the true risks of the ballooning credit bubble. We leave aside the "greed" part here and focus on the second part of the argument, confidence in quantitative models.

Quantitative portfolio models are condensed formal descriptions of how all risk factors that we judge as relevant for the problem at hand may act simultaneously on aggregated portfolio return, given that all material factor interaction has been adequately mapped into formulas and parameters. Thus, especially with credit portfolio analysis, there is always considerable model risk, which might be difficult to assess for nonspecialists. The following observation of Rebonato (2007, p. 137) concerning current financial risk management practice certainly applies to frequent discussions in CPM units:

> [A] dangerous disconnect is forming between specialists (statisticians, mathematicians, econometricians, etc.) on the one hand, who are undoubtedly discovering more and more powerful statistical techniques, and policy makers, senior managers, and politicians on the other, who are ill-equipped to understand when, and how, and to what extend these sophisticated techniques should be used and relied upon.

Statistical portfolio distributions and its derived risk metrics, like return volatility, value-at-risk, expected shortfall, or marginal risk contributions of individual portfolio positions should better be understood not as the goal of CPM but as resources of the CPM function to derive sound decisions and choices between available management alternatives. To ensure sustained value of these resources a formal model-validation process should always be implemented [see IACPM (2005)]. Sustained compliance of the quantitative portfolio model with the institution's fundamental understanding about basic relationships between significant risk factors can thus be reached.

However, even if sound models are agreed upon, the core challenge of credit portfolio *management*, namely, to derive consistent financial decisions, is still to be solved. There is no portfolio management by numbers, only. Again, Rebonato's worries can be adapted to credit portfolio management: "It is forgetting that managing risk is about making decisions under uncertainty. It also seems to hold on two dangerous beliefs: first, that our risk metrics can be estimated to five decimal places; second, that once we have done so the results will self-evidently guide our risk management choices. They do not," (Rebonato, 2007, p. ix).

CONCLUSION

Even if the chosen business model for CPM does not generate additional profit on its own, like reactive controller or active advisor mentioned above, it usually impacts the institution's performance in a positive and measurable way. McKinsey & Company (Beitel et al., 2006) estimate the benefits of applying the complete scope of active CPM instruments by 20 to 150 bps (on risk-weighted assets). This includes additional returns from better pricing new business, optimizing capital consumption, investing, and provisions from structuring and repackaging credit risk. Although these figures were derived prior to the downturn of the credit markets in 2007, they still show considerable earnings potential: Nearly half of the additional spread income is generated by optimizing origination, pricing, and growth of the corporate credit business.

A surprise at first sight might be the finding of McKinsey's study that, obviously, those institutions are more successful in harvesting the benefits of CPM activities that follow the more sophisticated approaches right from the start. An explanation for this might be that the decision to build up a sophisticated CPM function is usually taken by the top management or the board. Once the decision is made, it is likely that as a "top project" the implementation will be endowed with plenty of resources and a sustained backing by the board and the top management. It is probably this broad commitment within the institution that makes the difference in later success of the CPM function.

REFERENCES

Beitel, P., Dürr, J., Pritsch, G., and Stegemann, U. (2006) Actively Managing the Credit Portfolio. In *Banking in a Changing World*. New York: McKinsey & Company.

De Servigny, A. and Renault, O. (2004) *Measuring and Managing Credit Risk*. New York: McGraw-Hill.

Felsenheimer, J., Gisdakis, P., and Zaiser, M. (2006) *Active Credit Portfolio Management. A Practical Guide to Credit Risk Management Strategies*. Hoboken, NJ: John Wiley & Sons.

International Association of Credit Portfolio Managers (2005). *Sound Practices of Credit Portfolio Management*. New York (www.iacpm.org).

Jeffrey, C. (2006) Credit Model Breakdown. *Risk*, November, 19(11): 21–25.

Lando, D. (2004). *Credit Risk Modeling. Theory and Applications.*
Princeton, NJ: Princeton University Press.

McNeil, A.J., Frey, R., and Embrechts, P. (2005) *Quantitative Risk
Management. Concepts, Techniques, Tools.* Princeton, NJ:
Princeton University Press.

Rebonato, R. (2007) *Plight of the Fortune Tellers.* Princeton, NJ:
Princeton University Press.

Wolcott, R. (2006) Reconstructing Loan Management. *Risk*, December,
19(12): 19–21.

CHAPTER 2

Credit Portfolio Management: Accounting Implications

Christian Burmester

ABSTRACT

Existing credit portfolio management models are based on a theoretical framework and focus very much on risk–return optimization in a mathematical sense. However, they do not capture a bank's real-life constraints sufficiently, such as return on equity and accounting policies. Because senior management is held accountable for both economic and externally reported profit and loss statement (P&L), portfolio managers should understand the accounting implications for a given strategy and how these might manifest themselves in the external financial reported P&L. We focus on the International Financial Reporting Standards and briefly capture the accounting provisions for credit portfolio management. We further explain the implications of hedge accounting and fair value option in some detail and highlight the differences between trading and investment approaches. We conclude by commenting on how the alternative approaches can influence financial reporting under International Financial Reporting Standards.

INTRODUCTION

Over the last 20 years credit portfolio management has become more sophisticated. The objective of the portfolio manager is no longer to invest in assets
that generate a benchmark yield and are expected to be redeemed at par. The
potential profit and loss volatility generated during its life due to the change
in the creditworthiness of the obligor must also be considered. As a consequence, when selecting a potential asset, a portfolio manager not only has to
assess the creditworthiness of the obligor but also needs to formulate expectations on how this could change within the time frame of the investment
and how this change will be reflected in the reported accounting results.
Furthermore, the portfolio manager must understand the possible accounting
treatments as this could have a significant impact on the way in which the
performance of the portfolio is measured.

Credit portfolio management typically includes investments in securities, synthetic products such as credit default swaps, and structured
credit products such as credit linked notes and asset-backed securities. In
some organizations the range of products can include loans, particularly
those that can be readily traded, although we shall concentrate on securities for the purpose of this chapter. In particular, we discuss the accounting considerations a portfolio manager should take into account when
pursuing an investment strategy. Appropriate tools need to be available to
the portfolio manager to enable him or her to assess dynamically and
accurately the credit profile as well as the value of the portfolio so that he
or she can make ongoing investment decisions when carrying out his or
her investment strategy.

This investment strategy will depend upon a number of factors
inter alia:

- Appetite for risk of the portfolio manager and of the organization
- Type of assets the portfolio manager is authorised to trade
- Sophistication of the tools available to manage the portfolio
- Amount of capital available
- Accounting regime (or regimes), which are applied by the
  organization and the accounting policies applied to the
  portfolio

The financial markets and the range of products traded have increased significantly over the last 20 years. This growth has been fueled by the rapid expansion of the derivatives markets, coupled with advances in financial engineering and information technology. During this time the financial reporting standard-setting bodies have struggled to keep the pace with the developments. Until a few years ago the accounting standards relating to financial instruments were predominantly cost based. In particular, since there was little guidance given for derivatives, they were effectively removed from balance sheets. Furthermore, a number of high-profile financial scandals (e.g., Enron, WorldCom, and Procter & Gamble) highlighted the requirement for a more transparent valuation-based accounting framework. Consequently, the two main financial reporting standard authorities, the International Accounting Standard Board (IASB) and the Financial Accounting Standard Board (FASB), issued specific accounting standards covering financial instruments: International Accounting Standard (IAS) 39 and Financial Accounting Standard (FAS) 133, respectively. Although there are differences between these two standards, they share the same fundamental concepts. In February 2006 FASB and IASB issued a "Memorandum of Understanding" including a program of topics on which the two bodies will seek to achieve convergence by 2008.

The accounting framework we consider is the International Financial Reporting Standards (IFRS) and, in particular, we consider the implications of IAS 39—Financial Instruments: Recognition and Measurement. After a description of the IFRS framework, we shall examine the range of the possible accounting policies and how they may be applied to ensure that the financial performance of the credit portfolio is reported in an appropriate manner.

INTERNATIONAL FINANCIAL REPORTING STANDARDS

Background

As of January 1, 2005 all companies listed on a regulated market within the European Union (EU) are required to produce their consolidated financial statements in accordance with IFRS. This decision is part of an effort by the European Commission to enhance transparency and comparability of companies' financial statements, leading to improved access to capital and cross-border investment.

International Accounting Standard 39—Financial Instruments: Recognition and Measurement

International Accounting Standard 39 (IAS 39) is at the heart of the IFRS accounting framework for financial institutions and prescribes the accounting treatment for financial instruments. International Accounting Standard 39 represented a first step towards a fair value-based accounting model for financial instruments. This move toward a fair value-based model represented a radical change in the accounting approach and not surprisingly was subject to some resistance from interested parties. As a result, there was much discussion and numerous revisions, resulting in the final IAS 39 standard being somewhat of a compromise from the full fair value economic model. A full fair value model would effectively be accounting for all transactions as though they were held for trading purposes, thus generating extreme volatility in the reported profit and loss that would not necessarily be a true reflection of the performance of a portfolio held for the longer term. Nevertheless, even where assets or liabilities are not shown in the balance sheet at fair value under the provisions of IAS 39, their fair values are required to be disclosed in the notes to the financial statements under IFRS 7.

Under IAS 39 the initial recognition of a financial instrument is at cost, i.e., the fair value of whatever was paid or received to acquire the financial asset or liability. The standard requires that each financial asset and liability must then be classified under one of the following categories set out in Table 2.1. These categories determine how the financial instrument is subsequently measured after its initial recognition and where any changes in the carrying value are reported (either in the profit and loss account or equity reserve).

As an example we should consider a credit portfolio composed of bonds, structured securities (e.g., credit linked notes, asset-backed securities), and synthetic products (e.g., credit default swaps), whereby the assets are purchased as long-term investments. The credit portfolio manger will typically use swaps and options to hedge interest rate and foreign exchange

T A B L E   2.1

Classification of financial instruments according to IAS 39.45

Classification	Subsequent Measurement	Changes in Carrying Value
Financial assets and liabilities at fair value through profit or loss:	Fair value	Profit and loss
• Instruments held for trading		
• All derivatives		
Available for sale financial assets	Fair value	Equity
Loans and receivables	Amortized cost	Profit and loss
Held to maturity investments	Amortized cost	Profit and loss
Other financial liabilities	Amortized cost	Profit and loss

risks. The investments are intended to be held for the longer term, possibly to maturity, but are definitely not held for trading purposes. The investments will comprise long positions with no selling short. Typically interest rate and foreign exchange risk are hedged by swaps or options to leave credit risk as the principal exposure.

When considering the classification of products within the portfolio detailed in Table 2.1, there are two categories available for the classification of securities, namely as "available for sale financial assets" and as "held to maturity investments." An important provision for held-to-maturity investments is that, in principle, they cannot be sold or reclassified until maturity (IAS 39.50). If a sale or reclassification occurs, all remaining held-to-maturity investments in the portfolio are deemed to be "tainted" and have to be reclassified as available for sale (IAS 39.52). In practice this restriction is too onerous for the portfolio manager to dynamically manage the portfolio. Hence the available-for-sale category is the only suitable classification. Under this approach the variation in the fair value is deferred to an equity reserve (IAS 39.55).

Figure 2.1 displays how the classification process is essentially a decision tree based upon the portfolio manager's intention at inception of the trade. The classification of derivatives is straightforward as they are only permitted to be designated as "financial assets and liabilities at fair

Decision tree to classify financial instruments

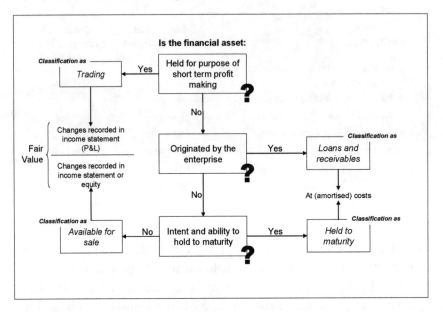

value through profit or loss" with mark-to-market changes shown in the profit and loss account. This treatment covers not only derivatives used to create synthetic risk, such as credit default swaps, but also hedging derivatives, e.g., interest rate swaps.

Where a derivative is embedded into a nonderivative financial instrument, IAS 39.11 requires that the embedded derivative is separated from the host contract if the economic characteristics and risks do not closely resemble those of the host, e.g., convertible bonds or callable bonds. Once separated, the embedded derivative must be designated consistently with outright derivatives, thus being valued through the profit and loss account. This ensures that institutions cannot mask derivative exposures through nonderivative products. This is particularly relevant to the credit portfolio manager where investments in structured credit-linked notes such as synthetic collateralized debt obligations (CDOs) are required to be separated into the host and embedded derivative elements. However, the valuation of the embedded derivative element is often difficult to model as it references a dynamically changing credit portfolio. International Accounting Standard provides for this situation by stating that whenever separation is not possible, the entity should value the hybrid financial instrument (i.e., host contract and embedded derivative) at fair value with changes reported in the profit and loss account (IAS 39.12).

When applying the accounting treatment outlined above to a typical credit portfolio comprising a range of standard products, it is clear that identical risk exposures may have different accounting treatments depending upon the type of products used to generate the risk. In some ways this is the consequence of the compromise from the theoretical full fair value accounting model to an approach that allows a mixture of accounting treatments within a portfolio. This can be seen below by a simple example whereby a credit portfolio manager can undertake identical corporate credit exposures in three different ways: as a floating rate note (FRN), as an asset swap package (i.e., synthetic FRN), and as sold protection default swap (i.e., unfunded FRN).

Table 2.2 demonstrates that the general IFRS provisions for financial assets, liabilities, and derivatives result in an inconsistent profit or loss

T A B L E   2.2

Possible accounting treatment for same credit exposure with different products

Product	Classification	Disclosure of Fair Value Changes Due to Movements in	
		Credit Risk	Interest Rate Risk
FRN	Available for sale	Equity	N/A[1]
Asset swap:			
• Security	Available for sale	Equity	Equity
• Swap	Fair value through profit or loss	N/A	Profit and loss
Credit default swap	Fair value through profit or loss	Profit and loss	N/A

---

[1] It is assumed that no interest rate movement within the FRN period occurs; otherwise, movements will be shown in equity.

recognition that would not reflect the economic reality of these transactions. Furthermore, the fully hedged interest rate component of the asset swap exposure would be reported in the profit and loss account and equity reserve, effectively producing an asymmetrical accounting result that would increase the volatility of reported results. Fortunately, IAS 39 recognizes this issue by permitting two methods to mitigate this asymmetric accounting treatment:

1. Hedge accounting
2. Fair value option (FVO)

Hedge Accounting

Hedge accounting is effectively a matching concept that seeks to correct the profit and loss difference by altering the timing of recognition of gains and losses on the hedged item or the hedging instrument thereby avoiding much of the volatility that arises from using the normal accounting principles. IAS 39 sets out detailed criteria that must be met in order for hedge accounting to be applied. This criteria includes the following key items reproduced from IAS 39:

- Hedging relationship must be formally designated and documented at inception of the hedge and must cover the risk management objective, the hedged item, the hedging instrument, nature of risk being hedged, and how the effectiveness will be measured.
- Hedge must be expected to be highly effective at the inception of the hedge.
- Effectiveness result (defined as changes in fair value or cash flows of the hedge as compared to the change in value of the hedged item) must fall within a range of 80 to 125 percent to remain effective at the relevant testing dates.

In practice these criteria prove to be an administrative burden, and in particular the effectiveness testing requires appropriate systems and market data. IAS 39 requires two types of effectiveness tests to be performed at the financial reporting date and are reproduced as follows:

1. **Prospective test** looks at whether a hedging relationship is likely to be effective in future periods.
2. **Retrospective test** looks back over the past period to assess whether the hedging relationship has been effective.

The IAS 39 does not prescribe a single method for assessing hedge effectiveness prospectively or retrospectively. However, the four most common methods used are reproduced from IAS 39 and are as follows:

- **Critical terms comparison**: This is a simple test which does not require any calculations as it is purely a comparison to ensure that all principal terms such as notional, currency, maturity etc. match. This method is only permitted to assess the prospective hedge effectiveness with a separate assessment required for the retrospective effectiveness test.

- **Sensitivity scenario analysis:** This is a quantitative method of assessing prospective effectiveness by comparing the underlying value of the hedged item and hedging instrument given a hypothetical shift in the hedged risk.

- **Dollar offset method**: This is a quantitative method that compares the change in fair value of the hedging instrument with the change in fair value of the hedged item attributable to the hedged risk. The calculation can be performed on a cumulative basis (i.e., since inception of the hedge) or on a period-by-period basis. A cumulative basis has the advantage that it is less likely to give rise to small movements that can lead to ineffectiveness as there is no materiality threshold applied to the 80 to 125 percent calculation. This method can only be used to assess the retrospective effectiveness.

- **Regression analysis**: This is a statistical method that assesses the strength of the statistical relationship between the hedged item and the hedging instrument. The regression analysis essentially involves determining a "line of best fit" and the "goodness of fit" of the line. The slope of the line must be between -0.8 and -1.25, the coefficient of determination (R^2) must be greater than 0.96, and the F statistic must be "significant."

In practice the critical terms comparison is a highly efficient and effective prospective effectiveness method, where all critical terms match such as with an asset swap package. The choice of whether to apply the dollar offset or regression method is often based upon system constraints. However, the portfolio manager should bear in mind that since there is no de minimis materiality threshold for IFRS testing and small fair value changes can lead to ineffectiveness, the regression approach is much safer.

International Accounting Standard 39 identifies three different types of hedges:

1. **Fair value hedge** is used where the risk being hedged is the change in fair value of the underlying asset or liability (e.g., a fixed bond hedged with an interest rate swap to generate a variable rate);

2. **Cash flow hedge** is used where the risk being hedged is the exposure to variability in cash flows (e.g., a variable deposit hedged with an interest rate swap to generate a fixed rate); and

3. **Hedge of a net investment in a foreign operation** is used where an entity is exposed to currency risk arising from its overseas operation.

The interest rate hedges within a typical credit portfolio are most likely to be fair value hedges although it would be possible to apply cash flow hedge accounting to match the floating rate funding. If all of the conditions outlined above are met, hedge accounting modifies the way gains or losses are recognized as follows:

- **Fair value hedges** are the gains or losses due to the hedged risk and are recognized directly in the profit and loss account for both the hedging instrument and the hedged item. In particular, a fair value hedge modifies the carrying amount and/or gains or losses recognition whenever subsequent measurement of the hedged item is at cost or deferred into the equity reserve (available-for-sale assets) (IAS 39.89).

- **Cash flow hedges** are the gains or losses on the hedging instrument that effectively hedge the risk and are deferred into the equity reserve while the ineffective portion is recognized in the profit and loss account (IAS 39.95). Therefore, cash flow hedges modify the accounting treatment of the hedging

F I G U R E   2.2

Schematic representation of fair value hedge accounting

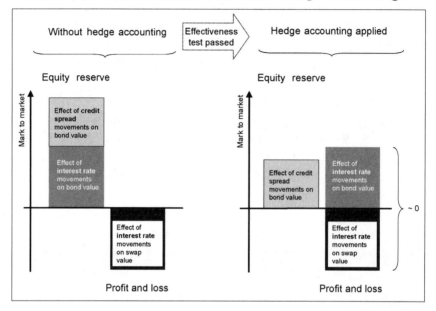

instrument, which in most cases is a derivative by deferring gains or losses due to the hedged risk in the equity reserve.

Fair value hedges can be considered schematically as illustrated in Figure 2.2 above.

Although hedge accounting undoubtedly produces a much more symmetrical accounting result, it has a high administrative burden and unless the more complex regression method is used, there is always a risk of ineffectiveness. Furthermore, hedge accounting does not solve the problem that there is inconsistent accounting treatment when derivatives are used to create synthetic positions within the portfolio as the mark-to-market movement on all derivatives must be shown in the profit and loss account.

The Fair Value Option

The provisions about FVO allow an entity to designate any financial asset or liability at fair value with changes recognized in the profit and loss account. FVO is the only possible for instruments containing embedded derivatives or when it results in more relevant information because it reduces or eliminates an accounting inconsistency with the risk management or investment strategy (IAS 39.9, IAS 39.11A). To impose discipline with this optional classification, FVO designation can be only made at initial recognition of the financial instrument, and subsequent to initial recognition, it is not possible to reclassify any financial asset or liability into or out of this category (IAS 39.IN16).

In the notes to the financial statements the entity has to disclose the financial assets and liabilities for which it has adopted the FVO, indicating the reason for the designation and its consistency with the risk management or investment strategy. Fair value option is forbidden only when a quoted market price for the financial instrument is not available or where the fair value cannot be reliably measured. Adopting the FVO for some of the financial instruments within certain transactions, it is therefore possible to align the accounting treatment of the overall transaction to reflect its economic reality. This can be shown schematically as explained in Figure 2.3.

FIGURE   2.3

Schematic representation of FVO

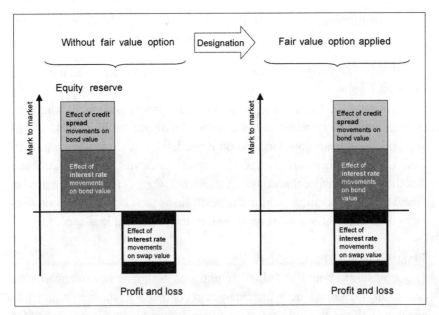

F I G U R E   2.4

Comparison of fair value option and hedge accounting

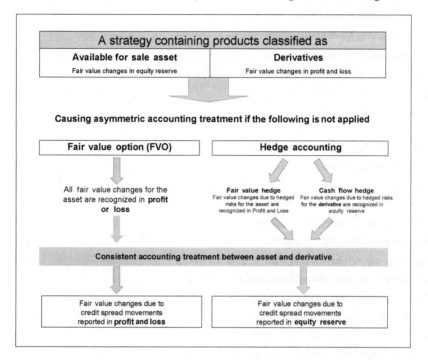

Figure 2.4 summarizes how FVO and hedge accounting modifies the general rules about gains and losses recognition.

An example with tangible figures may highlight the differences of the various accounting treatments available to a portfolio manager (see Box 2.1). The economic results of scenario A are as follows:[2]

- +€231,000 for the bond (of which +€78,000 is due to the fall in interest rates and +€153,000 due to the tightened credit spread)
- −€80,000 for the swap due to the fall in interest rates

---

[2] Results are simplified due to didactical reasons. It is assumed that a 10-bp interest rate shift changes the value of the €10m swap by €10,000 p.a. over the next 10 years. Each of the sum of all changes (10 × 10,000) is then discounted with the appropriate discount factor resulting in a net present value change, say €80,000. The change in value of the bond attributable to interest rate movements is assumed to be €78,000.

B O X   2.1

Data and assumptions of accounting example

Assumptions

1. On January 1, 2008 a bank purchases a fixed-term bond with a notional value of €10m at par paying a coupon of 5 percent per annum and a maturity of 10 years.
2. Interest is swapped into floating rate with a payer swap, i.e., the interest rate risk is hedged and the bank receives London Interbank Offered Rate (LIBOR) + 50 bps.
3. Initially the swap has a market value of zero; thus the implicit credit spread is 50 bps.
4. In the course of the year, the following market movements are observed:

Scenario A

- Interest rates fall by 10 bps.
- Credit spreads narrow by 20 bps.

Scenario B

- Interest rates fall by 10 bps.
- Credit spreads widen by 20 bps.

The economic results of scenario B are as follows:

- −€75,000 for the bond (of which +€78,000 is due to the fall in interest rates and −€153,000 due to the widened credit spread)
- −€80,000 for the swap due to the fall in interest rates

From an accounting perspective the results will depend upon the accounting treatment (see Tables 2.3 and 2.4):

T A B L E   2.3

Results of scenario A for different accounting treatments

	Standard Treatment (€K)		Fair Value Hedge Accounting (€K)		Fair Value Option (€K)	
	Profit and Loss	Equity Reserve	Profit and Loss	Equity Reserve	Profit and Loss	Equity Reserve
Swap	−80	−	−80	−	−80	−
Bond	−	+231	−	+231	+231	−
Hedge adjustment	−	−	+78	−78	−	−
Result	**−80**	**+231**	**−2**	**+153**	**+151**	**−**

T A B L E   2.4

Results of scenario B for different accounting treatments

	Standard Treatment (€K)		Fair Value Hedge Accounting (€K)		Fair Value Option (€K)	
	Profit and Loss	Equity Reserve	Profit and Loss	Equity Reserve	Profit and Loss	Equity Reserve
Swap	−80	−	−80	−	−80	−
Bond	−	−75	−	−75	−75	−
Hedge adjustment	−	−	+78	−78	−	−
Result	**−80**	**−75**	**−2**	**−153**	**−155**	**−**

To conclude, the standard treatment leads to an asymmetrical result in the bank's accounts. While the changes in value of the swap are shown in the profit and loss account, the changes in the fair value of the bond are recorded in the equity reserve, although the position is economically hedged and interest rate changes are neutralized.

The use of hedge accounting significantly reduces these effects and only a small residual net loss is shown in the profit and loss account after applying hedge accounting. The net loss is termed the *hedge ineffectiveness* and arises because the change in the fair value of the bond attributable to interest rate movements does not exactly offset the change in the value of the swap resulting from the fixing of the floating rate leg of the swap. Hence, compared to the standard treatment, the volatility of the equity reserve is reduced as well because hedge accounting transfers the bond revaluation due interest rate movements into the profit and loss account. The residual balance in the equity reserve represents the changes in the credit spread of the bond. The FVO approach is straightforward as all changes in value of both instruments are recorded in the profit and loss account and the accounting result is therefore identical to the economic result.

With regard to portfolio management, the asset manager has to anticipate the "desired" effects of profit and loss changes before investing:

- Which components should contribute to the profit and loss (carry, interest rate changes, credit spread movements)?
- The resource required to apply a specific accounting treatment should be regarded in the context of the portfolio size. If the

manager deals with a fairly small portfolio and the organization
has not implemented hedge accounting, then it may be
appropriate to avoid hedge accounting because such a treatment
will incur implementation and documentation costs as well as the
requirement to perform regular ongoing hedge effectiveness tests.

- If the portfolio manager believes that spreads may be volatile
  during the life of the assets, then a FVO approach will result in
  profit and loss volatility, and hence, it is important to perform
  scenario and sensitivity analysis in order that senior management
  are aware of potential profit and loss swings.

- If hedge accounting is applied, then the portfolio manager
  should be aware that any corporate initiatives to realize profit
  could put pressure on him to sell assets as this would be the only
  way to realize profits.

CONCLUSION

International Financial Reporting Standards are extremely technical and
often not simple to understand comprehensively; however, the options
available to the credit portfolio manager are relatively straightforward.
Although there is no best generic accounting treatment that should be
adopted, asymmetric accounting should be avoided at all times as this
could lead to accounting results that would be unacceptable to senior
management and in turn could lead to the portfolio manager's investment
strategy being jeopardized. Hedge accounting and the FVO should be
used to ensure a symmetrical profit and loss result. They both have their
own merits, and it is possible to use a combination of these treatments to
produce the most appropriate solution. The appetite of the organization
to profit and loss volatility must also be considered when deciding upon
the appropriate treatment. It is vital that the accounting decisions are
made at inception of the trade as the designation cannot be made retrospectively. In summary, the credit portfolio manager does not need to be
an accounting expert but should have a good understanding of the
accounting implications and work closely with the accountants within the
organization to ensure an appropriate treatment of the transactions within
the portfolio.

ACKNOWLEDGMENTS

I am deeply grateful for the support I received from Nick Stevens, Head of Finance, and Paul Beard, Head of Financial Control of Landesbank Berlin, London Branch.

CHAPTER 3

The New Basel Capital Framework (Basel II) and Its Impact on Investment Decisions: An Overview

Martin Knocinski

ABSTRACT

This chapter covers the impact of the new rules on capital adequacy published by the Basel Committee on Banking Supervision referred to as *Basel II*, which took effect at the beginning of 2008 and will play an important role in the asset management sector. After a brief introduction of the basic principles of credit risk limitation behind Basel II, this chapter focuses on a detailed discussion of the newly introduced rules on the regulatory treatment of securitizations and credit risk mitigation techniques using credit derivatives and other instruments. Subsequent to that, the chapter looks at some important amendments regarding the regulatory treatment of investments in funds according to the new rules. The chapter concludes with an outlook on possible future developments in the area of banking regulation as well as a brief description of open issues in the Basel II framework.

INTRODUCTION

By signing the Capital Requirements Directive (CRD) for credit institutions and investment firms (which itself is comprised of Directive 2006/48/EC[1] and 2006/49/EC[2]) and amending the formerly existing Banking Directive (2000/12/EC) and Capital Adequacy Directive (93/6/EEC), the Council and the European Parliament replaced the well-established and widely accepted earlier version of the supervisory framework, commonly known as *Basel I*. While this rather long juridical phrase describes the results of a long-lasting consultation process, it does not reflect the actual implications of the recently introduced set of regulatory standards.

There have been discussions about Basel II for several years now. However, given that the final postponement in terms of a one-year transition period[3] (in Europe at least) after the introduction of the new supervisory rules on January 1, 2007 has expired, it is essential that all concerned parties are familiar with the new rules of the game. The basics of Basel I as well as Basel II are straightforward (i.e., banks have to hold 8 percent regulatory capital for different types of risks). However, already under Basel I, understanding how exposure to credit and market risk is determined and how regulatory capital is to be calculated was far more complex and quite often required expert knowledge. In fact, the introduction of Basel II even increased the complexity of banks' minimum capital requirements. Hence, this chapter provides an overview of which segment of the current banking regulation law is particularly affected by Basel II and how the framework has changed and will change in the future in credit asset management.

THE BASEL ACCORD'S GENERAL PRINCIPLES

In order to mitigate the risk of bank crises and to strengthen the confidence of the general public in the stability of the international financial system,

---

[1] Directive 2006/48/EC of the European Parliament and the Council of 14 June 2006 relating to the taking up and pursuit of the business of credit institutions (recast)
[2] Directive 2006/49/EC of the European Parliament and the Council of 14 June 2006 on the capital adequacy of investment firms and credit institutions (recast)
[3] Directive 2006/48/EC (2006), Article 152 Sec. 8, and Directive 2006/49/EC (2006), Article 50

Basel I and Basel II are limiting credit and market risks that banks, which are subject to supervision,[4] are allowed to expose themselves to on the basis of their individual regulatory capital situation. This particular limitation is expressed as a minimum capital ratio banks must maintain at all times. While according to Basel I, banks must comply with the same rather less risk sensitive rules and processes regarding the relevant capital calculations, the approach of Basel II is more sophisticated (Figure 3.1). The new rules take into account that banks' business models, their individual size, international focus as well as their organizational structures can differ significantly and that a "one size fits all" approach is not adequate in the long run.[5] Basel II leaves the regulations regarding the capital requirements for market risk unchanged compared to Basel I. However, banks face significant changes with respect to their capital requirements for credit risk in the banking book. Basel II now allows for three different approaches to measure credit risk in the banking book.

The Standardized Approach of Basel II is primarily an enhanced version of the widely known approach used to determine the minimum capital requirements in Basel I. While under Basel I determination of individual

FIGURE   3.1

Approaches to measure credit risk according to Basel II

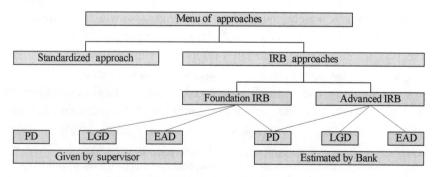

---

[4] Despite the fact that the supervisory rules and hence Basel II are not limited to banks, this chapter will refer to supervised entities only as *banks* for reasons of simplicity.
[5] Basel Committee on Banking Supervision (2001), p. 2.

T A B L E   3.1

Risk weighting of rated corporate claims

External Rating	AAA to AA−	A+ to A−	BBB+ to BB−	Below BB−	Not rated
Risk Weight	20%	50%	100%	150%	100%

capital requirements was done using a broad-brush approach,[6] under Basel II the risk weight is determined based on the credit assessment of an external credit assessment institution (ECAI). In order to allow for a more adequate risk weighting of different kinds of exposures, the Basel II Standardized Approach requires that all relevant credit exposures are divided into 13 groups, eventually into additional subgroups. Each of these groups is provided a table that shows a risk weight to any exposure depending on the relevant external credit assessment. Table 3.1 shows how a risk weighting is assigned to a corporate claim.

Depending on the individual category to which a claim is assigned, in most cases the risk weights range from 20 to 150 percent.[7] It is particularly noticeable that for several categories of claims unrated exposures receive a lower risk weighting than exposures, which are assigned a relatively bad credit assessment. Even if this does not appear to be very reasonable at first glance, the logic behind it is straightforward: By assigning a 100 percent risk weight, the supervisory authorities avoid discrimination of unrated exposures. However, in order to avoid the problem of adverse selection, the supervisory authorities reserve the right to assign higher risk weights than 100 percent in individual cases when appropriate.

As an alternative to the Standardized Approach, banks can measure their credit risk exposure and hence determine their minimum capital

---

[6] Using risk weights as an indication of an exposure's individual credit risk is based on the differentiation of debtors into governments and public sector entities, financial institutions (basically banks) and other corporates or private debtors, and whether these debtors are domiciled in an Organisation for Economic Co-operation and Development (OECD) member country or not as well as the exposure's individual time to maturity.

[7] Lower risk weights of 0 or 10 percent, respectively, are applied to claims against governments and covered bonds with an external rating of AA−/Aa3 or better. Higher risk weights of 350 or 1,250 percent are applied to securitization exposures with an external rating of BB−/Ba3 or below. For a more detailed discussion, refer to the Introduction of this chapter.

requirements using an internal rating-based approach (IRB approach),[9] which is subject to approval of the bank's supervisor. Banks which comply with strict supervisory rules regarding the application of an IRB approach and obtain their supervisor's approval, may determine the credit risk using their own estimations. In this context, banks have to calculate the expected loss (EL) using the functional relationship between the input parameters probability of default (PD), loss given default (LGD), exposure at default (EAD) and maturity (*M*) as shown below.

$$EL = EAD \times f(PD, M) \times LGD$$

The key difference between the Advanced Internal Rating-Based Approach and the Foundation Internal Rating-Based Approach is the fact that a bank using the Advanced Internal Rating-Based Approach is allowed to estimate not only the input parameter PD but also the input parameters EAD and LGD. Hence, using the Advanced Internal Rating-Based Approach (i.e., making more extensive use of own estimations than in the Foundation Internal Rating-Based Approach) results in a significantly larger number of individual risk weights and in the ideal case in a far better risk sensitivity as compared to Basel I.

SELECTED AMENDMENTS IN BASEL II

In addition to the improvements described in the previous section, Basel II introduces many more very complex as well as significant changes.[10] Despite the significance of the new Basel framework in general, as well as the significance of individual issues in particular, the scope of this article must be limited to a small number of developments due to (1) the ever growing significance of securitization transactions, (2) the recent trend of

---

[8] Within the IRB approach, Basel II distinguishes between the Foundation Internal Rating-Based Approach and the Advanced Internal Rating-Based Approach.

[9] For a more detailed discussion, compare Felsenheimer, J., Gisdakis, P., and Zaiser, M. (2006), pp. 534–538.

[10] Representing other changes under Basel II, it is referred to as the introduction of the supervisory review process (pillar 2), the so-called market discipline or extended disclosure requirements (pillar 3), as well as the introduction of regulatory capital requirements for operational risks.

financial engineering to structure more and more complex financial instruments (in most cases with the intention to achieve a preferential regulatory and/or accounting treatment as compared to plain vanilla instruments), and last but not least (3) the credit crisis we experienced during the third and fourth quarters of 2007. This chapter will discuss the new rules regarding the regulatory treatment of securitization transactions and credit risk mitigation techniques.[11] Moreover, this chapter will provide detailed information on the impact of the amendments of the regulations regarding the regulatory treatment of shares in a fund.

Securitization Transactions According to Basel II

The Basel framework from 1988 did not include any specific rules regarding the regulatory treatment of exposures, which have been originated in the context of a securitization transaction. Such regulations were developed—first for so-called true sale transactions and for synthetic transactions in a second step—during multilateral discussions between banks, representatives of supervisory authorities, and other stakeholders in the second half of the 1990s, i.e., a long time after the introduction of the Basel I framework. From a regulatory point of view, there are two key questions when looking at securitizations: (1) Do the securitized assets (in the following: securitization exposures) still attract capital charges for the securitizing bank? (2) How does the bank, which purchases the assets, have to account for the securitization exposures from a regulatory perspective, i.e., which risk weight has to be applied to the exposure?

In order to achieve regulatory relief, i.e., to be released from the obligation to hold capital against securitization exposures, banks are required to show that they have effectively transferred the credit risk from the securitization exposures to another party.[12] The rationale is that banks shall be granted regulatory relief if and only if the credit risk cannot fall

---

[11] Despite the fact that banks in most cases had not applied Basel II rules at that time, in the aftermath of the subprime crisis there have been many discussions among banks and their supervisors as well as other organizations whether Basel II adequately reflects today's business models and product range. As the outcome of these discussions was still unclear at the time of printing, the discussion below is based on the rules as agreed upon in 2006. Compare Basel Committee on Banking Supervision, 2006.

[12] For an overview, compare Struffert, R. (2006), pp. 178–181.

back to the originating bank for any contractual and/or factual obligation after it has been transferred to a third party for the first time.[13] While this is not very difficult to comprehend, it is more difficult to determine which criteria must be fulfilled for an effective risk transfer to exist. However, shortly after true sale securitizations became a quite popular instrument within the banking industry, a catalogue containing different principles[14] and guidance when a risk transfer to be considered effective was developed. While this catalogue was developed under the regime of Basel I, the basic principles are still valid under Basel II as well.

When considering the regulatory treatment of purchased securitization exposures,[15] Basel II entails quite a number of amendments. Securitized assets that are sold in a true sale transaction are transferred to the acquirer for balance sheet purposes as well as for regulatory purposes. Hence, the acquirer is required to treat the securitization exposure in the same way as the originator was required to treat the exposures before their securitization. Determining an adequate risk weight for securitization exposures in the case of synthetic transactions, however, is far more complex. Because it is not possible to match an exposure that is acquired in a securitization with an individual debtor in a synthetic transaction, such exposures are assigned the highest possible risk weight under Basel II of 100 percent. If the exposure meets the relevant criteria[16] in order to qualify as securitization exposure and hence falls under the securitization framework of Basel II, in the Standardized Approach the exposure's risk weight is determined based on its individual external rating as shown in Table 3.2.

---

[13] Compare Lutz, P. (2005), p. 105.

[14] In order for a risk transfer to be considered effective, there must be a legally binding transfer of significant credit risk associated with the securitized exposures. Recourse against the seller of the securitized assets, other than recourse based on the liability for the legal existence, must be excluded. Substitution of receivables between the purchaser and the seller after the transfer must be prohibited, and the securitizing bank has no right to repurchase transferred assets except for cases where the size of the residual portfolio is less than 10 percent of the originally transferred portfolio.

[15] Standard securitization exposures have to be distinguished from so-called first loss positions (FLP). First loss positions are usually not sold to investors by the securitizing bank but kept on the securitizing bank's own books in order to reduce moral hazard issues. Such first loss pieces have to be fully deducted from regulatory capital according to Basel I (or more specifically, the several principles regarding the treatment of securitization exposures under Basel I that were developed subsequent to the introduction of Basel I) as well as according to the new supervisory framework Basel II.

[16] Basel Committee on Banking Supervision (2006), p. 120.

T A B L E   3.2

Risk weighting of rated securitization exposures

External Rating	AAA to AA−	A+ to A−	BBB+to BBB−	BB+ to BB−	B+ or below/ not rated
Risk Weight	20%	50%	100%	350%	1,250%

   When considering the risk weights for securitization exposures in the Standardized Approach of Basel II as shown in the Table 3.2, it becomes apparent that securitization exposures as compared to other exposures are playing a particular role within the new banking supervision rules. In contrast to the fixed 100 percent risk weighting under Basel I, it is possible under Basel II that highly rated securitization exposures receive a preferential risk weight of 20 (external rating of AA−/Aa3 or better) or 50 percent (external rating of A−/A3 or better). However, securitization exposures that have a non-investment grade rating of BB+ or below are assigned much higher risk weights of 350 or 1,250 percent as compared to identically rated nonsecuritization exposures.[17] By applying a wider range of individual risk weights to securitization exposures based on the individual credit risk of the respective exposures, the Standardized Approach in Basel II allows for a more adequate risk weighting of synthetic securitization exposures than Basel I, while using the same simple methodology that is applied for other exposures as well. Nevertheless, the Basel Committee on Banking Supervision was aiming at further improving the risk sensitivity of capital charges for securitization exposures. If a bank applies one of the Internal Rating-Based Approaches, then it can choose one of the three different methods for determining the risk weights of securitization exposures as follows:

---

[17] Furthermore, Basel II treats exposures differently if held by the originator or an investor. In contrast to Figure 3.2, banks which are originators in a securitization exposure have to apply a 1,250 percent risk weight to all positions (i.e., fully deduct the exposure from regulatory capital) without investment-grade rating and that the originating banks keeps on its books. This regulation was not adopted during the European Implementation of Basel II (Capital Requirements Directive) and insofar was not considered during the national adoption in many EU member states.

1. Ratings-based approach (RBA)
2. Supervisory formula approach (SFA)
3. Internal assessment approach (IAA)

However, that does not necessarily mean that banks can choose freely between these three approaches. In fact, Basel II sets out a strict hierarchy as to which approach may be used and which may not.

If an external rating is available or if a rating is inferred,[18] the RBA must be applied to securitization exposures. When using the RBA, the risk weight for securitization exposures is determined in a similar way as compared to using the Standardized Approach for securitization exposures, i.e., the individual risk weight is based on the external or inferred credit assessment. In contrast to the Standardized Approach for securitization exposures however, the RBA also considers the seniority of an individual exposure in relation to the other exposures of the same securitization transaction as well as the granularity of the pool of securitized assets. In this context, higher seniority of the relevant exposure and higher granularity of the pool of the securitized assets reflect lower credit risk and higher risk diversification and hence reduce the applicable risk weight. The individual risk weights for securitization exposures that have a long-term[19] credit rating under the RBA are displayed in Table 3.3.

In essence, exposures are treated as senior positions if those positions have the highest priority in the waterfall, i.e., the highest rated position in case of true sale transactions, super senior swaps in synthetic transactions, as well as liquidity facilities in case of conduit exposures if these facilities are sized to cover all the outstanding commercial paper. According to Basel II, a pool of securitized assets is considered granular if there are at least six different debtors. In this context, debtors that are related to each other in a way that makes it likely that financial problems of one debtor lead to financial problems of the other debtor count as one single debtor and hence do not improve a pool's granularity.

Table 3.3 clearly implies that the qualification of a pool of securitized assets as granular or nongranular has a significant effect on the securitization

---

[18] Basel Committee on Banking Supervision (2006, p. 136). In this case, an unrated position is assigned the external rating of another securitization exposure, which is subordinated as compared to the original exposure in every respect.

[19] For securitization exposures, which have a short-term credit rating, Basel II provides a similar table.

TABLE   3.3

Risk weighting of rated securitization exposures
under the RBA

External Rating	Risk Weights for Senior Positions and Eligible Senior IAA Exposures (Senior, Granular Pool)	Base Risk Weights (Non-Senior, Granular Pool)	Risk Weights for Tranches Backed by Nongranular Pools (Senior/Non-Senior, Non-Granular Pool)
AAA/Aaa	7%	12%	20%
AA+ to AA−/ Aa1 to Aa3	8%	15%	25%
A+/A1	10%	18%	35%
A/A2	12%	20%	35%
A−/A3	20%	35%	35%
BBB+/Baa1	35%	50%	50%
BBB/Baa2	65%	75%	75%
BBB−/Baa3	100%	100%	100%
BB+/Ba1	250%	250%	250%
BB/Ba2	425%	425%	425%
BB−/Ba3	650%	650%	650%
Below BB−/Ba3 or not rated	1,250%	1,250%	1,250%

exposure's individual risk weighting, especially if the relevant position has
an external rating of BBB+ or better. The Basel Committee on Banking
Supervision justifies this with the effect of risk diversification and the resulting reduction of risk concentrations in the case of granular pools. In order
to determine if the underlying portfolio is treated as granular or nongranular,
the Basel II framework refers to the effective number of underlying exposures (N) comprised in the securitized portfolio. Banks can choose between
two alternative methods as to how to calculate N using one of the following
formulas:

$$N = \frac{\left(\sum_i EAD_i\right)^2}{\sum_i EAD_i^2} \quad \text{or} \quad N = \frac{1}{C_1}$$

T A B L E   3.4

Effective number of underlying exposures

	Portfolio 1	Portfolio 2	Portfolio 3
Asset 1	10,000	1,000	780
Asset 2	0	1,000	880
Asset 3	0	1,000	1,390
Asset 4	0	1,000	1,050
Asset 5	0	1,000	900
Asset 6	0	1,000	1,300
Asset 7	0	1,000	1,800
Asset 8	0	1,000	650
Asset 9	0	1,000	800
Asset 10	0	1,000	450
Total Exposure	10,000	10,000	10,000
Effective Number of Underlying Exposures	1	10	8.75

In the formula above, EAD_i stands for the sum of all credit risk positions against the debtor i and C_1 stands for the share that the credit risk position with the highest basis for assessment has in the total of all individual basis for assessment in the securitized portfolio. Thus, both formulas for the calculation of the effective number of underlying exposures not only consider the total number of exposures within the pool but also the concentration within the pool. Table 3.4 illustrates this feature using three different pools as an example.

If an external rating is not available and an external rating cannot be inferred, banks using the Internal Rating-Based Approach for securitization exposures have to apply either the Internal Assessment Approach or the Supervisory Formula Approach. The Internal Assessment Approach may only be used for liquidity facilities and credit enhancements as well as other securitization exposures that were extended to a qualifying asset-backed commercial paper (ABCP) program. If specific minimum requirements[20]

[20] Basel Committee on Banking Supervision (2006), pp. 136–139

for using the Internal Assessment Approach are met, banks may use their internal assessments of the credit quality of the securitization exposure to determine the risk weights. In order to do that, the bank's own estimations are mapped to an external credit rating and applied to Table 3.3 in the RBA for securitizations. In addition, Basel II will introduce other new regulations, e.g., the application of higher capital charges for liquidity facilities depending on their individual structure as compared to Basel I. In particular, under Basel II it is will no longer be allowed to apply a 0 percent risk weight, i.e., not applying capital charges at all, to loan commitments with a maturity of less than one year or loan commitments, which can be canceled without further notice. Despite the fact that under Basel II there will still be 0 percent risk weights for specific loan commitments or liquidity facilities, due to the stricter requirements for qualification as a "0 percent risk weight commitment," overall these will be exceptional cases.

If an external and/or inferred rating is not available and the Internal Assessment Approach cannot be used, IRB banks are required to determine the risk weights of their securitization exposures using the Supervisory Formula Approach. In this case, the capital charge is calculated based on the functional relationship of several input parameters using the formula below.[21]

$$S[L] = \begin{cases} L & \text{when } L \leq K_{IRB} \\ K_{IRB} + K[L] - K[K_{IRB}] + \left(d \times K_{\frac{IRB}{\omega}}\right)\left(1 - \frac{\omega(K_{IRB}-L^e)}{K_{IRB}}\right) & \text{when } K_{IRB} < L \end{cases}$$

The risk weights calculated according to the formula above are floored—similarly to the RBA—to a minimum risk weight of 7 percent.

If none of the three approaches for determining the risk weight of a securitization exposure under the IRB approach of Basel II can be applied, the relevant exposure must be fully deducted from regulatory capital, hence resulting in a 1,250 percent risk weight. As is the case in the

[21] The most important input parameters are (1) the IRB-capital charges for the securitized exposures before securitization including expected loss, (2) the tranche's credit enhancement level, (3) the tranche's thickness, (4) the pool's effective number of underlying exposures, and (5) the pool's exposure-weighted average loss given default. For more details, please refer to Basel Committee on Banking Supervision (2006), pp. 139–143.

Standardized Approach for securitization exposures, the total capital charge for any securitization exposure is limited to the capital that is required before the securitization.

Credit Risk Mitigation Techniques According to Basel II

The definition of credit risk mitigation techniques in the new Basel framework includes all instruments suitable to reduce the credit risk of exposures banks have to hold regulatory capital against. Provided that certain criteria were met, under Basel I, the range of credit risk mitigation techniques that banks were allowed to use was limited to the use of collateral and guarantees in the form of cash deposits and/or certificates of deposit, securities or credit derivatives issued by qualified counterparties (which usually had to have a risk weight of either 0 or 20 percent), netting agreements for derivative contracts or repo-style transactions, and residential (and, based on discretion of the national supervisor, commercial) property.

Depending on the approach banks use to determine their individual capital requirements, the range of eligible credit risk mitigation techniques is significantly enlarged in Basel II. This is reflected in a larger number of eligible types of credit risk mitigants on the one hand and a wider range of eligible protection sellers on the other hand. In theory, banks using the Advanced Internal Rating-Based Approach are not limited at all with respect to the use of credit risk mitigation techniques, provided these banks have the ability to determine the value of the credit risk mitigant reliably. As a result of the broader range of credit risk mitigation techniques banks may use and the higher complexity of the calculation of capital requirements, Basel II poses comprehensive requirements for the use of these techniques (so-called minimum conditions for the use of credit risk mitigation techniques).

The regulatory treatment of credit risk mitigation techniques is discussed for each type and/or group of credit risk mitigant in separate sections of the new Basel framework. The two important groups "financial collateral" and "guarantees and credit derivatives" will be discussed below in detail.[22] As mentioned earlier, the Standardized Approach and the IRB approaches

---

[22] A detailed discussion of different amendments in the Basel II framework with respect to other areas of credit risk mitigation is outside the scope of this article.

use different methodologies. Thus, the provision for the use of credit risk mitigation techniques must be completed differently in the Standardized Approach and in the IRB approach.

For the treatment of financial collateral, there is a simple and a comprehensive approach. The methodology of the simple approach is very similar to the way collateral was treated under Basel I, i.e., substituting the risk weighting of the collateral instrument collateralizing or partially collateralizing the exposure for the risk weighting of the counterparty. In addition to collateral instruments such as cash deposits or certain securities, which are issued by qualified counterparties and already considered eligible collateral under Basel I, Basel II also recognizes gold, rated debt securities with an external rating of BB− or better (issued by sovereigns or public sector entities that are treated as sovereigns by the national supervisor) and BBB− or better (issued by other debtors), respectively, unrated debt securities (where these are issued by a bank, listed on a recognized stock exchange, or classified as senior debt and where all rated issues of the same seniority are rated at least BBB- and the supervisor is adequately certain about the market liquidity of the security), equities, convertible bonds, and shares in a fund that are part of a main index where the unit price is quoted daily and the fund is limited to investing in the instruments. However, in Basel I as well as Basel II when using the simple approach for financial collateral, financial collateral is only eligible provided that it has at least the same time to maturity as the exposure to be collateralized. The risk weight of the collateralized part of an exposure in general[23] cannot be reduced below 20 percent. In contrast to Basel I, under Basel II only banks that do not have an IRB admission will be allowed to use the simple approach for credit risk mitigation techniques.

If banks use a comprehensive approach to determine the suitable risk weight for a transaction secured by financial collateral (or if banks are required to do so because they have their supervisor's authorization to use an IRB approach), then the effect of the credit risk mitigation techniques is not determined by using the simple approach's substitution model.[24] In

---

[23] There are exceptions for transactions that fulfill certain criteria, over-the-counter (OTC) derivatives as well as other secured exposures if particular criteria are met.

[24] In contrast to the simple approach, equities, which are not included in a main index, are considered eligible financial collateral as well in the comprehensive approach. The same holds true for shares in a fund where the fund is invested in equities that are not included in a main index.

fact, under the comprehensive approach, the amount of an exposure against which a bank would have to hold regulatory capital (the basis for assessment) is reduced by offsetting the exposure with financial collateral. In order to account for changes in the market price of the collateral as well as the exposure itself, when using the comprehensive approach for financial collateral, banks have to adjust the amounts of the received collateral as well as the exposure by applying so-called haircuts. If, in addition currency mismatches between the exposure and the financial collateral exist, then the amount of the collateral that is already adjusted for market price volatility must be further adjusted to reflect the foreign exchange risk. As a result, the adjusted amount of the exposure is larger than the amount of the original exposure, while the adjusted amount of the collateral is smaller than the original amount of the collateral. The capital requirement of a collateralized exposure (or the exposure value after risk mitigation) is calculated as the difference in the amount of the adjusted value of the exposure and the adjusted amount of the collateral multiplied by the risk weight of the counterparty as shown in the following formula:

$$E^* \times RW \times 8\% = \text{capital requirement}$$

where E^* is the exposure value after risk mitigation, which is itself calculated using the following formula:

$$E = \max \{0, [E \times (1 + H_e) - C \times (1 - H_c - H_{fx})]\}$$

where E is the exposure's current value and H_e is the haircut appropriate to the exposure.[25] The current value of the collateral received is represented by C. H_c stands for the haircut appropriate for the collateral and H_{fx} for the haircut appropriate for the currency mismatch between the collateral and the exposure. When determining the haircuts under the comprehensive approach, banks again face two different methods on how to do that. On the one hand, banks can use standard supervisory haircuts, which are given in the Basel II framework. Nonetheless, banks can calculate haircuts using their own internal estimates of market price volatility and

---

[25] The size of the haircut depends on the type of underlying exposure as well as on other factors, e.g., the frequency of the revaluation and/or remargining.

foreign exchange volatility or even their own value at risk (VaR) model if they have permission from their supervisor.[26]

While under Basel I maturity mismatches between the secured exposure and the financial collateral were not allowed in order to receive regulatory capital relief when securing exposures with collateral, a bank that is using the comprehensive approach for financial collateral under Basel II might receive capital relief even if there are maturity mismatches. However, in the case of any maturity mismatch, the exposure value after risk mitigation and application of all relevant haircuts needs to be adjusted according to the following formula:[27]

$$P_a = P \frac{t - 0.25}{T - 0.25}$$

The maturity of the exposure and the maturity of the hedge should both be defined conservatively, i.e., the effective maturity of the underlying exposure that is to be secured should be gauged as the longest possible time before the counterparty is scheduled to fulfill his obligation, while for the hedge the shortest possible time to maturity should be considered.[28] The minimum time to maturity for a hedge is three months. However, if the remaining time to maturity is shorter than one year, a bank is only allowed to consider the credit risk mitigation if there is no maturity mismatch between the underlying exposure and the hedge. For any combination of underlying exposures and hedges with remaining time to maturity of between 1 and 10 years, the application of the formula above translates into the adjustment factors as shown in Table 3.5.

In addition to financial collateral as described above, banks can also use guarantees or credit derivatives as credit risk mitigation techniques, provided that these risk mitigants and the bank that is buying protection meet strict criteria, as stipulated in the Basel II framework. Apart from certain operational requirements regarding the risk management system of

---

[26] A detailed discussion of the different approaches is not within the scope of this article.

[27] Where P_a = value of the credit protection adjusted for maturity mismatch; P = credit protection adjusted for any haircuts; t = min$\{T$, residual maturity of the credit protection arrangement$\}$, expressed in years; T = min$\{5$, residual maturity of the exposure$\}$, expressed in years.

[28] Compare Hahn, R. (2007), p. 151.

T A B L E   3.5

Adjustments for maturity mismatches

Maturity Exposure (years)

		1	2	3	4	5	6	7	8	9	10
Maturity Collateral (years)	1	100%	42.86%	27.27%	20%	15.79%	15.79%	15.79%	15.79%	15.79%	15.79%
	2	100%	100%	63.64%	46.67%	36.84%	36.84%	36.84%	36.84%	36.84%	36.84%
	3	100%	100%	100%	73.33%	57.89%	57.89%	57.89%	57.89%	57.89%	57.89%
	4	100%	100%	100%	100%	78.95%	78.95%	78.95%	78.95%	78.95%	78.95%
	5	100%	100%	100%	100%	100%	100%	100%	100%	100%	100%
	6	100%	100%	100%	100%	100%	100%	100%	100%	100%	100%
	7	100%	100%	100%	100%	100%	100%	100%	100%	100%	100%
	8	100%	100%	100%	100%	100%	100%	100%	100%	100%	100%
	9	100%	100%	100%	100%	100%	100%	100%	100%	100%	100%
	10	100%	100%	100%	100%	100%	100%	100%	100%	100%	100%

the bank (i.e., that is buying protection), Basel II further requires legal certainty in order to obtain regulatory capital relief as well as the right and ability to liquidate or take legal possession of collateral. In addition, legal separation of the collateral from the legal property of a custodian as well as the absence of a material positive correlation of the credit quality of the counterparty and the value of the collateral is required.[29] In order to be eligible for credit risk mitigation purposes according to Basel II, the definition of the credit event of credit derivatives must at least comprise default, insolvency, bankruptcy, and restructuring.[30]

While the 1988 Basel Accord did not contain any rules regarding the regulatory treatment of credit derivatives in general or nth-to-default credit derivatives in particular, there have been many questions as to how such positions have to be accounted for from a regulatory perspective. Basel II

---

[29] For structured products in particular there are further important requirements, e.g., the fact that guarantees or credit derivatives have to be settled in a timely manner after the credit event occurs, the fact that guarantees cannot be limited to individual parts of the claims against a debtor, and the fact that agreements according to which the cost of protection can be increased after the protection was bought initially due to deterioration of the credit quality of the debtor are prohibited.

[30] If credit derivatives do not cover restructuring as a credit event, the credit risk mitigant can only be recognized partially.

for the first time provides guidance on how such instruments have to be treated.[31] If, for example, a bank wants to protect a basket of assets using first-to-default credit derivatives, then the protection in the amount of the credit derivative's guaranteed amount is recognized against the asset in the basket with the lowest risk weighted amount. In the case a bank purchased second-to-default credit derivatives in order to protect a basket of different assets, the protection can only be recognized if either first-to-default protection was purchased as well or there already has been at least one default in the basket. Provided the guarantees or credit derivatives meet the relevant minimum requirements and are thus considered eligible credit risk mitigants, their effect on the capital requirements is determined using the same substitution approach as in the simple approach for financial collateral. Currency mismatches and maturity mismatches in the case of eligible guarantees and credit derivatives are treated the same way in the comprehensive approach for financial collateral.

REGULATORY TREATMENT OF SHARES IN A FUND ACCORDING TO BASEL II

The regulatory treatment of shares in a fund is another field where Basel II introduces some major changes. Before Basel II came into force, shares in a fund were treated from a regulatory perspective like common equity shares or other non-fixed rate securities and were thus assigned a risk weight of 100 percent. This procedure has been criticized long before[32] Basel II was implemented because it inadequately reflects the true credit risk that an investor in a share in a fund faces. One reason is that an investment company's fund assets are legally separated from the investment company and thus assume no liability for payments of the debts of the investment company itself. Consequently, the credit risk of a share in a fund equals the credit risk of the individual investments in a fund. Many national supervisory authorities within the EU consider determining the

---

[31] Despite the fact that the first Basel accord did not provide any explicit rules regarding the regulatory treatment of credit derivatives, most national supervisors soon developed a generally accepted set of rules. Compare Schulte-Mattler, H. and Meyer-Ramloch, D. (2005), pp. 537–561.

[32] The German Supervisory Authority BaFin allowed the use of the so-called look-through approach as an allowed alternative as early as 1993.

risk weight of a share in a fund by "looking through" the fund to the individual investments and applying the average risk weight based on the actual asset allocation of the fund. This principle is referred to as *look-through approach*. If banks intend on using the look-through approach, then they are required to meet the following criteria:

1. Consistent application for all shares in one particular fund (i.e., the decision of whether to apply a standard risk weight of 100 percent or to use the look-through approach can be made for each investment fund).
2. Banks must ensure that the average risk weight of the fund is calculated at least monthly.
3. The investment company's auditor must confirm that the calculation of the average risk weight is performed according to the relevant rules three months after the end of the investment company's financial year.

In the Standardized Approach of Basel II, the risk weighting of shares in a fund—as is true for other exposures—in general, depends on the external rating of the relevant exposure and can be derived from Table 3.6.

In addition to determining the appropriate risk weights for shares in a fund based on Table 3.6, banks can examine the fund's individual investments. Within the look-though approach there are two different ways how banks can calculate their individual capital requirements. If the actual composition of the fund is known, then the calculation of the risk weights of the shares in a fund is done in the same manner as compared to Basel I. Therefore, banks would be required to assign each underlying asset to one of the different asset classes given in Basel II and assigning the respective risk weights.

T A B L E   3.6

Risk weighting of shares in a fund

External Rating	AAA to AA−	A+ to A−	BBB+ to BB−	Below BB−	Not rated
Risk Weight	20%	50%	100%	150%	100%

In contrast to the rules of the 1988 accord, under Basel II banks can now use an average risk weight for the risk weighting of shares in a fund even if the actual composition of the fund is unknown. In this case, the calculation of an average risk weight is done assuming that the fund, based on the fund's prospectus, is invested up to the maximum possible amount in such assets with the highest risk weight (in descending order of risk weights). The requirement for using the look-through approach is that the shares in a fund are issued by an investment company subject to supervision as set out in the Undertakings for Collective Investment in Transferable Securities (UCITS) directive.[33] However, the fund prospectus contains sufficient information to calculate the average risk weight according to model-based approach. For this purpose, the fund prospectus must at least provide information regarding the general asset classes the fund can be invested in, the relative limits up to which the fund can invest in a single asset class, as well as information on how these upper limits are recalculated.

If an external rating is not available and an average risk weight cannot be calculated either according to the actual composition of the fund or by using the described model-based approach, shares in a fund shall be applied a 100 percent risk weight. In order to avoid regulatory arbitrage and to allow for adequate capital charges, the national supervisory authorities have the right to apply risk weights of 150 percent or more to shares in a fund, which bear significantly higher risks. However, in some legislations there is still uncertainty if the look-through approach can be used for shares in a fund whether or not an external rating of a qualified rating agency is available. While the wording of the respective EU directive does not explicitly forbid the use of the look-through approach in cases where an external rating is available, the national implementation within many EU member countries is stricter, as the use of external ratings shall be preferred to other allowed alternative treatments.

For the Standardized Approach, the risk weight is determined by looking at the external credit assessments provided by eligible ECAIs. In the case of the IRB approach the risk weight is (as discussed in the

---

[33] Commission Directive 2007/16/EC of 19 March 2007 implementing Council Directive 85/611/EEC on the coordination of laws, regulations, and administrative provisions relating to undertakings for collective investment in transferable securities (UCITS) as regards the clarification of certain definitions

section The Basel Accord's General Principles) a function of different variables, e.g., the estimated probability of default, the estimated loss given default, and an adjustment factor for the remaining time to maturity of exposures. The individual value for each of these parameters depends on in which of the asset classes[34] the exposure is categorized. For the IRB approach, exposures to credit risk resulting from a long position in shares in a fund are treated identically to exposures that are not part of a share in a fund, provided that the bank either knows the composition of the investment fund or is able to make an assumption on the composition of the investment fund. The share in a fund is issued by an investment company that is subject to supervision as set out in the UCITS directive, and the underlying exposure itself would qualify for treatment according to the IRB approach.

The approach described here translates into an obligatory use of the look-through approach for shares in a fund in the IRB approach. Where the composition of an investment fund is known or can be determined according to the model-based approach (but at least one other requirement as described above is not met), the position with an equity exposure has to be treated as equity position and is applied a risk weight depending on the individual type of exposure. For example, 190 percent for non-publicly traded exposures that are part of a sufficiently diversified portfolio, 290 percent for publicly traded exposures, and 370 percent for other equity exposures.[35] If the relevant position is not an equity exposure, then it is categorized in the respective asset class according to the rules in the Standardized Approach. The applicable risk weight in this case is the risk weight that would have normally been applied to exposures with a credit assessment, which is one credit quality step worse.

If it is not possible to assign a credit assessment to the respective position, then the applicable risk weight (substitutional risk weight) depends on the risk weight that would have been applied to the position according to the Standardized Approach (preset risk weight). The applicable risk weight can be determined by Table 3.7.

---

[34] The asset classes comprise claims against (1) sovereigns, (2) banks, (3) corporates, (4) retail exposures with three subclasses, (5) equity, (6) securitized assets, and (7) other assets.
[35] If a clear classification is not possible, a 370 percent risk weight has to be applied.

T A B L E   3.7

Risk weighting for shares in a fund in the IRB approach

Preset Risk Weight	0%	10%	20%	35%	50%	75%	100%	150%
Substitutional Risk Weight	0%	10%	20%	35%	50%	75%	100%	200%

Shares in a fund where the composition is not known by the bank and which cannot be determined according to the prospectus-based approach is treated as other equity exposure and accordingly risk weighted with 370 percent.

OUTSTANDING ISSUES

Despite the significant increase in size and complexity, the new Basel Accord makes no claim to be a complete set of banking supervisory regulations that provides answers to every question possible. In fact, the success of Basel II is likely to depend on the current regulations and whether the inherent methodologies in Basel II will be flexible enough and applicable to a wide range of different exposures in order to keep up with the rapid developments in the international capital markets that we have experienced in the recent past. Several issues still leave room for uncertainty or interpretation and can be of particular importance in the near future. Some of these issues as well as possible solutions to existing problems will be discussed briefly.

In order to determine whether a credit risk mitigation technique attracts regulatory capital relief under Basel II, banks have to assess whether the credit quality of the debtor of the collateralized exposure and the credit quality of the financial collateral are positively correlated in a more than a just irrelevant way. The new Basel framework does not provide any information or guidance as to what level of correlation shall be considered material and when a correlation is negligible because of a lack of material correlation and how correlation has to be measured for regulatory purposes. While there is no doubt that it is not allowable to have an exposure against a counterparty collateralized by debt securities issued by the same counterparty, such issues can be difficult to decide in practice.

Until the initial adoption of the new Basel Accord at the beginning of 2008, many EU member countries and national supervisory authorities have not published detailed information on how banks should deal with these types of issues. However, it is likely that there are several appropriate approaches to complicate issues and to maintain a level playing field for all banks; it is helpful if the supervisory authorities can provide detailed guidance.

Furthermore, the question of whether interest rate risk in the banking book will play a more important role with respect to banks' minimum capital requirements in the future has not been sufficiently answered. According to Basel I, banks in general did not have to account for interest rate risk in the banking book when calculating their minimum capital requirements. Although Basel II does not deal with interest rate risk in the banking book within the rules regarding the minimum capital requirements (pillar 1), these risks are discussed within pillar 2 (supervisory review process) of Basel II. According to the wording of Basel II, national supervisors are expected to require banks to reduce their risks or hold specific additional amounts of capital in the case a bank's economic value declines by more than 20 percent of the sum of Tier 1 and Tier 2 capital as a result of a standardized interest rate shock (so-called outlier banks).

Many national supervisors have already adopted this regulation and have provided guidance on how the effect of the interest rate shock on the bank's economic value can be calculated. In order to implement measures, many national supervisors require banks to report the fact that they qualify as an outlier bank. However, there is uncertainty regarding the question as to which measures the national supervisor will take if a bank's economic value is at high risk in the case of an interest rate shock. In the case that the national supervisors will opt for a capital charge for interest rate risk in the banking book as well, it is still not clear how the capital charge itself will have to be calculated. While it is possible that supervisors will use the same approach to interest rate risk as in the trading book, they could also demand that banks use an approach that is different from the one in the trading book.

Against the background of the turmoil on international credit markets during the third and fourth quarters of 2007, it is likely that Basel II will be thoroughly analyzed to see if it passes the test or if the subprime crisis revealed shortcomings with respect to the new supervisory rules paving the way for future amendments of the Basel II framework. Many questions, primarily regarding accounting issues, have already been discussed. For example, there is a great deal of criticism regarding the accounting standards on the consolidation of special purpose vehicles (SPVs). From a regulatory perspective, certain liquidity facilities (time to maturity below one year or cancelable without further notice) that were extended to ABCP programs or other financing structures did not attract any capital charge under Basel I were subject to criticism. Moreover, there are doubts if external ratings in general are suitable instruments for determining an exposure's risk weighting if these ratings tend to be unstable in turbulent markets. If some of these criticisms are appropriate, then it is important to remember that at the time when isolated problems are developing into an international credit crisis, most banks still had a tendency to apply the old Basel I rules (because they were not yet required to adopt Basel II). Despite the fact that the Basel committee has already developed new rules regarding the treatment of securitization exposures and credit risk mitigation techniques (e.g., higher capital charges for extended liquidity facilities), it had a soothing effect on recent developments.

RELEVANT DEVELOPMENTS WITHIN OTHER FIELDS AND CONCLUSION

As discussed in the section Selected Amendments in Basel II, the regulatory capital requirements for securitizations will bring some major changes when compared with Basel I. In the Standardized Approach and in the IRB Approach, securitization exposures having an external rating of BBB+ or better, or BBB− or better, will attract lower capital charges going forward. Furthermore, securitization exposures with an external rating of AAA will attract a five times lower capital charge when using the Standardized Approach and up to a maximum of 14 times lower capital charge when using an IRB approach as compared to rules under the 1988 Basel Accord. At the same time, securitization exposures rated below investment grade will attract significantly higher capital charges under Basel II, exposures with an external rating of BB− or below have to be fully deducted from regulatory capital and are hence treated in the same manner as first loss pieces.

It is likely that the changed regulatory environment will affect the spreads of securitization exposures further. The new rules regarding the regulatory treatment of securitization exposures in terms of application of more risk sensitive risk weights, the capital charges for liquidity facilities as well as other credit enhancements used in securitization transactions will reduce the incentive for regulatory arbitrage. Nevertheless, also after the implementation of Basel II, securitizations will continue to be attractive and effective instruments for achieving a broad range of different aims, even if the economic rationale as compared with regulatory reasons will likely play an increasing role.

With respect to shares in a fund, Basel II will introduce a number of amendments to the previous rules, which might have a major impact on the relative attractiveness of this asset class. While the rules in the Standardized Approach of Basel II basically remain unchanged as compared with the rules according to Basel I, the introduction of the two IRB approaches leads to a factual obligation to use the so-called look-through approach. When considering this factual obligation in combination with the generally increased risk sensitivity of capital charges for shares in a fund, it is likely that Basel II will lead to more risk sensitive capital requirements. In this context, the actual composition of the fund will become more important for banks from a regulatory perspective. The rule in the new Basel framework requires banks to treat unknown exposures to a fund as other equity exposures. Hence, the resulting 370 percent risk weight (which is almost four times the capital charge that would have been applied under Basel I) will be a strong incentive for banks to know at all times what assets comprise the funds where the bank is invested instead of buying shares in a fund with unknown composition. Despite the fact that using average risk weights was allowed already under Basel I, the possibility to calculate the average risk weight based on the fund's prospectus or similar documents will simplify the regulatory treatment of shares in a fund to a certain extent.

Compared with previous regulations, Basel II introduced a comprehensive framework for the recognition of eligible credit risk mitigation techniques and the procedure on how to calculate the respective capital relief. In the Standardized Approach as well as in the IRB approach, the range of eligible credit risk mitigation techniques has been significantly increased. Due to the also increased complexity of capital requirement calculations, the requirements for the use of credit risk mitigation techniques became stricter and more formal.

Another important improvement in the advanced approach for financial collateral under Basel II is the fact that maturity mismatches between the collateralized exposure and the financial collateral itself no longer prejudices the eligibility of such collateral. In general, the credit risk mitigation framework in Basel II introduces several amendments with respect to the methods and procedures as to how regulatory capital relief can be achieved. Thus, the regulatory rules to manage different risk exposures comprised in Basel II and the current risk management practice of banks and other companies in the financial services sector are converging.

REFERENCES

Basel Committee on Banking Supervision (2001) The New Basel Capital Accord: An Explanatory Note. Basel.

Basel Committee on Banking Supervision (2006) International Convergence of Capital Measurements and Capital Standards—A Revised Framework Comprehensive Version. Basel.

Directive 2006/48/EC (2006) Directive 2006/48/EC of the European Parliament and the Council of 14 June 2006 relating to the Taking up and Pursuit of the Business of Credit Institutions (recast). Brussels, Strasbourg.

Directive 2006/49/EC (2006) Directive 2006/49/EC of the European Parliament and the Council of 14 June 2006 on the Capital Adequacy of Investment Firms and Credit Institutions (recast). Brussels, Strasbourg.

Felsenheimer, J., Gisdakis, P., and Zaiser, M. (2006). *Active Credit Portfolio Management — A Practical Guide to Credit Risk Management Strategies*. Weinheim, Germany: John Wiley & Sons.

Hahn, R. (2007) Kreditrisikominderungstechniken. In T. Cramme, T. Gendrisch, and W. Gruber (eds.), *Handbuch Solvabilitätsverordnung — Eigenkapitalunterlegung von Markt-,*

Kredit- und Operationellem Risiko, Stuttgart: Schäffer-Poeschel Verlag, pp. 137–158.

Lutz, P. (2005) Verbriefungstransaktionen aus dem bankaufsichtlichen Blickwinkel—Betrachtungen zu Eigenmittel-und Großkreditvorschriften. In D. Auerbach and J.-Z. Zerey (eds.), *Handbuch Verbriefungen*. Berlin: Verlag für Wirtschafts-kommunikation, pp. 103–128.

Schulte-Mattler, H. and Meyer-Ramloch, D. (2005) Bankaufsichtliche Behandlung von Kreditderivaten in Deutschland. In H.-P. Burghof, S. Henke, and B. Rudolph (eds.), *Kreditderivate — Handbuch für die Bank- und Anlagepraxis*. Stuttgart: Schäffer-Poeschel Verlag, pp. 537–572.

Struffert, R. (2006) *Asset Backed Securities-Transaktionen und Kreditderivate nach IFRS und HGB*. Wiesbaden: Deutscher Universitäts-Verlag.

CHAPTER 4

Basel II Expected Loss as a Control Parameter

Bernd Appasamy and Uwe Dörr

ABSTRACT

According to Basel II the total expected loss, i.e., the sum of the expected loss of active credits and the expected loss of defaulted credits, has to be covered by capital or provisions. Unlike the expected loss of active transactions, the expected loss of defaulted transactions does not refer to the one-year time horizon, and therefore, the economical interpretation of the total expected loss becomes difficult. We provide a practical economical interpretation of the different expected loss components and point out how this interpretation can be applied within credit risk management, i.e., in the context of loss forecasts, true sales, provisioning, and the calculation of risk premia.

INTRODUCTION

Recently, many institutions have invested considerably towards the implementation of the advanced Basel II approach. Over the course of the implementation process, internal experience in the measurement of credit risks has been developed. From the regulatory point of view, the main purpose of the internal measurement of credit risk is to determine the minimum capital provisions for credit risk. Besides, this application of the Basel II methods for internal risk management is mandatory for regulatory approval. The financial use of investing in the advanced Basel II approach has two aspects: improvement of internal control and (possibly) capital relief. While capital relief is not necessarily attained, improvement of internal control can always be used to enhance the institution's financial situation.

Part of internal control is the assessment of the overall risk situation of the bank in light of appropriate parameters, for example, expected loss (EL). Over the course of the Basel II implementation, a standardized and detailed definition of EL has been introduced. The way this definition should be interpreted from the economic point of view will be the main subject of discussion in this article. Based on the correct interpretation of EL, we illustrate how EL can be used for controlling credit risk. Here we concentrate on the control parameters write-off amount and loss provisioning.

DISCUSSION: USE OF EL IN RISK MANAGEMENT

Expected Loss Definition According to Basel II

Expected loss is an estimate for losses that occur within a specific future time horizon. Typically, the time horizon being considered is one year and coincides with the standardized, regulatory definition of the EL. When an institution calculates its portfolio EL according to the Basel II regulations, then evidently, it leaves us to interpret the result as a loss that is expected within the following year. However, this interpretation would be correct only if losses due to credit defaults were immediately realized, for example, through selling of the defaulted receivables. In order to further our understanding, first we consider the definition of the EL within Basel II more precisely.

Within the Basel II framework, active and defaulted receivables are treated separately. Although a default definition is given within the framework, this is rather coarse, thus leaving a certain degree of flexibility for the institution in defining a concrete default event. The same holds for the definition of economic loss; here, e.g., all essential costs associated with credit defaults, including, for example, refinancing costs, must be included.

Based on the definition of default and economic loss, the credit risk parameters are defined as follows within the Basel II framework:

- The *probability of default* (PD) is the probability that a default event occurs within a one-year time horizon.
- The *exposure at default* (EAD) is the outstanding amount at the time of default.
- The *loss given default* (LGD) is the expected economic loss in percent of the outstanding amount at the time of default.

In many cases, the defaulted receivables are not immediately written off or sold but are transferred to a recovery management process. As a consequence, the loss is not immediate but is only realized at the end of the recovery period. Hence, the bank finds a part of its portfolio to be already in default but has not yet completed the recovery process to reach termination (defaulted portfolio). By considering the relationship between the defaulted and active portfolio, one deduces that, in general, the size of the defaulted portfolio (B_D) is almost negligible compared to the size of the active portfolio (B_A). As a rule of thumb the following relationship applies,

$$B_D = B_A \, \mathrm{PD} \, T_{\mathrm{wo}}$$

The quantity PD denotes the average probability of default, and T_{wo} is the average time for the liquidation process in years (workout time). If defaulted receivables were immediately sold, the time duration of the liquidation process would be zero; hence, there would be no defaulted assets in the portfolio at all. In general, however, the average time of the liquidation process varies considerably over different business units. In automobile financing, for example, it has been observed that on average the length of the workout period is of the order of one year (or smaller), while for mortgage financing a period of around three years is observed. Assuming an average default probability of 1 percent, the above formula yields a 1 percent volume for the defaulted portfolio in automobile financing, and 3 percent in the case of mortgage financing.

As far as the EL is concerned, however, the ratio between active portfolio and defaulted portfolio is substantially different from the simple ratio of the sizes of the two portfolios. In order to understand this, we shall first clarify how the two parts of EL are calculated in a way that conforms to Basel II. For the active portfolio, the EL of a single position is calculated as the product of PD, LGD, and EAD. In order to take into account correlations between PD and LGD, LGD must be estimated conservatively (known as the *downturn requirement*). The EL for an active portfolio (EL_A) is obtained by summarizing the single positions. The quantity EL_A represents an estimate for the loss to be expected within the following year, independent of the time at which the single losses are realized.

To adhere to Basel II regulations, an estimation of the EL of each position within the defaulted portfolio has to be given that is as accurate as possible; this is known as the *best estimate EL* (BEEL). On the one hand, best estimation means that all available information (for example, the status in the liquidation process) is to be used. On the other hand, contrary to the LGD estimation for the active portfolio, there is no need to make particularly conservative assumptions. From the summation of the BEEL over all single positions in the defaulted portfolio, one obtains the quantity EL_D. Consequently, the quantity EL_D can be interpreted as an estimate for the total loss that is expected to arise from the positions that are already in default. Similarly, as for the EL of the active portfolio, this is independent of the time at which the single losses are realized.

Typically, values of both the EL_D and EL_A lie within the same order of magnitude. However, for a liquidation process with a long duration of well over a year and a correspondingly large defaulted portfolio, the EL_D can be significantly larger than EL_A. The meaning of the EL within Basel II, according to its definition, is summarized in Figure 4.1.

Write-off Amount

At this stage the EL according to the above definition cannot be used as a forecast for the losses to be incurred in the following year. The reason is that losses are usually not realized immediately at the time of default and hence a defaulted portfolio exists. How can EL be understood correctly and how can it be used for internal control purposes. It is indeed possible to use EL as a loss forecast for the following year—as long as EL_A is considered as the characteristic parameter. To understand this, use an example (see Figure 4.2).

FIGURE   4.1

The expected loss as defined in Basel II

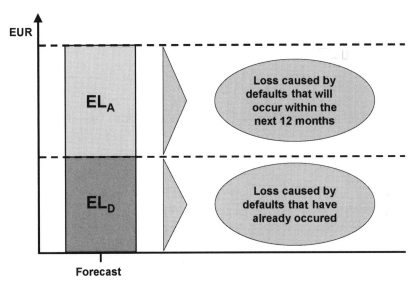

Forecast

The active and defaulted parts of the portfolio have to be treated separately.

Let us assume that receivables not paid are written off at the end of the recovery period (we do not distinguish between usage of provision and direct write-off). Furthermore, we assume that the workout time is the same for all defaults, say half a year. The portfolio shall consist of $N = 1,000$ credits, each of them amount to EAD = €1,000. Write-offs and expiring contracts are replaced by a new business so that the portfolio size remains constant. The same holds for the PD and the LGD. Let PD and LGD be 2 and 40 percent, respectively. For this sample portfolio, the relationship between EL_A and write-off amount is illustrated in Figure 4.2. The EL is calculated at time t_0, and the result for EL_A is

$$EL_A = N\,(EAD)\,(PD)\,(LGD) = 1,000\,(€1,000)\,(2\%)\,(40\%) = €8,000$$

We now compare this forecast with the write-off amount between t_0 and t_0 + one year. Since the workout time is exactly half a year the write-off events between t_0 and t_0 + one year correspond to the default events between $t_0 - 0.5$ years and $t_0 + 0.5$ years. This is just a one-year period,

F I G U R E   4.2

Schematic representation of ELA as loss forecast

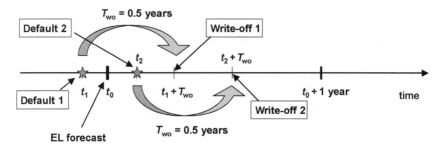

and thus we count PD $N = 20$ defaults. Each of the default events results in a loss of EAD LGD $= €400$, and hence, we arrive at a total loss amount of €8,000 between t_0 and the subsequent year, which equals EL_A as calculated at t_0. Note that half of the write-offs considered stem from contracts that are already in default at time t_0 (for example, default 1 in Figure 4.2). The other half corresponds to defaults which occur later than t_0 (like, for example, default 2 in Figure 4.2). This is a consequence of the 0.5-year workout time, but it is obvious that the result above is still the same when the workout time changes to arbitrary value.

It is obvious that the assumptions above are not realistic. However, we have shown within our projects that it is sufficient that the distributions of EAD, LGD, and the workout time among the portfolio remains stable and that the portfolio neither grows nor decreases strongly. These are reasonable assumptions for retail portfolios. For most retail portfolios, the correspondence between EL_A and the loss amount in the following can still be used as a rule of thumb, even if the assumptions are not met.

According to the Basel II framework, LGD and, hence, EL_A have to be estimated in a conservative manner, reflecting economic downturn conditions. Therefore, EL_A tends to overestimate the actual loss in the long-term average. In order to filter out this effect, banks should calculate a second LGD value that does not reflect downturn but long-term average economic conditions. By using this LGD estimate (instead of the regulatory "downturn LGD"), EL_A can be considered as an unbiased loss forecast that correctly predicts the loss in the long-term average, i.e., covering the whole economic cycle.

F I G U R E   4.3

Basel II EL as a projection of write-offs

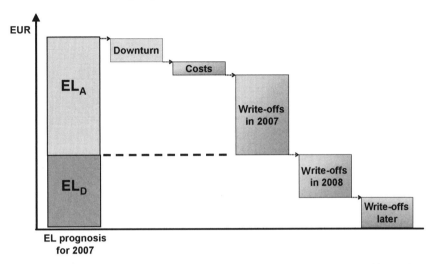

The block Downturn indicates the conservative LGD estimation required by the regulators. All costs that have not been taken into account as part of the write-offs are represented by the block Costs.

At this stage we face the question of whether EL_D can be interpreted in a similar way. According to its definition, the total EL (i.e., the sum of EL_D and EL_A) is the loss that is expected to result from the positions already in default and the positions that are going to default within the following year. Thus, when using the total EL as a loss forecast, we have to recognize in which way this loss is spread over the following years, as illustrated in Figure 4.3.

The total EL forecast as calculated at the beginning of 2007 is distributed among the years 2007, 2008, etc. It should be emphasized that the contributions assigned to the years 2008 and later do not represent the total loss expected for these years since the contributions from defaults occurring in 2008 and later are not included in the total EL as calculated at the beginning of 2007.

Therefore, the characteristic EL_D is of small use for profit and loss purposes. However, since the calculation of EL_D is based on all future cash flows resulting from the defaulted portfolio (and not only the cash flows within a certain time horizon), it can be used to determine the present value of the defaulted portfolio and thus plays an essential role in the context of true sales and securitization.

Loss Provisioning

Unless defaulted facilities are sold or securitized, specific provisions have to be recognized. The amount of specific provisions represents the loss the bank expects to incur from the facility. In the following, this obvious link between loss provisioning (as part of internal risk management) and EL shall be discussed in detail.

Within the Basel II framework itself, the link between EL and provisions is greatly emphasized, and a comparison between total EL (i.e., $EL_A + EL_D$) and the total amount of provisions is required (see *Treatment of EL and Provisions*, paragraphs 384 to 386). This is a consequence of the so-called UL-only calibration and can be summarized as follows: As a basic principle, both the EL and the UL have to be covered by capital. In this context, provisions can be recognized in the following way: If the total amount of eligible provisions exceeds the total EL, only the UL has to be covered by additional capital. Furthermore, in this case, the difference between provisions and EL may be recognized as Tier 2 capital up to a certain limit (see Figure 4.4). If, however, the total EL exceeds the total amount of provisions, the bank must compensate for the difference.

In the following, we shall analyze in detail the comparison between EL and total provisions especially with regard to EL as a control parameter. The main aspects are depicted in Figure 4.4. New business, expiries, and write-offs drive the dynamics of the portfolio. As far as write-offs are concerned, we do not distinguish between usage of provision and direct write-off. Within the treatment of EL and provisions two perspectives of the dynamic portfolio are contrasted. On the one hand, we have the perspective given by the internal model, and on the other hand, we have the accounting point of view. The dynamics of the accounting view is given by recognition and by release of provisions, while the dynamics of the internal model, and hence, the amounts of EL_A and EL_D is driven by all risk-relevant information including, for example, rating downgrades. Although there is no exact one-to-one correspondence between the elements of both perspectives, we observe close relationships.

Schematic illustration of the comparison between EL and
total provisions in a dynamic portfolio

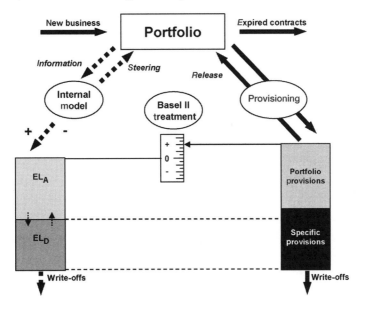

Obviously, there is a close relation between EL_D and the amount of
specific provisions since specific provisions reflect the loss the bank
expects to incur at the end of the liquidation process. This corresponds to
the definition of EL_D, but if we look in more detail, we have to notice
some differences. First, the rules for assessment of specific provision as
stated in the accounting standards slightly differ from the Basel II regulations for EL_D. Second, the definition of default according to Basel II does
not necessarily correspond exactly to the trigger event for specific provisions. One observes frequently that default according to Basel II occurs
before specific provisions are made, i.e., the Basel II default event is usually "softer" than the trigger event for specific provisions.

Neglecting these differences in detail we can conclude that if EL_D
corresponds to the amount of specific provisions, EL_A is a benchmark for
the amount of portfolio provisions. This benchmark follows the dynamics
of the internal model and thus reflects changes in the portfolio risk profile

immediately. In this way the EL calculation supports a profit and loss control that is risk sensitive since it has a strong forward-looking component.

Having a closer look at provisions and EL, we have to distinguish between different accounting standards. For example, according to the German commercial code (HGB) there are three different types of provisions called *specific loss provision* (EWB), *collective specific loss provision* (pEWB), and *collective general loss provision* (PWB). How can we assign these types of provisions in the scheme of Figure 4.4? Specific provisions are usually assigned to defaulted credits ("black portfolio") and, hence, to EL_D, while collective general loss provisions are made for the "white portfolio" consisting of all transactions that do not show any indication of impending default. Collective general loss provisions reflect the fact that the bank expects some losses from the white portfolio as well. Typically, PWB are calculated as a fixed percentage of the total receivables, and by definition they obviously correspond to EL_A. Thus, as a benchmark for risk adequate PWB, EL_A is more appropriate than a fixed percentage that cannot be as sensitive to portfolio changes as the internal rating system. Collective specific loss provisions are usually assigned to the "gray portfolio." The gray portfolio represents the credits that exhibit some indications of impending default like, for example, payment delinquencies, but have not defaulted yet. Depending on the trigger event for pEWB, they should be attributed either to EL_A or EL_D. For example, in a retail portfolio pEWB maybe recognized for each past due contract automatically, independent of the amount overdue. In this case, pEWB are attributed to the EL_A provisions. For example, if pEWB are made only after 70 or more days overdue, they correspond to EL_D.

According to the International Financial Reporting Standards (IFRS), impairments do not represent *expected* losses, but only *incurred* losses. This means that recognition of impairment shall only be possible if a trigger event, such as payment delinquency, is observed. At first sight, this seems to be in contradiction to the Basel II approach since no impairments can be recognized for the white portfolio. However, in practice, this is not the case. According to IFRS, we have to distinguish between individual and collective impairments. While individual impairments are more or less equivalent to EWB according to HGB and therefore correspond to EL_D, collective impairments may be recognized for losses incurred but not yet observed.

This opens the possibility of impairment recognition on the white portfolio since, even if no outstanding debts are observed, some obligors may already face financial difficulties. In practice banks usually make use of this opportunity, and we get the full picture of Figure 4.4. Similar to pEWB, collective impairments may sometimes rather be assigned to EL_D, depending on the definition of the trigger event. Concerning IFRS, Figure 4.4 does not show the complete dynamics of the accounting perspective since the so-called unwinding is neglected. Unwinding means that the impairment amount changes over time due to the changing time value of money—even if no changes in credit risk are observed. Despite all differences in detail and independent of the particular accounting standard, Basel II will lead to convergence of provisions and EL. In this way, provisioning is put on an objective basis.

Risk Premia

The importance of the convergence between EL and provisions shall be illustrated by the example of risk premia. In the preliminary costing process risk premia are calculated to cover expected future losses in the portfolio. To perform this calculation in a highly sophisticated way one can use PD, LGD, and EAD values for each transaction. Hence, the preliminary calculation is based on Basel II EL. As a side note, it should be mentioned that not only one-year PDs and current LGD and EAD values may be used in some approaches, but also assumptions about how these parameters evolve over the lifetime of the transaction.

In the postcalculation process, risk costs as the sum of net change of provision and direct write-offs are calculated in a backward-looking manner. It is obvious that precalculation and postcalculation can only be brought in line when provisioning is based on the same parameters and thus on EL. In other words, if the bank wants to make use of its Basel II investment for internal purposes like the calculation of risk premia, provisioning has to be based on EL.

SUMMARY AND OUTLOOK

To summarize, one could say that the EL within Basel II serves internal control purposes. However, this requires a precise understanding of this parameter. In particular, it is important to distinguish between the EL of the active portfolio, EL_A, and the EL arising from the default portfolio, EL_D. EL_A can be interpreted as the estimated amount of loss realized within the next coming year, disregarding whether the incurred losses actually stem from defaults within the active portfolio or rather stem (due to a nonzero workout time) from defaults that occurred prior to the observation period.

Under some mild homogeneity assumptions (such as constant work-out time), the loss arising from defaults within the next year is a good estimate for the losses to be actually incurred during the next year. As such EL_A can be used for profit and loss planning. In contrast, EL_D can be used for valuation of the defaulted portfolio or parts of it and, hence, plays an essential role in the context of true sales and securitization. The total EL, i.e., the sum of EL_A and EL_D represents an economically sensible benchmark for the total amount of provisions. Here EL_D and EL_A more or less correspond to specific (individual) and portfolio (collective) provisions, respectively. We strongly recommend that banks establish a provisioning system on the basis of EL, which is, for example, of particular importance in the context of the calculation of risk premia.

Last but not least, the EL represents an important part of the disclosure requirements according to pillar three of Basel II. In particular, a comparison between EL estimates and realized losses as observed over several years has to be reported. In order to avoid misunderstandings or misinterpretations of the figures reported, a detailed understanding of EL is required.

CHAPTER 5

Credit Risk Capital Allocation and Performance Measurement in Banking Institutions

Valerio Poti

ABSTRACT

We review alternative credit risk capital attribution methodologies and how they are used to evaluate the performance of financial intermediaries and their business units. Special attention is paid to the implications of credit risk exposures distributional features for the choice of the credit risk capital allocation methodology and for performance measurement.

INTRODUCTION

The performance of a firm and of its business units is often defined and measured according to some version of the residual income model,[1] such as Risk-Adjusted Return on Capital (RAROC), originally developed at Banker's Trust, and Economic Value Added (EVA), developed by the

---

[1] One of the earliest to mention the residual income concept was Marshall (1890), who defined *economic profit* as total net gains less the interest on invested capital at the current rate.

consulting firm Stern Stewart & Co. In residual income models, the goal of optimizing economic agents is to maximize income net of the cost of capital.[2] This requires that only investments with nonnegative expected residual income be undertaken and, in the presence of mutually exclusive investment opportunities, that the ones with the highest expected residual income be selected first. The application of residual income models to select the investments to be undertaken or to monitor the performance of those already undertaken requires the attribution of the firm's capital to the investments under consideration and the specification of the cost of capital. We might refer to these tasks as the *capital attribution problem* and the *cost of capital determination problem*, respectively. Both industry and consulting practice and the academic literature treat the two problems somewhat differently in the case of banks and other financial institutions relative to nonfinancial firms.

In applications of residual income models to financial institutions, in fact, performance measures are typically designed to underpin a capital budgeting process that is similar to the operation of an internal capital market, whereby businesses are allocated risk capital with the objective of making the best possible use of costly equity financing. In this approach, the relevant notion of capital is closely related to the institution's equity, rather than to a weighted average of equity and debt as in the case of non-financial firms. Examples of this approach are the applications of RAROC in a banking setting studied by James (1996) and Zaik et al. (1996), and the application of EVA to measure value creation in banking institutions considered by Uyemura et al. (1996).

Since the role of equity capital is to provide creditor protection, it is typically allocated to each business with a view to cover unexpected losses (UL) with a desired confidence level; see, for example, Chorafas (2004). This approach aims to ensure that the financial institution to which the business units belong is solvable with a desired probability, given the riskiness of its investments. The relevant notion of capital in capital attribution applications is therefore the amount of own resources required to withstand

---

[2] The cost of capital, following standard asset pricing theory, is often a function of the systematic riskiness of the business unit (possibly the entire bank) or project being evaluated.

UL that might occur with a certain probability, (i.e., the "buffer" required to withstand such losses), without incurring into bankruptcy. This buffer plays the role of risk capital, i.e., the amount of capital that shareholders put at risk in the conduct of the business, and it equals a given percentile of the cumulative distribution of UL, with the percentile depending on the probability of becoming insolvent deemed acceptable by the management (on behalf of the shareholders, at least in principle). Turning to the cost of capital determination problem, the expected return on allocated equity capital is often defined as a function of the correlation between the investment or business unit under consideration and the market portfolio, as in the capital asset pricing model (CAPM) and in standard applications to nonfinancial firms, even though some authors specify it as a function of the total risk of the investment or as a function of the investment correlation with the existing bank portfolio, as in James (1996) and Zaik et al. (1996).

In the next sections, we review and discuss alternative credit risk capital attribution methodologies and their use in evaluating the performance of financial intermediaries and of their business units, paying special attention to the relation between industry practice and the normative implications of extant financial theory. We first deal, in the second section of this chapter, with issues related to the capital attribution problem. One such issue is the extent to which diversification benefits can and should be taken into account in the determination of the amount of risk capital absorbed by the business units. Another related issue pertains to whether allocated capital or absorbed capital should be considered for capital attribution purposes. In the third section, we then deal with issues concerning the cost of capital determination problem, such as the choice between using a differentiated instead of an undifferentiated cost of capital. In the former approach, the cost of capital of each unit reflects its riskiness. In the latter approach, it is the definition of the allocated risk capital to be adjusted in order to reflect such riskiness (this is, de facto, the approach adopted by the Basel II regulators). In the fourth section, we discuss credit risk capital measurement and estimation issues, paying special attention to the distributional features of credit risk exposures and their implications for performance measurement. The final section presents our conclusions and suggests directions for future research.

CREDIT RISK CAPITAL

If capital markets were perfectly competitive and "frictionless," i.e., if transactions took place under conditions of perfect information and there were no taxes, bankruptcy costs, or conflicts of interest between managers and shareholders, "...the pricing of specific risks would be the same for all banks and would not depend on the characteristics of an individual bank's portfolio" (James, 1996, p. 4). In these circumstances, managers would allocate capital to uses that offer an expected return at least equal to the expected return on investments of equivalent risk, and given market prices of risk, investment decisions would be independent of how investments are financed (a classical separation result). These considerations, however, do not explain the emphasis on equity in the allocation of financial institutions' capital.

As highlighted by Matten (1996), one of the main sources of finance for banks, namely, customer deposits, cannot be viewed as external funding but rather as one of the main inputs of the business. Since the bank's own capital acts as a buffer against future, unidentified losses, thereby protecting depositors, it is a crucial resource for banking institutions, more so than for nonfinancial firms. This, at least in part, explains the emphasis on the efficient use of equity capital and other internal sources of finance and why the performance of banking institutions is typically defined in terms of how well the bank's own capital is remunerated, rather than in terms of returns on a weighted average of internal and external capital as for nonfinancial companies. On a more formal note, Froot and Stein (1998) assume that banks have some technological advantage allowing a higher expected return on capital than the market, but this advantage levels off as a function of the amount of external capital used. As remarked by Høgh et al. (2006), this mechanism implies that if the aim is to maximize shareholder's wealth, investment payoffs should be evaluated against the amount of internal capital they use up.

In agreement with this analysis, there is evidence that, when equity capital is not sufficient to cover credit risk capital, i.e., it is not sufficient to ensure solvability at the desired confidence level, banks reduce lending rather than raise new, expensive equity capital. This is demonstrated, for example, by Houston et al. (1997), who examine the relation between loan growth, internally generated funds, and external financing costs and by

James (1996) and Houston and James (1997), who demonstrate that loan growth at "... subsidiaries of bank holding companies depends on the capitalization of the holding company and on the earnings of other subsidiaries ..." (James, 1996, p. 10) within the same banking group. Further, albeit indirect, empirical evidence on the crucial role played by credit risk capital is provided by studies on the usage of credit derivatives by financial institutions. For example, Minton et al. (2005) examine the use of credit derivatives by U.S. bank holding companies. Suggestively, they state "... banks are more likely to be net protection buyers if they have lower capital ratios" (Minton et al., 2005, p. 1). They also tend to buy credit risk protection if they engage in risky activities that absorb relatively high amounts of risk capital, such as the origination of foreign loans and lending to commercial and industrial borrowers. This evidence suggests that, while the use of credit derivatives for the typical banking credit exposures is limited because adverse selection and moral hazard problems make the market for these instruments illiquid, the opportunity to reduce the use of costly equity capital renders the purchase of credit protection on certain exposures, such as commercial and industrial loans, convenient. Ultimately, this implies that, at least to some extent, credit derivatives protection is used as a substitute for scarce and costly credit risk capital.

In bank capital management literature [see, for example, Ong (1999), Matten (1996), and Saita (2007)], there is a long-standing debate on the relation between regulatory and economic capital. In spite of recent attempts made by regulators to bring regulatory capital more in line with economic capital in setting Basel II capital requirements, the two definitions of capital, as noted by Allen (2006), refer to the amount of equity required to meet the needs of different primary stakeholders. In the case of "... economic capital, the primary stakeholders are the bank's shareholders, and the objective is the maximization of their wealth. In the case of regulatory capital, the primary stakeholders are the bank's depositors, and the objective is to limit their probability of incurring losses" (Allen, 2006, p. 45). The tendency of capital-constrained financial institutions to purchase credit risk protection and limit lending, reported by Minton et al. (2005), Houston et al. (1997), James (1996), and Houston and James (1998), might be evidence that regulatory capital is not in line with economic capital, at least under the Basel I capital standards, thus creating incentives to modify the mix of exposures. In fact, Minton et al. (2005) find evidence that purchase of credit risk protection goes hand in hand with a high propensity to engage in asset securitization.

Elizalde and Repullo (2006) formally compare economic and regulatory capital in the context of Basel II internal rating-based (IRB) approach to setting capital requirements. They define *regulatory capital* as the minimum amount of capital required by regulation. *Economic capital* is defined as the capital level that bank shareholders would choose in absence of capital regulation ". . . to maximize the value of the bank, taking into account the possibility that the bank be closed if the losses during the period exceed the initial level of capital. This closure rule can be motivated by the assumption that a bank run may take place before the shareholders can raise new equity to cover losses" (Elizalde and Repullo, 2006, p. 1). This assumption, in turn, is consistent with the idea that adjusting equity capital may be costly, as in Malijuf and Mayers (1984) and Stein (1998), and it appears empirically well founded in light of the evidence [see for example Keeton (1994) and Jacques and Nigro (1997)] that banks find it difficult to raise new equity capital to meet capital requirements. Finally, they introduce the notion of actual capital, defined as the capital chosen by bank shareholders taking into account the regulatory constraints, such as the possibility of closure imposed by regulatory authorities in case capital requirements are not met. In Elizalde and Repullo's (2006) analytical framework, it is actual capital that represents the risk capital that should be allocated to different business units and investment projects for use in selecting investments and in performance measurement and attribution.

Elizalde and Repullo (2006) set regulatory capital equal to the capital charges in the Basel II IRB approach, while to compute economic capital, they calibrate a dynamic model in which shareholders choose, at the beginning of each period, the optimal level of capital. They show that while actual capital, for realistic values of the variables of their model, is closer to regulatory capital than to economic capital, the regulators' threat of closing undercapitalized banks generates significant capital buffers. These results suggest that both economic and actual capital are in general different from regulatory capital and that the widespread practice of using the latter as a proxy in residual income calculations rests on shaky theoretical foundations.

The merit of the definition of risk capital used by Elizalde and Repullo (2006) is that it does not rely on an exogenous and somewhat arbitrary confidence level, as it is typically the case in the extant literature [see, for example, Jones and Mingo (1998) or Carey (2001)]. In this literature, in fact, *risk capital* is "… usually defined as the amount of equity that is required to cover the bank's losses with a certain probability or confidence level, which is related to a desired rating and does not take such desired solvency standard as a primitive, but which derives it from an underlying objective function, i.e., the maximization of the market value of the bank" (Elizalde and Repullo, 2006, p. 1).

In principle, this approach is general enough that it allows actual capital, and thus risk capital, i.e., the notion of risk capital relevant in capital attribution and performance measurement exercises, to be identified with regulatory capital under appropriate circumstances. Under the definition of capital used by Elizalde and Repullo (2006), the notion of capital relevant in the capital allocation process, namely, actual capital, would coincide with regulatory capital in the case of capital-constrained banks. This is important, as there is evidence [see, for example, Keeton (1994) and Jacques and Nigro (1997)] that banks reduced their portfolio of loans in response to the introduction of Basel I capital requirement, suggesting that regulatory capital matters from an asset allocation point of view. Jacques's (2007) stylized theoretical model of how banks adjust the mix of their commercial loans in response to capital shocks neatly outlines the key relations between equity capital, regulatory capital constraints, and lending activity. It predicts that capital-constrained banks, i.e., banks that hold less economic capital than the capital requirements set by Basel II, respond to capital shocks by decreasing loans to high-risk commercial and industrial borrowers. While, under certain circumstances, lending to low-risk borrowers might increase, this leads to a decrease in overall lending.

CAPITAL ALLOCATION, COST OF CAPITAL, AND PERFORMANCE MEASUREMENT

Froot and Stein (1998) show that in the presence of capital markets frictions, such that not all risk can be hedged using traded instruments, and of market imperfections, e.g., agency problems, such that banks face increasing marginal costs of external financing, maximization of shareholders' wealth requires that equity capital be allocated to uses that offer an expected return above a rate that is a function of both undiversifiable and diversifiable risk and related risk premia. The required expected return depends in fact not only on the undiversifiable risk of the investment under consideration, i.e., its covariance with the market portfolio as in the classical CAPM, but also on a portion of the investment idiosyncratic risk, namely, the covariance between its nonhedgeable part and the existing portfolio of the bank. This consideration provides some theoretical support to the practice of allocating equity capital on the basis of the total risk of individual business units.

The performance attribution methodology prescribed by Froot and Stein (1998), however, is quite different from typical applications of RAROC or EVA. For a start, in their analysis, capital management matters only in relation to investments that cannot be hedged on the capital market. In a credit portfolio setting, these would be represented by large loans for which it is impossible to purchase credit risk protection due to the lack of a sufficiently liquid credit derivatives market. Additionally, the benchmark return for calculating risk-adjusted performance is not the CAPM equilibrium return for the project but a hard-to-estimate function of a certain "risk aversion" parameter. This parameter is not related to investors' risk aversion, but instead captures the extent to which the increasing marginal cost of external financing induces a risk averse type of behavior in banks that pursue the goal of shareholders' wealth maximization.

Stoughton and Zechner (2007) ground the use of RAROC and EVA in more solid theoretical foundations. They derive optimal capital allocation under asymmetric information and in the presence of outside managerial opportunities, such as the possibility for managers of setting up their own practice or hedge fund or simply of moving to a better paid job. These external opportunities create the incentive for managers of using good performance to represent themselves as a higher "type," i.e., managers with differential private information and exceptional skill. On the other hand, managers without outside managerial opportunities, faced with a capital charge that increases in the amount of risk taken, might have the incentive of underrepresenting their investment opportunity set, i.e., their skills, in order to be assigned a lower capital charge and thus a lower and easier-to-exceed target performance.

In spite of this information asymmetry, Stoughton and Zechner (2007) show that a financial institution can decentralize the investment decision and use compensation schemes based on RAROC and EVA to create an incentive structure that leads the managers to reveal their investment opportunity set, thus eliminating the problem of over- or underinvestment, while at same time taking the optimal amount of risk. In their model, risk is observable ex post. The decentralization leads to a charge for economic capital based on the division's own realized risk. This result is reminiscent of recent contributions that have attempted to use the so-called Euler allocation principle to define more rigorously the risk contribution of individual business units [see, for example, McNeil et al. (2005) and, more recently, Tasche (2007b)]. As far as hurdle rates are concerned, Stoughton and Zechner (2007) show that they have a common component, in contrast to the standard perfect markets result with division-specific rates [see, for example, Saita (2007)]. In fact, in their model, the hurdle rate tends to the cost of equity for a diversified multidivisional firm. Interestingly, this is consistent with the widely adopted practice of using an undifferentiated cost of capital as the hurdle rate.

CREDIT RISK CAPITAL MEASUREMENT

Kupiec (2002) shows that in risk capital calculations, UL must be measured relative to the initial market value plus accrued interests on funding debt. This requires augmenting UL to account for the interest income required by investors. While the need for such an adjustment has been known for some time in a market risk setting, it has received less attention in the credit risk literature, in spite of the fact that its impact is arguably more important in the measurement of credit risk capital than in the measurement of market risk capital. This is because credit risk exposure is typically measured over a much longer horizon (usually a year) than market risk exposure (often measured over a 10-day period). For example, the Creditmetrics Technical Document, Wilson (1997), and Saunders (1999) all advocate that UL relative to the initial market value of the debt instrument is the appropriate measure of credit risk capital at the chosen confidence level, while this is also the definition of credit risk capital underlying Basel II credit risk capital requirements according to the advanced internal rating-based (AIRB) approach.

Typical risk capital calculations, therefore, produce biased estimates as they are based on the UL relative to the initial market value of loans, bonds, or loan-equivalent of other credit risk exposures, without an adjustment to account for the interest income required by investors. Introducing such an adjustment, however, is not a trivial matter as it requires the specification of the interest payment on funding debt, which is in general stochastic. To address this issue, Kupiec (2007) uses Merton's (1974) option model of risky debt to determine jointly the rate of interest on funding debt and the UL. Kupiec (2007) then derives capital allocation rules that maximize leverage, thus maximizing expected profitability while maintaining a target solvency rate for credit portfolios. In Kupiec's (2007, p.103) model "... risk is driven by a single common factor and idiosyncratic risk is fully diversified. Equilibrium conditions then ensure that capital allocations depend on interest earnings as well as probability of default (henceforth, PD), endogenous loss given default (henceforth, LGD), and default correlations." In particular, Kupiec (2007) derives explicit capitalization rates for both the average and the marginal credit, i.e., the amount of capital to be held for each unit of loan or equivalent credit exposure already in the portfolio or to be added to the latter at the margin, respectively. Capitalization rates are the same in both cases because idiosyncratic risk is assumed to be fully diversified away, and they can be approximated as

$$k \cong \frac{YTM + LGD}{1 + YTM} \Phi\left(\frac{\sqrt{\rho}\Phi^{-1}(\alpha) + \Phi^{-1}(PD)}{\sqrt{1 - \rho}} \right)$$

Here, YTM denotes the yield to maturity on the credits in the bank portfolio, $\Phi(x)$ denotes the cumulative standard normal distribution evaluated at x, and α represents the desired solvency rate, i.e., the desired probability that the bank will meet its obligation. The capitalization rate derived by Kupiec (2007) differs from the minimum capitalization rate implied by Basel II capital requirement under the AIRB approach in that the latter ignores the adjustment for accrued interest on funding debt.

A number of measures are used to estimate risk capital, i.e., the equity that is required to limit the default rate on funding debt. The most popular among such measures are value at risk (VaR) and, more recently, expected shortfall (ES) or conditional VaR. Value at risk at an α percentage confidence level is defined [see, for example, Jorion (2001)] as the maximum UL with an α percent probability. The ES at a percentage level α is defined as the expected loss that exceeds the expected return on the portfolio in the worst α percent of the cases. Unlike VaR, it is a coherent risk measure, as shown by Acerbi and Tasche (2002a; 2002b). Kalkbrener et al. (2004) compare VaR-based and ES-based capital allocation schemes and argue that expected shortfall is a superior measure for the allocation of capital in credit portfolios.

In spite of its shortcomings, VaR is widely used as a risk capital measure. For example, in Stoughton and Zechner's (2007) model, the division's own realized risk capital is measured as incremental VaR at a chosen confidence level, defined as the contribution of each business unit to the overall VaR of the bank. As shown by Gordy (2003), single-factor credit risk models, where there is only a single systematic risk factor driving correlations across obligors, have the "... property that the contribution of a given asset to VaR (and hence the corresponding capital charge) is portfolio invariant, that is, it depends on each asset's own characteristics and not on those of the portfolio in which it is included" (Elizalde and Repullo, 2006, p. 5), as long as no exposure in a portfolio accounting for more than an subjectively minute share of the total entire exposure. The portfolio-invariance property facilitates their use in credit-rating-based capital allocation models, such as Basel II IRB approach to setting capital requirements. In these models, obligors' probabilities of defaults implied by internal credit ratings or by ratings issued by external specialized agencies are translated into capital requirements designed to ensure the bank's solvency at a desired confidence level.

Kupiec (2007), however, shows that Gaussian credit loss models, such as the model introduced by Vasicek (1991) and extended by, among others, Finger (1999), Schönbucher (2000), and Gordy (2003), are unable to accurately reproduce the negative return tail of a credit portfolio's return (loss) distribution. The inaccuracy arises in part because these models assume fixed LGD, i.e., because of a failure to model LGD as an endogenous variable. To address this problem, Kupiec (2007) proposes a full equilibrium structural model, broadly based on Merton's (1974) option model of risky debt, where the LGD of a particular obligor is determined endogenously, alongside its dependence on the obligor PD as well as on the LGD of other obligors. Interestingly, the endogenous dynamics of LGD, of the interactions between the LGD and PD, and of the interactions between the LGD of different obligors generate return distribution characteristics that cannot be accurately reproduced in the simplified single-factor Gaussian framework. As shown by Kupiec (2007), this implies that the single-factor Gaussian credit loss model is biased and underestimates UL. An important implication of Kupiec's (2007) analysis is that credit risk capital requirements under Basel II AIRB approach do not provide a sufficient buffer against credit losses, as this approach is essentially based on a Gaussian credit loss model.

> Determining contributions by sub-portfolios or single exposures to portfolio-wide economic capital for credit risk is a difficult estimation task. When economic capital is measured as either the VaR or ES of the portfolio loss distribution, under many of the credit portfolio risk models used in practice, see for example Crouhy et al. (2000), the contributions have to be estimated from Monte Carlo samples . . .

(Tasche, 2007a, p.1), and these tend to be rather volatile. When using simulation methods to estimate credit risk exposure, Xiao (2002) advocates importance sampling as a variance reduction technique, to mitigate sampling error. Kalkbrener et al. (2004) use an importance sampling algorithm for estimating ES in Merton-type models of credit risk exposure, which increases the precision of Monte Carlo estimates. Tasche (2007a, p. 1) suggests combining ". . . kernel estimation methods with importance sampling to achieve more efficient (i.e., less volatile) estimates of VaR contributions."

FINAL REMARKS AND DIRECTIONS FOR FUTURE RESEARCH

The academic literature on bank capital management is relatively recent. Under the influence of the perfect capital market paradigm, that can be traced back to Modigliani and Miller's (1958) propositions and Fama's (1970; 1976) efficient market hypothesis, the academic literature has trailed behind industry practices and consulting advice in understanding the role of risk capital in financial institutions and its implications for performance attribution. There are, however, recent efforts to develop a richer theory of capital management in financial institutions, such as the pioneering work of Stein (1997, 1998) and Froot and Stein (1998) on capital allocation, risk management, and performance attribution or, more recently, Elizalde and Repullo's (2006) risk capital determination model. These attempts bear the promise, on one hand, to explain industry practices within a systematic theoretical framework and, on the other hand, to provide richer and more coherent advice on how to efficiently organize the capital budgeting and performance measurement process within financial institutions. Much, however, remains to be done to ascertain the empirical success of these attempts.

For example, future research might seek to quantify certain empirically rather obscure parameters of the Froot and Stein's (1998) model, especially the bank's risk aversion and its relation with the marginal cost of external financing. Another fruitful avenue for future research is the investigation of relative merits of using a differentiated instead of an undifferentiated cost of capital in performance attribution applications, as both approaches are recommended by different strands of the literature [see, for example, the contrast between the implication of Stoughton and Zechner's (2007) analysis and Saita's (2007) advice]. A further, perhaps obvious, promising avenue for future investigation is the search for empirically more successful credit risk models and more accurate credit risk exposure estimators. For example, as shown by Kupiec (2007), failure to model in a multivariate and multi-obligor setting the complex relations between PD and LGD might lead to underestimate credit risk capital requirements. Besides having possible unpleasant implications for financial stability, it might also lead to suboptimal risk-taking policies, in contrast with the objective of shareholders' wealth maximization. Further research is also needed to develop less "noisy" credit risk exposure estimators, i.e., more efficient estimators that exhibit lower sampling error, especially in the context of credit risk capital models based on ES, along the lines of Xiao (2002) and Kalkbrener et al. (2004).

ACKNOWLEDGMENTS

The author is grateful to Fabio Fedel and Michele Zannini from Ambrosetti Stern Stewart for helpful discussions and comments. Any remaining error or omission is the author's sole responsibility.

REFERENCES

Acerbi, C. and Tasche, D. (2002a) Expected Shortfall: A Natural Coherent Alternative to Value at Risk. *Economic Notes*, 31(2): 379–388.

Acerbi, C. and Tasche, D. (2002b) On the Coherence of Expected Shortfall. *Journal of Banking and Finance*, 26(7): 1487–1503.

Allen, B. (2006) Internal Affairs. *Risk*, June, 19: 45–49.

Chorafas, D.N. (2004) *Economic Capital Allocation with Basel II: Cost, Benefit and Implementation Procedures*. Oxford, UK: Elsevier.

Crouhy, M., Galai, D., and Mark, R. (2000) A Comparative Analysis of Current Credit Risk Models. *Journal of Banking and Finance*, 24(1): 59–117.

Elizalde, A. and Repullo, R. (2006) Economic and Regulatory Capital in Banking: What is the Difference? Working paper available from www.abelelizalde.com/pdf/economic regulatory actual.pdf

Fama, E. (1970) Efficient Capital Markets: A Review of Theory and Empirical Work. *Journal of Finance*, 25(2): 383–417.

Fama, E. (1976) *Foundations of Finance*. New York: Basic Books.

Finger, C. (1999) Conditional Approaches for CreditMetrics Portfolio Distributions. *CreditMetrics Monitor*, April, pp. 14–33.

Froot, K. and Stein, J. (1998) Risk Management, Capital Budgeting and Capital Structure Policy for Financial Institutions: An Integrated Approach. *Journal of Financial Economics*, 47(1): 55–82.

Gordy, M. (2003) A Risk-Factor Model Foundation for Ratings-Based Bank Capital Rules. *Journal of Financial Intermediation*, 12(3), 199–232.

Høgh, N., Linton, O., and Nielsen, J.P. (2006) The Froot and Stein Model Revisited. *Annals of Actuarial Science*, 1(1): 37–47.

Houston, J.F. and James, C. (1998) Do Bank Internal Capital Markets Promote Lending? *Journal of Banking and Finance*, 22 (6–8): 899–918.

Houston, J.F., James, C., and Marcus, D. (1997) Capital Market
Frictions and the Role of Internal Capital Markets in Banking.
Journal of Financial Economics, 46(2): 135–164.

Jacques, K.T. (2007) Capital Shocks, Bank Asset Allocation, and the
Revised Basel Accord. *Review of Financial Economics*
(Forthcoming).

Jacques, K. T. and Nigro, P. (1997) Risk-Based Capital, Portfolio Risk,
and Bank Capital: A Simultaneous Equations Approach. Journal of
Economics and Business, 49(6): 533–547.

James, C. (1996) RAROC Based Capital Budgeting and Performance
Evaluation: A Case Study of Bank Capital Allocation. Working
paper, Wharton Financial Institutions Center. Available from
fic.wharton.upenn.edu/fic/papers/96/p9640.html

Jorion, P. (2001) *Value at Risk: The New Benchmark for Managing
Financial Risk.* 2nd ed., New York: McGraw-Hill.

Kalkbrener, M., Lotter, H., and Overbeck, L. (2004) Sensible and
Efficient Capital Allocation for Credit Portfolios. *Risk*, 17(1):
519–524.

Keeton, W.R. (1994) Causes of the Recent Increase in Bank Security
Holdings. *Economic Review*, 79(2): 45–57.

Kupiec, P.H. (2002) Calibrating Your Intuition: Capital Allocation for
Market and Credit Risk. IMF, Working paper, No. 02/99.

Kupiec P.H. (2004) Estimating Economic Capital Allocations for Market
and Credit Risks. *Journal of Risk*, 6(4).

Kupiec, P.H. (2007) Capital Allocation for Portfolio Credit Risk. *Journal
of Financial Services Research*, 32(1): 103–122.

Malijuf, N. and Mayers, S. (1984) Corporate Financing and Investment
Decisions When Firms Have Information That Investors Do Not
Have. *Journal of Financial Economics*, 13(2): 187–221.

Marshall, A. (1890) *Principles of Economics*. London: Macmillan
Press Ltd.

Matten, C. (1996) *Managing Bank Capital: Capital Allocation and Performance Measurement.* Chichester, UK: John Wiley & Sons.

McNeil, A., Frey, R., and Embrechts, P. (2005) *Quantitative Risk Management.* Princeton, NJ: Princeton University Press.

Merton, R. (1974) On the Pricing of Corporate Debt: The Risk Structure of Interest Rates. *Journal of Finance*, 29(2): 449–470.

Minton, B.A., Stulz, R., Williamson, R. (2005) How Much Do Banks Use Credit Derivatives to Reduce Risk? Working paper, available for download from www.cob.ohio-state.edu/fin/dice/papers/2005/2005–17.pdf.

Modigliani, F. and Miller, M.H. (1958) The Cost of Capital, Corporation Finance and the Theory of Investment. *American Economic Review*, 48(3): 261–297.

Ong, M.K. (1999) *Internal Credit Risk Models: Capital Allocation and Performance Measurement.* London: Risk Books.

Saita, F. (2007) *Value at Risk and Bank Capital Management.* Burlington, MA: Elsevier.

Saunders, T. (1999) *Credit Risk Measurement.* New York: John Wiley & Sons.

Schönbucher, P. (2000) Factor Models for Portfolio Credit Risk. Working paper, Department of Statistics, Bonn University, Bonn, Germany.

Stein, J (1997) Internal Capital Markets and Competition for Corporate Resources, *Journal of Finance*, 52(1): 111–133.

Stein, J.C. (1998) An Adverse-Selection Model of Bank Asset and Liability Management with Implications for the Transmission of Monetary Policy. *Rand Journal of Economics*, 29(3): 466–486.

Stoughton, N.M. and Zechner, J. (2007) Optimal Capital Allocation Using RAROC and EVA. *Journal of Financial Intermediation*, 16(3): 312–342.

Tasche, D. (2007a) Capital Allocation for Credit Portfolios with Kernel Estimators. Fitch Ratings Working paper, available from www.defaultrisk.com/pp_other_39.htm.

Tasche, D. (2007b) Euler Allocation: Theory and Practice. Fitch Ratings Working paper, available from www.defaultrisk.com/_asp/rd_fitch_other159.asp.

Uyemura, D., Kantor, C., and Pettit, J. (1996). EVA for Banks: Value Creation, Risk Management and Profitability Measurement. *Journal of Applied Corporate Finance*, 9(2): 94–113.

Vasicek, O.A. (1991). Limiting Loan Loss Probability Distribution. Working paper, KMV Corporation, San Francisco, CA.

Wilson, T. (1997) Portfolio Credit Risk (I). *Risk*, 10(9): 111–117.

Zaik, E., Walter, J., Kelling, G., and James, C. (1996) RAROC at Bank of America: From Theory to Practice. *Journal of Applied Corporate Finance*, 9(2): 83–93.

Xiao, J.Y. (2002) Importance Sampling for Credit Portfolio Simulation. *RiskMetrics Journal*, 2(2): 23–28.

PART TWO

Evaluation of Credit Risk

Characteristics of Credit Assets and Their Relevance for Credit Asset Management

Stephan Bucher and Jochen von Frowein[1]

ABSTRACT

In this chapter the authors present the characteristics of the most relevant credit assets and their role in credit asset management. We start by defining the most common types of credit assets and provide an overview of their key characteristics. On the basis of the most common credit types we describe the most relevant purposes of credit that asset managers have to consider for their hedging and their credit trading strategies. The results build the basis for further credit asset portfolio considerations.

INTRODUCTION

Credit is one of the most fundamental functions of banks and has been around for centuries. The types and forms of credit have evolved over time, and today, credit still forms an integral part of nearly all banking relationships. Standardized credit products often provide low returns but

---

[1] The following article represents the authors' opinions and does not necessarily reflect the view of Dresdner Kleinwort or its staff.

offer the potential of cross-selling. Structured credit products, on the other hand, promise considerably higher returns, but often carry higher risk. For the client relationship manager (CRM) it is, therefore, essential to understand the various credit products and to view them as part of both the overall client relationship and as part of the credit portfolio of the bank.

The credit market is highly complicated, and the pricing of a loan is not fully explained by the economic model of supply and demand. Instead, Stiglitz and Weiss (1981) argue that due to information asymmetry between borrower and lender, moral hazard and adverse selection result in a rationing of the credit market. In contrast to other products, supply and demand will not result in a price that clears the market; some borrowers will fail to obtain loans despite their willingness to pay higher prices in the form of higher interest rates. In order to make more reasonable credit decisions, lenders have to reduce this information asymmetry.

The basis for obtaining additional information is a strong relationship between lender and borrower, which Ongena and Smith (1998) define as a ". . . connection between a bank and a customer that goes beyond the execution of simple, anonymous, financial transactions." Intensive relationship banking is, therefore, not only the key to provide the clients with the products they need and to promote cross-selling, but it also allows the bank to gather information on the client over time. The result is increased willingness of the lender to provide the borrower with credit, with increasing amounts and maturities and decreasing prices.[2] For single credit transactions that are not based on an existing banking relationship, such as leveraged finance transactions, lenders often use covenants, both affirmative and financial, to overcome the existing information asymmetry (Hartmann-Wendels et al., 2004).

In order to reduce the credit risk, banks often require collateral as a prerequisite for the provision of a loan. The collateral does not reduce the repayment risk of the loan but the loss in case of default. The security types that serve as collateral range from personal securities, such as guaranties, to physical collateral of both movables and real estate. The collateral type is often closely related to the credit types it is used for.

---

[2] For a comprehensive literature overview on the effect of relationship intensity on loan pricing, see Fredriksson (2007).

Finally, the lender may reduce his credit risk after the disbursement of the funds via a funded or unfunded sale of the credit risk. The key to selling an asset in the secondary market is the transferability of the asset. This transferability is achieved either by the inclusion of a transferability clause in the credit agreement, which is often the case in leveraged finance transactions or multilateral loans. Large corporate borrowers may, however, deny the transferability of their debt, due to the fear of potential damage to their reputation if a bank sells the debt in a secondary market. Securitization of debt is an alternative to reduce the credit risk without selling the individual asset.

This chapter will provide an overview of the spectrum of the types and purposes of the loans in the market. These loans may be classified by a wide range of factors, including the following (Hartmann-Wendels et al., 2004):

- Borrower (corporate, private, etc.)
- Term (short, medium, long)
- Purpose (working capital, mortgage loan)
- Collateral
- Repayment (amortizing, bullet)
- Transferability
- Conditions

We focus on the factors that are most relevant for each credit type and, at the same time, important for credit asset management. As most loan types exist in a wide variety of characteristics, we focus on the standard parameters for each loan type. The chapter is structured as follows. In the second section, several credit types are analyzed based on the most relevant factors. Next, we introduce several credit purposes and show how these are related to the underlying credit types. Finally, we conclude with an overview of our results.

CREDIT TYPES

Term Loan

A term loan is a business loan that is fixed for a specific period of more than one year, typically for 3 to 10 years. Term loans are often granted for the financing of fixed asset investments; other purposes include the financing of general working capital needs or company acquisitions. The loan is usually repaid with interest in regular installments or, alternatively, loans may be repaid in form of a bullet payment at maturity. The interest rate is commonly calculated based on the current market rate plus a margin; banks also offer fixed interest rates based on clients' request.

The revenue resulting from a term loan includes both interest rate and additional fees whereby the former is usually higher relative to short-term financing due to higher risk. In addition, the interest rate differs greatly based on the parameters of the loan. On the one hand, factors that, ceteris paribus, lead to an increase of the interest cost are loan inherent factors such as longer maturity, smaller amounts, poor risk profile of the borrower, weak loan documentation, the absence of collateral, and the borrower's access to alternative financing sources. On the other hand, external factors also affect the interest rate level, such as the current market rate, the liquidity in the market, and the demand for this credit type in the market. In addition, the lender may charge fees, which depend on the complexity of the product, e.g., arrangement fees are very common for syndicated loans and leveraged finance transactions.

For the bank, term loans are essential for the relationship to business clients. Bilateral term loans, even at rates that do not cover the bank's cost, are considered a door opener into new relationships and the base for cross-selling activities. Key correspondent banks are also expected to participate in multilateral facilities. Therefore, most term loans are considered an investment in an important current or future relationship. In structured transactions, term loans carry higher interest rates and high upfront fees for the lead banks, so they are used as a profitable product of investment banks. The predefined repayment and interest rate schedules of term loans offer long-term planning security for both the borrower and the bank. This planning security, combined with the high risk-valued assets calculated on term loans, makes this product highly attractive for portfolio considerations of credit asset management (CAM).

The credit risk arising from term loans is the counterparty risk of the borrower, which is high in comparison to other loan types as an effect of the longer commitment for the lender. Due to strong competition, unsecured term loans have become the market standard. Collateral and covenants are applied mainly for high-risk transactions, such as leveraged finance. In addition to credit risk, term loans are also subject to repayment risk, which may be covered by breakage fees charged to the borrower. Finally, in case of fixed interest rate loans, the lender is subject to changes in the market interest rate.

Overdraft

An overdraft credit is an uncommitted, usually uncollateralized bank credit that results from the overdrawing of a bank account and can be utilized in varying amounts by a client up to an agreed maximum limit. The respective interest is calculated based on daily utilization and paid on a regular basis, i.e., monthly, quarterly, semi-annually, or annually. The total limit available is not reduced by repayments but may be redrawn. The overdraft limit is a credit limit that can be freely utilized by the client fully, partially, or not at all. As an effect, the varying utilization of the limit is characteristic for this credit type. Overdraft facilities are general-purpose facilities that may be used by the borrower for any short-term financing needs. Private clients often use the limit for consumer financing, while companies typically finance their working capital needs with this facility. Other uses for corporate borrowers include short-term bridge financing or seasonal financing.

Overdraft credits are formally short-term in nature; however, it is important for banks to observe the use of the funds granted under the overdraft facility because by extending the loan the borrower can, in effect, use the overdraft for long-term financing. As the bank would not be able to cancel its overdraft without hurting their client, the bank may offer the borrower to refinance the overdraft with a term loan in order to avoid the abuse of the facility. Alternatively, in order to prevent long-term utilization, some loan contracts include a clean up period, i.e., a period during which the utilization must be reduced to zero.

The overdraft facility is an essential product for most account relationships, irrespective of the client group. It offers the client financial flexibility and improved liquidity management. Due to its flexible character, clients can respond to spending peaks without maintaining large amounts of expensive cash reserves or the commitment to long-term loans to, in fact, only finance short-term needs. As the overdraft permits the client to utilize (and pay interest on) only the amount needed, overdrafts often result in reduced cost for the client, despite high interest rates.

The most important benefit of the product for the bank is its role in the relationship to the client. In addition, banks are able to charge considerably higher interest rates than for most other loan types, especially for private clients. While banks often do not charge a commitment fee for overdrafts, the main income is generated through interest paid on the utilized credit. Overdrafts of private clients are mostly charged with fixed interest rates, while in corporate banking, variable interest rates, based on market rate and margin, are more common. The interest rates depend on the clients' risk profile and on their market position. In addition, banks charge fees and higher interest rates for unauthorized overdrawing of the limit.

The counterparty risk of an overdraft is limited due to the short maturities of the credit. However, the credit is usually not collateralized; therefore, the lender carries the full credit risk. Borrowers also tend to draw their overdraft limits in situations of poor liquidity; at the same time, the overdraft is, on average, not fully utilized, thereby generating lower revenues than comparable term loan facilities. The varying utilization levels result in a low predictability of the credit risk for the portfolio. This insecurity, and the low risk-weighted assets (RWAs) resulting from low utilization periods can reduce the efficiency of the securitization of this credit type.

Revolving Credit

A revolving credit, similarly to an overdraft, consists of an approved credit limit that may be utilized by varying amounts, according to the clients financing needs. As the funds are drawn by the borrower, the available limit decreases. Based on the repayments by the borrower, the total limit is not reduced; in consequence, the repayments result in an increase in limit availability. However, in contrast to an overdraft, the revolving credit is not directly tied to a bank account. Instead, the borrower has the right to utilize his revolving credit limit based on a loan contract.

Revolving credit facilities are an important product in the corporate banking sector for general purpose and working capital financing. The facilities play a vital role both in bilateral and syndicated loans, as well as in leveraged finance operations. Corporate revolving credit facilities are short- to medium-term in nature. Similar to overdrafts, revolving credit inhibits the risk of being used for long-term financing based on constant renewals. As a consequence, loan agreements often include a clean up period. The utilization of the limit is regulated in the loan documentation, including minimum amounts and a maximum number of drawings under an existing credit limit. The lender may only cancel the limit at the contractual maturity date or based on a breach of the loan contract by the borrower, such as a breach of covenants or material deterioration. In private banking, revolving structures are used for, e.g., credit cards loans.

Interest is paid only on the amount drawn under the revolving credit limit, not on the unutilized part. In addition, the borrower may be charged with a commitment fee for the unutilized part, which is typical for corporate revolving loan facilities, while not the case for credit card loans. If drawings are prepaid before their maturity date, then the bank may also charge the borrower with a handling fee as well as breakage costs resulting from interest losses due to prepayment. Due to the close relation of revolving credit and overdrafts, revolving credits are subject to the same risk factors. While carrying the full credit risk, the lender receives lower interest payments than the lender in a term loan transaction and the varying utilization negatively affects the efficiency of this credit type for a portfolio approach.

Documentary Credit

As world trade is growing, documentary credit (also referred to as *letter of credit*) has become the classical instrument for handling and safeguarding payments in commercial business worldwide.

> A documentary credit is issued at the request of the applicant (buyer/importer) by a bank (issuing bank), who undertakes to pay for the account of its client and through a second bank (beneficiary's bank) to the beneficiary (seller/exporter) a certain amount within a specified period against presentation of certain required documents and in compliance with the terms and conditions specified in the documentary credit.[3]

---

[3] Dresdner Bank AG (1995) *Foreign Trade Related International Banking Services*. Economia Verlag GmbH.

The majority of documentary credits is established on the basis of an underlying trade in goods or commodities and is, therefore, rather short-term (i.e., below 360 days). In addition, documentary credits may also be used to safeguard periodical payments for services not relating to trade. The only precondition for the use of a documentary credit is that the actual payment event can be documented. There are various types of documentary credits, however, the most common types shall be classified according to the type of obligation on the part of banks, their availability to the respective beneficiary, their transferability, and revolvability.

Depending on the form of documentary credit used, there are specific obligations assumed by banks. As a matter of principle the credit can be revocable or irrevocable. While revocable credits are rarely used in practice, irrevocable credits may be either confirmed or unconfirmed. In an unconfirmed irrevocable credit the issuing bank only offers a commitment to pay the beneficiary. In cases where the creditworthiness of the issuing bank is not known to the beneficiary or the conversion or transfer risk appears to be too high, the beneficiary will ask the advising bank to add a confirmation. In a confirmed irrevocable credit the confirming bank (usually the advising and/or exporter's bank) then makes a definite undertaking to pay—even in the event that no payment is obtained from the issuing bank.

Alternatively the exporter can also obtain a silent confirmation from a bank. In this case the credit is transferred from the issuing bank to the advising bank. The bank providing the undertaking to pay bears the risk and responsibility of honoring the documents. The commitment made upon opening an irrevocable credit cannot be amended or rescinded without the consent of the issuing bank, the beneficiary, or if confirmed, the confirming bank.

There are three basic types of usage under a documentary credit: credits providing for payment, documentary acceptance credits, and negotiable credits. Credits providing for payment are either payable at sight or foresee a deferred payment. A deferred payment credit and a sight credit (also known as clean credit) differ only in their respective maturity, i.e., the date on which payment is due. By opening a sight credit, the issuing bank is obliged to pay against presentation of compliant documents. In a deferred payment credit the beneficiary grants the applicant a specified time for payment (once the documents are presented as specified).

If payment is to be made by acceptance credit, then the beneficiary draws a bill on the bank specified in the documentary credit. At some determinable future date when the payment is due, a draft is accepted in place of the payment. The accepting bank is under an irrevocable obligation to honor payment of the draft on the due date. In a negotiable documentary credit, the beneficiary of the credit draws a sight draft or a usance draft on the bank named in the credit. In this case the issuing or confirming bank agrees to honor the payment on the due date or to negotiate the draft with a different bank. Transferable credits are typically arranged for trading houses which do not wish to disclose the name of their subsupplier. Therefore, the beneficiary may request the authorized bank to transfer the credit (in whole or in part) to one or more third parties (second beneficiaries). In a non-transferable credit the issuing bank must exclusively pay to the beneficiary. Revolving documentary credits are used for trades that foresee several shipments under a particular delivery schedule. Until the limited total amount is used up, a revolving credit can usually be drawn several times. In case of a non-cumulative revolving credit the period of validity for partial shipments is limited. If unused credit can be availed of subsequent to final shipment, then it is referred to a revolving cumulative credit. Legal basis for documentary credits in virtually all countries are the Uniform Customs and Practice for Documentary Credits (UCP).[4]

For banks, documentary credits offer fee income for negotiation and handling as well as credit fees depending on the underlying risk. Documentary credits are a key product in commercial banking. From a CRM perspective they serve as a basis for various products in commercial business and offer cross-selling potential within the client relationship. Examples of such are forfaiting, cash advances, undertakings, revolvers, or short-term trade finance as a whole.

While banks need to fully address the counterparty risk of the borrower, the fact that the documentary credit is subject to the underlying commercial trade may be considered as a risk-mitigating factor when compared to a clean credit. It can be anticipated that the borrower intends to fulfil his

[4] For further information on UCP please see International Chamber of Commerce: *www.iccwbo.org/*.

or her commitment under the commercial trade. Furthermore, the liquidity and fungibility of the underlying goods may also bear a considerable mitigating character; examples are crude oil, precious metals, cotton or crop.

For securitization purposes, the attractiveness of the respective documentary credit very much depends on the financials and reputation of the borrower, the country of origin as well as the characteristics of the underlying goods. With the features outlined above, RWA usage of Documentary Credits is rather low. Hence, from a CAM perspective the effect on RWA relief via securitization is limited.

Guarantees

Like documentary credits, guarantees are used as instruments for safeguarding payments and performance obligations in commercial business. By issuing commercial guarantees, banks take the role of a guarantor offering risk protection to their clients who may be buyers or sellers in a commercial contract. For the description of guarantees we follow Bishop (2003) and distinguish between guarantees that have a "true" guarantee character and those that have an "on-demand" character.

We define true guarantees as guarantees where a guarantor undertakes the liability of a third party. Unlike on-demand guarantees, true guarantees are always linked to a primary debt to which the guarantor becomes secondarily liable. When the primary debt is being reduced or cleared the guarantee expires accordingly. In essence, guarantee types are usually governed under local law jurisdictions of the country the guarantee is issued.

Bishop (2003) describes on-demand guarantees as an undertaking by a bank "to pay the beneficiary a certain sum to cover the action or default of a third party. [...] In this form of guarantee, the guarantor is primarily liable; the beneficiary has only to make a demand, worded precisely as indicated in the guarantee and he will be paid." Thereby the guarantee is autarkic and independent from the underlying transaction between the buyer and seller, between debtor and debtee. Essentially, guarantees are covered under the terms and conditions of the issuing bank.

In practice, banks prefer to accept guarantees that are independent from the underlying transaction. The on-demand character is therefore the most commonly type used in commercial guarantee business. Internationally there can be different meanings for the word guarantee. In the Anglo-American jurisdiction a guarantee is subject to an underlying liability, while a general and/or on-demand guarantee as described above will be in form of a Contract of indemnity or a Standby Letter of Credit. In other jurisdictions the term guarantee comprises both forms. Due to this, banking practice uses standard wordings for international guarantee business. The payment instruction "on first demand," for instance, is commonly used by banks to structure guarantees with an on-demand character.

The most common types of on-demand guarantees used in international trade are Bid Bonds, Performance Bonds, Advance Payment Guarantees, and Standby Letters of Credit. Bid bonds are required in large (mostly public) tender offers from a supplier or contractor—guaranteeing for a compensation amount in case he withdraws from his bid. Effectively these guarantees amount to 1 to 5 percent of the offer value and have maturities of three to six months. In a Performance Bond a bank undertakes to compensate the beneficiary in the event that the supplier does not satisfy his obligations in the underlying contract. A compensation amount of 10 percent of the contract value is guaranteed. The maturity depends on the underlying contract and will mostly be two or more years. In commercial transactions of high volume, the buyer is usually asked to make an advance payment for raw material or manufacturing costs. In return the buyer receives an Advance Payment Guarantee which guarantees the repayment of the advance payment in the event that the supplier does not fulfil his obligations under the contract. These guarantees are usually limited to the date of shipment. In a Standby Letter of Credit the beneficiary is guaranteed a payment for the event that a third party fails to carry out the contract as specified. In their form as a documentary credit, Standby Letters of Credit are subject to and governed under the international standard and rules of the UCP.

Due to their flexibility, guarantees offer a large scope for design and purpose. They may serve as instruments for securing payment flows or may simply be used with the intention to upgrade a transaction by using the good name of the bank (guarantor) backing the guarantee. Standard guarantee types are usually very competitive in pricing. From a CRM perspective, commercial guarantees mainly function as a supplementary product offered in trade finance and present cross-selling benefits.

As long as the guarantee is not drawn, RWA will be low and there will be no cost of capital for the bank as the guarantor. When securing or selling off the risk in the market, however, banks might have to pay a high price for the actual (counterparty) risk that is being sold. In such a case, securitization will not be attractive in terms of an efficient use of capital.

Leasing

A lease is an alternative source of financing whereby a lessor (owner of an asset) licences the right to use and obtain possession of the asset to a so-called lessee (user) in exchange for regular rental payments. The lease is based on a legal contract that is usually non-callable for the fixed period of the lease. Historically, companies use leasing as an alternative to buying capital equipment. Leasing the equipment offers them the possibility of optimizing the allocation of their capital and making use of cash flows available. Thereby the equipment is often leased from a leasing company or from the manufacturer directly.

In the financial industry, lessors such as banks offer unique leasing structures in connection with tax-efficient finance or as an investment product offering extraordinary investment returns. Generally, the underlying assets may comprise anything from movable property (such as printing machines, power plants, or incineration plants) or real property (such as premises, warehouses or convenience stores) to intangible assets (such as trademarks, patents, and film distributions rights).

There is a wide variety of possible arrangements. The most common structures typically found in a bank's leasing portfolio are any kind of sale-and-lease-back structures. In such structures the lessor acquires the asset from the lessee and leases it back to the lessee. This way the lessee has the ability to retain use of the asset and additionally raises cash from the sale. Depending on the structure, there may be various further benefits arising from a sale-and-lease-back structure. As the lessor is entitled to capital allowances, the lessor will be able to provide the lessee with tax-efficient finance for the cost of the equipment. The tax advantage arises from the timing benefit from receipt of capital allowances by the lessor prior to paying tax on the rental receipt. This post-tax enhanced term finance structure is mostly used by large corporates with high-value assets that have a modest appreciation. In this case the source of further benefit arises from capital allowances that are based on the sale price less the clawback of capital allowances capped at the assets' original costs. In this product type the leasing period equals to the economic life of the asset.

In a long-term-funding-lease finance the lessee is typically granted the right to acquire the asset at maturity at the price of the residual book value and thereby benefit from fully participating in hidden reserves. The counterparty risk is reflected in the ability to perform the regular rental payments. Depending on the structure, the lessor also bares the risk in the residual value of the asset when the leased asset reverts to the lessor at the end of the lease period. Constant maintenance and inspection by an assessor will therefore be incorporated in the lease contract. Whereas leasing companies structure the lease based on the asset, banks usually demand covenants such as liquidity, profitability, net worth, and debt–coverage ratio of their client.

Standard lease products are usually high in volume, have long maturities, and are of noncallable character during the lifetime of the lease. As such, standard lease products offer attractive characteristics for long-term customer retention as well as securitization purposes. While structured leasing products on the other hand may offer attractive fee income, they become unplaceable in the market the more complex and sensitive they are in their character.

CREDIT PURPOSE

By offering financing solutions, banks address the very special needs of their clients. Making use of the full product range available, finance solutions are built of a combination of various types of loan products. The latter are structured to best suit the individual needs of the banks' customers.

Syndicated Loans and Club Deals

Syndicated loans are loans that are provided by a group of lenders, the consortium, in contrast to bilateral loans with a single lending party. The banking consortium is formed and cooperates for a single transaction only where the most common loan types used in syndicated transactions are revolving loan facilities and term loans. The loan is often divided between several tranches, with the tranches varying according to credit type, term, or seniority.

The credit process begins with the borrower mandating a lead bank or several lead banks to arrange a multilateral loan. The lead banks will structure the transaction and negotiate the details with the borrower, such as credit type, maturity, terms, and conditions. Once the structure is agreed between lead banks and borrower, the syndication process will take place.[5] During the syndication, the lead banks invite other banks to join the transaction. The participants receive different titles in the consortium, such as arrangers, managers, or participants, depending on their participation in the transaction. One bank is selected as the agent, who administers the transaction and coordinates the consortium throughout the lifetime of the loan.

The lead banks chose between several syndication approaches, based on the borrower's request and the transaction size. In a programmed syndication, only banks that already maintain a relationship with the borrower are invited. If the group is extended to include other selected banks, then the approach is called *ad hoc syndication*. In a broadcast syndication, large numbers of banks are invited (Büschgen, 1998).

The syndication of loans, and the participation in syndicated loans, allows a bank to increase the number of borrowers in its credit portfolio, thereby reducing concentration risk. Another benefit of the syndication process is the comprehensive loan documentation and the disclosure thereof throughout the process. These factors facilitate a secondary sale of syndicated loans, making them very attractive for credit portfolio transactions. Syndicated loans have become an important instrument in financing both medium and large corporations as well as financial institutions.

Syndicated loans generate both interest and fee income for the banks involved in the transaction. Each bank receives interest payments based on their participation in the various tranches. In addition, the lead banks receive upfront fees for the structuring and syndication of the loan. These fees represent the most lucrative aspect of loan syndication, as the interest often hardly covers the cost for the bank.

---

[5] If no other banks are invited to participate, the transaction is called a *club deal*.

The main risk in a syndicated loan, as in any term or revolving loan, is the counterparty risk. The risk is reduced in comparison to bilateral loans, as each bank retains a smaller share of the risk. In addition, by providing the loan as a consortium, the banks avoid the risk of obtaining a subordinated status in comparison to other lenders. The downside of participating in a consortium is that the individual bank might encounter difficulties in enforcing its position within the group, as many decisions will require the consent of the majority or all consortium members.

The second risk, which arises for the lead banks, is the syndication risk. In order to acquire the mandate, the lead bank often underwrites the full loan amount. In case of major market shifts, as seen in the financial markets during the second half of 2007, the lead banks are not able to syndicate the full expected amount and, thereby, retain a larger risk share than intended. Banks try to avoid the syndication risk by negotiating the syndication of the loan on a "best effort" basis, allowing them to reduce or cancel the loan if they are unable to place the necessary loan volume.

Consumer Finance

Consumer finance, in a broad sense, includes loans from banks and other financial institutions to consumers. In the United States, the term is commonly used in a more narrow sense as subprime lending, i.e., lending to private clients with a poor credit quality. The term *consumer finance* will be used in the broader sense, synonymous to the term *consumer loans*.[6] The term of these loans is mostly short to medium, ranging from six months to six years, depending on the credit quality of the borrower, and the purpose of the loan, e.g., the lifetime of an asset that is being financed. Most consumer loans are amortizing, i.e., the payments by the borrower remain constant over the lifetime of the loan, with each payment consisting of principal repayment and interest. Consumer loans are normally provided in amounts of up to €25,000, with larger amounts possible.

---

[6] Residential mortgages, which may also be included in the definition, are excluded here for analytical purposes and discussed separately in the section Mortgage Loans. For a historical perspective on the U.S. market as well as a comparison with other international mortgage markets, see Green and Wachter (2005).

Consumer loans offered by banks and financial institutions are mostly general-purpose loans. In contrast, loans by nonfinancial corporations, such as car producers or large retail chains, are characterized by their explicit relationship to the underlying assets, such as consumer goods, journeys, and house repairs. In this case, large corporations provide their clients, directly or via cooperating financial institutions, with amortizing loans to acquire their products.

The only income that consumer loans generate for the lender is interest income. Additional fees, such as administration fees, are typically not charged separately but included in the interest rate. The interest rate level varies widely, based on the purpose of the loan and the credit quality of the borrower. Loans for the purchase of a specific asset are often subsidized by the seller in order to promote the asset sale. General-purpose loans are processed on a standardized basis and, therefore, at low administrative cost. The major single factor influencing the interest rate is the credit quality of the borrower.

The main risk involved in consumer finance is the credit risk of the private borrower. The lender's intent is to reduce the credit risk through advanced, standardized credit processes in order to identify eligible borrowers. In addition, lenders may require their clients to provide collateral, such as the pledging of salary or the granting of security interests in the acquired assets. In addition to individual credit risk, consumer finance is subject to systemic risk, as the credit process is standardized with limited focus on individual borrowers. In conclusion, consumer loans are comparably small loans that cannot be syndicated on an individual basis; instead, portfolio transactions, such as basket or securitization approaches, have proven more viable for the risk reduction of consumer loan portfolios.

Credit Card Loans

Credit card institutions emit credit cards, directly or in cooperation with commercial banks. Clients use the credit card to purchase goods, services, or obtain cash at partners cooperating with the credit card issuer, up to an approved limit. This credit card limit represents the maximum credit card loan available to the client. Structurally, the credit card limit is a revolving credit facility. If the money owed is not repaid on a monthly basis, then it is converted into a consumer loan that is amortized over a longer period. The credit card is, therefore, used for both convenience and credit purposes.

Credit cards provide both fee and interest income to the issuing institution. With any purchase paid for with the credit card, a certain percentage (usually 1 to 5 percent) is charged directly to the seller of the goods or services. For the client, the credit card loan is interest rate free if the loan is repaid on a monthly basis. If the loan is not repaid but converted into an amortizing loan, then very high interest rates are charged on the outstanding loan balance. In addition, many credit card providers charge an annual fee for the credit card.

Credit card loans are subject to the counterparty risk of the private client. As for other revolving loans, the percentage drawn under credit card limits increases when clients are faced with liquidity shortages. In addition, credit card issuers face fraud risk in the case of abuse of the credit card. Similar to consumer loans, credit card loans are relatively small, resulting in portfolio transactions being the most adequate tools for the securitization of credit cards.

Mortgage Loans

A mortgage is a pledge of property that is used to collateralize a long-term loan, the mortgage loan. The collateral assets may be either residential properties, such as apartments and houses, for residential mortgages, or commercial properties, such as warehouses or office buildings, for commercial mortgages (Fabozzi and Modigliani, 2003). Mortgage loans are not tied to a particular financing object; the proceeds from the loan are used either to finance the acquisition of the property or for other long-term investments. The most common structure is a conventional mortgage, which is a mortgage loan that serves to finance the residential real estate that is used as collateral.

Mortgages exist in a variety of terms, rates, repayment, and amortization structures, the description of which extends beyond the scope of this chapter. The focus of the following description will, therefore, be on the current conventional mortgage structures in the U.S. market.[7] Today,

---

[7] For a historical perspective on the U.S. market as well as a comparison with other international mortgage markets, please see Green and Wachter (2005).

most mortgages have a maturity of 5 to 30 years. The maximum amount is not limited in absolute terms but is related to the underlying collateral. The average loan to value is in the range around 75 percent; however, some mortgage lenders provide loans of over 100 percent of the asset value. The loan is also limited by the financial strength of the borrower, as the maximum mortgage rate is based on the personal income situation.

The repayment period is usually divided among fixed-term periods of up to 10 or 20 years; afterwards, the interest rate will be renegotiated. For commercial mortgages, variable interest rates based on market rate and margin are more common; in some countries, conventional mortgages are also dominated by variable rates. In addition, there are mixed interest rate schedules, with low fixed interest rates during the first periods and higher fixed or variable interest rates later on. This interest rate system has achieved dubious fame due to its role in the overheating of the mortgage market in the United States in 2007.

Mortgages often amortize over the maturity of the loan; however, bullet payments at maturity are a feasible alternative if the borrower expects are large cash flows to coincide with the maturity of the loan. In addition to the scheduled repayment, the borrower often has the opportunity to effect prepayments. The prepayment option depends both on the national mortgage standards—private borrowers in the United States may prepay any part of the mortgage at any time without additional cost—and the individual mortgage loan contract—prepayments in Germany usually incur breakage costs, unless a prepayment clause is included in the mortgage loan contract, possibly resulting in higher interest cost over the term of the loan. Based on expected prepayment rates, an average repayment rate is calculated by the lender. Prepayment options result in a prepayment risk for the lender, as the loan will be reduced in a low-interest environment (contraction risk) and extended under high interest rate environment (extension risk), compared with the expected average repayment schedule.

Mortgages are among the key financing tools for borrowers, as they provide low-cost, long-term financing that is not available otherwise. For banks, mortgage loans offer the opportunity of long-term stable income. The main income component is the regular interest payment. Fees are mostly built into the interest rate. Other cost that might be included comprises legal or collateralization charges, credit insurance or the cost for the prepayment option.

The counterparty risk for residential mortgages depends on the income situation of the borrower, while commercial mortgages are repaid from income generate by the underlying asset; in that case, the asset quality is the key determining aspect for the repayment risk. The risk is, in any case, mitigated by the option to sell the collateral in case of default. The arising security risk depends, on the one hand, on the current market situation, as a downturn in real property markets will result in a lower than expected value of the property. On the other hand, it is affected by the loan to value ratio of the transaction, as a relatively small loan will be covered by the proceeds from the sale even under difficult market conditions. The recent subprime mortgage crisis in the United States resulted, therefore, from the granting of mortgages with a very high loan to value ratio to borrowers with weak credit quality. As the property prices started to decline, the banks were hit by repayment failures combined with reduced property prices, resulting in the write-off of large mortgage portfolios.

Conventional mortgage loans are usually too small to be considered by CAM on an individual basis. Therefore, and due to their long-term and stable cash flows, mortgages are an important product for portfolio transactions. The key challenge for these transactions is the dealing with the prepayment option inherent in many mortgage loans. In addition, the recent mortgage market turmoil has resulted in valuation problems and a lack of confidence in the secondary mortgage market. The consequence is a temporarily inefficient market with unreliable prices.

Structured Finance

Globalization and challenging market conditions require banks and their clients to identify new ways of financing. Market trends show bilateral loans being substituted by large syndicated loans. At the same time leverage in financing is increasing and financial covenants are being accepted on weaker basis. Banks offer structured finance solutions by making use of various types of loan products that are structured to best suit the individual needs of their customers. Doing so, they primarily focuses on the capacity of the financed operation to generate sufficient cash for the repayment of the financing.

Typical target clients are internationally orientated corporations as well as financial institutions. For banks, financing on a structured basis secures higher returns and offers cross-sell opportunities with their international clients. The most relevant features of structured finance shall be described on the basis of trade finance and leverage finance.

Structured Trade Finance

In structured trade finance (STF), banks provide their clients with financing along the international supply chain of commercial business—anywhere from production to the processing, warehousing, and trading. Such finance structures are built around existing or future contracts for commercial goods. These are usually of high demand and fungible character and may comprise anything from commodities to merchandise, mass consumer goods, or interchangeable services like tourism or logistics. The tenor of the structure depends on the character of the underlying good as well as the production and off-take characteristics and is mostly short- to medium-term.

Most STF product types provide loans in the form of cash lending, but they may also choose the form of a guarantee. There is a broad range of product types that is offered according to the individual needs and financing phases in the supply chain. Structured trade finance comprises pre-finance, inventory finance, trade finance, or hedging business and is typically built of the credit types named earlier in this chapter such as term loans, overdrafts, or revolvers. What is common to all STF products is the fact that the debtor is a party to one or more (future) commercial contracts that when fulfilled will originate cash flow in sufficient volume to repay the financing. In a pure transaction-based credit it is not the borrower that pays back the loan with his or her own funds; but it is the fulfillment of the underlying contract that results in repayment. Here a variety of other commercial products such as documentary credits or draft discounting and forfaiting is offered as supplementary financing instruments.

As the repayment depends on the fulfillment of the underlying commercial contract, the borrower's financials may only be of ancillary importance. The ability of repayment is assessed via track records and the market reputation of the borrower rather than on its financials. Especially for borrowers with weak financials, this allows to structure financing at reduced risk premiums and longer tenors—even in non-investment grade countries. Due to their complexity, transactions costs can sum up quite high. The transactions, therefore, tend to be high in volume.

Collateralization in STF is mainly provided by the goods underlying the financing. They are being pledged, assigned, guaranteed, or hedged in various forms. As explained above, the unique character of STF is that the goods that serve as collateral are also the source of the funds for the repayment of the financing. As the borrower is anticipated to be able to fulfill the commitment under the commercial contract, the same goes for the underlying finance structure.

Depending of the fungible goods traded and liquidity of the market, the goods can be turned into cash at anytime. Price volatility can be managed by respective hedging instruments. Insurance can be put in place for losses and claims that could endanger due fulfillment of the contracts. However, cost of collateral may become a considerable factor. The bank's role in STF is not restricted to offering financing solutions. With their well-known names in the respective market and business segment, banks establish contacts between their clients and potential trading partners. From a CRM perspective this helps to establish long-term customer relationships.

While the characteristics described above make STF products an attractive source for securitizations, the same is limited under the following aspects. Due to their complexity, STF transactions require market expertise, manual handling, and monitoring. A securitization will therefore be considered only for a certain loan or guarantee product of the financing structure, rather than for the transaction as a whole. Thereby, the market reputation of the parties involved becomes a crucial aspect. Securitization during the initial phase of financing, for instance, inheres performance risk (inability to duly produce and/or deliver the goods underlying the structure). For the latter a potential buyer might demand for a higher price, irrespective of the risk characteristics of the structure. This in turn puts constrains on the whole STF structure as—in such a case—the desired financing at reduced risk premiums cannot be achieved.

Leverage Finance
Leverage finance products are common in acquisition finance where leverage is used as a means to allow large acquisitions without having to

commit a lot of equity. As described by Brealey and Myers (1996) a common feature to all such structures is that a large fraction of the purchase price will be debt financed.[8] After the takeover, the shares will no longer trade on the open market. The equity will be privately held by a small group of usually institutional investors. After the financed takeover, debt appears on the acquired company's balance sheet and its free cash flow is used to repay the debt. As long as the operational return is higher as the cost of debt, the debt-to-equity ratio is leveraged to achieve a positive effect on the internal rate of return. As in STF, leverage finance is being provided on the basic cash flow generated by the underlying. Ideal acquisition candidates therefore typically generate stable cash flows, have low business risk, and offer some kind of upside to the financial sponsor.

The different types of leverage finance structures can be distinguished depending on the type and role of the equity investors. Examples are leverage buy out (LBO), management buyout (MBO), or institutional buy-out (IBO) structures. In the following, the most relevant features shall be discussed on the basis of an LBO. In an LBO the equity component of the purchase price usually marks up 25 to 35 percent and is typically sponsored by a pool of private equity investors. The major portion of the purchase is financed through a combination of debt facilities arranged by banks and institutional investors as well as public or privately placed bonds. While mezzanine and junior debt usually ranges between 20 and 30 percent, the role of senior secured loans has become of increasing importance in recent years and can mark up more than 50 percent.

The European LBO market for senior loans has grown more than six-fold in terms of volume over the past seven years.[9] The demand for senior debt has been bolstered by increasing leverage multiples and an increasing trend in recapitalization structures.[10] At the same time tenors for senior debt term loan tranches have increased to maturities over seven to nine years. In international competitive markets banks need to address the special needs of their customers by offering highly structured finance solutions. In order to maximize the visibility with their clients and in the

---

[8] Compare Brealey, A. and Myers, C. (1996, p. 937).

[9] Source: *LCD European Leveraged Buyout Review* (Q3 2007).

[10] Standard & Poor's Ratings Direct (August 7th, 2006) *The Dividend Recap Game: Credit Risk vs. the Allure of Quick Money.*

market, they are compelled to follow the trend of increase in transaction size and leverage, accompanied by weaker covenants.

In a market study by the Banking Supervision Committee of the European Central Banks, German banks state that in 90 percent of their five largest transactions they have been part of a syndicate.[11] In face of the market developments, banks try to limit their risk exposure by holding only a small portion of the LBO financing debt—just enough to show commitment and realize cross-selling potential for the client relationship. Making active use of syndicating the credit risk, banks place most of the arranged financing with other market participants—increasingly institutional investors. The existence of a liquid secondary market allows the selling of debt even after the arrangement of the LBO. The features of senior secured debt financing in the form of syndicated loans are described in the first part of this chapter. In addition to the spreads on the individual products offered via a structure, fees for advising, arranging, handling or placing offer an attractive source of revenue income, both, from a CRM as well as the CAM perspective.

CONCLUSION

In this chapter we have provided an overview of the most relevant credit types and credit purposes in the current credit market. Based on the most important features of each credit type or structure we derived their relevance for both client relationship management and credit portfolio management of banks. In our analysis we have shown that certain factors such as a long-term, constant utilization and stable cash flows facilitate the management of credits from a portfolio perspective. When analyzing a credit, CAM focuses on these features and the effect of the credit on the existing credit portfolio. The CRM, on the other hand, is interested in sustainable high income and focuses on the overall client relationship, considering all products that a single client utilizes. As a result, the two points of view often diverge in their analysis of credit structures.

Credit asset management has succeeded in playing an increasingly important role in the decision-making process in relationship banking.

---

[11] Source: Deutsche Bundesbank, monthly report (April 2007).

This emergence of CAM has allowed the banks to increase the efficiency of their credit portfolio by involving CAM early in their credit decisions. However, for a proactive portfolio management, both CAM- and CRM-relevant factors have to be considered. Therefore, it is important for CAM to also maintain a broad perspective and consider the economic relevance of client relationships. Only if both CAM and CRM perspectives are accounted for in credit and credit portfolio decisions, will modern banks be able successfully to support cross-selling, maximize earnings, manage risk and sustain efficient use of capital.

REFERENCES

Bishop, E. (2003) *Finance of International Trade*. Burlington, MA: Elsevier.

Brealey, A. and Myers, C. (1996) *Principles of Corporate Finance*. New York: McGraw-Hill.

Büschgen, H.E. (1998) *Bankbetriebslehre*. Wiesbaden, Germany: Gabler Verlag.

Fabozzi, F. and Modigliani, F. (2003) *Capital Markets*. Upper Saddle River, NJ: Pearson.

Fredriksson, A. (2007) The Effect of Relationship Intensity and Value on Loan Pricing. Turku School of Economics, Working Paper Series.

Green, R.K and Wachter, S.M. (2005) The American Mortgage in Historical and International Context. *Journal of Economic Perspectives*, 19(4): 93–114.

Hartmann-Wendels, T., Pfingsten, A., and Weber, M. (2004) *Bankbetriebslehre*. Berlin, Germany: Springer-Verlag.

Ongena, S.R.G. and Smith, D.C. (1998) Bank Relationships: A Review. Available at SSRN: ssrn.com/abstract=139933 or DOI: 10.2139/ssrn.139933.

Stiglitz, J.E. and Weiss, A. (1981) Credit Rationing in Markets with Imperfect Information. *The American Economic Review*, 71: 393–410.

CHAPTER 7

Default Dependency Modeling: An Introduction to Theory and Application

Sabine Bank and Mathias Schwarz[1]

ABSTRACT

This chapter deals with the measurement of credit risk in loan portfolios and the application in structuring collateralized debt obligations. When assessing credit risk in a portfolio of loans the measurement and modeling of dependencies or correlations of credit events is of crucial importance. After briefly describing the basics of underlying mathematical concepts that often rest on the Gaussian copula approach, we go on to demonstrate how these concepts are applied by practitioners in structuring and rating collateralized debt obligations by analyzing a sample collateralized debt obligation (CDO) composed of small- and medium-sized enterprise loans.

---

[1] This article represents the authors' opinions and does not necessarily reflect the view of KfW Bankengruppe or its staff.

INTRODUCTION: DEFAULT DEPENDENCY

When modeling credit portfolio losses as opposed to defaults on individual loans, one has to take into account that defaults among different borrowers are often related. This can result from several factors such as when borrowers belong to the same industry, region, or country. One of those factors can be the general state of the economy, and accordingly during a recession, default probability increases for many companies.

Whereas default dependencies considerably complicate the task of finding a portfolio loss distribution, their modeling is a crucial step in rating and pricing pools of such credit risky assets as collateralized debt obligations (CDOs). This has become obvious during the subprime crisis. Furthermore, default dependency matters from a regulatory point of view. Normal rates of default are not what cause problems for the financial sector—these are normally covered by margins and loss provisions. Rather, it is the simultaneous default of multiple borrowers that threatens lenders as well as the entire financial system. Unfortunately, this risk can only be partially mitigated by diversification especially during crises when correlations tend to increase considerably via contagion effects.

Several concepts of dependency are employed in the context of modeling credit defaults. The measure most often used is doubtlessly the correlation coefficient according to Bravais and Pearson.[2] This measure is the linear correlation coefficient of two indicator variables each of which takes the value one if the corresponding borrower defaults on its loan within a certain time period and zero otherwise. However, this measure has several drawbacks. Most of all, while independence of two random variables implies zero correlation, the reverse generally does not hold. Other measures of dependency such as Kendall's τ or Spearman's rank correlation coefficient overcome those limitations to some extent.[3] Li (2000) introduces the concept of default time correlation, which is described in the next section.

---

[2] The correlation coefficient of two random variables X, Y is defined as, $\rho_{XY} := \mathrm{COV}\,(X, Y)/(\mathrm{SD}(X)\text{-}\mathrm{SD}(Y))$, where SD() and COV() denote the standard deviation and covariance, respectively. Despite this narrow statistical definition, the term *correlation* is often used in the broader sense of dependency as in Lucas et al. (2006) who define *default correlation* as "the phenomenon that the likelihood of one obligator defaulting on its debt is affected by whether or not another obligor has defaulted on its debt" (pp. 301 and 302).

[3] See, e.g., De Servigny (2007a) for a description of various dependency measures.

The remainder of this chapter is organized as follows: The second section of this chapter provides an introduction to the theory of default dependency modeling. One popular approach builds on factor models that derive default dependency from the co-movement of common underlying factors. We show how different assumptions regarding the underlying distribution and correlation level affect the resulting loss distribution of a portfolio consisting of credit risky assets and then introduce copulas. Copulas are an elegant way to separate the problem of dependency modeling from the problem of calibrating the marginal distributions. The third section of this chapter demonstrates how these concepts are applied by practitioners in structuring and rating CDOs by analyzing a sample CDO composed of small- and medium-sized enterprises (SME) loans.

MODELING DEFAULT DEPENDENCIES

There are broadly speaking two ways of modeling default dependencies, *reduced form* and *structural* models. In reduced form models the companies' hazard rates follow a stochastic process that is linked to common (e.g., macroeconomic) drivers. As a result, the hazard rates of two companies have a tendency to move in the same direction. However, the degree of default correlation that can be achieved with reduced form models is limited. CreditRisk+ of Credit Suisse First Boston is a well-known example of a reduced form model. Another model is Moody's BET model that transforms a portfolio of n correlated heterogeneous loans into a portfolio of $D < n$ independent homogeneous loans on which the binomial distribution is applied.[4] All such approximations work better the more granular (i.e., more diverse and homogeneous) the actual portfolio is.

Structural models[5] are based on a Merton (1974) asset value approach. The models assume some stochastic process of the firm's asset value, and a firm defaults when the asset value falls below the level of outstanding debt. In other words, equity is viewed as being long a call option on the asset value of the firm with a strike price equal to the debt, and default correlation

---

[4] Binomial expansion technique. D is the diversity score that accounts for the fact that the assets in the actual portfolio are correlated. See Moody's (1996) or Bluhm et al. (2003).

[5] KMV's Portfolio Manager and CreditMetrics as well as the CDO rating tools of the major rating agencies belong to this type of model.

stems from the correlation of asset values. Depending on the size and the diversification of the pool, structural models are implemented using either a Monte Carlo simulation or some analytical approximation like the Vasicek distribution described later.

Factor Models

In what follows, we describe the basic framework of factor models and their implementation using Monte Carlo simulations. Factor models are an elegant way to incorporate default correlations into structural models. To their advantages belong that they are economically meaningful and that they drastically reduce the number of correlations needed. As mentioned, factor models build on a Merton (1974) model. The asset value A_i of a company i is explained by the movement of several factors, which are either common to all companies or only to subgroups, and by an idiosyncratic shock.[6] Default correlation stems from the correlation of the asset values and therefore from the movements of the common factors. Moody's CDOROM, for example, uses the following three-factor approach:

$$A_i = \sqrt{\rho_G}X_G + \sqrt{\rho_I}X_I + \sqrt{\rho_{IR}}X_{IR} + \sqrt{1 - \rho_G - \rho_I - \rho_{IR}}\varepsilon_i, \quad (7.1)$$

where X_G, X_I, X_{IR}, and ε_i are independently normally distributed random variables with zero mean and unit variance.[7]

According to Equation (7.1), the asset value is driven by a global factor X_G, an industry-specific factor X_I, and by a regional industry factor X_{IR}. Thus, asset value correlation depends on whether the companies are located in the same industry or region, whereas the region should be interpreted in terms of country. Correlation is the highest for companies within the same sector and region ($\rho_G + \rho_I + \rho_{IR}$) and the lowest for companies of different industries and regions (ρ_G).

---

[6] We use a somewhat simplified approach here in which the asset price directly depends on the factors, whereas in Vasicek (1987) asset prices follow a geometric Brownian motion with an stochastic component driven by a the factor model.

[7] See Moody's (2006) manual for CDOROM v2.3. Fitch uses a similar three-factor approach in its VECTOR model. See Fitch (2006) or Fitch (2007).

For ease of exposition, we now turn to the case of only one common factor X:

$$A_i = \sqrt{\rho}X + \sqrt{1-\rho}\varepsilon_i. \qquad (7.2)$$

Given the default threshold d_i, company i defaults whenever $A_i < d_i$. Assuming normality and uniform individual default probability, the probability of default conditional on the value of the common factor is

$$p_i := \text{prob}\left(A_i < d \mid X = x\right) = \text{prob}\left(\varepsilon_i < \tfrac{d-\sqrt{\rho}x}{\sqrt{1-\rho}}\right) = \Phi\left(\tfrac{\Phi^{-1}(p_i)-\sqrt{\rho}x}{\sqrt{1-\rho}}\right), \quad (7.3)$$

where Φ denotes the cumulative normal distribution. Conditional on the realization of the common factor X, individual defaults are independent from each other, and one can calculate the probability of n defaults in a portfolio consisting of N obligors by using Equation (7.3) in a binomial distribution and integrating over the common factor:

$$\text{prob}(n \text{ out of } N \text{ defaults}) = \int_{-\infty}^{\infty} \binom{N}{n}\left(\Phi\left(\tfrac{\Phi^{-1}(e_i)-\sqrt{\rho}x}{\sqrt{1-\rho}}\right)\right)^n$$
$$\left(1 - \Phi\left(\tfrac{\Phi^{-1}(e_i)-\sqrt{\rho}x}{\sqrt{1-\rho}}\right)\right)^{N-n} d\Phi(X). \qquad (7.4)$$

Factor models can be implemented by using a Monte Carlo simulation which is the most flexible but also the most time consuming way. For this reason semi-analytical approaches like those discussed in De Servigny (2007b) are often adopted, if possible.

The steps of implementing a factor model are as follows:

1. Estimate the individual default probabilities p_i for a given time horizon, e.g., one year.
2. Determine the distribution of the underlying factors. In Equation (7.2) this has been the standard normal distribution and translates into what is known as a *Gaussian copula model*. However, other distributions and/or copulas that exhibit more weight on the tails are possible.[8]

---

[8] See section on copulas or De Servigny (2007b) for other examples.

3. Evaluate Equation (7.4) to obtain the portfolio loss. This has to be done numerically either by using numerical integration or Monte Carlo simulation.

The procedure results in a default correlation between companies i, j of

$$r_{ij} = \frac{p_{ij} - p_i p_j}{\sqrt{p_i(1 - p_i)p_j(1 - p_j)}} \tag{7.5}$$

and depends, via the probability of common default p_{ij}, on the asset correlation ρ. In general, it is much smaller than ρ.

One of the drawbacks of Monte Carlo simulations is that they can become computationally intensive—especially for large portfolios. Fortunately, for large portfolios it is possible to find a good analytical approximation if the obligors are homogeneous (e.g., the case for a portfolio of consumer loans). In this case, Equation (7.4) can be further simplified by using the law of large numbers, which ensures that the proportion of defaults almost surely equals the uniform individual default probability $p(y)$. The probability distribution and density functions of the share of defaulted loans $\theta = n/N$ are as follows:

$$F(\theta) = \Phi\left(\frac{\sqrt{1 - \rho}\ \Phi^{-1}(\theta) - \Phi^{-1}(p)}{\sqrt{\rho}} \right), \tag{7.6}$$

$$f(\theta) = \sqrt{\frac{1 - \rho}{\rho}} \exp\left(\frac{1}{2}\left[\Phi^{-1}(\theta)\right]^2 - \frac{1}{2\rho}\left[\Phi^{-1}(p) - \sqrt{1 - \rho}\Phi^{-1}(\theta)\right] \right). \tag{7.7}$$

This result is due to Vasicek (1991) and is sometimes called the *Vasicek distribution*.[9] Other terms include *homogeneous large portfolio Gaussian copula (HLPGC) model*[10] or *normal inverse function*.[11] Whereas Equation (7.4) can in principle incorporate multiple factors, the HLPGC

---

[9] See Schönbucher (2007) or Bluhm et al. (2003) for a more elaborate discussion.
[10] See Felsenheimer et al. (2006).
[11] See Moody's (2007).

model considers only one common factor. Nevertheless, Moody's (2007) shows that this methodology leads to a good approximation of the full simulation approach for a reasonable (but not infinitely) large portfolio and uses it for evaluating CDOs of loans to small- and medium-sized companies. Finally, Equation (7.6) forms the basis for the Basel-II asymptotic single risk factor (ASRF) framework for calculating regulatory capital requirements under the advanced IRB approach.[12]

Copulas and Default Dependence

So far, we implicitly used the Gaussian copula approach. It is worth having a closer look on the concept of copulas. The central idea is not new and dates back to Sklar (1959). A copula $C(U)$ links a vector of univariate marginals $U = (U_1, U_2, ..., U_n)$ to their multivariate distribution function. Therefore, copulas are also called *dependency functions*. Formally a copula is defined as

$$C\left(u_1, u_2, ..., u_n\right) := \mathrm{prob}(U_1 \leq u_1, U_2 \leq u_2, ..., U_n \leq u_n). \qquad (7.8)$$

By Sklar's theorem copulas link the marginals with a joint distribution:

$$C\left(F_1\left(x_1\right), F_1\left(x_2\right), ..., F_n\left(x_n\right)\right) = F\left(x_1, x_2, ..., x_n\right). \qquad (7.9)$$

Unfortunately, while it is possible to deduce a unique copula and dependence structure from a given multivariate distribution, provided certain conditions are satisfied, the opposite is generally not possible.

The concept of copulas is useful for analyzing dependencies, because a copula entails only the dependency information but no individual information. This allows the user to separate the process of calibrating the individual default probability distribution from the process of finding the joint distribution. Two popular copulas in the field of credit risk modeling are the *Gaussian* and the *Student's t copula*. We briefly introduce them and demonstrate how to reproduce them with spreadsheet software. The results are displayed in Figure 7.1.

---

[12] See Basel Committee on Banking Supervision (2005).

F I G U R E   7.1

Comparison of the Gaussian and the t-copula (3 df.),
ρ = 50 percent, 5,000 draws

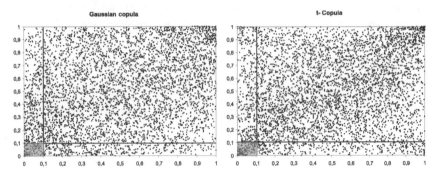

Gaussian copula: Consider a vector **X** of n standard normal distributed random variables X_i with a correlation matrix R. Then the Gaussian
copula is defined as

$$C_R^G(\mathbf{u}) = \mathrm{prob}\big(\Phi(X_1) < u_1, ..., \Phi(X_n) < u_n\big) = \Phi_R\big(\Phi^{-1}(u_1), ..., \Phi^{-1}(u_n)\big) \quad (7.10)$$

where Φ and Φ_R denote the univariate and multivariate standard normal
distribution functions. To simulate a Gaussian copula, one has
to generate a vector of jointly standard normal distributed random variables X with a correlation matrix R. The vector $U = (\Phi(X_1), ..., \Phi(X_n))$
then has a Gaussian copula $C_R^G(U)$. This is what we do in our factor
model (7.2), since asset prices A_i are jointly normally distributed random
variables.[13]

Student's t Copula: To obtain a t copula, one has to slightly modify
the above procedure. Recall that a t-distributed random variable is the
ratio of a standard normal variable and the square root of a chi squared
random variable divided by the degrees of freedom. Correspondingly, if
the vector **X** is jointly standard normal distributed with correlation
matrix R and W is chi squared with ν degrees of freedom, the vector
$\mathbf{Y} = \sqrt{W/\nu} \cdot \mathbf{X}$ is jointly t distributed with ν degrees of freedom and a

---

[13] The correlation matrix in the one-factor model (7.2) is $\mathbf{R} = \begin{pmatrix} 1 & \rho \\ \rho & 1 \end{pmatrix}$.

correlation matrix R. Denote this distribution $F^t_{\nu,R}$. Then the t copula is defined as

$$C^t_{\nu,R} = \text{prob}\left(F_\nu(Y_1) < u_1, ..., F_\nu(Y_n) < u_n\right) = F^t_{\nu,R}\left(F_\nu^{-1}(u_1), ..., F_\nu^{-1}(u_n)\right). \quad (7.11)$$

With the degrees of freedom ν, the t copula exhibits an additional parameter compared to the Gaussian copula, and the dependence structure is largely influenced by this additional parameter (see Figure 7.4). The implementation of the t copula resembles that of the Gaussian copula, but the correlated standard normal vector X must be transformed into the corresponding jointly t-distributed vector Y. Then, $U = (G_\nu(Y_1), ..., F_\nu(Y_n))$ has the t copula $C^t_{\nu,R}(U)$. In our factor model, if we divide each realization of asset values A_i by $\sqrt{W/\nu}$, the individual default probabilities p_i have a t copula $C^t_{\nu,R}$.

As previously mentioned, the resulting default dependency as well as the shape of the portfolio loss distribution crucially depends upon the choice of the underlying copula and its parameters. For example, the loss distributions derived with a t copula exhibit much more weight on the tails of the distribution and a higher level of skewness compared to a Gaussian copula, especially for low degrees of freedom. This translates to a higher probability of extreme losses in a loan portfolio. For example, the 99 percent quantile, i.e., the portfolio loss that on average is exceeded only once in a hundred times, is 26 percent for the t copula with 10 degrees of freedom and only 19 percent for the Gaussian copula, assuming an asset value correlation of 10 percent and a individual default probability of 5 percent.

Thus, the choice of the copula and the calibration of its parameters introduce an added amount of flexibility, but they also introduce the problem of an extra parameter to estimate. In addition to the two specific copulas presented here, there are numerous others discussed in the literature on credit risk modeling,[14] amplifying the problem of finding and calibrating the "right" copula. This may explain the popularity of the Gaussian copula, which is completely specified by its expectation and covariance matrix.

Figure 7.1 may help to visualize default dependence and displays 5,000 random draws from a Gaussian (left panel) and a t copula with three degrees of freedom (right panel) for a portfolio consisting of two loans.

---

[14] See De Servigny (2007b).

F I G U R E   7.2

Impact of asset value correlation on default correlation

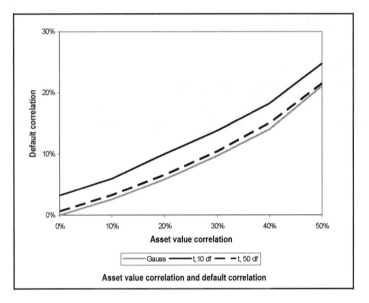

We observe that the *t* distribution exhibits more simultaneous realizations on the extremes, which translates into fatter tails of the portfolio loss distribution. Given a default probability of 10 percent for each loan, obligor 1 defaults if the realization is located left from the 10 percent line, and obligor 2 defaults if it is located below the 10 percent line. Accordingly, the probability of simultaneous default corresponds to the share of realizations within the shaded area, and one can see that this share is larger for the t copula. Figure 7.2 shows how asset value correlation translates into default correlation. The latter is generally smaller than the former.

Figure 7.3 shows how different correlation assumptions translate into different portfolio loss distributions.[15] As expected, the higher the correlation, the more skewed to the right is the portfolio loss distribution, i.e., the probability of large losses increases. For $\rho = 0$ we end up with the

---

[15] For simplicity we assume a zero recovery rate. Since we further assume a portfolio of 100 equal-sized loans, the portfolio loss distribution equals the distribution of the number of defaulted loans.

Asset value correlation and portfolio loss distribution

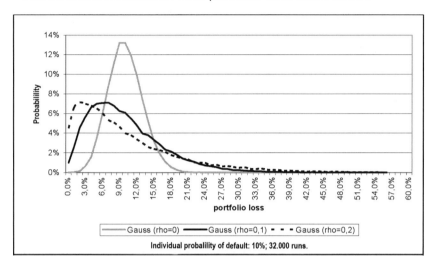

Individual probalility of default: 10%; 32.000 runs.

typical bell-shaped normal density (gray line). Note that this was not the case for the t copula, i.e., even for $\rho = 0$ jointly *t*-distributed random variables are not independent, and accordingly there is some default dependency. While asset correlation significantly impacts the shape of the loss distribution, the expected loss remains constant. However, in a CDO the expected loss of the different tranches depends on correlation.

Finally, Figure 7.4 shows how the choice of the copula affects the shape of the portfolio loss distribution. We observe that the loss distribution created with the t copula is more skewed to the right, especially for lower degrees of freedom.

Default Time Correlation

Another approach to modeling default dependencies introduced by Li (2000) and adopted, e.g., by Standard & Poor's (S&P) within its CDO Evaluator[16] is to use survival analysis[17] and time to default. In this

---

[16] See Standard & Poor's (2005).

[17] See Kiefer (1988) or Greene (2002) for an introduction to survival theory and estimation methods.

F I G U R E   7.4

Portfolio loss distribution using the Gaussian and the *t*-copula

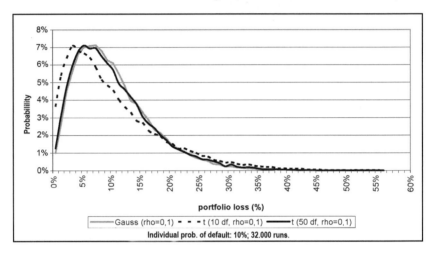

approach a default occurs if the survival time is shorter than the maturity. Default correlation here is viewed as the correlation of survival times T_i:

$$r_{12} = \frac{\text{COV}(T_1, T_2)}{\text{SD}(T_1)\text{SD}(T_2)}. \tag{7.12}$$

Li (2000) denotes Equation (7.12) survival time correlation as opposed to the discrete default correlation according to Equation (7.5). Employing the copula approach to the correlated default or survival times leads to the concept of *survival copulas*. Thereto, we define $S_i(t) = \text{prob}(T_i > t)$ as the individual survival function of obligor i and $S(t_i, t_j) = \text{prob}(T_i > t_i, T_j > t_j)$ as the joint survival function of obligor i and j. Then we can define the survival copula:

$$\tilde{C}_R\left(S_i(t_i), S_j(t_j)\right) := S(t_i, t_j) = S_i(t_i) + S_j(t_j)$$
$$-\left[1 - C_R\left(1 - S_i(t_i), 1 - S_j(t_j)\right)\right] \tag{7.13}$$

The process of generating correlated default times involves the following steps: First, use the survival copula to generate a vector u of uniformly distributed random variables as described above. Second, use the inverse of the individual cumulative credit default curves to obtain a vector of correlated default times t. The individual credit curves contain the term structures of the cumulative default rates and can be obtained by using historical default rates provided by the rating agencies or bond spreads, if available, or some type of Merton (1974) model.[18]

MEASURING CREDIT RISK OF CDOs

In the remainder of this chapter we apply the theory of default dependency to structuring and rating of CDOs. Here, we will focus on synthetic transactions securitizing a portfolio consisting of SME debt obligations in order to demonstrate how rating agencies usually analyze the inherent credit risk and the impact of asset correlation on the portfolio loss distribution and the risk profile of different tranching levels.

There are several reasons for taking synthetic SME transactions as an example to illustrate the impact of asset correlation. First, this asset class is characterized by a different risk profile than standard consumer asset-backed securities (ABS) transactions. This is due to its lower level of granularity, the heterogeneity of the underlying assets, and the obligors' higher dependence on macroeconomic factors. Hence, the manner in which the dependency structure of this asset class is modeled is crucial for measuring the inherent credit risk in such a CDO. Second, the advantage of focusing on *synthetic* CDOs is that we can prescind from modeling the often complicated cash-flow structure (waterfall) of cash CDOs.

Typical Structure of Synthetic CDOs

In a typical synthetic CDO transaction, the credit risk of a predefined reference portfolio, i.e., the asset side of a CDO, is transferred via a credit default swap (CDS) to a special-purpose vehicle (SPV). In a second step,

---

[18] See De Servigny and Sandow (2007).

the SPV issues notes of differing seniorities in order to provide investors with varying, leveraged credit risk exposures to the portfolio. The proceeds of the issuance are used to purchase collateral for the SPV's obligations under both the CDS and the notes. In case of a predefined credit event, the SPV pays the protection buyer, i.e., originating bank, an amount linked to the loss incurred on the reference entity. This loss in turn is passed on to investors by writing down the notes by an equal amount in reverse order of seniority. Repayments in the reference portfolio, on the other hand, lead to an amortization of the notes side starting with those of highest seniority: The more senior the creditor, the less risky the investment, and hence the smaller the risk premium received. This risk premium on the notes is paid with the CDS premium received by the SPV.

The link between the asset and liability side of a CDO is given by the structural definition of the transaction. Collateralized debt obligations can vary significantly in terms of predefined events that trigger payments under the CDO and in the way how losses are allocated. Very often a replenishment period is in place, e.g., the principal of repaid assets in the reference pool can be used to refill the reference portfolio with new assets. Another feature is the use of a so-called synthetic excess spread, which provides additional credit enhancement beyond the subordination.[19]

Rating of SME CDOs by Moody's, S&P, and Fitch: General Approach

In general, the risk of the single tranches is indicated by a risk assessment provided by rating agencies such as S&P, Moody's, and Fitch. This assessment is given by assigning a particular rating to each tranche ranging, in the case of Moody's, from Aaa as the highest rating category to C as the lowest. In contrast to ratings assigned by S&P and Fitch, which give an assessment of the probability of the full and timely payment of interest and principal, Moody's ratings address the probability of default (PD) as well as the expectation of loss in the event of default, i.e., the expected loss (EL) concept. Whereas, the PD approach of Fitch and S&P focuses on determining the credit enhancement necessary to support the desired

---

[19] See Lucas et al. (2006) for a more elaborate description of the various types of CDS.

rating and to a lesser degree on the thickness of tranches, in Moody's EL concept the tranches' size plays a significant role. In addition to the different modeling approaches employed by the rating agencies to capture the credit risk of single rating classes, one should bear in mind the differing rating concepts, i.e., the PD- and EL-based rating approaches.

When rating an SME transaction, rating agencies generally differentiate between an ABS and CDO approach depending on the granularity[20] and homogeneity of the portfolio backing the transaction. If the transaction exhibits a low level of granularity in terms of number of obligors and diversity, a Monte Carlo–based CDO approach[21] is normally employed. In contrast, an actuarial ABS approach is applied to transactions with an adequate degree of granularity and homogeneity.[22] The ABS approach relies on a default distribution with parameters derived from vintage data of the originator. Moody's usually assumes in its ABSROM model a normal inverse distribution.[23] In contrast to ABS transactions with well-diversified portfolios of homogeneous assets, where the idiosyncratic risk stemming from single obligors is of less importance, CDOs are considered more "lumpy." Accordingly, the modeling of idiosyncratic as well as systemic risks plays a key role in their analysis.

To determine the loss distribution, one needs to make an assumption on the recovery value and the time of recovery. Fitch and S&P determine a recovery assumption for a so-called base case scenario. This base case recovery rate will be decreased by the use of a tiering factor that will increase the higher the desired rating. The rationale behind this increasing loss given default is that S&P and Fitch assume that in case of a depression, the value of a company's assets will suffer from less demand and therefore result in

---

[20] Granularity and homogeneity are often measured by the use of the Herfindahl index $H = \Sigma_{i=1}^{n} E^2_i$, where E_i is the relative exposure of each obligor, industry, or region i in a portfolio of n obligors, industries, or regions. Thus, the higher the index, the less granular or homogeneous the portfolio is. Moody's calculates the "effective number" by taking the reciprocal of the index. If, for instance, all obligors have the same exposure, $E_i = 1/n$, the effective number will be n. Another popular concentration measure is the already mentioned Diversity Score of Moody's.

[21] The Monte Carlo models used by the rating agencies are Moody's CDOROM, S&P CDO Evaluator, and VECTOR (SME) by Fitch. Whereas CDOROM is a single-period model, Fitch's VECTOR and S&P CDO Evaluator are based on a multiperiod default model.

[22] In general, Moody's classifies SME portfolios with more than 1,000 assets and no major concentration as SME ABS. See Moody's (2007).

[23] See the section Modeling Default Dependencies for further details.

lower recovery prices. To determine the assets' individual base recovery rates, Moody's and S&P assume stochastic recovery rates, whereas Fitch relies on a fixed recovery rate. Whereas in its ABS approach a normal distribution for the portfolio recovery rate is used, Moody's usually assumes stochastic recovery rates on a loan-by-loan basis under its CDO approach. There, individual recovery rates are assumed to follow a beta distribution, and recovery dependency is incorporated by adopting a factor model.

In case of synthetic transactions that exhibit a replenishment option or other features such as synthetic excess spread, rating agencies often conduct a cash-flow analysis. The rationale for setting up a transaction-specific cash-flow model is to study the impact of different timing scenarios on the ability of the structure to cope with a given amount of defaults and losses.

Impact of Correlation on Portfolio and Tranche Loss

In this section we discuss the impact of a higher correlation level on the loss distribution of a given reference portfolio. In a second step we will tranche this portfolio and study the sensitivity of single tranches to increases in the global correlation level. The tranching and the respective loss distributions will be derived using Moody's CDOROM model.

Let us assume a fictitious portfolio consisting of 450 German SME loans with a weighted average obligor exposure of 0.2 percent and a maximum single obligor exposure of 1 percent. In order to model a representative SME portfolio, we constructed a portfolio with an industry diversification in terms of Moody's sectors with a maximum sector exposure of 11 percent, which is typical for SME CDOs seen on the market. As our reference portfolio consists only of German assets, and Moody's regional factor only differentiates between different countries, the intersector variable impacts all assets in the same way.[24] As a simplifying condition, we assume that the asset pool is static and consists of bullet loans with a maturity of five years and a weighted average Moody's rating of Ba2. In order to abstract from the

---

[24] In German SME CDOs, it is quite common that more than 20 percent of the portfolio assets are located in one federal state. As this would not be reflected in a higher correlation, Moody's often increases its standard industry correlation assumption by 1 to 3 percent in order to capture the additional geographical concentration usually encountered in SME [see Moody's (2007)].

impact of stochastic recovery rates, we assume a fixed recovery rate of 45 percent, which is in line with Moody's mean recovery assumption for senior unsecured loans in Germany.

In our analysis, we rely on Moody's standard assumptions of intra-sector asset correlation. Therefore, differences in terms of asset correlation stem from the industrial correlation factor only. We will illustrate the effects of a higher asset correlation by increasing the global correlation factor from 1 percent in our base case to 3 and 8 percent. The cumulative expected loss of the portfolio equals 3.69 percent, which corresponds to a Ba2 Moody's portfolio rating.

In Figure 7.5 one can see the impact of an increase of the global correlation level on the loss distribution of the given portfolio. As we already know, an increase in asset correlation does not impact the expected portfolio loss but the shape of the loss distribution—the higher the global correlation, the fatter the tails of our loss distribution. This means that due to a higher dependency between the obligors, it becomes more likely that in a bad state of the economy several obligors suffer a loss whereas in a boom fewer obligors default together.

In a second step, we study the impact of a higher correlation level on single tranches. For this purpose, we derive a tranching of our reference portfolio by use of Moody's CDOROM under our base case assumption of a global correlation of 1 percent. For our purposes, we sliced the portfolio

F I G U R E   7.5

Portfolio loss distribution for different levels of global correlation (exp. loss of 3.69%)

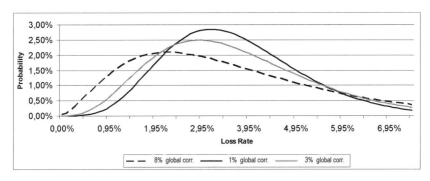

in three different risk classes: a senior tranche with an Aaa rating (91 percent), a mezzanine tranche with a Ba2 rating (3.5 percent) and a junior tranche, that compensates the first losses of the reference portfolio. The tranching was derived by determining the minimum required subordination (attachment level) thus ensuring the desired rating, starting with the senior tranche. The necessary subordination of the Ba2 tranche determines the volume of our first loss tranche.

In our base case, the junior investor compensates the first portfolio losses up to a volume of 5.5 percent, i.e., he covers the expected portfolio loss (3.69 percent) in particular. Therefore, it is not surprising that the default probability of this tranche is close to 1 [see Table 7.1(a)]. As a result the expected loss (EL) and the loss given default (LGD) of this

T A B L E   7.1

PD, LGD, EL, and σ for different levels of correlation

(a) Base Case: Global Correlation 1%

Reference Portfolio	Duration	Rating	PD	LGD	EL	SD
	5 years	Ba2	6.72%	55.00%	3.69%	1.48%

Tranche	Rating	Attachment Level	Tranche PD	Tranche LGD	Tranche EL	SD
Senior	Aaa	9.00%	0.28%	0.88%	0.00%	0.06%
Mezzanine	Ba2	5.50%	11.68%	28.34%	3.31%	12.41%
First loss	Ca	0.00%	100.00%	65.00%	65.00%	22.56%

(b) Stress Case: Global Correlation 8%

Reference Portfolio	Duration	Rating	PD	LGD	EL	SD
	5 years	Ba2	6.72%	55.00%	3.69%	2.36%

Tranche	Rating	Attachment Level	Tranche PD	Tranche LGD	Tranche EL	SD
Senior	Aa3	9.00%	3.36%	2.02%	0.07%	0.51%
Mezzanine	B2	5.50%	18.97%	48.36%	9.18%	24.13%
First loss	Ca	0.00%	99.95%	60.22%	60.19%	29.06%

Impact of an increase of global correlation from 1 percent to 8 percent and tranche loss profiles

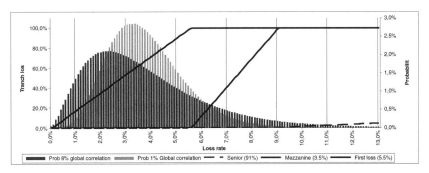

tranche are nearly identical, whereas these figures differ in case of the mezzanine and senior tranche.

Let us now assume that the portfolio exhibits a higher asset correlation level than expected. Figure 7.6 displays the loss profile of the different tranches derived in our base case and the density of the portfolio loss distribution in respective cases of low and high correlation levels. In contrast to our base case, where the majority of probability mass is concentrated around the mean, the probability density function in case of a higher global correlation becomes flatter and the probability mass is "pushed" to more extreme loss realizations.

From the senior investors' point of view, this shift of probability mass to higher loss rates is unfavorable, as it becomes more likely that his tranche suffers a loss, whereas the junior investor can benefit from a higher probability of scenarios where lower losses are realized. Given the tranching derived in our base case, an increase of the correlation level results in a lower expected loss of the junior tranche (60 percent instead of 65 percent) and an increase in the expected loss of the senior tranche leading to a lower rating of Aa3 instead of Aaa. Even though the mezzanine investor suffers a higher expected loss in our stress case, this result cannot be generalized to all mezzanine tranches due to the fact that the amount of probability mass attributed to the range of losses covered by the mezzanine tranche is dependent on its thickness and the shape of the loss distribution. We can infer from our example that even if the expected loss and the corresponding rating of two investments are the same, the risk profile of the investments can differ markedly in terms of higher moments of their loss distributions. This can be seen in Table 7.1 if one compares the distribution parameters of the Ba2 rated mezzanine tranche with those of the Ba2 portfolio, and the sensitivity of this tranche to an increase in the global correlation level.

Another important result we can derive from Figure 7.6 is that the risk profile of thinner tranches displays a higher sensitivity to an increase in the underlying loss rate. Whereas the reaction of the senior tranche to an increase in the portfolio loss rate is essentially marginal, the loss profile of the mezzanine tranche with a volume of just 3.5 percent exhibits a higher gradient which implies a higher volatility as well. As ratings in CDOROM are determined by adding the standard error of the loss distribution to the expected loss derived in the simulation, and multiplying this adjusted expected loss with the risk adjusted discount factor, the rating sensitivity of small tranches in relation to an increase in global correlation is quite high.

As we have seen, the assessment of the risk and return of a specific tranche is dependent not only on the underlying model, but is also very sensitive to changes in the underlying correlation assumptions. Furthermore, the thickness of the tranches can have a huge impact on the risk profile in terms of higher moments of the loss distribution and therefore on the rating sensitivity which may result in a higher volatility of its market value.

CONCLUSION

We provided a brief introduction to the theory and application of default dependency modeling. Factor models and the copula approach are elegant ways to model default dependency and caution should be exercised in their application. The number of available copulas offers much flexibility but also introduces some degree of arbitrariness and hence model risk. Therefore, the Gaussian copula has become a standard, and the CDO rating tools of the major rating agencies all rely on this approach. Whereas the increase of systemic risk (in terms of correlation) leaves the expected portfolio loss unchanged it adversely affects the return of the upper tranches in a CDO. During the subprime crisis of 2007, many investors in very secure supersenior tranches have experienced this not as a purely theoretical consideration but rather as a highly relevant threat. In spite of the simplicity of the models introduced, one should not oversee the problems associated with their calibration and implementation. In particular, correlations are not stable over time. As we have witnessed during the subprime crises, there are contagion effects even between seemingly unrelated asset classes, which are further aggravated by liquidity effects and trigger events. Therefore, complementary stress tests are important and more effort should be devoted to estimating dependency structures.

REFERENCES

Basel Committee on Banking Supervision (2005) An Explanatory Note on Basel II IRB Risk Weight Functions. Basel, Switzerland.

Bluhm, C., Overbeck, L., and Wagner, C. (2003) *An Introduction to Credit Risk Modeling.* London: Chapman & Hall/CRC.

De Servigny, A. (2007a) Modeling Credit Dependency. In De Servigny, A. and Jobst, N. (eds), *The Handbook of Structured Finance.* New York: McGraw-Hill.

De Servigny, A. (2007b) Collateral Debt Obligation Pricing. In De Servigny, A. and Jobst, N. (eds), *The Handbook of Structured Finance.* New York: McGraw-Hill.

De Servigny, A. and Sandow, S. (2007) Univariate Risk Assessment. In De Servigny, A. and Jobst, N. (eds), *The Handbook of Structured Finance.* New York: McGraw-Hill.

Felsenheimer, J., Gistakis, P., and Zaiser, M. (2006) *Active Credit Portfolio Management.* Weineim, Germany: John Wiley & Sons.

Fitch (2006) *The Fitch Default VECTOR 3.0 Model—User Manual.*

Fitch (2007) *European SME CDO Rating Criteria.* London.

Greene, W.H. (2002) *Econometric Analysis*. Upper Saddle River, NJ: Prentice Hall.

Kiefer, N.M. (1988) Economic Duration Data and Hazard Functions, *Journal of Economic Literature,* 26: 646–679.

Li, D. (2000) On Default Correlation: A Copula Function Approach, *Journal of Fixed Income*, 9(3): 43–54.

Lucas, D.J., Goodman L.S., and Fabozzi, F.J. (2006) *Collateralized debt Obligations, Structures and Analysis.* Hoboken, NJ: Wiley.

Merton, R. (1974) On the Pricing of Corporate Debt. *The Journal of Finance*, 29(2): 449–470.

Moody's (1996) The Binomial Expansion Method Applied to CBO/CLO Analysis. New York.

Moody's (2006) CDOROMv2.3 User Guide. New York.

Moody's (2007) Moody's Approach to Rating CDOs of SMEs in Europe. London.

Schönbucher, P. (2003) *Credit Derivatives Pricing Models: Models, Pricing and Implementation.* Chichester, UK: John Wiley & Sons.

Sklar, A. (1959) Fonctions de repartition a n dimensions et leurs marges. *Publications de l'Institute Statistique de l'Universite de Paris,* 8: 229–231.

Standard & Poor's (2005) CDO Evaluator Version 3.0. Technical document, New York.

Vasicek, O. (1987) Probability of Loss on Loan Portfolio. KMV Corporation, San Francisco, CA.

Vasicek, O. (1991) Limiting Loan Loss Probability Distribution. KMV Corporation, San Francisco, CA.

A Credit Contagion Model for the Dynamics of the Rating Transitions in a Small- and Medium- Sized Enterprises Bank Loan Portfolio

Antonella Basso and Riccardo Gusso

ABSTRACT

In this chapter we analyze the effects of credit contagion on the credit quality of a portfolio of bank loans issued to small- and medium-sized enterprises. To this aim we start from the discrete time model proposed in Barro and Basso (2005) that considers the counterparty risk generated by the business relations in a network of firms, and we modify it by introducing different rating classes in order to manage the case of firms with different credit qualities. The transition from one rating class to another occurs when a proxy for the asset value of the firm crosses some rating specific thresholds. We assume that the initial rating transition matrix of the system is known, and compute the thresholds using the probability distribution of the steady state of the model. A wide Monte Carlo simulation analysis is carried out in order to study the dynamic behavior of the model and, in particular, to analyze how the default contagion present in the model affects the output rating transition matrix of the portfolio.

INTRODUCTION

In this chapter we study the effects of credit contagion on the credit quality of a portfolio of bank loans; in particular, we investigate how credit contagion can affect the credit quality downgrade/upgrade of the firms in the portfolio. As it is done in practice, we identify the credit quality of a firm with a "rating" associated to it, as the ones assigned by rating agencies such as Standard & Poor's or Moody's or obtained by internal bank rating systems, and we investigate the downgrades and upgrades of the ratings of the firms in the portfolio in a dynamic discrete time setting by means of the dynamic rating transition matrix.

A number of different approaches have been recently proposed in the literature for modeling the credit risk of a portfolio of bank loans; see, for example, Giesecke and Weber (2004), Frey and Backhaus (2004), Egloff et al. (2007), and Neu and Kühn (2004). Among these different approaches, the counterparty risk model proposed in Barro and Basso (2005) models the asset value of a firm following a structural approach, and can be generalized in such a way as to take into account the presence of different rating classes.

In such a model, a proxy V_i for the asset value of firm i is described as the sum of three terms: a macroeconomic component, which considers the influence of the business cycle through a factor model; a microeconomic component, which models the business connections with other firms; and a residual idiosyncratic random term. The microeconomic component takes into consideration the direct business connections between the firms in the bank portfolio and their clients and explains how the default of a client may cause financial distress to its suppliers and a possible downgrade of their credit quality. In this way a contagion mechanism is introduced in the model.

We consider a portfolio of bank loans issued to small- and medium-sized enterprises (SMEs), and we assume that they have been assigned a rating class that reflects their credit quality. We estimate from historical data, using a maximum likelihood method under a time homogeneity assumption, an initial rating transition matrix for the system, whose elements are the probabilities of the transition from a rating class to another. The transition of a firm from a rating class to another occurs when the value V_i crosses some rating-specific thresholds, which are computed using the probability distribution of the steady state of the model. In such a way the model enables to describe the evolution in time of the ratings of all the firms in the portfolio.

In order to analyze how the default contagion affects the system and influences the credit quality of the firms in the portfolio, we apply a Monte Carlo simulation technique and carry out a wide simulation analysis. In particular, we simulate the behavior of the model for different values of the parameters on a 10-year time horizon, and we analyze the results obtained for the defaults and the rating transitions of the firms in the portfolio.

The chapter is structured as follows: In the chapter's second section, we present a brief review of the literature on counterparty risk and contagion models; in the third section we present the model proposed, which generalizes that presented in Basso and Barro (2005) and allows us to model the rating transitions of the portfolio positions year after year. In this chapter's fourth section we describe the simulation procedure applied in the empirical analysis and discuss the results obtained. Finally, the concluding section presents some closing remarks.

COUNTERPARTY RISK AND CREDIT CONTAGION MODELS

In most of the popular credit risk models, both in reduced form and structural models, the dependence among the defaults and the credit quality downgrades of different firms is modeled using state variables that represent the major macroeconomic factors. In the reduced form models the default intensities depend on these factors, while in the structural models it is the asset value of firms in the portfolio that depends on them. In both approaches, the common dependence on these macroeconomic variables, which reflect the state of the economy and the business cycle, introduces some dependence in the rating transitions and in the default probabilities.

Nevertheless, some recent empirical results have pointed out that the dependence on common macroeconomic factors fails to explain properly the clustering of defaults observed when the economy is in a recession period; see, for example, Jarrow and Yu (2001) and Das et al. (2007). This suggests that a firm-specific risk term could be introduced, which accounts for the changes in the firms' health due to some microeconomic effect, for example, as that generated by the business relations with firms' counterparties.

Jarrow and Yu (2001) introduced the notion of *counterparty risk*, defined as the risk that the default of a firm's counterparty affects its default probability. In a wider sense the counterparty risk can be defined as the risk that the default of a client causes a change in the credit quality of a firm. If the firms in a portfolio are strongly interdependent in terms of their business relations, as it is often the case in portfolios of bank loans issued to SMEs operating in the same geographical area, then the counterparty risk may play an important role. In this case the default of one firm induces a contagion effect on other firms through the network of the business relations, which can lead to the deterioration of their credit quality and even to their default.

Subsequently, several recent papers have introduced a counterparty risk term to model a microeconomic dependence in terms of direct inter-firm relationships, often jointly with the dependence on the business cycle. Along these liens, Giesecke and Weber (2004) present a model in which firms interact with their business partners in a lattice-type economy. Here the contagion effect is modeled as liquidity shocks generated when some counterparties fail to honor their obligations; firms in the economy jump from a "good" state to a "bad" one, and vice versa, with an intensity that is proportional to the number of their counterparties in the opposite state. The empirical investigation of this model shows that the contagion process leads to additional fluctuations of the portfolio losses around their averages.

In Egloff et al. (2007), microstructural data obtained from a bank's credit risk department are used to build a topological risk map of the bank's credit portfolio, which is represented by a weighted graph connecting firms in the portfolio, where the weights are related to the business relations between the firms. Then Monte Carlo simulation is used to analyze the effects of different interdependence microstructures on the correlation structure and on the risk figures of the credit portfolio; their findings show that the tail behavior of the portfolio credit losses is significantly modified by the presence of the contagion effect.

Neu and Kühn (2004), in analogy with a lattice gas model used in physics, model the correlations between sequential defaults by introducing functionally defined couplings between mutually dependent counterparties. The paper focuses on the estimation of the impact of the counterparty risk on the capital allocations in loan portfolios; the outcomes obtained by a simulation analysis of the model suggest that corporate dependency introduces an additional source of risk and can significantly amplify the portfolio losses.

MODELING CREDIT CONTAGION AND RATING TRANSITIONS IN A PORTFOLIO OF BANK LOANS

The main goal of this contribution is to propose a model that allows the study of the effects of the counterparty risk not only on the clustering of defaults in a SME bank loan portfolio but also on the co-movements of the credit quality of firms. We relate the credit quality of a firm i (for $i = 1, ..., N$), to the value of a proxy for the firm's asset value at time $t, V_i(t)$, and model $V_i(t)$ as the sum of three components: a macroeconomic one F_i, influenced by the business cycle; a microeconomic component M_i, which accounts for the contagion effects produced by the defaults of the major clients of a firm; and an idiosyncratic random term ε_i.

As in Barro and Basso (2005), the macroeconomic component $F_i(t)$ is described by a factor model

$$F_i(t) = \sum_{j=1}^{J} \beta_j^{s(i)} Y_j(t) \quad t = 0, 1, \ldots \qquad (8.1)$$

where $Y(t) = (Y_1(t), Y_2(t), \ldots, Y_J(t))$ is the vector of the values at time t of the driving factors, $s(i) \in \{1, \ldots, S\}$ is the economic sector of firm i, and β_j^s is the weight of factor j for the firms of sector s. The driving factors $Y_j(t)$ are assumed to follow some stochastic process with covariance matrix $\Sigma_Y(t)$.

In order to model the microeconomic component $M_i(t)$, let us define the following measure $D_i(t)$ of the distress suffered by firm i at time t as the difference between the average default rate of the economy $p(t)$ and the percentage of the turnover of firm i sold to clients that defaulted at time t:

$$D_i(t) = p(t) - \left[\sum_{k \in C_i(t)} \delta_k(t) w_{ik}(t) + p(t) r_i(t) \right] \qquad (8.2)$$

where $C_i(t)$ denotes the set of the major clients of firm i at time t, w_{ik} is the percentage of the sales to major client k on the turnover of firm i, $r_i(t) = 1 - \sum_{k \in C_i}(t) w_{ik}(t)$ is the percent value of the turnover of firm i sold to all the minor clients, and $\delta_k(t)$ is a binary value that takes value 1 if client k defaults at time t and 0 otherwise. Note that the distress measure $D_i(t)$ has a positive value if the percentage of the turnover of the firm sold to clients that defaulted at time t is lower than the average default rate in the economy and a negative value if it is higher. The basic idea is that the distress component affects the health of a firm with a one-period delay, and its effects decay exponentially in time.

The microeconomic component $M_i(t)$ can be modeled in the following way:

$$M_i(t) = \mu_{s(i)} \sum_{\tau=1}^{\infty} \lambda_{s(i)}^\tau D_i(t - \tau) \qquad (8.3)$$

where $\mu_s \in R_+$ is a real parameter dependent on the economic sector of the firm and $0 \leq \lambda_s < 1$ is the dampening factor that determines the distress memory of the firms in sector s. The residual idiosyncratic terms $\varepsilon_i(t)$ are assumed to be normally distributed with zero mean and standard deviation $\sigma_{s(i)}$, mutually independent and independent of the driving factors $Y_j(t)$.

Therefore, $V_i(t)$ is given by

$$V_i(t) = F_i(t) + M_i(t) + \varepsilon_i(t) = \sum_{j=1}^{J} \beta_j^{s(i)} Y_j(t) +$$

$$\mu_{s(i)} \sum_{\tau=1}^{\infty} \lambda_{s(i)}^\tau D_i(t - \tau) + \varepsilon_i(t) \qquad (8.4)$$

To analyze the credit quality upgrades and/or downgrades of the firms in the portfolio we adopt the commonly used *rating* approach. Let us consider an ordered set of rating classes $\{1, \ldots, K\}$ that reflect the credit quality of the firms in the portfolio through a mapping $i \to r_i \in \{1, \ldots, K\}$, where 1 represents the best rating class and K the worst one, $K + 1$ representing then the absorbing default state. We assume that the initial classification is determined a priori by some rating system, either external (e.g., provided by an external rating agency as Moody's or Standard & Poor's) or internal (when a bank internal rating systems is used).

As it is generally done in the framework of structural models, let us assume that there exists a set of sector-specific thresholds

$$-\infty = d^s_{j,K+1} \leq d^s_{j,K} \leq \cdots \leq d^s_{j,1} \leq d^s_{j,0} = +\infty \qquad (8.5)$$

for the proxy $V_i(t)$ of the value of firms in the kth rating class, such that if $r_i(t) = k$, then $r_i(t + 1) = k'$ if and only if $V_i(t + 1) \in [d^{s(i)}_{k,k'}, d^{s(i)}_{k,k'-1}]$.

The determination of these thresholds becomes a crucial point in our model. We observe that we can estimate the probability $p^s_{k,k'}$ of transition in one year from rating k to rating k' from historical data referring to large populations of firms. If taken over a sufficiently long period of time, these estimates give an approximation of the *unconditional* rating transition probabilities since they may be considered as free of cyclical effects connected to the current state of the economy.

We use time series of the one-year credit transition matrices for years $1, \ldots, T$. The arithmetic mean of the one-year rating transition frequencies gives an estimate of the unconditional rating transition probabilities that underestimates the default probabilities in the best rating classes. In order to avoid such a drawback, following an idea similar to that discussed in Lando and Skødeberg (2002), we could use the following maximum likelihood estimator for Markov chains under a time homogeneity assumption:

$$P = \exp(\Lambda) \quad \text{with} \quad \Lambda_{i,j} = \frac{N_{i,j}(T)}{\int_0^T N_i(t)\,dt} \qquad (8.6)$$

where $N_i(t)$ is the number of firms in rating class i at time t and $N_{i,j}(T)$ is the total number of transitions from rating i to rating j over the time horizon of interest.

In addition we observe that $E[M_i(t)] = 0$ for all t, so that the estimate of the unconditional rating transition probabilities, if based on a sufficiently large sample of firms, may also be considered as free of contagion effects. Hence, if Equation (8.4) has a stationary state, the rating transition matrix (8.6) gives an estimate of the unconditional transition matrix of the model in this stationary state. The macroeconomic part is described by a single factor model that follows this mean reverting $AR(1)$ process

$$Y(t+1) = Y(t) + a(b - Y(t)) + \sigma_Y u(t+1) \qquad (8.7)$$

where $u(t) \sim N(0,1)$, $a, b \in R$, $\sigma_Y > 0$, and let $\beta^s = 1$ for all sectors. In the stationary state the macroeconomic component is normally distributed with mean equal to the long-term mean b of $Y(t)$ and standard deviation σ_Y.

As for the microeconomic term, we assume that it is approximately normally distributed with mean 0 and standard deviation σ_M and that it is independent both of the stationary state macroeconomic component and of the idiosyncratic term. Under these assumptions, the value of $V_i(t)$ when the macroeconomic term is in stationary state is normally distributed with mean b and standard deviation $\sqrt{\sigma_Y^2 + \sigma_M^2 + \sigma_s^2}$.

In general, let G denote the probability distribution function of $V_i(t)$ when the macroeconomic term is in the stationary state; if G is invertible, then the rating transition thresholds $d^s_{k,k'}$ can be computed as follows:

$$d_{k,k'} = G^{-1}(p_{k,K+1} + p_{k,K} + \cdots + p_{k,k'+1}) \qquad (8.8)$$

where

$$G(d^s_{k,k'-1}) - G(d^s_{k,k'}) = p^s_{k,k'} \qquad (8.9)$$

SIMULATION ANALYSIS OF RATING TRANSITIONS

In order to test the model proposed in the previous section and study its dynamic behavior, we carry out a wide simulation analysis by randomly generating a portfolio of bank loans with $N = 10,000$ positions issued to SMEs.

For each firm in the portfolio the number of clients has been randomly generated according to a normal distribution with mean 50 and standard deviation 25, while the volume of sales to each client has been generated according to a lognormal distribution with parameters 5 and 2.

The default or survival status of each client at each time period has been generated according to a Bernoulli random variable with mean equal to the average default rate of the economy; $p(t)$ moreover, each time a major client defaulted, we assumed that in time it is replaced by another client with the same business volume.

The number of rating classes considered is $K = 7$, corresponding to the classes from AAA to C in the S&P classification, and each firm was assigned an initial rating class randomly generated according to the S&P rating distribution reported in Table 8.1.

Once the initial composition of the portfolio was generated, in the simulations the defaulted obligors were replaced by new randomly generated obligors, so that the number of positions in the portfolio was kept constant in time.

As in Equation (8.7), for the macroeconomic term (8.1) we have considered a single factor that follows a mean reverting AR(1) process with, $a = 0.5, b = 1$, and $\sigma_Y = 0.08$. As regards the parameters μ and σ, which represent the relative impact of the microeconomic and the idiosyncratic

T A B L E   8.1

Relative distribution of obligors in the rating classes AAA to C

Rating Class	Relative Weight
AAA	0.043730
AA	0.141370
A	0.273947
BBB	0.224433
BB	0.151319
B	0.158029
C	0.007173

Source: Standard & Poor's (2003) technical report.

T A B L E 8.2

One-year rating transition matrix estimated using the MLE (8.6)

	AAA	AA	A	BBB	BB	B	C	D
AAA	0.9243	0.064	0.0091	0.0005	0.002	0.0001	0	0.0001
AA	0.0061	0.9109	0.0761	0.0057	0.0006	0.0004	0	0.0001
A	0.0004	0.0129	0.9368	0.0436	0.0047	0.0011	0.0002	0.0002
BBB	0.0003	0.0023	0.0479	0.9024	0.0393	0.0063	0.0008	0.0008
BB	0	0.0012	0.009	0.0869	0.8268	0.0612	0.0084	0.0065
B	0.0001	0.0022	0.0024	0.0084	0.0643	0.8252	0.0534	0.0440
C	0.0025	0.0003	0.0053	0.0017	0.0215	0.0674	0.4539	0.4474

components on $V_i(t)$, respectively, the simulations have been carried out for a set of different values, namely, $\mu = 0, 10, 20, 30, 40, 50$ and $\sigma = 0.3, 0.4, 0.5, 0.6, 0.7$. First, for the determination of the thresholds $d^s_{k,k'}$ we estimated the one-year rating transition matrix from the time series of S&P historical rating matrices in the period 1988 to 2002 using the maximum likelihood estimation (MLE) estimator (8.6); the resulting transition matrix is presented in Table 8.2.

Second, we have carried out a first set of Monte Carlo simulations in order to analyze the distribution of the microeconomic part $M_i(t)$ for different values of μ and σ and compute the rating thresholds for the different rating classes. The firm-specific information about the past (for $t < 0$) were assumed to be not available, and accordingly, in Equation (8.3) we set $D_i(t) = 0$ for $t = -1, -2, \ldots$

For each couple (μ, σ) we generated 10,000 paths for $Y(t)$ and $\varepsilon_i(t)$ on a time horizon of 10 years, with a one-year time step. The empirical results obtained confirm that in each period $M_i(t)$ can be considered as approximately normally distributed with mean 0. As far as the value of the standard deviation σ_M is concerned, it turns out to be not only linearly dependent on μ [which can be immediately seen from Equation (8.3)] but also approximately linearly dependent on σ (see Table 8.3).

Using the values obtained for σ_M in this first set of simulations, we have computed the rating transition thresholds $d^s_{k,k'}$ for each rating class according to Equations (8.8) and (8.9). An example of the thresholds

T A B L E   8.3

Values of σ_M for different values of μ and σ

σ	10	20	30	40	50
0.3	0.000137	0.000256	0.000386	0.000513	0.000647
0.4	0.000414	0.000824	0.001238	0.001631	0.002057
0.5	0.000743	0.001489	0.002239	0.002971	0.003725
0.6	0.001041	0.002084	0.003143	0.004173	0.005211
0.7	0.001298	0.002595	0.003865	0.005164	0.006459

obtained for the different rating classes is presented in Table 8.4. These rating thresholds were held constant over time in the simulations carried out in the second step.

Third, we have carried a second set of simulations in order to study the dynamic behavior of the model and to analyze the values of the main quantities of interest as time varies. Again, we generated 10,000 paths of the macroeconomic and of the idiosyncratic component for each couple (μ, σ), as in the first step simulations. In this set of simulations we focused our attention on the analysis of the one-year rating transition matrices, the default rate for each rating class and the resulting average default rate of the portfolio, and the distribution of the firms in the portfolio in the different rating classes.

T A B L E   8.4

Rating thresholds of the different rating classes for $\mu = 30$ and $\sigma = 0.3$

AAA	0.5548	0.2972	0.13619	0.11575	−0.09914	−0.15469	−0.15469
AA	1.77638	0.56972	0.23383	0.04936	−0.02166	−0.15469	−0.15469
A	2.02165	1.68754	0.4887	0.22362	0.07857	−0.04099	−0.09914
BBB	2.09915	1.87154	1.5095	0.48068	0.25065	0.08474	0.02014
BB	$+\infty$	1.94253	1.71998	1.40309	0.55545	0.3254	0.22883
B	2.15473	1.87985	1.80637	1.69028	1.44175	0.59745	0.4703
C	1.87154	1.86014	1.74652	1.72464	1.57813	1.40021	0.95894

As regards the one-year rating transition matrices, the simulation results indicate that on average it takes three years for the system to get rid of the initial conditions. After this initial period the behavior of these matrices is quite stable in time, in the sense that the average transition matrices, computed by averaging the transition matrices obtained over all the 10,000 paths simulated for the macroeconomic factor, do not change significantly as time varies. Two examples of the matrices observed at different times are shown in Tables 8.5 and 8.6.

T A B L E   8.5

Rating transition matrix obtained with $\mu = 30$ and $\sigma = 0.3$ at time $t = 4$

	AAA	AA	A	BBB	BB	B	C	D
AAA	0.92575	0.06182	0.00914	0.00054	0.00223	0.00013	0	0.00039
AA	0.00671	0.90788	0.07751	0.00621	0.00072	0.00056	0	0.00042
A	0.00056	0.01366	0.93356	0.04486	0.00518	0.00131	0.00028	0.00059
BBB	0.00023	0.0025	0.04946	0.89804	0.04058	0.00688	0.00095	0.00136
BB	0	0.0013	0.00951	0.08879	0.82138	0.06241	0.00890	0.00770
B	0.00011	0.00241	0.00256	0.00884	0.06576	0.81990	0.05394	0.04649
C	0.00275	0.00033	0.00566	0.00178	0.02212	0.06830	0.45034	0.44873

T A B L E   8.6

Rating transition matrix obtained with $\mu = 30$ and $\sigma = 0.3$ at time $t = 10$

	AAA	AA	A	BBB	BB	B	C	D
AAA	0.92753	0.06038	0.00883	0.00051	0.00221	0.00015	0	0.00039
AA	0.00682	0.90852	0.07685	0.00613	0.00071	0.00056	0	0.00041
A	0.00058	0.01391	0.93377	0.04449	0.0051	0.00131	0.00027	0.00058
BBB	0.00024	0.00257	0.05011	0.89788	0.04013	0.0068	0.00093	0.00134
BB	0	0.00136	0.00971	0.08958	0.82094	0.06198	0.00882	0.00761
B	0.00012	0.00245	0.00261	0.00894	0.06645	0.81976	0.05358	0.04607
C	0.00279	0.00034	0.00569	0.00187	0.02248	0.069	0.45224	0.44557

We have also measured the distance between the average of the rating transition matrices obtained with the simulation at times $t = 3, 4, \ldots, 10$ and the initial rating transition matrix estimated using the MLE (6) and presented in Table 8.2; as a measure of the distance between two matrices P and Q we used $d(P,Q) = \Sigma_{i,j} \, |p_{i,j} - q_{i,j}|$.

As can be seen in Figures 8.1 and 8.2, it turns out that the distance is quite small for the smaller values of μ, while it increases as μ increases, and it is also very sensitive to the increments of σ. Moreover, it can be observed that when μ has a strictly positive value, the distance increases with σ, while the converse holds when μ is equal to 0, i.e., if the microeconomic component is not present in the model. In addition, the simulation results tend to give rating transition matrices with smaller diagonal elements and higher off-diagonal elements than the initial transition matrix, with the effect to increase the probability of changing class (including the default probability for the different rating classes) and to reduce that of staying in the same class.

F I G U R E   8.1

Distance between the average rating transition matrices obtained with the simulation and the initial matrix as μ varies for different values of σ

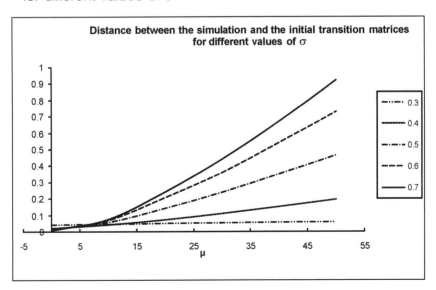

F I G U R E   8.2

Distance between the average rating transition matrices
obtained with the simulation and the initial matrix as σ varies
for different values of μ

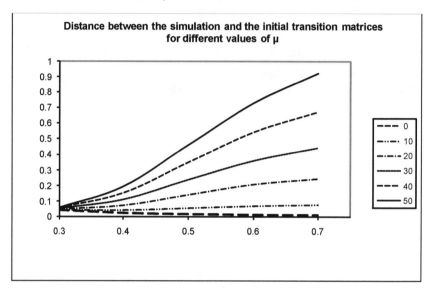

As far as the dynamic behavior of the average default rate of the
portfolio is concerned, the simulation outcomes indicate that it tends to
converge to a limit value as time increases. For small values of both μ and
σ, this limit value is very close to the initial average default rate obtained
using the estimated initial transition matrix, while it is significantly higher
for higher values of μ and especially of σ. An example of the dynamic
behavior of the portfolio average default rate is shown in Figure 8.3.

Furthermore, we have analyzed the dynamics of the distribution of
the firms in the different rating classes as time varies. The results suggest
that the model shows the tendency to increase in time the population of
the "central" rating classes A and BBB and to slightly decrease the others,
except for the extreme classes AAA and C, whose relative weight keeps
nearly constant. This behavior can be observed for all pairs of values for
μ and σ. An example of this tendency is shown in Figure 8.4.

F I G U R E   8.3

Average default rate of the system as *t* varies for μ = 30, σ = 0.3

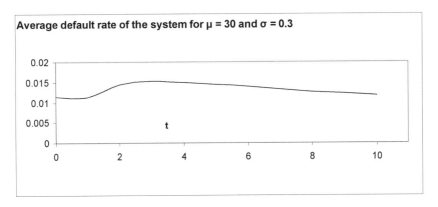

F I G U R E   8.4

Dynamics of the relative distribution of the firms in the rating classes for μ = 30 and σ = 0.3

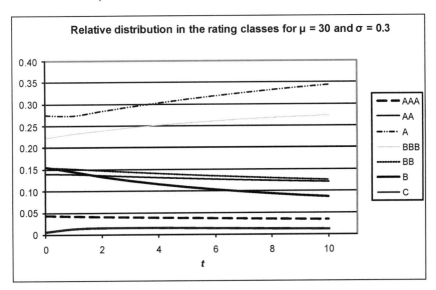

CONCLUSION

In this chapter we proposed a credit contagion model that explicitly takes into account both a macroeconomic effect and a microeconomic term describing the counterparty risk. In a structural approach, we introduce a set of thresholds for the value of a firm whose passage induces either a downgrade or an upgrade of the credit quality of the firm considered and leads to a change in the rating class assigned to it. The dynamic properties of the model and the effects of the counterparty risk on a portfolio of bank loans are studied by means of a of a wide Monte Carlo simulation analysis.

REFERENCES

Barro, D. and Basso, A. (2005) Counterparty Risk: A Credit Contagion Model for a Bank Loan Portfolio. *Journal of Financial Risk Management*, 2(4): 34–52.

Das, S., Duffie, D., Kapadia, N., and Saita, L. (2007) Common Failings: How Corporate Defaults Are Correlated. *Journal of Finance*, 62(1): 93–117.

Egloff, D., Leippold, M., and Vanini, P. (2007) A Simple Model of Credit Contagion. *Journal of Banking and Finance*, 31(8): 2475–2492.

Frey, R. and Backhaus, J. (2004) *Portfolio Credit Risk Models with Interacting Intensities: A Markovian Approach*. Preprint, Department of Mathematics, University of Leipzig, Leipzig, Germany.

Giesecke, K. and Weber, S. (2004) Cyclical Correlations, Credit Contagion and Portfolio Losses. *Journal of Banking and Finance*, 28(12): 3009–3036.

Jarrow, R. and Yu, F. (2001) Counterparty Risk and the Pricing of Defaultable Securities. *Journal of Finance*, 56(5): 555–576.

Lando, D. and Skødeberg, T.M.S. (2002) Analyzing Rating Transitions and Rating Drift with Continuous Observations. *Journal of Banking and Finance*, 26(2–3): 423–444.

Neu, P. and Khun, R. (2004) Credit Risk Enhancement in a Network of Interdependent Firms. *Physica A*, 342(3–4): 639–655.

Standard & Poor's (2003) Rating Performance 2002. Technical report, New York.

CHAPTER 9

Copula-Based Credit Rating Model for Evaluating Basket Credit Derivatives

Nicolas Papageorgiou, Bruno Rémillard, and Jean-Luc Gardère

ABSTRACT

In this chapter we present a credit risk model that can be used to multi-name credit derivatives. The model is an extension of earlier work by Hamilton et al. (2002) and not only captures default events but also can be used to price the risk of single or multiple downgrades on a given portfolio of issuers. We use the CreditGrades model to measure the credit quality of individual firms while the dependence between different issuers is modeled using copulas. We highlighted the impact of the choice of copula on the pricing of the different credit derivatives.

INTRODUCTION

Over the course of the last few years, significant advances have been realized in the field of credit risk measurement and management. The recent implementation of Basel II has provided great incentive for banks and regulators alike to appropriately model the risk of holding securities whose prices are sensitive to the creditworthiness of the obligor and/or the counterparty.

Academics and practitioners have contributed considerable time and effort in better understanding the factors that affect the structure of credit spreads, and numerous models have been put forth for the valuation of credit risky securities. These models are generally divided into two broad categories: structural models and reduced form models. Structural models rely on the approach of Black-Scholes (1973) and Merton (1974) in which the process driving default is the value of the firm. On the other hand, the reduced form class of models views defaults as an exogenously unspecified process, rather than as a predictable process. Although the structural model is conceptually important as it provides a causality for default, reduced form models are often more tractable mathematically, rendering them potentially useful in applications.

The main empirical problem with credit risk is that unlike market risk, where daily liquid price observations allow a direct calculation of value-at-risk (VaR), credit risk is more complicated to quantify. Apart from the obvious lack of market data, the most significant difference pertains to the horizon for which we are calculating VaR. For market risk, we usually consider a one-day horizon, and the portfolio of securities is marked to market on a daily basis. Credit VaR calculations consider a longer time horizon (usually one year), rendering it more difficult to properly estimate and back test the VaR model. As a result, these credit risk models generally use a combination of historical data and simulation techniques in order to estimate the required parameters needed for the VaR calculations [see Nickell et al. (2000) and Gordy (2000) for a more thorough discussion of the problem]. In essence, credit risk managers seek to construct what they cannot observe—the price distribution of credit risky securities.

In this chapter we present a hybrid model that takes into account the credit quality of the firm and incorporates rating-specific information. Using copula functions, we allow for the pricing of multiname credit derivatives. It is a direct extension of the model of Hamilton et al. (2002).

LITERATURE REVIEW

Reduced form models emerged in recent years as an alternative approach following the difficulties to implement structural models due to the non-clearly defined default boundaries and the complexity of capital structures. In these models, default is no longer linked to the market value of assets. Instead, default is considered as an unpredictable event and occurs in an exogenous way. Because the literature on reduced form models is quite vast, we limit our overview to the few important papers to which our model relates.

Jarrow and Turnbull (1995) introduced a methodology for pricing derivatives subject to credit risk. The authors use a foreign currency analogy to decompose the payoff of a credit risky security into a certain payoff and payoff ratio similar to a spot exchange rate. Under this framework, the price of a risky zero-coupon bond $v(t, T)$ is expressed as

$$v(t, T) = p(t, T) e(t, T)$$

where $p(t, T)$ and $e(t, T)$ are the price of a risk-free zero-coupon bond and the payoff ratio, respectively. This payoff ratio follows a stochastic process with pseudo-probability of default $\lambda \mu_t$. In the event of default, bondholders receive an exogenously given constant δ of face value, and the value of their bond following bankruptcy is a fraction, δ, of the price of a default-free bond. This assumption is known as the *recovery of treasury* and implies as suggested by the authors that in the event of bankruptcy, the term structure of the risky debt collapses to that of the default-free bonds. Under this setting, the price of a risky zero-coupon bond becomes

$$v(t, T) = p\,(t, T)[\delta + (1 - \delta)\,\tilde{Q}_t\,(\tau^* > T)]$$

where $\tilde{Q}_t\,(\tau^* > T)$ is the probability, under martingale measure $\tilde{Q}$, that default occurs after period T.

Building on the methodology presented in Jarrow and Turnbull (1995), Jarrow et al. (1997) develop a contingent claims model that incorporates credit ratings as an indicator of the likelihood of default. The authors model the default time distribution using a discrete time, time-homogenous Markov chain on a finite state space $S = \{1, 2, ..., K\}$. The different credit classes are represented in the state space S, with 1 and $K - 1$ representing the highest and lowest classes, respectively. The state K represents the event of default. The finite state space Markov chain is specified by a $K \times K$ transition matrix Q defined by

$$Q = \begin{pmatrix} q_{11} & q_{12} & \cdots & q_{1K} \\ q_{21} & q_{22} & \cdots & q_{2K} \\ \vdots & & & \\ q_{K-1,1} & q_{K-1,2} & \cdots & q_{K-1,K} \\ 0 & 0 & \cdots & 1 \end{pmatrix}$$

where q_{ij} represents the actual probability of going from state i to state j in one time step, with $q_{ij} \geq 0$ for all $i, j, i \neq j$ and $\sum_{j=1} q\hat{ij} = 1$ for all i. The authors assume that the state of bankruptcy is an absorbing state; so the probability for a bankrupt firm to move on to a higher credit class is zero, i.e., $q_{Ki} = 0$ for $i = 1, \ldots, K - 1$ and $q_{KK} = 1$.

Next, the authors introduce an n-step transition probability of going from state i at time 0 to state j at time n, which they denote $q_{ij}(0, n)$. The resulting transition matrix from time t to time $t + 1$ is as follows:

$$\tilde{Q}_{t,t+1} = \begin{pmatrix} \tilde{q}_{11}(t, t+1) & \tilde{q}_{12}(t, t+1) & \cdots & \tilde{q}_{1K}(t, t+1) \\ \tilde{q}_{21}(t, t+1) & \tilde{q}_{22}(t, t+1) & \cdots & \tilde{q}_{2K}(t, t+1) \\ \vdots & & & \\ \tilde{q}_{K-1,1}(t, t+1) & \tilde{q}_{K-1,2}(t, t+1) & \cdots & \tilde{q}_{K-1,K}(t, t+1) \\ 0 & 0 & \cdots & 1 \end{pmatrix}$$

Transition probabilities for a one-year time step can be obtained from rating agencies such as Moody's and Standard & Poor's and used to construct the transition matrix discussed above. The authors note that movements of more than one credit class in one year are rare. The probability of solvency or the probability that default occurs after time T, maturity, is expressed as $\tilde{Q}_t^i(\tau^* > T) = \Sigma_{j \neq K} \tilde{q}_{ij}(t, T) = 1 - \tilde{q}_{iK}(t, T)$.

Under this setting, the price of a zero-coupon bond issued by a firm belonging to credit class i is $v^i(t, T) = p(t, T)(\delta + (1 - \delta) \tilde{Q}_t^i(\tau^* > T))$. The forward rate for the risky zero-coupon is defined with the following expression $f^i(t, T) = -\log(v^i(t, T + 1)/v^i(t, T))$ and the credit risk spread for a particular credit class i is obtained from $f^i(t, T) - f(t, T)$, where $f(t, T)$ is the forward for a risk-free zero-coupon bond with maturity T. As in their previous work, the authors assume independence between the default-free term structure and the default process.

Duffie and Singleton (1999) develop a model for pricing defaultable bonds that is similar to the procedure for pricing default-free securities. They show that under a risk-neutral probability measure Q, the value of a defaultable corporate bond making a series of payments X with maturity T can be obtained as follows:

$$V_t = E_t^Q \left[\exp\left(-\int_t^T R_s \, ds \right) X \right]$$

where R denotes a default-adjusted rate. The default-adjusted rate accounts both for the probability of default and the severity of losses in the event of default and is expressed as $R_t = r_t + h_t L_t$, where r is the short-term interest rate process, h is the hazard rate, and L is the expected fractional loss. In the event of default, the authors assume that the losses L are a fraction of the market value of the obligation instead of a fraction of the face value. This assumption known as *recovery of market value* (RMV) differs from the assumption of recovery of treasury presented in Jarrow and Turnbull (1995) and simplifies the valuation problem since the joint probability distribution of the expected recovery value, the hazard rate, and the short-term rate is no longer required. Using the pricing framework developed by Duffie and Singleton, it is possible to recover the implied risk-neutral hazard rates from corporate bond prices given a constant fractional loss rate L.

Hamilton et al. (2002) propose a model that incorporates the credit migration approach of Jarrow et al. (1997) and the flexibility of the Duffie and Singleton (1999) framework. The default intensity in their model varies between 0 and 1, and this interval is further subdivided into rating-specific subintervals. The authors model the default intensity using a Cox–Ingersoll–Ross process to which they add a jump process to capture the possibility of unforeseen default. Each rating has its own default intensity and the interest rate, the default rate, and the recovery rate are assumed to be independent.

THE PROPOSED MODEL

Our model is an extension of Hamilton et al. (2002). We adopt the CreditGrades framework in order to model the credit quality of a firm. We integrate credit ratings in order to model the probabilities of default and rating transitions, and we use copulas for modeling the dependence between the different issuers in the portfolio.

Modeling the Credit Quality

Following Hamilton et al. (2002), the credit quality q_t is modeled as a stochastic process that can depend on a number of underlying variables and that is contained in [0, 1]. $q_t^{(i)} = 1$ represents the state of default for the issuer, and $q_t^{(i)} = 0$ represents an issuer that has a zero probability of default (no default risk). q can be loosely interpreted as a default probability. In contrast to Hamilton et al. (2002), we do not directly model q as a stochastic process; we assume that q is derived from the firm value, which in turn is determined by an underlying stochastic process.

We therefore have $q_t = h(V_t)$, where $dV_t = \mu_V V_t \, dt + \sigma_V V_t \, dW_t$ and W is standard Brownian motion. By applying Itô's lemma, we obtain $dq_t = \alpha(t, V_t) \, dt + \beta(t, V_t) \, dW_t$. Similarly to Hamilton et al. (2002), we allow for a random default time, that is, $q_t = 1$ if $t \geq \tau$, where τ Exp (λ) is a random stopping time that is independent of W. This gives $dq_t = \alpha(t, V_t) \, dt + \beta(t, V_t) \, dW_t + (1 - q_t) \, dN_t$, where $N_t = I_{t \geq \tau}$. However, since q is a strictly decreasing function of V, we can express V in terms of q; so we have $dq_t = \alpha'(t, q_t) \, dt + \beta'(t, q_t) \, dW_t + (1 - q_t) \, dN_t$.

In this chapter we have opted to use the (corrected) CreditGrades to model the credit quality q. CreditGrades is a kind of structural model with a stochastic barrier developed by RiskMetrics group that estimates credit quality using equity returns and volatility as well as the leverage ratio of the firm. Justifications can be found in the RiskMetrics Group (2002) technical report. However, the correct value of $P_t = P(V_s > LD$, for all $s \leq t)$ is

$$P_t = \Phi_2\left(-\frac{\lambda}{2} + \frac{\log b}{\lambda}, -\frac{A_t}{2} + \frac{\log b}{A_t}; \frac{\lambda}{A_t}\right) - b\Phi_2\left(\frac{\lambda}{2} + \frac{\log b}{\lambda}, -\frac{A_t}{2} - \frac{\log b}{A_t}; -\frac{\lambda}{A_t}\right)$$

where $\Phi_2(x, y; r)$ is the joint distribution function of two standard Gaussian copulas with correlation r, $b = V_0/\overline{L}D)\, e^{\lambda^2}$, $A_t^2 = \lambda^2 + t\sigma_V^2$, where $\mu_V = 0$, $L = \overline{L}e^{\lambda Z} - \lambda^2/2$ is the stochastic recovery rate with

$Z \sim N(0, 1)$ independent of W and D is the debt per share. Thus the probability of default by time t is $1 - P_t/P_0$.

Credit Rating

The credit rating c_t is an indicator of the company's credit risk. However, unlike q_t, $c_t \in [1, ..., C]$, where $c_t^{(i)} = 1$ is the lowest credit risk state and $c_t^{(i)} = C$ is the highest default risk state. The credit ratings used here are the ones issued by Moody's.

Copula

In the model the correlation between the level of credit risk across different issuers is introduced through the credit quality. More specifically, the dependence between the different issuers in the portfolio is modeled directly through $V_t^{(i)}$, where $i = 1, ..., m$, as in Hull and White (2001) and Li (1999). In effect, since the credit quality is a function of the firm value, $q_t^{(i)}$ and $V_t^{(i)}$ share the same copula and hence the same dependence structure.

Combining Discrete and Continuous Credit Information

Our model attempts to integrate a discreet model based on credit rating into a continuous credit quality model. In order to achieve this, we associate each credit rating c_t to an interval of q_t. These intervals are bounded by b_{k-1} and b_k, representing the lower and upper bounds, respectively, for credit rating k. We also have $b_0 = 0$ and $b_C = 1$. Let us recall that $q_t \in [0, 1]$, and so

$$q_{t,k} \in \left[b_{k-1}, b_k\right] \quad k = 1, ..., C$$

where $q_{t,k}$ is the credit quality at time t given credit rating k. However, the credit rating is not continuously observable but rather is only updated at discrete intervals. The time between ratings follows an exponential hazard rate $\lambda^{(R)}$, and each credit rating has its own hazard rate. We therefore have $\tau_i^{(k)} \sim \text{Exp}(\lambda_i^{(k)})$, and we assume that the rerating intervals are independent. In order to model the default time, we follow Hamilton et al. (2002), and assume that it follows a nonhomogeneous exponential distribution with default intensity $\lambda_t^{(D),\,i}$, which is a function of the credit quality.

$$\lambda_t^{(D),i} = \lambda^{(D)}\varphi(q_t^i) \quad i = 1, ..., m$$

where $\varphi(q_t^i)$ is an increasing function. The default intensity is greater for issuers that have a lower credit quality. Similarly to Hamilton et al. (2002), we define $\varphi(q_t^i) = q_t^i/(1 - q_t^i)$. We therefore obtain

$$Pr(\tau^{(D),i} < t) = 1 - \exp\left(\int_0^t - \lambda_t^{(D),i}\, dt\right) \quad i = 1, ..., m$$

In a multibond framework, we obtain the following stochastic differential equations:

$$dV_t^{(i)} = \mu_V^{(i)}V_t^{(i)}\, dt + \sigma_V^{(i)}V_t^{(i)}\, dW_t^{(i)} \quad i = 1, ..., m$$

where $W_t^{(i)}$ are standard Brownian motions that are correlated using a given copula function. The credit quality $q_t^{(i)}$ is driven by the following stochastic differential equation:

$$dq_t^{(i)} = \alpha\left(t, V_t^{(i)}\right)dt + \beta\left(t, V_t^{(i)}\right)dW_t^{(i)} + \left(1 - q_t^{(i)}\right)dN_t$$
$$i = 1, ..., m \quad and \quad j = 1, ..., C$$

where $\tau_j^{(i)}$ have the same dependence structure as $V^{(i)}$, similarly to Mashal et al. (2003).

CALIBRATION OF THE PARAMETERS

In this section we discuss how the parameters for each part of the model are calibrated.

The Credit Boundaries

In order to estimate the boundaries for the different credit ratings, we solve for the boundaries that allow for the greatest possible number of matches between the credit rating and the estimated boundaries. We need to solve

$$\max_{b_1,b_2...,b_{C-1}} \sum_{t=0}^{T} \sum_{i=1}^{I} I_{\{q_{t,k}^{(i)}\in[b_{k-1},b_k)\}}, \quad k = 1, 2, ..., C,$$

where $q^{(i)}_{t,k}$ is the credit quality at time t of bond i with credit rating k, $b_0 = 0$, and $b_C = 1$.

Rerating Interval

In our model we assume that the interval between rerating times follows a distribution with hazard rate with intensity $\lambda^{(R)}$, and this intensity is unique to each credit rating. We must estimate

$$\widehat{\lambda_j^{(R)}} = \sum_{i=1}^{I} T_j^{(i)} / \sum_{i=1}^{I} N_j^{(i)}, \quad j = 1, ..., C$$

where $T_j^{(i)}$ is the time spent by bond i in rating j during the sample period and $N_j^{(i)}$ is the number of times that bond i, with rating j, was rerated during the period.

Generating Random Rerating Times

We need to generate a vector of uniform independent random variables $V = (V_1, ..., V_m)$ over, $[0, 1]^m$, where m is the number of bonds in the portfolio, and then replace it in the following equation:

$$\tau_{ik}^{(R)} := -\lambda_k^{(R)} \log V_i \quad i = 1, ..., m \quad k = 1, ..., C$$

where $\tau_{ik}^{(R)}$ is the random rerating time for bond i with rating k and $\lambda_k^{(R)}$ is the rerating intensity for a bond rated k.

Default Times

Default times follow a nonhomogeneous exponential distribution. The default probability can be expressed as

$$Pr^{(D)} = Pr(\tau^{(D)} < t) = 1 - \exp\left(\int_0^T - \lambda^{(D)} \frac{q_t}{1-q_t} dt\right)$$

If we replace q_t by $a_k = b_{k-1} + b_k\, 2$, the midpoint of the ratings, we obtain an equation for each credit rating. Next, in order to estimate $\lambda_{(D)}$, one must find $\lambda^{(D)} = \text{argmin}_{\lambda^{(D)} \in [0,\, 1]}\, F(\lambda^{(D)})$, where

$$F(\lambda^{(D)}) = \sum_{k=1}^{C} \left\{ Pr_k^{(D)} - \left[1 - \exp\left(\lambda^{(D)}\, \frac{a_k}{1 - a_k} \right) \right] \right\}$$

and $Pr_k^{(D)}$ is the historical Moody's one-year default probability given rating k.

Generating Correlated Default Times

Since the default times in the model follow a nonhomogeneous Poisson distribution, it is difficult to directly generate correlated default times. To resolve this issue, we generate several different homogeneous Poisson distributions over a short interval Δt. We therefore have for $i = 1, \ldots, m$,

$$\lambda_{[t,t+\Delta t]}^{(D),i} = \int_{t}^{t+\Delta t} \lambda^{(D)}\, \frac{q_t^i}{1 - q_t^i}\, dt \approx \lambda^{(D)}\, \frac{q_t^i}{1 - q_t^i}$$

where $\lambda_{[t,\, t+\Delta t]}^{(D),\, i}$ is the default intensity of bond i over the time interval $[t,\, t + \Delta t]$. Also,

$$Pr_{[t,t+\Delta t]}^{(D),i} = 1 - \exp\left(-\lambda_{[t,t+\Delta t]}^{(D),i} \right)$$

where $Pr_{[t,\, t+\Delta t]}^{(D),\, i}$ is the default probability of bond i over the time interval $[t,\, t + \Delta t]$. Bond i will default $[t,\, t + \Delta t]$ if $Pr_{[t,\, t+\Delta t]}^{(D),\, i} > V_t^i$, where V_t^i is a randomly generated element of the uniform vector $V_t = (V_t^1, \ldots, V_t^m)$. Finally, we obtain

$$\tau^{(D),i} = \min\left\{ t^i \in \{ Pr_{[t,t+\Delta t]}^{(D)\,i} > V_t^i \} \Big| 0 < t^i < T^i \right\}$$

where $\tau^{(D),\, i}$ is the default date for bond i with maturity T^i.

Copulas

The calibration of the copulas is achieved using maximum likelihood with the method proposed by Genest et al. (1995). It is important to note that the procedure can vary depending on the type of copula function that is being estimated. In this chapter we will look at the Gaussian and Student copulas, as well as three copula functions from the Archimedean family (Frank, Gumbel, and Clayton).

Since defaults are rare events and hence there are insufficient data points to calculate dependence between these events, we will employ equity returns as a proxy for default probability. This is possible because there is a monotonic relationship between equity prices, the value of the firm, and the survival probability $1 - q_t$. Using the methodology proposed by Genest et al. (1995), the copula can be estimated using normalized ranks; hence, the margins are not important.

ESTIMATION RESULTS

We now present some details on the implementation of the model.

Data

Three sources of data are required in order to estimate the model. The first is a rating history that must be obtained from a credit rating agency (in our case Moody's). From the Center for Research in Security Prices (CRSP) we then need the equity prices for the firms that will be studied. Finally, from Compustat we need to obtain historical information about the debt structure of the firm to calculate the (corrected) CreditGrades default probability. For the sake of illustration we will focus our study on a portfolio of 10 firms, on which we will price a basket default product. Table 9.1 provides a summary of the firms.

Credit Rating Boundaries

To estimate the credit rating boundaries for the model, we combined the credit rating history of the bonds and the rating history given by Moody's. This allowed for 600 matches between credit rating and credit quality. The parameters are presented in Table 9.2.

T A B L E   9.1

Descriptive statistics for the 10 firms on January 31, 2005

Firm	Rating	Price	Reference Price	Debt per Share	Volatility
Alcoa	A2	28.93	30.12	12.06	15.77
Coca-Cola	Aa3	40.91	45.14	5.28	9.90
Dupont	Aa3	46.71	40.36	9.80	11.77
Exxon	Aaa	50.44	38.38	7.09	10.06
GE	Aaa	35.13	31.93	12.86	14.06
Honeywell	A2	35.99	31.33	8.88	17.12
IBM	A1	92.38	90.40	30.48	13.16
Procter and Gamble	Aa3	55.65	41.96	18.33	8.81
Boeing	A3	50.07	41.43	29.49	14.74
United Tech	A2	100.08	73.38	20.65	14.48

T A B L E   9.2

Estimated rating boundaries

Rating	Aaa	Aa	A	Baa	Ba	B	Caa,Ca,C	D
Lower Bound	0	1.11×10^{-16}	2.11×10^{-12}	1.46×10^{-8}	4.90×10^{-2}	3.45×10^{-2}	3.19×10^{-1}	1

Rerating Intervals

From Moody's database, we were able to extract over 5,000 ratings. Using this information we estimated the rerating intervals for the different credit ratings. The results are presented in Table 9.3.

T A B L E   9.3

Time interval between reratings for different credit ratings in years

Rating	Aaa	Aa	A	Baa	Ba	B	Caa,Ca,C
Estimate	3.66	1.83	1.53	1.45	1.19	1.24	0.96

T A B L E   9.4

One year default probability by credit rating

Rating	Aaa	Aa	A	Baa	Ba	B	Caa,Ca,C
Estimate	0.04%	0.16%	0.36%	1.69%	8.76%	27.83%	51.25%

Default Times

In order to estimate the default intensity $\lambda^{(d)}$, we used the historical default probabilities obtained from Moody's, conditional to the credit rating of the firm that defaults. The default probabilities are presented in Table 9.4.

Therefore, we obtain $\lambda^{(d)} = 0.6059$.

Copula Parameters

The copula parameters were estimated from the equity returns that have been adjusted for dividends and stock splits. The parameters for the five copula functions are given below.

Gaussian Copula

The (symmetric) dependence matrix for the Gaussian copula is

```
1.0000
0.4315  1.0000
0.2465  0.3104  1.0000
0.5405  0.4523  0.3384  1.0000
0.3669  0.3785  0.3674  0.4280  1.0000
0.4706  0.4413  0.4157  0.5131  0.4821  1.0000
0.4761  0.5315  0.3120  0.5487  0.3697  0.5249  1.0000
0.4137  0.3706  0.3000  0.4676  0.3697  0.5007  0.4556  1.0000
0.2655  0.3085  0.4045  0.3089  0.3840  0.4231  0.3299  0.3124  1.0000
0.4742  0.5681  0.3345  0.4883  0.398   0.4617  0.5858  0.3888  0.3109  1.0000
```

Student Copula

The (symmetric) dependence matrix for the Student copula is

1.00									
0.431	1.00								
0.245	0.310	1.00							
0.545	0.452	0.338	1.00						
0.369	0.378	0.367	0.428	1.00					
0.476	0.441	0.415	0.513	0.482	1.00				
0.476	0.531	0.312	0.548	0.369	0.524	1.00			
0.413	0.370	0.300	0.467	0.369	0.500	0.455	1.00		
0.265	0.308	0.404	0.308	0.384	0.423	0.329	0.312	1.00	
0.474	0.568	0.334	0.488	0.398	0.461	0.585	0.388	0.310	1.00

and the degrees of freedom are 13.323.

Archimedean Copulas

We obtain the parameters in Table 9.5 for the three Archimedean copulas.

PRICING MULTINAME CREDIT DERIVATIVES

In this section we will price two different multiname credit derivatives using the model. The first product is a straightforward Nth-to-default credit default swap, and the second will be a rating-dependent product whose payoff will be triggered by the downgrade of one or several issuers

T A B L E   9.5

Three Archimedean Copulas

Copula Family	Parameter Estimate
Clayton	0.419
Frank	0.766
Gumbel	0.097

in the basket. Both products will be written on the 10 names presented in the previous section, and the impact of the choice of copula on the price of these derivatives will also be investigated.

Nth-to-Default Swap

We will price both a first- and second-to-default swap. The first-to-default pays the purchaser in the event of the first default in the portfolio, whereas the second-to-default only pays out when the second default occurs in portfolio. The potential cash flow FM_t at time t for the first to default is

$$FM_t^{(D,1)} = \sum_{i=1}^{m} I_{t>\tau_i}(1 - R_{k_i})p_i, \quad t \leq T$$

while for the second to default it is

$$FM_t^{(D,2)} = \sum_{j=1}^{m} I_{t>\tau_j} \sum_{i=j+1}^{m} I_{t>\tau_i}(1 - R_{k_i})p_i, \quad t \leq T$$

where T is the maturity of the swap, τ_i is the default time for issuer i, R_{k_i} is the recovery rate in the event of default for bond i with credit rating, k and p_i is the weight of bond i in the swap. We assume they simultaneous defaults are not possible.

Nth-to-Downgrade Swap

We also evaluate a first- and second-to-downgrade option that pays out when the first (or second) downgrade below Baa occurs. The potential cash flow FM_t at time t for the first to downgrade is

$$FM_t^{(C,1)} = \sum_{i=1}^{m} I_{t>\alpha_i} H_{k_i^{s-1},k_i^s} p_i, \quad t \leq T$$

and for the second to downgrade, it is

$$FM_t^{(C,2)} = \sum_{j=1}^{m} I_{t>\alpha_j} \sum_{i=j+1}^{m} I_{t>\alpha_i} H_{k_i^{s-1},k_i^s} p_i, \quad t \leq T$$

where α_i is the moment at which bond i is downgraded below Baa and $H_{k_i^{s-1},\,k_i^s}$ is the loss resulting from the downgrade from k^{s-1} to k^s of bond i. Note that if default occurs prior to downgrade, that is, $\tau_i \leq \alpha_i$, the payout of the downgrade option is the same as the corresponding default swap.

Parameters

Tables 9.6 and 9.7 present, respectively, the recovery rates and the markdown in the event of downgrade that we employ for the pricing of the derivatives.

All recovery and markdown values are based on the face value of the bond and not its market values. The interest rate is assumed to be 3 percent and constant, the maturity of the derivatives is two years, and they have an equal exposure to each firm.

Table 9.8 presents the average price (in basis points) for the four derivatives using 10,000 simulations and five different copula functions. As expected, the choice of copula has an important impact on the price of

TABLE 9.6

Recovery rate by credit rating

Rating	Aaa	Aa	A	Baa	Ba	B	Caa,Ca,C
Estimate	0.95	0.90	0.80	0.70	0.50	0.40	0.30

TABLE 9.7

Markdown in the event of downgrade

	Ba	B	Caa, Ca, C
Aaa	0.25	0.35	0.50
Aa	0.20	0.25	0.35
A	0.15	0.25	0.30
Baa	0.10	0.15	0.25

T A B L E   9.8

Price of credit derivatives

Copule	First to Default	Second to Default	First to Downgrade	Second to Downgrade
Franck	98.9	42.7	122.8	63.6
Clayton	82.4	36.4	104.1	53.5
Gumbel	32.5	19.2	45.0	28.0
Student	21.0	4.5	32.0	8.4
Normal	18.0	3.3	29.0	7.0

the different credit derivatives. This result is consistent with the results of Berrada et al. (2006).

The price using Archimedean copula functions is greater than for the Student and Gaussian copulas for the Nth-to-default and Nth-to-downgrade derivatives. This is due to the higher dependence in the tails of these copula functions. As expected, we observe that the first and second to default are cheaper than the first and second to downgrade, respectively, as they represent insurance against a less likely (yet more costly) event.

CONCLUSION

In this chapter we have presented a credit risk model that can be used to multiname credit derivatives. The model is an extension of earlier work by Hamilton et al. (2002) and captures not only default events but also can be used to price the risk of single or multiple downgrades on a given portfolio of issuers. In our implementation we use the CreditGrades model to capture the creditworthiness of a given issuer and then overlay information about the credit rating of the company in order to estimate the appropriate default (and migration) intensity. In order to the capture the dependence between default times, we use five different copula functions. We highlighted the impact of the choice of copula on the pricing of the different credit derivatives.

REFERENCES

Berrada, T., D.J. Dupuis, E. Jacquier, N. Papageorgiou, and B. Remillard. (2006) Credit migration and derivatives pricing using copulas. *Journal of Computational Finance*, 10 43–68.

Black, F. and Scholes, M. (1973) The Pricing of Options and Corporate Liabilities, *The Journal of Political Economy*, 81, 637–654.

Duffie, D. and Singleton, K.J. (1999) Modeling Term Structures of Defaultable Bonds. *Review of Financial Studies*, 12(4): 687–720.

Genest, C., Ghoudi, K., and Rivest, L.-P. (1995) A Semiparametric Estimation Procedure of Dependence Parameters in Multivariate Families of Distributions. *Biometrika*, 82(3): 543–552.

Gordy, 2000 M. (2000) A comparative anatomy of credit risk models, Journal of Banking and Finance 24 (1–2), pp. 119–149.

Hamilton, D., James, J., and Webber, N. (2002) Copula Methods and the Analysis of Credit Risk. Working paper, Warwick Business School, University of Warwick, Coventry, UK.

Hull, J. and White, A. (2001) Valuing Credit Default Swap: No Counterparty Default Risk. *Journal of Derivatives*, 8(1): 29–40.

Jarrow, R.A. and Turnbull, S.M. (1995) Pricing Derivatives on Financial Securities Subject to Credit Risk. *Journal of Finance*, 50(1): 53–85.

Jarrow, R.A., Lando, D., and Turnbull, S.M. (1997) A Markov Model of the Term Structure of Credit Risk Spreads. *Review of Financial Studies*, 10(2): 481–523.

Li, D., (2000), "On default correlation: a copula function approach," Journal of Fixed Income 9, 43–54.

Mashal, R., Naldi, M., and Zeevi, A. (2003). Extreme Events and Multi-Name Credit Derivatives. In *Credit Risk: Models and Management*. London: Risk Waters Group.

Merton, R.C. (1974) On the Pricing of Corporate Debt: The Risk Structure of Interest Rates. *Journal of Finance*, 29(2): 449–470.

Nickell, P., W. Perraudin, and S. Varotto. (2000) "Stability of Rating Transitions." *Journal of Banking and Finance*, (24)1–2: 203–27.

RiskMetrics Group (2002) *CreditGrades—Technical document.* Available from www.riskmetrics.com.

Mark-to-Market Valuation of Illiquid Loans

Claas Becker

ABSTRACT

Market prices for illiquid loans are not directly observable. In this chapter a methodology is presented how to derive loan prices from observable market prices for tranches of collateralized loan obligations. This methodology is based on the internal rating the bank assigns to the borrower and takes into account collateral, a feature typically encountered in small- and medium-sized enterprise business.

INTRODUCTION

This chapter describes a methodology for valuing illiquid loans. This methodology is based on observable prices for tranches of collateralized loan obligations (CLOs) and on observable credit spreads for actively traded names. The main input variables are the borrower's internal rating, tenor of the loan, and a recovery rate assumption based on the degree of collateralization. This methodology has been developed by Deutsche Bank's

Loan Exposure Management Group and is used in the context of pricing loans to small- and-medium-sized enterprises (SMEs) in Germany.

This chapter is organized as follows: In the second section, we describe how "average" spread curves are built based on market observations. We call these average spread curves liquid generic curves as they are constructed from observed market spreads. The next step is the construction of illiquid spread curves based on liquid curves. This topic is covered in the third section. The fourth section of this chapter describes the loan pricing algorithm. Finally, the concluding section contains some results about back testing this pricing methodology.

BUILDING LIQUID GENERIC CURVES

For a traded name, a spread curve is the credit spread as a function of time. Credit spread is the observable spread paid for a credit default swap (CDS) contract of given tenor. In the context of this chapter, we shall not differentiate between bid and ask curves.

Given observable spreads for discrete points in time t_1, ..., t_n, e.g., today + 1 year, today + 2 years, ..., today + n years, we can calculate risk-neutral survival probabilities Q_1 ..., Q_n. More precisely, the survival probabilities Q_1, ..., Q_n are chosen in such a way that the n CDS contracts simultaneously trade at par. This involves solving a system of n equations with n variables.

Since the main focus of this chapter is the pricing of illiquid loans, we will not dwell on the precise formula for pricing CDSs. Nevertheless, let us emphasize that in order to arrive at risk-neutral default probabilities and consequently at risk-neutral survival probabilities, we have to make an assumption about recovery rates. Obviously, for a given real-world default probability, the credit risk increases with declining recovery rates, and thus spreads increase as well. Moreover, since swap premiums for protection until t_j are not necessarily due exactly at t_1, ..., t_{j-1}, we also need a convention on how to interpolate between adjacent survival probabilities Q_k and Q_{k+1}.

Having constructed the spread curves for the universe of actively traded names, we can now construct liquid generic curves. A generic spread curve is the spread regarded as a function of time, and it averages the market

Averaging market observations

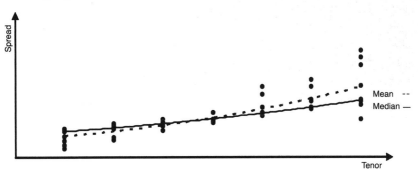

observations for a given rating (and potentially geographic region). As an example, the BBB Western Europe liquid generic curve is the average of all market observations for BBB-rated companies in Western Europe. When averaging, we must be careful not to give too much weight to statistical outliers. Thus, taking the median is more appropriate than taking the arithmetic average, as depicted in Figure 10.1.

The next step is to build series of liquid generic curves for different ratings. The generic curves initially obtained may contain kinks and may cross over curves for other rating categories, which is illustrated in Figure 10.2.

Thus, we may need to apply a "smoothing" algorithm to remove such kinks and crossovers. Such an algorithm will contain elements of subjectivity. Finally, after these adjustments, we construct a system of liquid generic curves.

BUILDING ILLIQUID GENERIC CURVES

The next step is to construct a system of illiquid generic curves. Illiquid generic curves are intended to be used for pricing large corporates and financial institutions that are not actively traded in the CDS market but may be traded on a bilateral basis between market participants. Consequently, traders will charge an additional illiquidity premium.

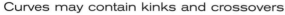

F I G U R E   10.2

Curves may contain kinks and crossovers

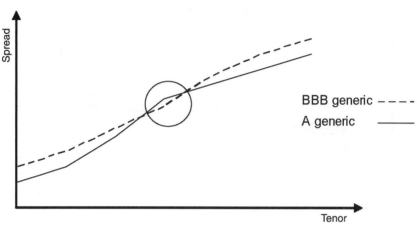

For given rating and tenor, the relative illiquidity premium is *ill_relative = spread_illiquid/spread_liquid,* and the absolute illiquidity premium is *ill_absolute = spread_illiquid – spread_liquid.*

We assume that traders have a good idea about the relative illiquidity premium for a given rating, say single A. It may be inappropriate to choose the same illiquidity premium across all rating categories: While a charge of 50 percent might be adequate for an investment grade name, e.g., increasing the CDS premium from 50 bps to 75 bps, charging the same 50 percent for a non-investment grade name would result in, e.g., 450 bps instead of 300 bps. One would assume that the relative illiquidity premium decreases with lower credit ratings, while the absolute illiquidity premium increases.

We will presume that the relative illiquidity premium is a function of rating only (and not of tenor) and now construct a series of illiquid generic curves (for different ratings) by solving the following:

Minimization problem: *Minimize the total absolute illiquidity premium (for all ratings) subject to the following constraints:*

   1. The relative illiquidity premium for the given rating is the numerical value based on traders' opinions.

2. *The relative illiquidity premium decreases with lower credit ratings.*
3. *The absolute illiquidity premium increases with lower credit ratings.*

The minimization problem can be solved with standard linear optimization packages and the result is a series of illiquid generic CDS curves. The algorithm for constructing illiquid generic curves contains elements of subjectivity. Ultimately, the pricing results obtained from such curves should be subject to back testing, a topic which is discussed in the last section of this chapter.

In the remainder of this section, we construct another set of illiquid generic curves suitable for valuing SME loans. For SME loans, we cannot expect that they could be traded on a bilateral basis. Furthermore, banking secrecy laws may restrict the disclosure of borrower names to potential buyers. In such cases, the only viable hedging instrument is a blind pool CLO. The idea is to infer the relative illiquidity premium by comparing the hedging costs for a CLO with a corresponding data point in the system of liquid generic curves.

Table 10.1 depicts the capital structure of a typical blind pool SME CLO with only moderate single obligor concentrations. Spread estimates relate to the situation before the subprime crisis.

T A B L E   10.1

Capital structure of a typical blind pool CLO

Tranche	Lower Bound	Upper Bound	Size	Spread BPS	Costs per Annum	BPS
Supersenior	12.50%	100.00%	875,000,000	10	875,000	9
AAA	9.00%	12.50%	35,000,000	15	52,500	1
AAA	7.00%	9.00%	20,000,000	25	50,000	1
AA	5.75%	7.00%	12,500,000	40	50,000	1
A	5.25%	5.75%	5,000,000	60	30,000	0
BBB	4.25%	5.25%	10,000,000	130	130,000	1
BB	3.50%	4.25%	7,500,000	400	300,000	3
Equity	0.00%	3.50%	35,000,000	1275	4,462,500	45
			1,000,000,000		5,950,000	60

Note that during the life of the CLO, part of the equity tranche will be lost due to defaults. We have converted the coupon payments to equity investors into a "riskless" coupon paid on the initial outstanding amount of the tranche. This conversion is done using the assumption that the internal rate of return (net of defaults) stays the same.

Apart from spreads paid for the different tranches of the capital structure, we also have to take into account up-front costs, e.g., for rating agencies and legal advisors. Let us assume for the sake of simplicity that annualized up-front costs are 5 bps per annum. In practice, the actual up-front charges tend to be relatively stable. Thus, relative up-front costs vary significantly with deal size.

In our example, spreads and up-front charges amount to 65 bps per annum. We have to relate these to a specific rating and tenor. The tenor we use is the weighted average life of the loans, which is the average tenor of the hedge. The legal tenor of the CLO may be much longer but is inappropriate in this context.

The rating we use is the weighted average rating of the securitized assets, but we would like to be a little bit more precise and take collateral into consideration. For this purpose, we use the average expected loss as computed by an internal credit risk model: average $EL = PD$ (average rating) LGD_{CLO}.

We can determine the cost of securitizing uncollateralized loans by linear scaling with LGD_{uncol} / LGD_{CLO}, where LGD_{uncol} is the LGD assigned to loans that are not collateralized. This is illustrated in Table 10.2.

T A B L E   10.2

Some parameters of a typical blind pool CLO

Average rating	BBB–
Average tenor	3 years
Average expected loss	20 bps
PD (BBB–)	40 bps
Weighted average spread and up-front costs	65 bps

We arrive at LGD_{CLO} = 20 bps/40 bps = 0.5, and assuming LGD_{uncol} = 0.6, the final data point for BBB–, 3 years, is 65 bps · 0.6/0.5 = 78 bps. By comparing this data point with the corresponding data point on the liquid generic curve, we can determine the numerical value of the illiquidity premium. We now have the prerequisites to apply the preceding algorithm based on the minimization problem to obtain a set of illiquid generic curves, which we will call *illiquid generic CLO curves*.

Let us mention that this approach only works for pricing loan portfolios that are fairly granular and can be securitized in a standard blind pool CLO. For loans that exceed the single obligor concentrations of such a CLO, one might want to charge a size add-on. The numerical value of such a size add-on can be determined by comparing the weighted average spread of the capital structure of a diversified pool with the weighted average spread for a "lumpy" pool. As an example, table 10.3 shows the single obligor concentrations for Deutsche Bank's GATE 2006–1 SME CLO (granular) and Deutsche Bank's CART 1 Ltd. CLO (lumpy). The equity tranches for both CLOs have been privately placed, and the coupon is not publicly known.

Note that both deals are fairly comparable in terms of weighted average rating and weighted average life of the assets. The only significant difference is the size of the single obligor concentrations. As single obligor concentrations are increased, the attachment points of the tranches shift upward. Secondly, investors ask for additional spread. This is illustrated in Table 10.4: The BB GATE 2006–1 tranche yields 275 bps over EURIBOR,

T A B L E   10.3

Comparison of a granular and a lumpy CLO

	GATE SME 2006–1		CART 1 Ltd.	
Portfolio Size	€2,100,000,000		€1,700,000,000	
Single Obligor Concentrations	AAA to A–	1.75%	AAA to A–	5.0%*
	BBB+ to BBB–	1.2%	BBB+ to BBB–	5.0%
	BB+ to BB–	0.7%	BB+ to BB–	3.0%
	B+	0.3%	B+	1.5%

* 7.0% for top five groups.

TABLE 10.4

Capital structure of a granular and of a lumpy CLO

| | GATE SME CLO 2006–1 Ltd | | | | | CART 1 Ltd | | | |
Class	Ratings S&P/FITCH	Attachment Point	Detachment Point	Spread over 3m EURIBOR bps	Class	Ratings S&P/FITCH	Attachment Point	Detachment Point	Spread over 3m EURIBOR bps
A	AAA/AAA	6.81%	8.81%	15	A+	AAA/AAA	14.50%	15.50%	25
B	AA/AA	5.55%	6.81%	25	A	AAA/AA+	14.00%	14.50%	30
C	A/A+	5.19%	5.55%	35	B	AA/AA−	11.00%	14.00%	50
D	BBB/BBB+	4.24%	5.19%	65	C	A/A+	10.00%	11.00%	70
E	BB/BB+	3.50%	4.24%	275	D	BBB/BBB+	7.75%	10.00%	130
F	NR	0.00%	3.50%		E	BB/BB	4.90%	7.75%	450
					F	NR	0.00%	4.90%	

NR = not rated

whereas the BB CART 1 Ltd tranche yields 450 bps. As a result of these two effects, the weighted average spread for CART 1 Ltd is significantly higher than for GATE 2006–1.

In this section we have described how to construct liquid generic curves, illiquid generic CDS curves, and illiquid generic CLO curves at one point in time. These curves can be updated regularly, e.g., weekly, as new market observations become available. While CDS spreads can be directly observed, an update of the spreads for CLO tranches must be based at least partly on "expert opinion."

THE LOAN PRICING ALGORITHM

In this section we briefly describe the loan pricing algorithm. Our main focus will be the estimation of recovery rates based on collateral information. Let us assume that the loan consists of contractual cash flows p_i (principal) and r_i (interest) due at times t_i, $i = 1, \ldots, n$. We put $t_0 =$ today.[1] Assuming recoveries of zero, the mark-to-market value of the loan is $\sum_{i=1}^{n} D_{0i} (p_i + r_i) Q_i$, where D_{0i} is the discount factor for the period $[t_0, t_i]$ and Q_i is the risk-neutral survival probability until time t_i.

We now incorporate recoveries into the model. Let R_i denote the recovery rate if default occurs at t_i. This recovery rate is supposed to relate to principal cash flows only, and we assume that the recovery occurs instantaneously after default. The mark-to-market value of the loan now becomes

$$\sum_{i=1}^{n} D_{0i}(p_i + r_i)Q_i + \sum_{i=1}^{n} D_{0i}R_i \sum_{j=i}^{n} p_j(Q_{i-1} - Q_i) \qquad (10.1)$$

where we have used the convention $Q_0 = 1$.

The remainder of this section focuses on the relationship between recovery rates and collateral. The general idea is to treat collateral in a

---

[1] Note that if we know the numerical values of interest cash flows today, this implies that the loan is a fixed-rate loan. The generalization to floating-rate loans can be done by discounting payments first with respect to (w.r.t.) the period [next fixing date, t_i] and then w.r.t. the period [t_0, next fixing date].

way similar to the bank's internal credit risk model. This approach has the advantage that one can rely on parameters already calibrated in the context of Basel II. Collateral is very important in the SME lending business, and the types of collateral are manifold. Examples are cash collateral, land charges, chattel mortgages, cessions, and financial guarantees by third parties. Thus, it appears to be reasonable to put the different types of collateral into at least three groups:

- Impersonal collateral, with decreasing value over time, e.g., chattel mortgages
- Impersonal collateral, constant in time, e.g., land charges or cash collateral
- Financial guarantees.

It may be useful to refine these groupings, for instance, by assigning different recoveries to cash collateral and cessions.

A typical situation in the SME lending business is an amortizing fixed-rate loan secured by a land charge. As the principal is paid back over time, the loan runs into a higher degree of collateralization. Thus, we do not want to assign one recovery rate to the loan as such, but rather individual recovery rates to each cash flow.

Let col_1 be the estimated liquidation value of the collateral with decreasing value over time. We will assume linear depreciation over a period T. Let col_2 be the estimated liquidation value of the collateral with constant value over time. Let $b_i = \Sigma_{j=i}^{n} p_j$ be the outstanding balance at time t_i. The collateralized portion of the balance b_i is $b_{i col} = \min(b_i, \max(1/T[T - (t_i - t_0), 0] col_1 + col_2)$.

We further assume that we have a financial guarantee and that the joint default probability between borrower and guarantor is JDP. Such a joint default probability is usually estimated in the context of internal credit risk models. The expected loss for uncollateralized exposure with a given PD is $EL = LGD_{uncol} PD$.

Given a financial guarantee, this changes to

$$EL = LGD_{uncol} JDP = LGD_{uncol} \frac{JDP}{PD} PD$$

Thus $LGD_{uncol} JDP/PD$, is the appropriate LGD for exposure secured by a financial guarantee. Let the guaranteed amount be g. The guaranteed portion of the balance b_i is $b_{i\ gar} = \min(g, \ b_i - b_{i\ col})$, and the remainder $b_{i\ uncol} = b_i - b_{i\ col} - b_{i\ gar}$ is not collateralized at all. Thus, we have the following expression for the recovery rate R_i:

$$1 - R_i = LGD_i = \frac{1}{b_i}(b_{i\ col}LGD_{col} + b_{i\ gar}LGD_{uncol}\frac{JDP}{PD} + b_{i\ uncol}LGD_{uncol}) \quad (10.2)$$

Based on the preceding analysis, we can now substitute equation (10.2) into equation (10.1) and do a mark-to-market valuation of an illiquid SME loan. We can also use equation (10.1) for pricing a loan at origination. In order to do so, we determine the interest rate that makes the loan value at par. Subtracting this interest rate from the bank's internal funding rate, we arrive at the break-even margin.

Table 10.5 shows the break-even margin for an amortizing six year loan in the non-investment grade area. As can be seen, the break-even margin is heavily influenced by collateral. Since the liquidation value of machinery is depreciated over time, a chattel mortgage results in less risk reduction than a land charge, a view that credit practitioners are likely to share.

T A B L E   10.5

How collateral impacts pricing

	Break-even Margin (bps)
No collateral	145
Chattel mortgage (pledge of machinery) initial liquidation value 50% of loan	88
Land charge initial liquidation value 50% of loan	37

BACK TESTING

As mentioned before, our methodology for deriving generic curves contains elements of subjectivity. We have back tested this methodology on a diversified portfolio of SME loans of various ratings, tenors, and degrees of collateralization, booked into Deutsche Bank's loan book over a period of time.

If all loans in the portfolio under consideration were bullet loans of the same rating and tenor, then there would be no reason for back testing. However, for a real-life portfolio, the CLO contains amortizing loans of various ratings and tenors. The break-even margin of the different loans depends on the illiquid CLO curves. For example, the steepness of the CLO curves (as a function of tenor) might be too high or too low so that the equation

$$\text{Weighted average break-even margin} \\ = \text{weighted average CLO spread} \\ + \text{upfront costs} \qquad (10.3)$$

may not hold. In the sequel, we describe the back testing algorithm in several steps.

Step 1: We used Standard & Poor's CDO Evaluator to derive a tranching of this portfolio and have made assumptions about spreads for the various tranches of the capital structure. Thus, we derived the weighted average spread of the capital structure and added annualized up-front costs on top. We arrived at a data point for a weighted average rating of BBB− and a weighted average life of three years.

Step 2: We have used this data point to derive generic CLO curves.

Step 3: We have used these generic CLO curves to price each loan of the portfolio. Thus, we were in the position to compute the weighted average break-even margin of the loan portfolio.

Step 4: We verified whether equation (10.3) holds. Note that the assumptions about the CLO tranche spreads affect both the weighted average spread of the capital structure and, via the generic CLO curves, the weighted average break-even margin. This implies that the results will not be very sensitive to inaccuracies in the CLO tranche spreads. The results show that CLO costs and weighted average break-even margin are quite close, but overall the weighted average break-even margin is a bit low. The conclusion is that at origination we charge a little less than the actual hedging costs.

A closer investigation shows that the recovery rate assumptions made by rating agencies and investors are more conservative than the internal credit risk model. While internal credit risk models usually use recovery rates of 90 percent and more for the collateralized portion of a loan, the assumptions made by rating agencies usually are in the 60 to 70 percent range. When we adjusted the recovery rate for the collateralized portion in the loan pricing model and re-ran our analysis, we arrived at a closer match. We could calibrate the recovery rate for the collateralized portion such that a perfect match could be achieved. Thus, we believe that the loan pricing model we have presented in this article is quite satisfying from both a practical and a theoretical perspective.

SUMMARY

In this chapter we have shown how to construct liquid generic curves from observable CDS spreads. Based on these liquid generic CDS curves, illiquid generic CDS curves can be built. Another class of illiquid curves are illiquid generic CLO curves, which are based on observable spreads for tranches of blind pool CLOs. These generic CLO curves are used for pricing SME loans. Such an SME loan typically is an amortizing fixed-rate loan. For each contractual payment of the loan, an individual recovery rate is computed based on collateral information.

Disclaimer

This chapter is purely academic in nature. It is not intended as an instruction to build a loan pricing model. Neither the author nor Deutsche Bank AG can be made liable for any damage or lost business opportunity resulting from loan pricing based upon this chapter.

REFERENCES

Becker, C. (2006) Transfer Mittelständischer Kreditrisiken. *Zeitschrift für das Gesamte Kreditwesen*, 59(21): 1151–1153.

PART THREE

Managing Credit Exposure

CHAPTER 11

A Holistic Approach to Risk Management of Credit Portfolios

Christian Burmester

ABSTRACT

Risk management of credit portfolios is regarded as a multidimensional task that has to satisfy both the objectives of the portfolio manager and the strategy set by the bank. Beyond the classical tasks to manage risk and return, the portfolio manager has to be aware of regulatory and accounting constraints. Given these boundaries, we review briefly how risk can be measured and then focus on ways to contain risks: to set limits for significant risk drivers, to run stress tests in order to identify potential harm to the going concern of the bank, and to define the risk capacity of the bank. Management must ensure that concentrations of risk are avoided as often the greatest potential damage to a bank arises from disproportionate risk drivers.

INTRODUCTION

Over the past decades, risk management has improved significantly, both on an individual product and portfolio level. It is now common to assess both the creditworthiness and price movements with statistical methods. Whereas the early methods assumed normal distribution of all market movements, more sophisticated methods are being developed to capture the more erratic movements. How come the huge market disruptions in late 2007 and 2008 nevertheless led to massive provisions?

The conclusion is that regardless of how sophisticated price and risk calculations are, it is still impossible to identify unforeseen future market development. Thus, ways to go beyond finite exact computation of prices and risks. Risk management has to capture unthinkable events and to introduce efficient but readily acceptable means to contain risks. The most recent market turmoil—triggered by U.S. subprime mortgages—shows that although the risk of structured products may have been individually assessed correctly, it has not prevented the industry from ending up in deep water. Therefore, the following chapter explains managerial ways to contain risks beyond the classical risk calculations, such as value-at-risk (VaR).

PORTFOLIO MANAGEMENT IN THE CONTEXT OF A BANK'S MANAGEMENT

At a corporate level the board of directors has to make sure that the overall objectives are met, which usually means to earn the highest possible yield on the invested capital given an accepted level of risk. Certain constraints also have to be considered, e.g., regulatory framework, compliance matters, cost targets, and accounting policies. To support these objectives, the overall risk and yield aims are allocated to the various business lines of the bank, thus requiring a credit portfolio manager to act within this framework of (delegated) risk appetite, yield target, and ancillary constraints. Figure 11.1 briefly captures the framework within which the bank and each portfolio manager have to operate.

The following sections describe how the overall targets are delegated to a dedicated portfolio and how risk is measured and contained. First, the bank's management has to ensure that sound processes are implemented in order to manage the framework. Second, the risk capacity of the bank and the subset delegated to the portfolio manager has to be identified. Third, the risk measurement methodology will be briefly examined. Note that both risk capacity and risk quantification are strongly

Methodological framework of portfolio management

Management of credit portfolios based on four targets

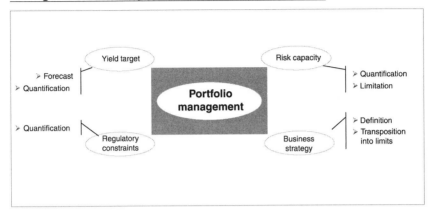

linked to each other because the bank can not define the risk capacity without knowing the risk methodologies. Fourth, different ways to contain the risks are discussed. The two major ways are to run additional stress tests to identify the main risk drivers that could harm the going concern of the bank and to set and enforce appropriate limits.

RISK MANAGEMENT OF PORTFOLIOS
Segregation of Duties

In a typical (bank) environment the various responsibilities are segregated between the portfolio management itself and the controlling functions like risk control, compliance office, and financial accounting. These sound practices make sure that conflicts of interest are unlikely to arise and that the true measures of risk, present value, and return are assessed independently.

Risk Capacity

To allocate risk limits, banks should adopt a top-down approach. The board of directors should determine the risk capacity first. The *risk capacity* is defined as the maximum amount of risk the bank (or group) can maintain without going bankrupt should the risk materialize, or in other words, how big could the risk appetite be without risking the bank to fail? The answer depends on the level of equity and the (subjective) risk appetite the bank might have.

There is a very elegant although theoretical way to determine the risk capacity. Based on external ratings, a certain level of probability of default—say 0.1 percent p.a.—can be used to set the maximum risk level the bank can maintain. Equity should be adjusted to such a level that "allows" a bankruptcy only once in 1,000 years (which is the reverse of 99.9 percent). In technical terms, it is the reverse-engineered loss distribution, as shown in Figure 11.2, where the shortfall (or value at risk) at 99.9 percent confidence level is equivalent to the equity a bank should maintain. The higher the bank is rated, the more equity is necessary to support a certain level of risk and to maintain the going concern. If the bank wants

F I G U R E   11.2

Risk assessment and terminology

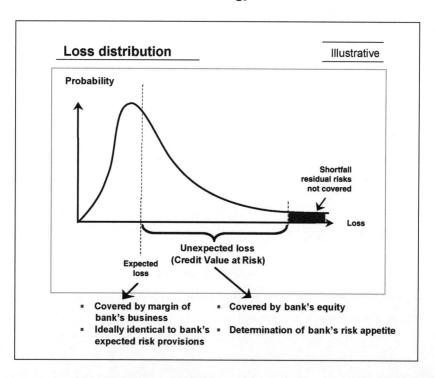

to adjust its risk capacity, it can reduce its (typically most) risky assets, raise fresh capital, or manage both together.

It has to be acknowledged that this is a statistical concept that may be difficult to interpret in real economical terms—no bank will last for thousands of years. However, the method is compatible with the risk methodologies of market and credit risk measurement and thus most appropriate to be used. The overall risk capacity should then be broken down to the various risk categories and further to divisions or even desks (see Figure 11.3).

Risk Measurement

The risk is usually measured in value-at-risk (VaR) terms, which is an assessment of the likelihood of a shortfall by a certain amount. There are various methods available that encompass market, credit, and operational risk. At a group level all categories are amalgamated into one figure to compare the actual risk with the risk capacity of the bank. There is an extensive array of literature that covers the mathematics of these models, which would be too much to discuss in this chapter. Therefore, the reader is referred to comprehensive technical documents such as Bielecki and Rutkowski (2002), Lando (2004), Gordy (2000), or Bluhm et al. (2003).

The VaR methodology comes across with certain criticism and the following points should be considered when calculating VaR figures (see Figure 11.2). First, all VaR models are statistical models based on certain

F I G U R E   11.3

Concept of the risk capacity

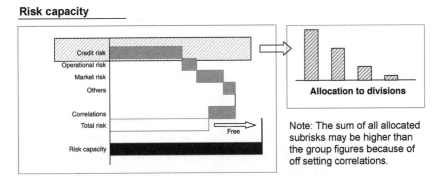

assumptions and are not perfect when measuring risk. For example, it is very difficult to assess the true figures of the probability of default, correlations of assets, and confidence levels. If the amount of data is sufficient, then it will be possible to obtain these figures at a reasonable confidence level, but they represent merely the past development of financial markets. When interpreting VaR figures, the reader should consider that historic market developments serve as a proxy to assess the risk of future developments. This concept has its limitations when market patterns change.

Second, the VaR results are definite figures, i.e., they do not exhibit any kind of volatility. However, most of the VaR models for credit portfolios are based on simulation and randomization techniques (especially if they have to deal with complex products) and thus have an intrinsic volatility. Whenever a new simulation run is started, a new and more or less different result will appear, simply because no randomization function is perfect. Furthermore, the most valuable figure is the shortfall—also called *fat tail* of the distribution—which fluctuates because it caters to unique or very seldom events. Each risk quant has to pay special attention to these fat tails and to make sure that the simulation technique is as robust as possible. When using normal distributions as an input parameter, the kurtosis is important. It is often observed that the assumed normal distribution does not capture the outliers of the factual market event. Again, the fat tails challenge the suitability of the risk model.

Third, special attention has to be given to structural changes in the pattern, e.g., caused by a change of legislation. In these cases the existing parameters of the well-known risk models will be immediately obsolete and need to be validated again.

Ways to Contain Risk

Outline of a Limit Management System

In a perfect world, only one limit—which is the risk—may be deemed enough. On an aggregated portfolio level, comprehensive assessment has to be given to the estimation of correlations and concentrations of risk. From a practical point of view, however, this one-dimensional management is not sufficient, predominantly because of the shortcomings of the VaR methodology detailed above. Thus, it is necessary to look at a broader way to contain risk, which is to set up a grid of various limits. The fundamental idea is that these limits should protect the bank from losses as a result of adverse and extreme incidents, which VaR models could not fully capture. The following example may help the reader to understand the concept.

A credit portfolio manager may invest solely in the emerging markets to the maximum possible amount until his VaR limit is reached. If a military coup occurred and currency control was imposed, all assets would have to be provisioned at once. To mitigate such an event, it is helpful to diversify investment and to restrict oneself because no portfolio model can cater to such singular events. These limits should protect the bank and their shareholders from rare and unique events. Another actual example is the liquidity crisis of securitized assets of 2007 and 2008, whereby billions of assets were provisioned, and German, US and UK banks nearly collapsed. Without going into too much detail, had they limited their exposure to the U.S. subprime market and securitized assets more restrictively, they would not have faced billions of provisions. Thus, "simple" exposure limits could effectively prevent banks from facing troubles or going bankrupt if limits are set appropriately, when compared to the bank's capital (or in other words, the risk capacity). Value-at-risk models are overstrained with singular events, and best practice is to limit the following risk drivers (see Table 11.1). To conclude, the purpose of these sublimits is to contain the operational risks in absolute terms because no credit risk portfolio model can be regarded as perfect in a business sense.

Limit structures can be understood as a multidimensional grid; up to three dimensions can be displayed as a cuboid (see Figure 11.4). Every individual transaction has to satisfy all dimensions simultaneously. Limits should be suggested and monitored by departments that are independent of the front office. Depending on the size of the bank, the board of directors or levels below should authorize at cost limits.

While limits are finite figures, the limit usage is subjective and will depend upon the methods used to compute exposures:

1. How are trades going to be valued? An easy but outdated way is to take the figures of each trade only. As soon as derivatives are part of a portfolio, the at-cost valuation is no longer a sensible method, and it is recommended to mark-to-market all positions. Doing so, will result in fewer discrepancies between the external accounting reporting [e.g., International Financial

T A B L E 11.1

Summary of potential limits

Limit	Risk Driver	Notes
VaR	Overall credit risk of the portfolio	This is deemed the most important limit to contain both credit and market risk. Whereas credit risk may only focus on the likelihood of defaults, market risk captures the whole range of market price volatility. The input parameters of specific credit risk models are, among others, the probability of default of all individual assets, exposure at default, recovery rate after default, correlations of assets, and the (statistical) confidence level.
Country limits	Transfer risk	Country limits should narrow investments in foreign countries, whereas the countries of the Organisation for Economic Co-operation and Development (OECD) and the European Union (EU) may not be regarded as foreign because of their established polities.
Currencies	Risk of currency devaluation	If the foreign exchange (FX) risk is not hedged, it is recommended to limit the exchange downside.
Tenor	Future developments are uncertain	Because of the nature of uncertainty, future risk can be contained by restricting the maximum tenure, e.g., to set them to five or seven years.
Products	Operational risk	Especially for complex products, it may be difficult to get a fair market price because tradable price may not be available and mark-to-model techniques may be potentially insufficient. Additionally, product limits may capture liquidity risk as well.
Industries	Correlation risks	Correlations of default risk are captured principally by the Credit VaR models; however, the assessment of correlations are difficult and somehow not flawless. Reliable data is often not available, thus the analyst has to take best guesses or approximate figures, e.g., from the stock market. Correlations might not be very stable over the time, especially in the light of structural changes in economies.
Rating buckets	Default respectively risk provisions	Although rating classes are one of the major inputs of Credit VaR models (they are proxies for default rates), an additional limitation should capture the model risks that are intrinsic to all Credit VaR approaches and other inaccuracies.
Exposure size buckets	Maximum loss	If a sizable asset defaulted, this would have a significant impact on the bank's operating profit. It makes a big difference if a loan of 10 million or 1 billion defaults. With regard to off-balance vehicles like structured investment vehicles (SIVs) or special-purpose vehicles (SPVs), the exposure size has a huge impact on liquidity as seen in the recent 2007 credit crisis.

F I G U R E   11.4

Graphical depiction of a three-dimensional limit system.

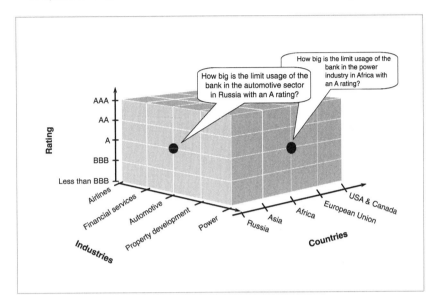

Reporting Standards (IFRS)] and the internal management reporting. There is also a downside because complex, leveraged, structured, or illiquid products cannot be measured on mark-to-market basis but require a mark-to-model approach. This model approach suffers from a number of well-known problems such as the setting of certain parameters, inaccuracies of the model itself, and the lack of tradable market opportunities at the calculated price. Embedded options (e.g., convertibles, callable bonds) have to be considered as well. To be on the safe side, "haircuts" (deductions of the value) are a reasonable way to make sure the calculated price is one at which the trade might be executable.

2. Should collaterals and hedges be recognized? Fundamentally such a question has to be answered yes; however, certain minimum requirements have to be satisfied:

   a. Collateral should be liquid and tradable on recognized markets.

   b. Hedges should be traded with a reputable, investment grade counterpart.

   c. Due to the fact that collateral and hedges are susceptible to mark-to-market movements, the remaining (operational) risk can be contained by additional haircuts that reduce the creditable amount.

    Alternatively, collateral and hedges can replace the original obligor if his or her creditworthiness is below the substituted one. The final limit usage is calculated by taking the actual market value and reducing this amount by recognizable collateral and hedge positions.

Stress Tests

Beyond the econometrical risk measurement, stress tests belong to the sound practices of risk control, and it is mainly risk control's task to define adverse market scenarios as well as to test how the portfolios of the bank might behave in these circumstances. The purpose is to capture extreme, unlikely, and rare events, which, if they occurred, would have a significant impact on the bank's going concern.

    Typically, the portfolio manager has to define extreme scenarios that should not prejudice any kind of market movements. As markets are diverse, the task is to define a set of scenarios to which the portfolio (and subsequently the bank) might be exposed. Each scenario should cover all markets, i.e., the stress test should focus not only on a single distress but on several at the same time. As banks may be exposed not only to declining market values but also to soaring markets, both sides have to be covered.

    The following scenarios in Table 11.2 are some examples to give the reader a better understanding. Although some of the them do not have a direct impact on credit portfolios—like "shortage of commodities"—they are still worth considering because there might be side effects that may then have an impact on credit. With regard to commodities, it might boost inflation and thus have an effect on interest rates. To benefit from these indirect implications, the stress test model has to capture this mechanism.

    The bank has to compute the effect of each of these scenarios on the profit and loss result, and its main purpose is to understand and get insight into the biggest risk drivers of the bank. Special attention should be given to those results that have a significant impact on the operating profit and going concern of the bank. If risks are not well balanced, then the exposure has to be limited. It is up to the bank to define suitable scenarios and the range of test for a given strategy. This can be seen as somehow

T A B L E   11.2

Examples of potential stress test scenarios

Historical simulations	• Data similar to the stock market crash in 1974 to 1987
	• Data similar to the oil crisis in 1979
	• Asian crisis (Baht devaluation) 1997
Fictitious scenarios (a) One dimension	• Decline of the U.S. dollar (±25%)
	• Soar of U.S. dollar volatility (+25%)
	• Interest rate rise/decline by 200 bps (10 y)
	• Inverse yield curve
	• Decline hedge funds value by 25%
	• European, U.S., and Asian stock markets soar and/or decline by ±25%
	• Correlations of stock markets and fixed income markets change by ±25%
(b) Multiple dimension	• Strategy "fear of inflation": Yield curve steepens by 100 bps, U.S. dollar gains plus 25%, stock markets drop by 20%, and volatility doubles.
	• Strategy "shortage of commodities": Oil price doubles, precious metals soar by 50%, stock markets in the United States and in Europe drop by 30% but remain stable in China and Asia.
Worst case	• All market data move in the "wrong" direction by 20%, i.e., causing losses in all positions.
	• If worse comes to the worst, this scenario can be topped by assuming that volatilities and correlations change adversely too.

subjective, but it serves the main aim to get greater transparency of the exposure. It may not be relevant whether, say, the yield curve steepens by 100 or 125 bp; its main purpose is to identify the main risk drivers. If the yield curve does not have a big impact, then the actual amount of change— be it 100 or 125 bp—can be neglected. If, however, it has a significant impact, then further tests should be carried out, and the exposure should be limited sensibly.

The credit crunch and subsequent liquidity crisis of 2007/2008 is a classical example to justify the need for a stress test—it has not happened in recent times and was widely ignored or seen as farfetched. Stress tests are the means to consider rare or unusual events.

CONCLUSION

Risk management is regarded as a holistic approach. While it is common practice to assess the risk of a portfolio by a VaR technique, portfolio management has to fit in a broader approach: Each portfolio contributes a certain portion of risk to the bank's overall exposure, which has to be limited by the bank's risk capacity. This capacity is governed by the need to keep the bank as a going concern and liquid. From a practical managerial point of view, VaR figures are not flawless and should not be used as the only measure but need to be supported by stress tests and robust, easy-to-implement limits for all risk drivers; which means a grid of limits has to be established. The major aim is to contain both known and unforeseeable risks by limiting exposure to any given scenario across the portfolio and the organization. This helps to establish a well-diversified set of portfolios that make the bank less sensitive to external shocks of any kind. For the going concern it does not really matter if the precision of VaR models is set to the "fifth digit after the decimal point," but it must be able to identify and capture all major risk drivers in a timely and comprehensive manner.

REFERENCES

Bielecki, R. and Rutkowski, M. (2002) *Credit Risk: Modeling, Valuation, and Hedging.* Berlin: Springer Finance.

Bluhm, C., Overbeck, L., and Wagner, C. (2003) *An introduction to Credit Risk Modeling.* Boca Raton, London, New York: Chapman & Hall.

Lando, D. (2004) *Credit Risk Modeling. Theory and Applications.* Princeton Series in Finance, Princeton University Press: Princeton (New Jersey).

Gordy, M.B. (2000): A Comparative Anatomy of Credit Risk Models. *Journal of Banking and Finance*, 24: 119 ff.

CHAPTER 12

How a Revolution in the Loan Sale Process Transformed the Secondary Market and Portfolio Management

J. Kingsley Greenland II and William F. Looney

ABSTRACT

In the past five years, a liquid secondary market for commercial debt has emerged and profoundly remade the management of commercial loan portfolios. The ability to buy and sell loans efficiently and cost effectively in both the United States and Europe has enabled portfolio lenders to improve diversification and risk management, free up capital for additional loans, and eliminate problem assets before they distract bankers from revenue-generating pursuits. Financial institutions that regularly leverage the secondary market to trade commercial debt continue to be rewarded with higher share prices and praise from regulators concerned about unhealthy concentrations of loans, particularly in commercial real estate. The liquidity in this global secondary market is accelerating because of technological and business process innovation, as well as the growing realization that portfolio diversification has strategic benefits as the global banking industry continues to consolidate.

INTRODUCTION

Over the past five years, a revolution has taken place in the way financial institutions manage their loan portfolios. A secondary market powered by technology and online marketplaces have created constant liquidity for whole loans or pools of loans that were once illiquid. Online marketplaces for debt have brought a new era of efficiency and transparency to the loan sale process, and as a result, the market is broader and deeper than ever before. Today, buyers and sellers from around the globe can not only bid on assets they never had access to previously, but also perform due diligence online at a fraction of the time and expense. The aggregation of loan sale data at online marketplaces has spawned a new generation of more accurate valuation models, which has brought more certainty to the challenging process of managing portfolios.

This historic transformation of the loan sale process has meant strategic and tactical benefits for all marketplace participants. For troubled institutions, the rapid elimination of problem debt has enabled some to survive when they couldn't before. For acquiring banks in particular, the knowledge that loans can be sold into a liquid market creates more opportunity to buy institutions whose shares are depressed due to poorly performing loan portfolios. For institutions that are performing well, the ability to efficiently sell debt has improved the bottom line by allowing them to proactively manage problems and risk.

From a diversification and risk management perspective, loan sales have allowed institutions to engage in active portfolio management, the discipline of properly optimizing portfolio performance by diversifying and avoiding over concentrations. Active portfolio management facilitates more systematic and strategic portfolio management that is regularly cheered by regulators and rewarded by shareholders. For all these reasons, the technology-driven secondary market represents a quantum leap forward in loan portfolio management. This chapter is designed to shed light on the loan sale transaction at online marketplaces and explore each step of the process in detail. To clear up any lingering questions, we will unravel some of the common misconceptions about online sales versus offline sales. Our objective is to provide portfolio managers and loan professionals with the information necessary to leverage the global loan marketplace, to improve performance, and to take advantage of strategic options.

EVOLUTION OF THE SECONDARY WHOLE LOAN MARKET

Before examining the impact of technology on the secondary whole loan market, it is important to define today's loan sale marketplace. Loans sold at online marketplaces are mostly whole loans that are not part of securitizations or syndications. The loans often have complex structures and are typically held by the originating institution. Commercial real estate (CRE), commercial and industrial (C&I) loans, residential loans, and consumer loans are the most common type of whole loans sold in online marketplaces. Technology-savvy institutions in the United States pioneered the practice of selling loans online; however, European institutions now account for a rapidly growing share of online loan sales. In both markets, large institutions were the first to sell loans online, but as fixed costs dropped, small- and mid-tier institutions entered the fray.

BUYERS: SMART, SAVVY, AND GLOBAL

To understand the dynamics of today's global loan marketplace, it is instructive to start on the buy side. The primary buyers of whole loans are institutional investors. These include commercial banks of all sizes, investment banks, and insurance companies, as well as structured investment vehicles like collateralized loan obligations (CLOs) and collateralized debt obligations (CDOs). Pension funds, hedge funds, and opportunity funds that focus on specific kinds of debt instruments are also buyers. High net worth individuals deemed as accredited investors are also buyers, although they represent a fraction of the market.

Buyers of whole loans fall into three distinct categories: Those interested in performing debt, those interested in subperforming debt, and those interested in nonperforming debt. The profile of each investor is different, although sub- and nonperforming investors tend to have more in common than investors buying performing loans. Investors in performing loans are driven mainly by yield considerations — what is the asset expected to yield now and in the future? Banks, insurance companies, and pension funds are the most frequent buyers of performing debt because of their conservative risk profile. These institutions tend to buy all types of performing loans across all market sectors. In purchasing performing debt, banks and insurance companies act much like traditional bond investors seeking a dependable income stream over time. In other words, these institutions are executing a classic buy-and-hold strategy. Because the loans are performing as agreed upon, there isn't anything further the purchaser can do to enhance their value.

By comparison, investors in sub- or nonperforming loans are seeking to increase the value of the loan over time and are less interested in the current yield. As a result, they tend to focus more narrowly, rather than buying across the entire marketplace. For example, investors experienced in CRE loans in the office sector may work with the borrower to raise rents or invest in building improvements. Buyers of a C&I loan from a middle market company may reposition the company or merge it, and the options are limited only by the buyer's imagination and capabilities. The common denominator is that investors are intending to add value by applying some special expertise.

SELLERS: ORIGINATORS OF ALL SIZES JOIN IN

The primary sellers of loans are financial institutions—commercial banks, investment banks, insurance companies, and finance companies. Larger institutions tend to originate more loans and are often more frequent sellers. However, many smaller institutions now sell loans regularly because technology has dramatically reduced the cost of the sale. Prior to the Internet, the minimum loan amount was approximately $50 million due to the fixed transaction costs, while the efficiencies of online marketplaces now allow for loan sales as small as $1 million.

In addition to private-sector financial institutions, government entities are also frequent loan sellers. The Federal Deposit Insurance Corporation (FDIC), in conjunction with the Resolution Trust Corporation (RTC), sold billions in loans acquired from failed thrifts and savings-and-loan associations in the 1990s. Institutions typically sell for three reasons: to actively manage their portfolio for proper diversification, to dispose of sub- and nonperforming loans, and to place sector bets based on an institution's outlook or appetite for a particular asset type. At any one time, institutions may be executing all three strategies.

Active Portfolio Management

Institutions actively manage their portfolios to achieve the proper diversification of performing assets. Much like equity investors rotating individual stocks for optimal diversification, active portfolio management allows institutions to achieve the right balance in their portfolio. Proper portfolio strategy dictates that institutions avoid being over weighted in any particular asset class or in any geographic region, length of maturity, or other investment criteria. Active portfolio management is one of the surest ways to achieve the optimal mix. Active portfolio management is increasingly essential to acquisition planning and to maintain competitiveness. After a merger or acquisition, institutions will frequently wind up with loans they would have never originated. Disposing of loans quickly eliminates portfolio mismatches. Likewise, active portfolio management lowers the likelihood that institutions will have to decline business from valuable customers or prospects because they have run into a lending limit for a particular type of loan.

Sector Bets

Institutions often sell loans to increase their concentration in a particular sector. Just as investors make judgments about future opportunities in the marketplace, institutions do the same about their portfolio exposure. By freeing up capital through a loan sale, institutions can originate more loans that support their current investment thesis. Increasingly, sector bets are being executed not only by originating loans, but also by purchasing seasoned performing loans in the secondary market. Both portfolio strategies complement each other, and many institutions implement them concurrently.

Sales for Performance Issues

Sales of sub- and nonperforming debt represent about half of the debt sold in the secondary marketplace, although they generate a disproportionate amount of attention. The reason is simple: Publicly announcing the sale of poorly performing loans frequently results in better performance for the selling institution and a higher stock price. Selling troubled loans is an increasingly common strategy because it is less onerous than managing the loan back to profitability. Because of greater liquidity due to the secondary market, institutions would rather sell than invest in time-consuming loan workouts. Workouts prolong problems and create a drag on performance. Loan sales can expedite a turnaround and create strategic opportunities unavailable to institutions burdened with a weak portfolio.

HOW BUYERS AND SELLERS ENGAGE ONLINE

Buyers and sellers have traditionally come together offline through investment banks or offline brokers. That process has largely remained the same over time: The agent for the seller finds prospective buyers through his referral network. Since the emergence of online marketplaces, that process has fundamentally changed for the better. The following section offers a step-by-step description outlining the role of the seller, the buyer, and the underwriter acting as the seller's agent at an online marketplace.

Initial Pricing

The loan sale process begins with a preliminary pricing analysis led by a senior loan sale professional that sets the seller's expectations by providing a snapshot of current market conditions. The price analysis takes into account a wide range of quantitative and qualitative factors, such as the dependability of the financial stream, quality of collateral, loan-to-value ratio, and debt service coverage, among others. The relevant financial factors considered include interest rate trends, yield and whether it is a fixed or floating instrument, and prepayment protection. Complementing this empirical data is the qualitative analysis gathered from a loan officer's narrative accompanying a loan and/or the written summaries provided periodically to management. As a general rule, the pricing process can take as little as a day for simpler loans, such as a pool of residential real estate loans, or it can take several days or even a week for more complicated loans, such as a CRE transaction. The reason is that residential transactions involve analysis of fewer variables than a CRE loan sale.

In setting the loan pricing, advisors have traditionally relied on their market savvy and experience, but online marketplaces have improved the art of loan pricing by aggregating data that can be used to develop more accurate valuation models. Loan sale advisers now analyze data from thousands of transactions before arriving at a starting price for a loan. Previously, it was difficult to obtain market comparables because sales data were scattered across the industry and were not stored in an easily usable or accessible format.

Portfolio Underwriting

Once a seller agrees to proceed after a pricing review, the next step is drafting the underwriting documents used to market the loan. The two-page to seven-page underwriting document summarizes all of the critical information. The synopsis is intended to give buyers enough information to quickly ascertain the asset's general value and decide if they should bid. Typically, the document doesn't include the price, which is to be decided later by bidders in the open market. Underwriting documents have become standardized into readily identifiable sections that allow buyers to find the same information in the same places for each transaction. The standardization of offering documents is one of the key reasons for greater liquidity in the secondary market. Standardization also reduces dead deal time and the associated costs.

Marketing Campaign

After the underwriting circular is prepared and due diligence information and transfer documents are completed, the underwriter kicks off the marketing program. To attract the greatest number of buyers, investors are contacted by phone, are met in face-to-face meetings, and receive e-mail and regular mail. The transactions are frequently advertised in leading trade journals, such as *American Banker* in the United States. Dedicated sales people contact investors who have expressed interest or would be ideal buyers for a specific loan type. At online marketplaces, loan sale advisors can reach prospective buyers very efficiently. When investors register online to participate in a sale, they will indicate the exact kinds of loans they want to buy in the future. Targeted, efficient marketing expands the pool of qualified investors; thus, the flexibility at an online marketplace also allows many individuals from the same institution to register.

Online Due Diligence

While underwriting documents are being prepared, a seller works closely with the underwriter to convert hundreds or even thousands of pages of loan documents into digital files. These documents, usually provided to an underwriter in hard copy or in various electronic formats, include original loan documents, collateral appraisals, operating statements, court proceedings, or other information that supports the original underwriting process. Once digitized, these documents are supplemented with search and spreadsheet capabilities, so information can be easily downloaded and analyzed. Underwriters also provide financial models to enable buyers to carefully analyze the revenue stream.

Preparation of Transfer Documents

To streamline the process, a selling institution uses a standardized purchase and sale agreement provided by the underwriter. The seller's consent to use this neutral, standardized document is another important factor in creating liquidity because it eliminates friction and facilitates more transactions. Once the seller has agreed to conduct a sale, transfer documents are posted online to allow a buyer's legal counsel to review the document ahead of time. By making documents available in advance, buyers and sellers minimize the possibility of litigation and help ensure that the transaction proceeds in a fair and straightforward manner.

Handling Investor Inquiries

As the marketing campaign continues, investors typically have some questions about a loan for sale. An account manager is assigned to a seller from start to finish of the transaction to answer many of those questions. At online marketplaces, the process of handling those inquiries is streamlined because information about the loans for sale is more accessible and can be communicated with greater ease electronically. By handling investor inquiries smoothly, online marketplaces remove another obstacle to the sale and motivate institutions to consider a loan sale when they otherwise wouldn't.

Competitive Bidding

Bids are submitted by investors through an online sealed bid or an electronic English auction ("e-cry") format. Typically, the seller and underwriter work closely to determine the format that will maximize the proceeds of the sale. That decision is based on recent market transactions and the underwriter's understanding of various bidding formats. The most common types of auctions are executed by a sealed bid, which can be done online, or by a live online auction. In the sealed bid, buyers generally give their best bid first and aren't allowed to increase it. In an open, e-cry auction, investors can increase their bid in response to other offers they are seeing in real time on their computer screen. Generally, quality performing loans will generate higher proceeds under an e-cry format, while underperforming loans tend to generate higher proceeds in a sealed-bid format.

Bid Award

Successful buyers are selected when bidding ends. In most cases a loan will be sold to the highest bidder, and in rare instances, a seller may choose another buyer if there is a question about the buyer's ability to close the transaction. With a live English auction, bidders observe the winning price at the conclusion of the session. In a sealed bid, the underwriter notifies the buyer shortly after the bid deadline.

Closing

As soon as the seller accepts the winning bids, the buyer must post a large, nonrefundable deposit, and closing usually occurs within five business days. Before standardized documents were incorporated into the online sale process, a closing normally took 40 to 50 days. At online marketplaces, it's now common to complete all the legal paperwork and close in five days. All loan sale participants at online marketplaces must agree up front to forgo individually negotiated documents and use the standardized templates.

The Benefits of Electronic Trading

The loan sale process outlined in the preceding pages represents a fundamental improvement from the traditional way loan sales have been executed. The

Internet, combined with the availability of low-cost technology worldwide, has transformed a largely manual, paper-intensive exercise into a streamlined process conducted electronically. At the same time, the process remains guided by human judgment and expertise. Technology, coupled with the experience of loan sale professionals, delivers compelling benefits. Improved portfolio diagnostics, faster due diligence, superior price execution, and expedited closes enable more transactions to occur. Online marketplaces also bring a new measure of transparency, security, and audit reporting to the loan sale process. Sellers and buyers now have a clear window into the transaction, which leads to greater accountability. The net effect is that technology and human expertise translate into better results for buyers and sellers.

BETTER PORTFOLIO DIAGNOSTICS

One of biggest benefits of online marketplaces is their positive impact in deciding whether to sell a loan in the first place. Today, many institutions must still make critical portfolio decisions based on models with anecdotal or outdated information. Because online marketplaces aggregate trade data each day, institutions are using that intelligence to make much better judgments about individual loans or entire portfolios. Rather than rely on internally generated valuation models, online marketplaces serve as a central repository of market data that enables sellers to value assets based on recent comparable sales. With improved portfolio diagnostics, the decision to sell or hold becomes clear and the guesswork is gone. Shareholders and regulators increasingly value an objective, third-party assessment because it leads to more effective risk management, a stronger balance sheet, and ultimately greater profitability.

Faster, Better Online Due Diligence

The due diligence process has also been transformed by technology and online marketplaces. Due diligence has typically been the most difficult part of the loan sale because buyers must wade through thousands of documents. The process often requires extensive travel at significant expense in out-of-pocket costs and lost management time. At online marketplaces, due diligence is done electronically and loan documents that are warehoused in war rooms are placed online. Technology built into online platforms allows investors to search and analyze documents, instead of making on-site visits to search boxes of loan documents. As a result, prospective investors can complete all of these tasks from the comfort of their own office. This efficiency enables investors to analyze a dozen or more deals in the time it formerly took to do one. Equally important, investors eliminate the sunk costs and lost management time in bids that are not accepted or could not be made for a variety of reasons.

Small Loan Sales Grow

The ability to sell small loans is another substantial benefit of online marketplaces. Lower transaction costs at online marketplaces allow smaller loans to be sold. Institutions also have the flexibility to break up large loans into small pieces at online marketplaces, and that allows investors to buy exactly what they want. In the past, investors often wound up with loans they didn't want but were forced to buy because they were bundled. Smaller loan amounts have also broadened the universe of buyers, and that has translated into more liquidity. When large loan sales were the only possibility, only institutions with large balance sheets and resources could buy loans. With face amounts regularly under $10 million, community and independent banks have now become active buyers. These institutions frequently bid on loans in their local area, where they have a built-in advantage over regional or national buyers because they understand the local market.

Superior Trade Execution

Of all the benefits of electronic trading, superior trade execution is the most important. The reason is that the bidding process at online marketplaces maximizes the sale price for sellers. In contrast to the traditional loan sale process managed by investment bankers and brokers, online marketplaces typically generate more bids per sale because investors can review more opportunities at lower expense. In addition, technology can also facilitate real-time bidding, as in the case of live English auctions. Dynamic bidding further maximizes the seller's proceeds, something not possible in a sealed-bid format. Superior price execution is also the result of transparency. At online marketplaces, the transaction is completely open, and all parties have all the information in front of them. There are no hidden brokerage fees that could mask the true sale price. Transparency allows buyers to determine fair market value with absolute certainty.

COMPARING THE TWO APPROACHES

While online marketplaces account for a growing share of loan sales, the majority of transactions are still executed by investment banks and brokers. For sellers, the M&A option is the most familiar, although there are significant drawbacks with that approach—particularly in maximizing price. The M&A approach favored by investment banks and offline brokers is largely opaque. Bids are usually sealed, and there is no ability for investors to make a counteroffer to match a competitor's bid. Thus, price execution can vary widely. The sale price is often distorted with back-end commissions not visible to buyers. The result is that only the largest loan sales can be executed.

Online loan marketplaces deliver transparency, efficiency, and liquidity not possible in offline, bilateral sales. Loans sold at online marketplaces are more accessible to buyers, and the pool of potential investors is global. The playing field is leveled. Investors big and small must abide by the same rules and have access to the same information. Although a high degree of expertise and hands-on service is delivered by loan sale professionals at online marketplaces and by investment banks and brokers, the key difference is the way the sale is bid and closed. The following section is designed to clear up common misperceptions about online marketplaces compared to the investment banking approach.

Misconception No. 1: A Bilateral Sale Leads to Better Prices

A bilateral sale—a transaction directly between two parties—may appear to be a fast, relatively confidential and profitable way to sell loans. In reality, sellers almost always realize higher proceeds on better terms through sales at online marketplaces. The reason is that selling institutions frequently overestimate the value of the bilateral approach in three ways: First, sellers are convinced that the buyers are obvious and that they will show interest. Second, sellers believe the bids among investors will be largely similar. Third, sellers are highly confident they can negotiate favorable terms in the loan sale agreement.

For large loan sales, the buyers may be obvious because there are fewer of them, but they do not have unlimited capacity to purchase. While sellers instinctively look to recent buyers as their next buyers, these investors are often precluded from bidding because they need to properly manage recently acquired assets to realize the expected return on investment. Moreover, as the offering amounts fall below $200 million, the pool of buyers expands almost exponentially. The law of large numbers makes it impossible to keep tabs on so many potential buyers unless the seller is constantly in the market and deploying sophisticated technology. With 10,000 community and independent banks in the United States alone—all of whom may be interested in buying a small loan—how can a seller anticipate where the high bid will materialize?

In terms of price, bilateral sales often result in inferior terms, particularly with the sale of nonperforming assets. Bids for nonperforming loans tend to have a wide standard deviation due to the fact that investor valuation assumptions often vary substantially to reflect the differing strategic objectives of the sellers. For example, one investor may purchase a subperforming loan with the intention of investing $10 million in the underlying property and then selling it in six months. In contrast, another investor may plan on simply cutting costs and selling the property in 18 months. These different strategies will yield a different set of assumptions and bids.

With regard to negotiating a better deal, buyers of nonperforming assets are often more experienced and skillful than banks in negotiating the asset sale agreement. Buyers of nonperforming assets are experts at this task because it is their primary focus. Most banks execute a nonperforming loan sale agreement infrequently. More often that not, the initial bid has the best terms the seller will likely see in a bilateral transaction. After that, the terms will deteriorate, as the buyer allows time to lapse to position for more favorable terms. In the following negotiations, the buyer most often winds up the winner.

Misconception No. 2: The Value of the Seller's Assessment

Another common misperception is that buyers want to review the seller's assessment of the loan's value. Investors do want to see the assessment, but not for the reasons most sellers think. Buyers use that assessment to spot holes in the underlying assumptions to negotiate more attractive terms.

Many sellers are wrongly convinced that the seller's analysis is critical to the sale because it is the foundation of the sales strategy by investment banks and brokers. This M&A approach is based on a significant effort to build the case for the valuation of the loan. Sellers mistakenly believe that the buyer will be persuaded to accept the bank's framework as the basis for its bid. Most investors simply don't value it, and sellers often incur an unnecessary expense that could just as well hurt their cause.

Misconception No. 3: Less Loan Information Is Better

Some sellers have been coached to believe that if the seller omits or withholds certain data, the bids will be higher. In reality, if an investor sees that a loan file has been purged of unflattering information, they will react negatively. Sales lacking complete information will most certainly be lower. Moreover, the seller's judgment as to what constitutes good due diligence information can often be wrong. For example, a combative series of correspondence with the borrower might indicate litigious inclinations. On the other hand, it could also demonstrate that the borrower is open to dialogue and persuade an investor to believe that a real opportunity exists.

Aside from the fallacy that less information will result in higher prices, more information—full disclosure—is the best way to eliminate the possibility of legal action. Because many of today's investors spend much of their time reviewing loan files, they know or can sense when materials are incomplete.

CONCLUSION: IT'S A NEW DAY FOR PORTFOLIO MANAGERS

Technology and electronic trading have been responsible for the accelerating liquidity in the marketplace. These process improvements represent a breakthrough for sellers of all sizes around the world because they open up a world of new options. The liquidity accessible at online marketplaces improves portfolio management, lowers risk, and provides the flexibility to execute a more far-reaching acquisition strategy.

CHAPTER 13

What Drives the Arrangement Timetable of Bank Loan Syndication?[1]

Christophe J. Godlewski

ABSTRACT

We investigate the influence of loan and syndicate characteristics as well as banking environment factors on the arrangement timetable of global bank loan syndications. Employing accelerated failure time models, we find that loan, syndicate, legal environment, and information disclosure characteristics that mitigate agency problems related to syndication reduce the arrangement timetable. Among the banking environment factors, information disclosure, which reduces moral hazard due to informational frictions between syndicate members, appears to be the most important driver of a faster deal arrangement timetable, while better creditor rights protection increases the arrangement timetable, consistently with recontracting risk issues.

---

[1] I thank Guillaume Horny for valuable advice regarding the econometric specification and Laurent Weill for his remarks and suggestions. The usual disclaimer applies.

INTRODUCTION

The global syndicated lending market has reached US$2.8 trillion and 6,580 issues in the third quarter of 2006.[2] Currently, syndicated loans are an important source of external finance for financial and nonfinancial companies, comparable to bond markets and often larger than equity markets. For instance, they represent 51 percent of total corporate financing in the United States.

Briefly, a syndicated loan is a loan granted jointly and under common terms by a group of banks to a borrower. Usually, the borrower mandates a lead bank (the arranger) to arrange the syndication. These two agents negotiate the terms of the loan agreement. The arranger then finds participant banks that grant a share of the loan, receiving compensation in terms of fees and/or spread for this activity. Consequently, every syndicate member has a separate claim on the debtor within a single loan agreement.

In syndication, apart from several borrower-related advantages[3] and lender-related advantages,[4] the deal arrangement timetable is of special interest in this chapter. Factors that can speed up the arrangement timetable of a loan syndication process allow obtaining funds more quickly. These factors are of primary interest for the borrower, who is the primary initiator and beneficent of the syndication. In a rapidly evolving economic and financial reality, fast and efficient funding arrangement provides a competitive advantage allowing the exploitation of existing investment opportunities.[5] Arrangers are also concerned by the arrangement timetable of a syndication, as quick and efficient deal arrangement and activation signals

---

[2] Syndicated Loans Review, Thomson Financial (2006).

[3] Borrower-related advantages include the ability to arrange cross-border transactions, the restriction of negotiation with one bank (the arranger), uniform terms and conditions, more competitive pricing resulting in lower spreads, lower fees compared to bond issues, more flexible funding structure, larger amount compared to public finance, and bilateral relationships with participants (Allen, 1990; Altunbas and Gadanecz, 2004).

[4] Syndication allows diversifying loan portfolios and thus avoiding excessive single-name exposure in compliance with the regulatory limits while maintaining a relationship with the borrower. It helps to exploit comparative advantages of syndicate members in terms of financing and eventually in terms of information sharing (Song, 2004). Syndication also allows one to diversify income sources through the collection of fees, as well as to tackle lack of origination capability and origination costs.

[5] Syndicated loan announcement has a positive impact on borrower's wealth through a positive stock market response [see Preece and Mullineax, (1996)].

a more efficient and reputable arranger and thus enhances the probability of further syndications and increases market presence. Furthermore, as the credit approvals remain an important piece of the arrangement timetable, efficient credit risk management decisions by the syndicate members are of primary concern during the timetable. Other syndicate participants are also concerned about arrangement timetable as a faster syndication process allows benefiting more quickly from the compensation related to funding a tranche of the deal as well as from potential bilateral relationships with the borrower. Finally, financial regulators can also gain valuable information from the knowledge of individual-and country-level characteristics which influence the arrangement timetable of loan syndication in order to set up appropriate regulatory environment for the development of syndicated lending.

Loan syndication has several drawbacks as it generates potential agency problems due to informational frictions between the senior (arrangers) and the junior (participants) members of the syndicate. These agency problems may influence the arrangement timetable of the syndication process. Following Diamond (1984), Gorton and Pennachi (1995), and Holmstrom and Tirole (1997), borrower monitoring by multiple creditors may lead to cost inefficiency and free riding. Hence, creditors usually delegate monitoring to one financial intermediary, the arranger in a syndicated loan context. As the monitoring effort is unobservable, the syndicate faces a moral hazard problem. Furthermore, the latter is exacerbated by the fact that all participating banks have fewer incentives for monitoring than one bank granting the full loan. Additionally, the arranger collects private information through due diligence or through a previous lending relationship. Therefore, he plays the role of an informed lender on who rely the other less informed lenders. If the information cannot be credibly communicated to the participants or verified by them, an adverse selection problem arises as the arranger may syndicate loans with the less favorable information.

We empirically investigate the factors that influence the arrangement timetable of global loan syndication. Former literature on syndicated lending is relatively scarce and focuses on other issues: identifying the factors driving the decision to syndicate a loan (Dennis and Mullineaux, 2000; Altunbas et al., 2005; Godlewski and Weill, 2008), the structure and composition of a syndicate (Lee and Mullineaux, 2004; Song, 2004; François and Missonnier-Piera, 2007; Godlewski, 2008), and the impact of a syndicated loan on borrower's wealth (Preece and Mullineaux, 1996).[6] We use a sample of more than 4,800 syndicated loans from 68 countries in the period 1992 to 2006. Employing accelerated failure time models, we test the influence of individual- and country-level characteristics, such as loan agreement and syndicate characteristics, as well as information disclosure and legal risk, on the arrangement timetable of bank loan syndications.

The rest of the chapter is organized as follows: The second section of this chapter presents the timetable of a loan syndication arrangement and discusses the determinants of the arrangement timetable. The third section presents the accelerated failure time model methodology and the data. Results are displayed and discussed in this chapter's fourth section. Our conclusions are presented in the final section.

DETERMINANTS OF LOAN SYNDICATION TIMETABLE ARRANGEMENT

Loan Syndication Process

Bank loan syndication can be considered as a sequential process, which can be separated into three main stages.[7] During the *pre-mandated stage*, the borrower solicits competitive offers to arrange and manage the syndication with one or more banks, usually its main banks.[8] From the proposals it receives, the borrower chooses one or more arrangers that are mandated to form a syndicate and negotiates a preliminary loan agreement.[9] The arranger is responsible for the negotiation of key loan terms

---

[6] The results show that the decision of loan syndication is notably related to the transparency of the borrower and the maturity of the loan. It appears also that poorly performing banks tend, on average, to be more involved in syndications. Syndicates are structured in order to enhance monitoring efforts and to facilitate renegotiation.

[7] See Esty (2001) for a detailed analysis of the syndication process.

[8] The borrower chooses an arranger taking into consideration placing power (ability to attract participants into the syndicated loan), structuring ability, and experience with arranging and pricing a deal.

[9] The syndication can be sole or joint mandated, the latter involving the participation of more than one lead bank. Such syndications are usually chosen by the borrower in order to maximize the likelihood of a successful syndication, in terms of loan characteristics, subscription, and duration of the syndication process.

with the borrower, the production of an *information memorandum*, the appointment of participants, and the structuring of the syndicate. The arranger's role is normally completed once the deal is signed, but it will often continue its involvement in the facility by acting as the agent who manages the syndicated loan. This role involves such tasks as funds administration, interests calculation, covenants enforcement, information sharing, and renegotiation management.

During the *post-mandated stage*, the borrower and the arranger execute a *commitment letter* that confirms key terms, duties, and compensation. This syndication stage also involves preparing a documentation package for the potential syndicate members, called an *information memorandum*, which is produced collectively by the borrower and the arranger. It usually contains information about borrower creditworthiness and loan terms. The initial set of targeted participants is strongly determined by the arranger. Their previous experiences with the borrower, the industry sector, or the geographic area are strong drivers for being chosen by the arranger to join the syndicate.[10] A *road show* is then organized to present and discuss the content of the information memorandum, as well as to announce closing fees and establish a timetable for commitments and closing. The participants can make comments and suggestions in order to influence the structure and the pricing of the loan. They are also free to make commitments on any tier offered. After the road show, the arranger makes formal invitations to potential participants. The final step is to determine the allocation given to each participant.

The third and last phase takes place after the *completion date* when the deal becomes active and the loan is operational, binding the borrower and the syndicate members by the debt contract. The latter sets out the terms and conditions of the loan: the amount, the purpose, the period, the rate of interest plus any fees, the periodicity, and the design of repayments and the presence of any security.

---

[10] However, Sufi (2007) shows that previous bank–borrower relationships play a more important role in the arranger's decision to invite a particular participant to the syndicate than previous arranger–participant bank relationships.

Determinants of Loan Syndication Arrangement Timetable

We investigate the factors that influence the arrangement timetable[11] of loan syndication—from the launching date until the completion day (when the deal becomes active)—measured in days for each syndicated loan.

Loan syndication is a complex process involving specific agency and recontracting risks. It involves several actors: the arranger, the participants, and the borrower. Agency problems can interfere with the arrangement timetable of the syndication process. First, the arranger possesses more information about the borrower either because of the private information collected through a previous lending relationship or through due diligence. This private information creates an adverse selection problem as the arranger may be inclined to syndicate loans from bad borrowers. However, such opportunistic behavior generates reputation risk for the arranger and affects negatively the success of future syndications (Pichler and Wilhelm, 2001). Second, the participant banks delegate some monitoring tasks to the arranger in charge of the loan documentation and notably of the enforcement of covenants and collateral. As the efforts of the lead bank are unobservable for participant banks, this results in a moral hazard problem, which is exacerbated with the opacity of the borrower. Nonetheless, the arranger has less incentive to monitor the borrower than if it were to lend the full amount of the loan (Pennachi, 1998). Another important issue is related to borrower's financial distress, which handling is more complicated in a syndicate setting because lenders must reach a collective decision. As shown by Bolton and Scharfstein (1996), the outcome of negotiations in debt restructuring are affected by the number of creditors, by the allocation of security among the set of creditors, and by the character of stringency of the voting rules among the creditors.

Hidden information problems should be positively related to the timetable. For instance, funding opaque borrowers is more complicated as such borrowers exacerbate adverse selection risk for the syndicate and thus increase the timetable. However, arranger's reputation risk can curb this effect as faster timetables can be considered as signals on arranger's

---

[11] For clarity purpose, we will use the term *timetable* in the rest of the chapter.

efficiency. Hidden action problems should also be positively related to the timetable as well as reorganization and recontracting risks. Here, borrower's risk profile, deal terms and structure, and arranger reputation play an important role, as well as country-level factors such as information disclosure and legal risk. Ultimately, arrangement timetable is affected by the factors that have an impact on the magnitude of agency problems related to syndicated loans. We discuss these factors in the following subsections.

Loan and Syndicate Characteristics

We first discuss the role of several loan and syndicate characteristics that might impact the timetable of the syndication process. Loan size (measured as the logarithm of the loan facility size) is expected to have a positive impact on the timetable as larger deals imply more risk, are more plagued by agency problems, and involve larger syndicates in terms of participants for diversification purposes. This makes the process more time consuming in terms of information memorandum and road show until the lenders reach a collective decision upon the deal terms as well as the final formation of the syndicate.

Lenders compensation also influences the timetable. The senior members earn an *up-front fee* (also called a *praecipium* or *arrangement fee*) in exchange for putting the deal together. The most junior syndicate members typically only earn the spread over the reference yield (such as six-month LIBOR). The level of the spread earned by these lenders is expected to positively influence the duration, as a higher spread signals a higher risk profile. As the up-front fee is a part of the arranger's compensation, we expect a negative coefficient for this variable parameter as larger fees provide incentives to the lead banks to complete the deal quicker.

Maturity of the loan is also considered, although whether it plays a positive or negative role is ambiguous. On the one hand, if we consider a positive relationship between maturity and credit risk (Flannery, 1986; Agbanzo et al., 1999), greater maturity should be associated with longer timetable. On the other hand, if credit risk and maturity are negatively related (Dennis et al., 2000), the timetable should be shorter.

The structure of a syndicate can be viewed as an organizational response to the agency problems (Pichler and Wilhelm, 2001; Lee and

Mullineaux, 2004; Sufi, 2007). Hence, the structure and size of the syndicate should also have an influence on the timetable. The size of the "core" of the syndicate is measured with the *number of arrangers* variable.[12] We expect the latter to have a negative influence on the timetable as a larger syndicate core implies better handling of agency problems related to monitoring of the borrower as several delegated monitors are present, reducing moral hazard related to private information, which is now spread among several arrangers (Lee and Mullineaux, 2004; Sufi, 2007). Furthermore, a larger number of arrangers are usually associated to a higher likelihood of successful syndication, of which an integral part is the speed of arranging the deal. Finally, it is likely that some of the arrangers will act as specialized agents during the syndication, thus contributing to a better handling of the process, through increased cost efficiency and reduced informational asymmetry (François and Missonier-Piera, 2007).

To account for the impact of publicly available information on the timetable of syndication process, we include in our regressions a dummy variable (*S&P Rating*) equal to one if a Standard and Poor's senior debt rating is available. We expect a negative coefficient since the existence of a rating mitigates the adverse selection problem due to hard information on borrower's creditworthiness, which reduces its opacity (Dennis and Mullineaux, 2000) and therefore allows one to reduce the timetable.

We take the presence of guarantors in the loan agreement into account, with a dummy variable equal to 1 if at least one guarantor exists (*Guarantor*).[13] A guarantor gives additional protection for the lenders, as it will honour a part or the totality of the claim in case of loan default, such as agency problems resulting from adverse selection are mitigated in line with the better information owned by the arranger on the borrower. If that holds, we should observe a negative coefficient associated with *Guarantor*. However, empirical literature on the role of collateral in loan contracts provides evidence in favor of the "observed-risk hypothesis," according to which banks would be able to sort borrowers from information they have

---

[12] The total size of the syndicate measured with the number of lenders is significantly correlated with the size of the loan; therefore, we do not include this variable in our estimations.

[13] Since information on the presence of collateral is strongly missing in the database, its inclusion in the estimations would have considerably reduced our sample.

on their quality (Berger and Udell, 1990; Jimenez and Saurina, 2004). As a consequence, banks would ask more protection schemes from riskier borrowers, and the presence of a guarantor may signal a riskier loan and, consequently, a loan plagued by greater agency problems, therefore increasing the timetable.

Additionally, we include a dummy variable (*Sponsors*) equal to one if the loan is sponsored. A sponsor is usually an individual capital investor who is involved in the project and might also act as an advisor and eventually as an additional monitor of the borrower. Its presence should reduce agency problems and therefore be negatively related to the timetable.

The presence of covenants, which aim at restricting the discretionary power of the borrower, providing the lender with an early warning signal and eventually triggering loan default, is taken into account with a dummy variable (*Covenants*) equal to 1 if the loan agreement includes financial covenants. The presence of covenants in a loan agreement is expected to reduce the risk of loan default (Rajan and Winton, 1995) and enhance the ability to monitor the borrower, thereby reducing the monitoring costs. Hence, covenants should be negatively related to the timetable, as they reduce potential agency problems from moral hazard behavior of lenders during the monitoring process. However, empirical evidence tends to show the opposite: a positive link between the presence of covenants and the probability of default of the borrower [e.g., Foster et al. (1998)]. This is in accordance with the observed-risk hypothesis, where riskier borrowers are offered more binding loan agreements, and implies a positive influence of covenants on the timetable.

We also take debt seniority into account through a dummy variable (*Senior Debt*) equal to 1 if the debt is senior. If it works as an effective protection for all the members of the syndicate, especially in case of borrower distress and reorganization, the timetable should be shorter. If the seniority does not apply equally to all syndicate members, then agency problems remain exacerbated, and the timetable might be longer. Furthermore, if the observed-risk hypothesis holds, the request for seniority may result from the perception of a higher risk of the borrower and therefore increases the timetable.

We also control for the type and the purpose of the loan through the inclusion of dummy variables. We include a dummy variable if the loan is a term loan and five dummy variables to describe the purpose of the loan, including corporate purposes, debt repayment, leveraged buyout, project finance, and working capital.[14] Finally, dummy variables taking benchmark rate (LIBOR and EURIBOR), facility issue year, geographical area, and industry into account are included in the estimations.

Country Characteristics

We now turn to the description of country-level variables that influence the duration. Qian and Strahan (2007) show that bank lending and financial contracts respond to legal and institutional environment, while Esty and Megginson (2003) show that institutional factors might influence the syndication process. Therefore, we also test the impact of legal environment, which affects both agency and recontracting risks, as well as of the level of information disclosure, which affects agency problems, on the timetable.

Our first category of country-level variables is related to information disclosure within the country of the borrower. Regulatory features enhancing information disclosure should have an influence on agency problems within the syndicate and should therefore allow for a shorter timetable. Indeed, as shown by Jappelli and Pagano (2002), information sharing among lenders reduces agency problems and lowers credit risk. We proxy the level of information disclosure through three variables. *Public Credit Registries* is a dummy variable equal to one if a public credit registry operates in the country of the borrower (Djankov et al., 2007).[15] This type of disclosure influences the level of informational frictions between the borrower and the syndicate. *Risk Management Disclosure* and *NPL[16] Definition* are two dummy variables equal to 1 if bank regulation requires public disclosure of risk management techniques and if the regulator provides a formal definition of nonperforming loans, respectively (Barth et al.,

---

[14] We do not provide variables for other purposes in our regressions since they represent less than 5 percent of our sample.

[15] The registries collect information on credit histories and current indebtedness of borrowers and share it with lenders. Public credit registries are databases managed by a government agency (usually the central bank).

[16] Non performing loans.

2005). That type of information disclosure influences the level of information asymmetry between the syndicate members. Public information regarding risk management of lenders is valuable for the arranger during the selection process of potential participants to the syndication as well as for further relationship within the syndication regarding risk diversification effects and borrower monitoring. A regulatory definition of NPL should also have a similar effect.

Syndicated loans agency problems and debt restructuring efficiency can be influenced by the country legal environment. Following a large body of research on law and finance pioneered by La Porta et al. (1997) and recently completed by Qian and Strahan (2007), legal institutions and legal risk can affect the way banks perform their governance function, mainly monitoring and recontracting, and in consequence the syndication process and its timetable. For instance, Esty and Megginson (2003) find that lenders structure the syndicates in order to facilitate recontracting in countries where creditors have strong and enforceable rights. Hence, our second category of country-level variables takes legal environment into account.

Two indicators for legal institutions are included in our estimations. Protection of creditor rights (*Creditor Rights*) and law enforcement (*Rule of Law*) are measured with the indexes provided by Djankov et al. (2007) and La Porta et al. (1997).[17] The expected sign of the coefficient for these both variables is ambiguous. If recontracting in countries where creditors have strong and enforceable rights is difficult, we can expect a positive coefficient for *Creditor Rights*. Similarly, if in high legal risk countries efficient reorganization of a distressed borrower is difficult, we can expect a negative influence of *Rule of Law* on the timetable. Apart from arguments regarding the handling of borrower default and recontracting, we can also consider the impact of legal risk on agency problems within the syndicate before the distress of the borrower. Indeed, as better legal protection of banks mitigates the moral hazard problem induced by syndication and decreases the need to monitor the borrower, we can also expect

---

[17] These indexes are scored on a scale from 0 to 4 and from 0 to 10, with a higher score indicating better protection and a better enforcement of the law, respectively.

the opposite coefficients. Finally, we also control for the legal origin into account with a dummy equal to 1 if legal origin is English.

METHODOLOGY AND DATA
Econometric Specification

Since the dependent variable is the timetable of a syndicated loan arrangement, the appropriate methodology is *survival analysis*, which is used to analyze data in which the time until the event is of interest, called an *event time*.

Survival data are generally described and modeled in terms of two related functions,[18] namely, the *survival* and *hazard* functions, respectively. Let T represent the duration of time that passes before the occurrence of a certain random event. Here T is the arrangement timetable of a loan syndication process. The *survival probability* $S(t)$ is the probability that the syndication process lasts from the time origin to a future time t and is defined as

$$S(t) = \Pr(T \geq t) = 1 - F(t) \tag{13.1}$$

where $F(t)$ is the cumulative distribution function for T.

The *hazard* is usually denoted by $h(t)$ and is the rate of transition of the syndication arrangement timetable to completion, given it has not been completed before. Put another way, it represents the *instantaneous event rate* for the syndication process that has already lasted to time t. The *hazard function* is defined formally by

$$h(t) = \lim_{\Delta t \to 0} \frac{\Pr(t \leq T < t + \Delta t \mid T \geq t)}{\Delta t} = \frac{f(t)}{S(t)} \tag{13.2}$$

where $f(t)$ is the probability density function of T evaluated at t. Since $\partial S(t)/\partial t = -f(t)/S(t)$, the hazard function can be expressed as

$$h(t) = -\frac{\delta \log S(t)}{\delta t} \tag{13.3}$$

the negative of the slope of the log of the survival function.

---

[18] See Kiefer (1988) and Harrell (2001) for a detailed description of survival analysis.

When estimating hazard functions, we need to assume a hazard function specification. The latter can be using parametric survival models known as *accelerated failure time* (AFT) models.[19] An AFT model specifies that the predictors act multiplicatively on the event time or additively on the log of event time. The effect of a predictor is to alter the rate at which the syndication proceeds along time axis (i.e., to accelerate the time to event). In this framework, the natural logarithm of the survival time In(t) is expressed as a linear function of the covariates X:

$$\ln(t) = a + X'\beta + \varepsilon \qquad (13.4)$$

where α is the intercept and ε is the error term with density $f(t)$. The distributional form of the error term determines the regression model.[20] The hazard function in an AFT model can be written as

$$h(t) = h_0 \exp(a + X'\beta)\left[1 + \exp(a + X'\beta)t\right] \qquad (13.5)$$

where h_0 is the baseline hazard rate. The hazard function is estimated using maximum likelihood methods.

Data

The sample of syndicated loans comes from the Dealscan database, provided by the Loan Pricing Corporation (LPC, Reuters). Data concerning information disclosure and legal risk come from La Porta et al. (1998), Barth et al. (2005), and Djankov et al. (2007).

The sample size is determined by information availability on the endogenous variable and exogenous variables used in the estimations. The timetable of the syndication process is measured in days since the launching date until the completion date, when the deal becomes active. We use only completed syndicated loans (no censoring), and we eliminate the

---

[19] Another possibility is to use the *proportional hazards* (PH) model, where $h(t) = h_0(t) \exp(X'\beta)$, given the predictors X and the baseline hazard rate $h_0(t)$. The latter can be left unspecified and estimated using the Cox's semiparametric partial likelihood (Cox, 1972; ibid., 1975) or take a specific parametric form such as Weibull or exponential distributions. Within this approach, the hazards are supposed to be proportional over time. This assumption is strongly rejected in our case (see the section Results and Discussion).

[20] With normal, logistic, extreme-value, and three-parameter gamma density functions, we obtain, respectively, lognormal, log-logistic, Weibull, and generalized gamma regressions.

outliers for the endogenous variable: deals with timetable greater than the
99-percentile, equal to 243 days (above eight months). We therefore have
a sample of 4,807 syndicated loans from 68 countries for the period
between 1992 and 2006. Mean duration of the syndication process equals
55.14 days (almost eight weeks) with a standard deviation of 37.02 days.

Table 13.1 lists descriptive statistics for endogenous and exogenous
variables computed on the dataset of loan facilities, with a distinction of
individual- (loan and syndicate) and country-level (information disclosure
and legal risk) determinants of the duration. Definitions of these variables
appear in Table 13.2, which provides a brief description and the sources of

T A B L E   13.1

Descriptive statistics

Variable	N	Mean	Standard Deviation	Minimum	Maximum
Descriptive Statistics for Individual-Level Variables					
Timetable	4,807	55.1367	37.0186	0	243
Loan size	4,807	375	1,100	0.9404	1,780
Maturity	4,807	53.8417	36.0990	1	324
Spread	4,807	110.6984	79.8330	2.12	910
Up-front fee	4,807	52.6986	43.6978	0	950
Number of arrangers	4,807	3.6004	3.6992	1	36
Guarantors	4,807	0.0957	0.2942	0	1
Covenants	4,807	0.1157	0.3199	0	1
Senior debt	4,807	0.2528	0.4346	0	1
Sponsors	4,807	0.0872	0.2821	0	1
S&P rating	4,807	0.0616	0.2404	0	1
Descriptive Statistics for Country-Level Variables					
Public credit registries	4,751	0.7116	0.4531	0	1
Public risk disclosure	3,814	0.4342	0.5175	0	1
NPL definition	3,978	0.5938	0.4912	0	1
Creditor rights	3,782	2.7343	0.9635	0	4
Rule of law	4,245	6.9136	2.0854	1.9	10

T A B L E   13.2

Variables definition

Variable	Description	Source
Individual-Level Characteristics		
Timetable	Duration of the syndication process arrangement timetable since the launching date until the completion date, measured in days	Dealscan
Number of arrangers	Number of arrangers in the syndicate	Dealscan
Loan size	Size of the loan in million U.S. dollars	Dealscan
Maturity	Maturity of the loan in months	Dealscan
Spread	Spread over the benchmark rate, measured in bps.	Dealscan
Up-front fee	Up-front fee, measured in bps	Dealscan
Guarantors	1 if there is at least one guarantor	Dealscan
Sponsors	1 if there is at least one sponsor	Dealscan
Covenants	1 if the loan agreement includes covenants	Dealscan
Senior debt	1 if debt is senior	Dealscan
Standard & Poor's rating	1 if the borrower has a senior debt rating by S&P	Dealscan
Country-Level Characteristics		
Public credit registries	1 if a public credit registry operates in the country	Djankov et al. (2007)
Public risk disclosure	1 if regulator impose to banks public disclosure of their risk management procedures	Barth et al. (2005)
NPL definition	1 if a formal definition of non-performing loans exists	Barth et al. (2005)
Creditor rights	An index aggregating four aspects of creditor rights. The index ranges from 0 (weak creditor rights) to 4 (strong creditor rights)	Djankov et al. (2007)
Rule of law	An index indicating the law enforcement. The index ranges from 0 (weak enforcement) to 10 (strong enforcement).	La Porta et al. (1998)

information for endogenous and exogenous variables, with a distinction of individual- (loan and syndicate) and country-level (information disclosure and legal risk) factors.

Syndicated loans come from six broad geographical areas: Africa, Asia and Pacific, Central and Eastern Europe, Latin America, Middle East, and Western Europe, which account, respectively, for 0.60, 80.03, 2.27, 0.37, 1.31, and 15.42 percent of the sample. The most important industry sectors are finance and insurance (32.51 percent), manufacturing (29.91 percent) and transport, communication and electricity (20.02 percent).

RESULTS AND DISCUSSION

As the proportional hazard assumption is strongly rejected with Schoenfeld residuals tests, we estimate an AFT model assuming a generalized gamma distribution, as the latter provides the lowest log likelihood, as well as Akayke and Schwarz information criterions.[21] Table 13.3 provides estimation results from the gamma model with different specifications [Equations (13.1) to (13.4)] in terms of covariates (individual- and country level characteristics). Definitions of variables appear in Table 13.2.

T A B L E   13.3

Estimations results

Covariate	Specification 1	Specification 2	Specification 3	Specification 4
Intercept	−24.3739*	−34.2232†	−81.5325‡	−81.5750‡
	(13.068)§	(13.207)	(15.842)	(15.408)
log(loan size)	0.0324‡	0.0309‡	0.0210*	0.0209*
	(0.011)	(0.002)	(0.013)	(0.012)
Spread	0.0014‡	0.0013‡	0.0008‡	0.0008‡
	(0.002)	(0.002)	(0.002)	(0.002)
Up-front fee	−0.0006†	−0.0006†	−0.0004	−0.0004
	(0.003)	(0.003)	(0.003)	(0.003)

---

[21] For all the estimations obtained with the gamma model that will follow, the magnitude and the significance of the covariates are very similar to those obtained with Weibull, log-logistic, and lognormal models. In order to not overload the chapter, we do not provide these results, but they are available from the author upon request.

Maturity	0.0020‡	0.0020‡	0.0019‡	0.0018‡
	(0.003)	(0.003)	(0.004)	(0.003)
Number of arrangers	−0.0113‡	−0.0109†	−0.0134‡	−0.0123‡
	(0.003)	(0.003)	(0.004)	(0.004)
Guarantors	−0.052	−0.0486	−0.0543	−0.0431
	(0.033)	(0.033)	(0.037)	(0.036)
Sponsors	−0.0575	−0.0583	−0.0761*	−0.0409
	(0.037)	(0.037)	(0.041)	(0.040)
Covenants	0.0760†	0.0763†	−0.0029	0.0170
	(0.038)	(0.038)	(0.043)	(0.040)
Senior debt	−0.1969‡	−0.2109‡	−0.2204‡	−0.2264‡
	(0.051)	(0.051)	(0.056)	(0.055)
S&P rating	−0.0225	−0.0200	−0.0070	−0.0253
	(0.042)	(0.042)	(0.048)	(0.046)
Public credit registries		−0.1322‡		−0.0032
		(0.031)		(0.033)
Public risk disclosure			−0.0731†	
			(0.032)	
NPL definition			0.3826‡	0.4103‡
			(0.035)	(0.033)
Creditor rights	−0.0777‡	−0.0689‡	0.0423†	0.0699‡
	(0.014)	(0.014)	(0.020)	(0.018)
Rule of law	0.0754‡	0.0375‡	0.0473‡	0.0344‡
	(0.025)	(0.007)	(0.008)	(0.008)
Scale	0.5684‡	0.5666‡	0.5586‡	0.5579‡
	(0.007)	(0.007)	(0.008)	(0.008)
N	3,418	3,418	2,648	2,786
log L	−3,055.99	−3,046.90	−2,344.26	−2,447.15
LR	554.64‡	572.81‡	657.95‡	659.69‡
AIC	6,187.97	6,171.80	4,768.52	4,979.66
SC	6,421.17	6,411.13	5,003.78	5,216.95

All syndications processes complete. Loan type (term loan), loan purpose (corporate, debt repayment, LBO, project finance, and working capital), benchmark rate (LIBOR and EURIBOR), facility active year, industry, and geographical areas dummies included but not reported.

* Coefficients of covariates significantly different from 0 at 10% level.

† Coefficients of covariates significantly different from 0 at 5% level.

‡ Coefficients of covariates significantly different from 0 at 1% level.

§ Standard errors in parentheses. N = number of observations, log L = log-likelihood, LR = likelihood ratio, AIC = Akaykle information criterion, SC = Schwarz information criterion.

As expected, the size of the loan, the spread, and the maturity have a positive influence on the timetable, while the number of arrangers has a negative influence. Larger loans imply a greater bulk of complexity, risk, and agency problems, and therefore more time-consuming arrangement. The result regarding the maturity of the loan confirms the positive relationship between the latter and risk. Concerned about the speed of loan activation and their own reputation as efficient arrangers, the latter have a negative impact on the timetable. Larger fees effectively function as an incentive device for the arrangers, with a negative and significant influence on the timetable. Debt seniority, presence of guarantors, and covenants have significant coefficients. The former suggests that seniority applies equivalently to all lenders and thus provide them with a protection scheme that reduces the timetable. *Covenants* have a sign consistent with the empirical evidence (Foster et al., 1998) in accordance with the observed-risk hypothesis. Guarantors' presence reduces adverse selections problems thanks to the better information about the borrower. Hard information availability through an external agency rating (*S&P Rating*) has no significant influence on the timetable, suggesting that most of the information is produced privately by the arrangers, and thus publicly available information does not contribute to reduce agency problems.

Regarding information disclosure variables, we observe that the presence of public credit registries reduces the timetable, according to its positive impact on the reduction of informational asymmetries between the borrower and the syndicate. Similarly, public risk management process disclosure has a negative influence on the timetable as it reduces information asymmetry between the lenders. On the contrary, a formal definition of NPL increases timetable. This result can be explained in several ways. First, financial institutions may not adhere to the regulatory standards, making the existence of a formal definition uninformative. Second, if binding, this formal definition can be counterproductive for syndications, as it might appear that a high fraction of participant banks actually carry an important burden of NPL.

Legal risk influences the timetable in a way suggesting that problems related to borrower's distress, reorganization, and recontracting are less of an issue for the syndication processes in our sample. The coefficients of *Creditor Rights* and *Rule of Law* are more consistent with our argumentation regarding the impact of legal risk on agency problems within the syndicate before the distress of the borrower, where better legal protection of banks mitigates the moral hazard problem induced by syndication and decreases the need to monitor the borrower. Alternatively, handling borrower distress might be less of an issue during the syndication arrangement, the latter being more driven by potential agency problems. However, the creditor rights index becomes positive in specifications 3 and 4. Also, when we take into account both type of information disclosure features, the information-sharing variable is not more significant. These results suggest that asymmetry of information between the syndicate members is more important for the syndication arrangement and that better transparency regarding the lenders is associated with an impact of stronger creditor rights on timetable, consistent with reorganization and recontracting issues related to borrower's distress. As the intrinsic moral hazard problem within the syndicate is reduced due to information disclosure imposed by regulation, the prospects of reaching a satisfactory collective agreement in case of borrower's distress might be more difficult in an environment where creditor rights are well protected (e.g., because of holdup problems). Alternatively, we can also explain this result stating that as better creditors' protection reduces the attraction of joining a syndicate (and enhances the motivation for bilateral lending), it increases the timetable in order for the arrangers to find participants and form a syndicate.

CONCLUSION

We have investigated the determinants of the arrangement timetable of bank loan syndications by analyzing the role of loan and syndicate characteristics, informational disclosure, and legal environment, inspired by recent literature on the role of institutions on bank loans behavior (Esty and Megginson, 2003; Qian and Strahan, 2007).

Overall, factors that mitigate agency problems related to syndicated loans reduce the timetable, while features that exacerbate moral hazard or adverse selection problems increase the timetable. Information disclosure through credit registries and regulatory features allows reducing the timetable, while legal environment has an impact consistent with agency problems mitigation rather than recontracting issues. Furthermore, when including both sets of factors, we find that information disclosure that influences moral hazard problems within syndicates is the main driver of syndication arrangement timetable, while creditor rights affects the latter in a manner consistent with recontracting risk issues related to borrower distress.

REFERENCES

Agbanzo, L., Mei, J., and Saunders, A. (1999) Credit Spreads in the Market for Highly Leveraged Transaction Loans. *Journal of Banking and Finance*, 22(10/11): 1249–1282.

Allen, T. (1990) Developments in the International Syndicated Loan Market in the 1980s. Bank of England, Quarterly bulletin, London.

Altunbas, Y. and Gadanecz, B. (2004) Developing Country Economic Structure and the Pricing of Syndicated Credits. *Journal of Development Studies*, 40(5): 143–173.

Altunbas, Y., Gadanecz, B., and Kara, A. (2005) Key Factors Affecting Internationally Active Banks' Decisions to Participate in Loan Syndications. *Applied Economic Letters*, 12(4): 249–253.

Barth, J., Caprio, G., and Levine, R. (2005) *Rethinking Bank Regulation: Till Angels Govern*. Cambridge, MA: Cambridge University Press.

Berger, A. and Udell, G. (1990) Collateral, Loan Quality, and Bank Risk. *Journal of Monetary Economics*, 25(1): 21–42.

Bolton, P. and Scharfstein, D. (1996) Optimal Debt Structure and the Number of Creditors. *Journal of Political Economy*, 104(1): 1–25.

Cox, D. (1972) Regression Models and Life Tables. *Journal of the Royal Statistical Society*, 24(2): 187–201.

Cox, D. (1975) Partial Likelihood. *Biometrika*, 62(2): 269–276.

Dennis, S., Bebarshi, N., and Sharpe, I. (2000) Determinants of Contract Terms in Bank Revolving Credit Agreements. *Journal of Financial and Quantitative Analysis*, 35(1): 87–109.

Dennis, S. and Mullineaux, D. (2000) Syndicated Loans. *Journal of Financial Intermediation*, 9(4): 404–426.

Diamond, D. (1984) Financial Intermediation as Delegated Monitoring: A Simple Example. Federal Reserve Bank of Richmond, *Economic Quarterly*, 82(3): 51–66.

Djankov, S., McLiesh, C., and Shleifer, A. (2007) Private Credit in 129 Countries. *Journal of Financial Economics*, 84(2): 299–329.

Esty, B. (2001) Structuring Loan Syndicates: A Case Study of the Hong Kong Disneyland Project Loan. *Journal of Applied Corporate Finance*, 14(3): 80–95.

Esty, B. and Megginson, W. (2003) Creditor Rights, Enforcement, and Debt Ownership Structure: Evidence from the Global Syndicated Loan Market. *Journal of Financial and Quantitative Analysis*, 38(1): 37–59.

Flannery, M. (1986) Asymmetric Information and Risky Debt Maturity Choice. *Journal of Finance*, 41(1): 19–37.

Foster, B., Ward, T., and Woodroof, J. (1998) An Analysis of the Usefulness of Debt Defaults and Going Concern Opinions in Bankruptcy Risk Assessment. *Journal of Accounting, Auditing and Finance*, 13(3): 351–371.

François, P. and Missionier-Piera, F. (2007) The Agency Structure of Loan Syndicates. *The Financial Review*, 42(2): 227–245.

Godlewski, C.J. (2008) Determinants of Bank Loan Syndication Structures for Emerging Market Borrowers, *Journal of Risk Management in Financial Institutions,* 1(3): 1–20.

Godlewski, C.J. and Weill, L. (2008) Syndicated Loans in Emerging Markets, *Emerging Markets Review*, forthcoming.

Gorton, G. and Pennachi, G. (1995) Banks and Loan Sales: Marketing Nonmarketable Assets. *Journal of Monetary Economics*, 35(3): 389–411.

Harrell, F. (2001) *Regression Modeling Strategies With Applications to Linear Models, Logistic Regression, and Survival Analysis.* New York: Springer.

Holmstrom, B. and Tirole, J. (1997) Financial Intermediation, Loanable Funds, and the Real Sector. *Quarterly Journal of Economics*, 112(3): 663–691.

Jappelli, T. and Pagano, M. (2002) Information Sharing, Lending and Defaults: Cross-Country Evidence. *Journal of Banking and Finance*, 26(10): 2017–2045.

Jimenez, G. and Saurina, J. (2004) Collateral, Type of Lender and Relationship Banking as Determinants of Credit Risk. *Journal of Banking and Finance*, 28(9): 2191–2212.

Kiefer, N. (1988) Econometric Duration Data and Hazard Functions. *Journal of Economic Literature*, 25(2): 646–679.

LaPorta, R., de Silanes, F.L., and Shleifer, A. (1998) Law and Finance. *Journal of Political Economy*, 106(6): 1113–1155.

LaPorta, R., de Silanes, F. L., Shleifer, A., and Vishny, R. (1997) Legal Determinants of External Finance. *Journal of Finance*, 52(3): 1130–1150.

Lee, S. and Mullineaux, D. (2004) Monitoring, Financial Distress, and the Structure of Commercial Lending Syndicates. *Financial Management*, 33(3): 107–130.

Pennachi, G. (1998) Loan Sales and the Cost of Bank Capital. *Journal of Finance*, 43(2): 375–396.

Pichler, P. and Wilhelm, W. (2001) A Theory of the Syndicate: Form Follows Function. *Journal of Finance*, 56(6): 2237–2264.

Preece, D. and Mullineaux, D. (1996) Monitoring, Loan Renegotiability, and Firm Value: The Role of Lending Syndicates. *Journal of Banking and Finance*, 20(3): 577–593.

Qian, J. and Strahan, P. (2007) How Laws and Institutions Shape Financial Contracts: The Case of Bank Loans. *Journal of Finance,* 62(6): 2803–2834.

Rajan, R. and Winton, A. (1995) Covenants and Collateral as Incentives to Monitor. *Journal of Finance*, 50(4): 1113–1146.

Song, W.-L. (2004) Competition and Coalition Among Underwriters: The Decision to Join a Syndicate. *Journal of Finance*, 59(5): 2421–2444.

Sufi, A. (2007) Information Asymmetry and Financing Arrangements: Evidence from Syndicated Loans. *Journal of Finance*, 62(2): 629–668.

CHAPTER 14

Credit Default Swap and Other Credit Derivatives: Valuation and Application

Ralph Karels

ABSTRACT

The chapter first introduces, analyzes, and valuates credit default swap in all its variations and then moves on to more sophisticated credit derivatives such as basket credit default swap derived from plain vanilla credit default swap. Copula methods are introduced to model the default correlation of dependent underlyings of a basket credit default swap. Analytical as well as numerical examples including Monte Carlo simulations are given to illustrate and calculate the joint distribution of dependent default times. Once the joint distribution is modeled, any basket credit derivative structure can be valuated and priced. Further, refined Monte Carlo methods incorporating importance sampling are discussed. The chapter finishes with a short market outlook and possible applications of "CDS & Co."

INTRODUCTION

Are "derivatives financial weapons of mass destruction," as Warren Buffett recently put it? Derivatives can indeed work destructively if one does not deal with them correctly. But you can also view them as "intelligent bombs," which help to eradicate any unwanted risk, as the Financial Times recently wrote. If deployed correctly, derivatives are indeed versatile instruments that are becoming more popular for good reason. This applies especially to credit derivatives (Figure 14.1). In this chapter we begin by presenting a number of typical credit derivatives, among them the central credit default swap (CDS). Then we analyze the significance of the correlation of payment defaults and derive from this both analytical valuation methods as well as pricing methods based on Monte Carlo simulations. This is because exact knowledge of the fair value of a derivative is crucial if it is to be meaningfully deployed.

Derivatives permit enterprises to reduce their market risk but expose them at the same time to a credit risk. For instance, if an enterprise wants to reduce the risk of a pending bond with flexible interest rate payments, then it can offer a swap with fixed interest rate payments. In this way, the enterprise reduces the interest rate risk—but only if the swap partner does not default. The interest rate risk on the bond turned into a credit risk on the swap. This credit risk can be hedged now with a credit derivative. However, the enterprise still has to bear the credit risk vis-a-vis the provider of the credit protection. Enron, for example, was an

F I G U R E   14.1

Global market for credit derivatives in billion U.S. Dollars

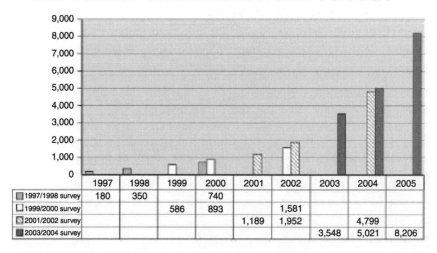

	1997	1998	1999	2000	2001	2002	2003	2004	2005
1997/1998 survey	180	350		740					
1999/2000 survey			586	893		1,581			
2001/2002 survey					1,189	1,952		4,799	
2003/2004 survey							3,548	5,021	8,206

important provider of credit derivatives. And we all know what happened in that case.

Credit Default Swap–the Central Credit Derivative: Analysis and Valuation

The term *credit risk* generally refers to the risk of incurring losses as a result of changes in a counterparty's credit quality. Credit derivatives, which in recent years have become increasingly popular and successful, allow this risk to be isolated and actively managed by providing a payoff upon a credit event arrival, be it a rating downgrade or default in form of failure to pay or bankruptcy of the reference credit. The International Swaps and Derivatives Association (ISDA) provides the definition of a credit event. The basic building block for more complex derivatives is the plain vanilla CDS.

A CDS offers protection against default of a certain underlying over a specified time horizon. A premium is paid on a regular basis as an insurance fee against the losses from default of the underlying. The premium is frequently a spread over the plain vanilla non-credit swap rate. The spread achieving a CDS present value of zero is called *fair CDS spread*. Hence, with this spread the (expected) discounted values of the payment (fee) leg and the contingent (protection) leg are identical. The payment of this premium stops either at maturity of the CDS or at the time of default, whichever comes first. In the case of default before maturity, the protection buyer receives a payment from the protection seller. This payment amounts to $(1 - R)$ percent of the underlying instrument carrying the credit risk, with R being the recovery rate (e.g., the recovery percentage of a corporate bond after default). Bear in mind that a CDS serves not only as an insurance against default but also as an insurance against changes in the rating of the underlying, since the market value of a CDS changes if the rating of the underlying changes.

One major reason for the increasing popularity of CDS is the possibility to separate the credit risk from the underlying credit relationship and thus the independent trading of risk. In other words, the CDS incorporates the specific risk premium, the part of a corporate bond generating additional value compared to government bonds. The main difference between a CDS and a total return swap (TRS) is that a TRS offers protection against all sorts of possible losses whereas a CDS only offers protection against credit events. The separate tradeability of these default risks enables an increasingly broader way of controlling risk and return. In former times, lacking liquidity of the "physically" traded asset prohibited interesting investments. However, nowadays by entering a CDS, a diversifying credit may be easily incorporated into the investors portfolio. Furthermore, the separation of interest and default risk via CDS opens new possibilities to translate market opinions exactly into investment strategies. For instance, if the credit risk is considered to be overvalued, then one can receive an attractive spread by entering a CDS contract as a security provider without having to buy a possibly illiquid corporate bond. Compared to the market for interest rate derivatives, the relatively young credit derivatives market[1] is still comparably small but shows high growth rates (see Figure 14.2). Single-name CDS make up for 50 to 85 percent (depending on the source) of the entire credit derivatives market. Two thirds of the underlyings for CDS are corporates.[2]

There are a number of variations of the plain vanilla CDS. In a digital or binary CDS, the payout following a credit event is not related to the

F I G U R E   14.2

Percentage share of different credit derivatives in the market

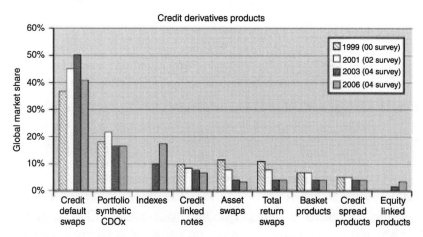

---

[1] The market for CDS emerged in the mid–1990s.
[2] See Deutsche Bundesbank (2004).

reference asset but aggregates to a specific predetermined cash amount. A contingent CDS requires next to the credit event itself an additional trigger, for example, regarding another underlying or a specific market parameter. In a dynamic CDS, the notional finally yielding the payoff is not constant but depends from the market value of a swap portfolio.[3]

Credit default swap spreads and interest rates are positively correlated: Increasing interest rates lead to liquidity flows from risky into riskless assets thus leading again to increased risk premiums—the CDS spreads. However, increasing implied volatilities are leading to higher CDS spreads as well since the probability of default increases in that case. In general, however, CDS spreads are determined to a large part by supply and demand structures depending on the market and economic trends. This leads to two different pricing problems: First, at origination the CDS premiums must be fixed so that the value of the CDS is zero. This is crucial for making markets, since otherwise no CDS transaction would be carried out. From no-arbitrage relations we observe that the fair CDS spread basically is the par spread or the asset swap spread. Second, after origination with changing credit quality and market interest rates, the current value of the CDS, expressed in terms of the difference between the current fair spread s_t and the fair spread s_0 at the time of engagement in the transaction, has to be determined, which is crucial for hedging.

We assume that the survival probabilities, interest rates, and recovery rates are independent and the interest rates deterministic. Let us denote with T_i the times of spread payment, τ the arbitrary time of default, $q(t) = P(\tau \geq t)$ the survival probability, $\mathrm{DF}(t)$ the discount factor for time t from the interest rate term structure curve, and Δ_i the length of the period $[T_{i-1}, T_i]$. Then we have to consider for the valuation of a CDS contract made in t_0 at time $t > t_0$ the following:

$$(s_t - s_0)\sum_{T_i > t}\Delta_i\mathrm{DF}(T_i)q(T_i)$$

The survival probabilities $q(T_i)$ are still unknown; however, they are contained implicitly in the CDS spreads quoted by the market and can be extracted by a bootstrapping procedure. A first insight into this is given by

---

[3] See Hull and White (2000).

the following example: A riskless 10-year zero bond at 4 percent is to be compared with a 10-year corporate zero bond at 4.5 percent, and both are paid back at time $t=1$. Hence, the present value of the default risk premium is $e^{-0.04 * 10} - e^{-0.045 * 10} = 0.6703 - 0.6376 = 0.027$.

If we further assume that in case of default there is no recovery and denote with p the risk-neutral default probability over the entire running time of the bond, it holds that $pe^{-0.045 * 10} = 0.032 \Rightarrow p = 5.13\%$.

In the general case, however, we have to cope with three hurdles. First, the recovery rate is not zero. Second, most corporate bonds are not zero bonds, and third, the default probabilities extracted from corporate bonds are to be considered with caution since there often is a significant difference between the cash market (asset swaps) and the CDS market.

We return to the general CDS valuation where we make an assumption on the recovery rate R, which we consider to be time invariant for our purposes here. Usually R takes values between 15 and 50 percent.[4] A mark-to-market valuation $V_R(s)$ of the CDS from the protection seller view yields (dependent from the spread s)

$$V_R(s) = s \sum_{i=1}^{n} \{\Delta_i \mathrm{DF}(T_i)q(T_i) + \Delta_i^* \mathrm{DF}(T_i^*)[q(T_{i-1}) - q(T_i)]\} - (1-R) \sum_{i=1}^{n} \mathrm{DF}(T_i^*)[q(T_{i-1}) - q(T_i)]$$

The first sum represents the spreads of the fee leg of the CDS, discounted with the discount factors and the survival probabilities where the factor marked with an * represents the accrued spread up until the arbitrary default time τ, discounted with the discount factors $\mathrm{DF}(T_i^*)$, which may be generated by interpolation of the interest rate term structure curve. Observe that the (positive) difference $q(T_{i-1}) - q(T_i)$ represents the probability of default occurring in the interval $[T_{i-1}; T_i]$. The second sum represents the contingent leg of the CDS, the discounted insurance payment ($= 1$) minus the recovery rate R, provided default occurs before T_n. Here we take into account that default may occur in every interval $[T_{i-1}; T_i]$. Hence, we have to sum up all intervals weighted by the respective survival probabilities. For the fair spread s_0 at inception of the contract, we have $V_R(s_0) = 0$, whereby a valuation after the inception of the contract is also possible. We set the default probabilities $q(T_{i-1}) - q(T_i)$ for past times T_i in the equation

---

[4] See Schmidt (2004).

for $V_R(s)$ to zero. The sensitivity of the valuation regarding the recovery rate R is marginal, since it is taken into account when calculating the survival probabilities and during the mark-to-market valuation. It can be empirically shown that these two movements neutralize each other. The valuation of a digital CDS, however, heavily depends on the assumption of the recovery rate R.

Basket Credit Default Swaps—A First Analysis

More sophisticated credit derivatives are linked not only to one but to several underlyings and include basket default swaps (BDS), such as kth-to-default swaps or collateralized debt obligations (CDOs). Similarly to a CDS, a BDS offers protection against the event of at least k defaults among a basket of $n \geq k$ underlying credit names against payment of a spread s_{kth}. The insured event only occurs if k of the n underlyings really default. In the case of a second-to-default-swap this means that insurance payment is received for a basket of, for example, 10 names as soon as any two names default. The insurance payment amounts to $(1 - R)$ percent with R being the recovery of the kth defaulted credit. Most popular are first-to-default swaps (FTDS), where the insured event already occurs upon the default of the first underlying contained in the basket. They offer highly attractive spreads (premiums) to a credit investor (protection seller). If the n credits inside a BDS are assumed to be independent, a FTDS is approximately equivalent to n CDS, and therefore, the spread s_{1st} is close to the sum of the n CDS spreads, provided the term structure of credit spreads s_j is flat for each credit in the basket since the likelihood of multiple defaults is now at a minimum, which is represented by Equation (14.1):

$$s_{1st} \approx \sum_{j=1}^{n} s_j \tag{14.1}$$

In the other extreme case—total dependence—the FTDS spread is the worst of all the CDS spreads, since in the case of perfect positive correlation the basket is dominated by the name with the worst spread and is represented by Equation (14.2).

$$s_{1st} = \max(s_1, \ldots, s_n) \tag{14.2}$$

Based on the dependence of issuers on several general economic factors or direct firm inter linkages, credit quality changes of several issuers are often (not perfectly) correlated. Hence we obtain[5]

$$\max(s_1, \ldots, s_n) \leq s_{1st} \leq \sum_{j=1}^{n} s_j$$

The higher the diversification rate of the basket, the higher the spread s_{1st} implying that for increasing positive default correlation, the spread is decreasing since the probability of multiple defaults increases and the degree of default protection provided by the FTDS diminishes. Investors holding positions with numerous counterparties are exposed to the aggregated risk of losses due to correlated credit events arrivals. Hence, a good reason why efficient modeling of default correlation becomes the most important part of credit risk valuation.

VALUATION OF CREDIT DERIVATIVES WITH SEVERAL UNDERLYINGS

Default Correlation—The Crucial Element

The estimation of aggregated loss distributions in credit risk measurement and the valuation of multi-name credit derivatives and CDOs require a model for the joint default behaviour of numerous credit-risky securities such as bonds or loans. The probability distribution of each of the underlyings is first analyzed and then pooled together via a mathematical process known as the copula concept into a joint distribution function.

The basis for modeling the correlation of payment defaults is the copula function. First, note that given a joint distribution of random variables (RVs), the marginal distributions and the correlation structure among the RVs can be extracted but in general not vice versa. An exception is the multivariate normal distribution, which can be fully described knowing only the marginal distributions and the correlation structure. There are many different techniques and ways to specify a joint distribution of RVs—which is by no means unique—with given marginal distributions

---

[5] See Schmidt and Ward (2002).

and a given correlation structure. Among these, the copula approach is a simple and convenient one. By definition, a copula function C simply is the joint distribution of a given number n of uniformly distributed random variables $U_1, \ldots, U_n$ with a given correlation structure. Note that in the special case of independence among the $U_1, \ldots, U_n$, we obtain

$$C(u_1, \ldots, u_n) := P(U_1 \leq u_1, \ldots, U_n \leq u_n) = \prod_{j=1}^{n} u_j$$

The probability that at the same time the RV U_1 lies below the value u_1 and the RV U_2 lies below the value u_2 and so forth can thus be easily calculated as the product of all of the u_j. The joint distribution is the product of the marginal distributions involved (in case of independence). An immediate application of this definition links arbitrary marginal distribution functions with F_j with the joint distribution function F via

$$C(F_1(x_1), \ldots, F_n(x_n)) = P(U_1 \leq F(x_1), \ldots, U_n \leq F_n(x_n))$$
$$= P(F_1^{(-1)}(U_1) \leq x_1, \ldots, F_n^{(-1)}(U_n) \leq x_n)$$
$$= P(X_1 \leq x_1, \ldots, X_n \leq x_n) = F(x_1, \ldots, x_n)$$

We use the simple stochastic fact where the distribution function of a RV $F^{(-1)}(U)$ with uniformly distributed random variable U is just F: $P(F^{(-1)}(U) \leq x) = P(U \leq F(x)) = F(x)$.

Hence, there are two ways to use the copula idea: First, copulas can be extracted from known multivariate distribution functions via $C(u_1, \ldots, u_n) = F(F_1^{-1}(u_1), \ldots, F_n^{-1}(u_n))$.

Once the marginal distributions F_j is known, then their inverse functions F^{-1}_j (which by definition exist for continuous F_j as they represent [strictly] increasing functions) and the joint distribution function F can be determined, and the copula C can be constructed according to the above formula. We then call C the copula of F, which remains invariant under strictly increasing component transformations—a property that is not shared by the correlation matrix. Second, new multivariate distribution functions can be created by joining arbitrary marginal distributions together with copulas.[6] The strength of copulas hence is the modeling of

---

[6] See Schmidt (2003).

joint distributions of dependent RVs. Contrary to the standard correlation measuring the degree of linear dependence, these dependencies also can be modeled in a nonlinear fashion.

Default correlation can be defined and modeled in various ways.[7] We will focus on the latent variable model approach, which is highly suitable to be generalized toward modeling multiple defaults involving a dependency structure.[8] It underlies the most important industry models such as those from KMV and CreditMetrics as well as the new Basel agreement. In the latent variable model the condition of the credit (distance to default), defaulting or (partially) failed, is modeled using a default indicator (the latent variables). This indicator is the basis for the decisive modeling of the joint likelihood distribution of the default times. The condition of the credit will be denoted with S, the default indicator (cutoff level) with D, and the latent variables (default times) with X. In equation format we introduce n obligors, a fixed time horizon T, and a vector $\underline{X} = (X_1, \ldots, X_n)$ of RVs with continuous marginal distributions representing the latent variables (which are, e.g., interpreted as asset values by KMV). At time T, obligor j is said to have status k (e.g., $k = 0$ means default) if the latent variable X_j falls into a certain range $[D^j_{k-1}, D^j_k]$ involving some deterministic cutoff levels D^j_k (with $j = 1, \ldots, n$ and $k = 0, \ldots, m$). As a formula we write

$$S_j = k \Leftrightarrow 1_{\{X_j \in [D^j_{k-1}, D^j_k]\}} > 0$$

In this context (X_j, D^j_k) is called a *latent variable model* for the state vector (default indicator) $\mathbf{S} = (S_1, \ldots, S_n)$.[9] Hence, obligor j defaults if $S_j = 0$, while k may be interpreted as its distance to default at time T. In an example with five obligors and six cutoff levels, a state vector $\mathbf{S} = (0, 2, 0, 2, 4)$, e.g., means that at time T obligors 1 and 3 default while the distance to default of obligors 2 and 4 is 2 and that of obligor 5—the best rated—is 4; all of which, of course, critically depend on the selection of

---

[7] After modeling the credit default times τ_j and the arbitrary losses L_j, one could either consider the correlation between the events $\{\tau_j < T\}$ and $\{\tau_k < T\}$ (where we still would have to choose a certain T), the correlation between the default times τ_j and τ_k, the correlation between the losses L_j and L_k, etc.

[8] See Giesecke (2001).

[9] See Frey et al. (2001).

cutoff levels D^j_k. If we simplify the model above by just regarding two possible cases—default and no default (hence, k may be just 0 or 1)—and set $D_j = T$ for all j, then the latent variables may be interpreted as times to default for all of the obligors.[10] If we further introduce time dependence and, e.g., a Black–Scholes-type process for $\mathbf{X}$, then it can be shown that assuming a suitable correlation structure, the joint default probability $P(\tau_i < T, \tau_j < T)$ can in fact be written as a Gaussian copula, $P(\tau_i < T, \tau_j < T) = N \left(N^{(-1)} (F_i (T)), N^{(-1)}(F_j(T)); \rho^a{}_{ij}(T) \right)$, with $\rho^a{}_{ij}$ denoting asset correlations.[11] This seems plausible but has drawbacks; since multivariate normally distributed risk factors (such as the X_j here) are asymptotically independent, joint large movements are a rare event, and therefore, Gaussian copulas may not necessarily be the best choice for modeling dependent defaults. In this case mixed copulas like the t copula are taken into account, which is based on the Student's t distribution incorporating fat tails, i.e., a stronger concentration of the probability distribution at the edges of a distribution compared to the normal distribution.[12]

Dependence among default events is modeled by dependence among the default times (the "latent" variables). The correlation matrix of these latent variables is often calibrated by using factor models that relate changes in asset value to changes in a small number of underlying economic factors. One of the advantages of latent variable models is that they can be derived analytically without having to resort to Monte Carlo simulations. Below, we derive the fair spread for the special case of a kth-to-default swap with any number of underlyings whose default times, however, do not correlate together. The method to use[13] is to first construct via bootstrapping from market data, such as the risky bond spread curve or CDS spreads, a credit curve (CC) $(q^j_0, q^j_1, ..., q^j_n)$ for each credit j with $q^j_k := P(\tau_j < k + 1 \mid \tau_j > k)$, denoting the probability of credit j defaulting in the time frame $[k, k + 1]$.[14] This provides the marginal

---

[10] KMV as well as Credit Metrics assume that the joint default distribution $\mathbf{X}$ of all underlyings contained in the basket follows a multivariate normal distribution, which leads to an equivalent model structure leaving possible differences only to the areas presentation, interpretation, and calibration.

[11] See Schmidt (2003).

[12] See Frey and McNeil (2001).

[13] See Karels (2003).

[14] See Li (1999).

default probabilities at any one time in the future. The extracted q^k_j reflect the market's judgement of the default probabilities—they are not equal to the true, unknown default probabilities. Nevertheless, based on the theory of no arbitrage and dynamic hedging, these default probabilities (or the respective survival probabilities) are best suited for the valuation of credit derivatives. Second, a joint distribution for the survival times is to be specified via a copula function. Since copulas may express a variety of nonlinear multivariate dependency structures, this problem obviously has no unique solution. If we assume mutual independence between the credits, then all related problems could be analyzed using the marginal default probabilities. However, an independence assumption among credit risks is far from being realistic since each credit is subject to the same set of macroeconomic environmental factors already inducing some form of positive dependence among the credits. If we consider n risky securities and let τ_j be the time until default of security j, then its distribution may be characterized by its hazard rate function $h_j(t)$ defined via $P(\tau_j \in [t + \Delta t] \mid \tau_j > t) =: h_j(t)\,\Delta t$, which is connected with the survival function $S_j(t) = 1 - f_j(t)$ via $S_j(t) = e^{-\int_0^t h_j(s)\,ds}$, where $F_j(t)$ is the distribution function of τ_j.

First, given the hazard rate function, also called a *default intensity function*, with no default until time t, the probability of default within a small time increment Δt is equal to the hazard rate times the increment Δt. Provided that the default intensity $h_j(t)$ of credit j is assumed to be constant over time, we can demonstrate that the amount of time until a credit event occurs conditional on no credit event yet is exponentially distributed with parameter h_j (the hazard rate). When using f_j as the density function of F_j, we obtain

$$P(\tau_j \in [t + \Delta t] \mid \tau_j > t) = \frac{F_j(t + \Delta t) - F_j(t)}{1 - F_j(t)} \approx \frac{f_j(t)}{1 - F_j(t)}\,\Delta t$$

$$h_j(t) = \frac{f_j(t)}{1 - F_j(t)} = -\frac{d/dt\,S_j(t)}{S_j(t)} = -\frac{d}{dt}(\ln S_j(t))$$

If the default intensity $h_j(t) \equiv h_j$ of credit j is constant over time, then the default intensity obviously is exponentially distributed with parameter h_j, i.e., $F_j(t) = 1 - e^{-h_j t}$.

The default time then can be characterized as the time of the first jump of a Poisson stochastic process with intensity h_j if the hazard rate for a credit event is seen as the arrival rate in the sense of a Poisson process. For example, a hazard rate of 200 bps then would correspond to a mean arrival rate of two times in 100 years. Further assuming horizontal interest rate and spread curves as well as continuous CDS spread payments s_j, the default intensity can be computed via $h_j = s_j/(1 - R_j)$, where R_j denotes the recovery rate of credit j.[15]

An Analytical Example

In a simplified case this can be used to price an m-year contract paying K units if the first default among n credits occurs during the period $[0, m]$ without having to resort to Monte Carlo simulation. If the contract is interpreted as a first to default swap with τ being the (random!) minimum of all default times τ_j involving a constant hazard rate h and payment of a constant swap spread s at dates $0 < t_1 < t_2 < \dots < t_n = m$, then the fee leg f of the FTDS has a present value of

$$f = \sum_{i:t_i \leq m} E(se^{-rt_i} 1_{\{\tau > t_i\}}) = s \sum_{i:t_i \leq m} e^{-(r+nh)t_i}$$

Proof: Since $\tau = \min(\tau_1, \dots, \tau_n)$ is the only random element under the sum, the spread s and the discount factor can be excluded from the expectation:

$$f = \sum_{i:t_i \leq m} E(se^{-rt_i} 1_{\{\tau > t_i\}}) = \sum_{i:t_i \leq m} se^{-rt_i} E(1_{\{\tau > t_i\}}) = s \sum_{i:t_i \leq m} e^{-rt_i} P(\tau > t_i)$$

We have also used the basic fact in probability theory that the expectation over an indicator function is equal to the probability of the event on which the indicator function is based. Furthermore, the probability $P(r > t_i)$ under the sum, provided there is stochastic independence among the τ_j, computes itself via

$$P(\tau \geq t_i) = P(\tau_j \geq t_i; j = 1, \dots, n) = \prod_{j=1}^{n} P(\tau_j \geq t_i) = \prod_{j=1}^{n} e^{-ht_i} = e^{-nht_i}$$

---

[15] See Schmidt (2001).

Hence, only the third equality in the above equation series still needs clarification, and we are done. However, this can easily be seen since the probability in question is nothing other than the survival function S_j, whose connection to the hazard rate function we know already. The fact that $h_j(t) \equiv h_j$ is constant completes the proof:

$$S_j(t_i) = P(\tau_j \geq t_i) = e^{-\int_0^t h_j(s)\,ds} = e^{-h_j t}$$

So f simply sums up the discounted (continuously with rate r) CDS spreads s up until maturity, conditional on the credit not defaulting yet. In detail, sum up the discounted spread cash flow se^{-rt_i} until default (product with $1_{\{\tau < t_i\}}$) or until maturity (sum over the set of all times $t_i \leq m$), whichever comes first. Since the default time $\tau = \min(\tau_1, \ldots, \tau_n)$ of the FTDS is random, the expectation E has to be computed. We are on purpose neglecting any possible accrued swap spread here for simplicity. The value of the contingent leg c of the swap assuming that investors are risk neutral is

$$c = E(Ke^{-rt} 1_{\{\tau < m\}}) = \frac{nhK}{r + nh}(1 - e^{-(r+nh)m})$$

which consists of the (expected) payment discounted with the (random!) default time τ provided it occurs before maturity.

Proof: Apart from the fact that this is a mere analysis exercise, the main problem here lies in the computation of the expectation since the RV τ is involved twice. As in the preceding proof, we again use the fact that τ is exponentially distributed with parameter nh. Hence, we have

$$c = E(Ke^{-rt} 1_{\{\tau < m\}}) = \int_0^{\infty} Ke^{-rt} 1_{\{\tau < m\}} nh e^{-nht}\,dt$$

$$= nhK \int_0^m e^{-(r+nh)t}\,dt = \frac{nhK}{r + nh}(1 - e^{-(r+nh)m})$$

Setting $c = f$, the fair spread s is calculated as

$$s = \frac{nhK(1 - e^{-(r+nh)m})}{(r + nh)\sum_{i:t_i \leq m} e^{-(r+nh)t_i}}$$

However, as you may have noticed already, this only holds if we assume the *n* credits to be pairwise independent, which, in general, is an unacceptable premise.[16] Hence, we have to search for a different, non-analytical way to derive solutions.

Dependence—Last Resort Monte Carlo?

The possibilities of analytically determining the joint default probability distribution are, however, quite limited. If the default times of the individual underlyings correlate with each other, an analytical derivation is generally no longer possible. When all analytical possibilities appear to have been exhausted, the key words *Monte Carlo* are again pulled out of the box of mathematical tricks. After all, nothing is analytically derived with the Monte Carlo method. Instead, tests are made until a large number of attempts offer sufficient assurance that the result is also correct. However, this alters nothing since this is a recognized method without which a valuation of derivatives in many cases would not be possible.

Among the numerical techniques to price derivatives, Monte Carlo simulation is one of three main methods including binomial tree approximation and finite differencing. Monte Carlo methods are flexible and easy to implement and modify. In finance the fair price of a derivative, in general, is a discounted expectation of a complex function under a complex probability measure.[17] In light of this, a Monte Carlo simulation often is the only method of choice if there is no analytical solution available. Any Monte Carlo simulation is based on the law of large numbers, which in the strong version (SLLN) states that the arithmetic mean of a series of *n* independent identically distributed (iid) random variables with mean μ and variance σ converges toward μ as *n* tends to infinity.

The procedure then is the following: Given a random variable $Z = F(X)$, where the function F may not be analytically representable but can at least be evaluated at certain points, we are in general interested in obtaining the expectation $E(Z)$ when pricing derivatives or the probability $P(Z \in B)$. For example, the event $\{Z \in B\}$ corresponds to $\{\tau > t\}$, as we have encountered during our analytical investigation when addressing

---

[16] See Giesecke (2002).
[17] See Robert and Casalla (1999).

credit default times. We simulate the RV X and calculate these values of interest according to

$$E(Z) \approx \frac{1}{n} \sum_{j=1}^{n} F(X_j)$$

$$P(Z \in B) \approx \frac{1}{n} \sum_{j=1}^{n} 1_{\{F(X_j) \in B\}}$$

Hence, when pricing a derivative with Monte Carlo methods, we sample the RV X many times, calculate the payoff $Z = F(X)$, and finally calculate the mean of those sample payoffs to get an estimate of the value of the derivative after discounting at the risk-free rate of interest. So Monte Carlo methods give at best a statistical error estimate. One may stop the simulation run at any time to obtain an estimate, but convergence only occurs at infinity. Hence, the goal must be to obtain a good approximation within a reasonable time. Judging this, the standard measure for the accuracy of a Monte Carlo method is the variance of the resulting numerical approximation. Monte Carlo methods are, in general, quite time consuming. Therefore, it is desirable to have a small variance estimator. Every estimator has a certain variance, and since there are infinitely many estimators[18] for any RV Z, the question of reducing and/or minimizing the variance of estimators naturally arises. This problem is treated in the research area labeled variance reduction techniques for Monte Carlo methods, and we will investigate importance sampling in the next section.[19]

For Monte Carlo simulation[20] we take historical infomation such as Moody's data or derive from current market data the survival function of the time of default of a security (credit) and repeat for all credits to address.[21] We then construct a credit curve for each, which characterizes the distribution of defaults over time. Assuming dependency (otherwise, we would be finished here already) among the default times, these are modeled via dependent uniformly distributed random variables that, on

---

[18] For example, the best linear unbiased estimator (BLUE) estimator in the class of linear and expectation true estimator.

[19] See Jäckel (2002).

[20] See Boyle et al. (2003) or Jäckel (2002).

[21] This is done via a bootstrapping technique.

the other hand, are derived from dependent normally distributed RVs. One possible joint distribution of these dependent default times is achieved by a special copula construction. For a single credit and its default time τ_i, and assuming a constant hazard rate $h_i (t) \equiv h_i$, the density f_i of τ_i denotes as follows: $f_i (t) = S_i(T)h_i(t) = h_i e^{-h_i t}$.

Hence, τ_i is exponentially distributed with parameter h_i, and the Monte Carlo simulation is done with uniformly on [0, 1] distributed sampling variables U_i via

$$\tau_i = F_i^{(-1)}(U_i) = \frac{R_i - 1}{s_i} \ln(1 - F_i(U_i)) \sim F_i$$

We obtain with m samples $u_{i1}, \ldots, u_{im}$ of U_i an estimation for the expected default time $\hat{\tau}_i = E(\tau_i)$ of the underlyings according to

$$\hat{\tau}_i = \frac{R_i - 1}{ms_i} \sum_{j=1}^{m} \ln(1 - F_i(u_{ij}))$$

Samples of a single uniform distribution are easy to obtain, and thus a Monte Carlo simulation of a CDS is quite simple. For a simulation of several dependent default times $\tau_1, \ldots, \tau_n$ it is more time consuming. First, we simulate independent normally distributed RVs $Y_1, \ldots, Y_n$ with correlation structure $\Sigma = (\rho_{ij})$ via the Box–Muller method[22] and use these to generate dependent normally distributed $X_1, \ldots, X_n$ and the desired dependent uniform random variables $U_1, \ldots, U_n$.[23] For $n = 2$ we choose $X_1 = Y_1, X_2 = \rho Y_1 + \sqrt{1 - \rho^2} Y_2$.

For $n \geq 3$ the effort increases with the Cholesky decomposition of the correlation Σ. Hence, for $i = 1, \ldots, n$, we obtain $\tau_i = F_i^{(-1)}(U_i) = F_i^{(-1)}(N(X_i)) = F_i^{(-1)}(N(g_i(Y_1, \ldots, Y_n))) \sim F_i$ with functions g_i originating from the Cholesky decomposition. This is used to valuate, e.g., FTDS with a Monte Carlo simulation run. There the following probabilities are encountered that are to be simulated: $P(\tau < T) = 1 - P(\min_{1 \leq i \leq n} \tau_i \geq T) = 1 - P(\tau_1 \geq T, \ldots, \tau_n \geq T)$ with τ denoting the default time of the FTDS. We then specify the joint distribution function of the τ_i with a copula

---

[22] See Robert and Casalla (1999).
[23] See Arvanitis and Gregory (1999).

construction, and the FTDS can be valuated. With a normal copula we obtain, e.g., for the case $n = 2$,

$$P(\tau < T) = F_1(T) + F_2(T) - C(F_1(T), F_2(T); \rho)$$
$$= P(F_1^{(-1)}(N(Y_1)) < T) + P(F_2^{(-1)}(N(\rho Y_1 + \sqrt{1 - \rho^2} Y_2)) < T)$$
$$- N(N^{(-1)}(F_1(T)), N^{(-1)}(F_2(T)), \rho)$$

with the normal copula itself being computed as

$$N(N^{(-1)}(F_1(T)), N^{(-1)}(F_2(T)), \rho) = N(N^{(-1)}(P(F_1^{(-1)}(N(Y_1)) < T)),$$
$$N^{(-1)}(P(F_2^{(-1)}(N(\rho Y_1 + \sqrt{1 - \rho^2} Y_2)) < T)); \rho)$$

Thus with samples of the independent normally distributed Y_1, Y_2 we achieve a Monte Carlo estimate of the first-to-default probability.

We observe that with the joint default time distribution achieved from the copula construction based on the dependent default times for the individual credits, any credit derivative structure can be priced.[24] However, the choice of the copula entails a significant amount of model risk. Joint default probabilities critically depend on the nature of the copula of the latent variables, and it is also important to note that the marginal distributions do not have to coincide with the nature of the copula.[25] In other words, any given single-name default probability model can be combined with an exponential correlation model. Returning to the simulation of our default times, we show that in a normal copula framework the correlations in the normal copula are in fact asset correlations. These can be estimated from empirical data about the asset values that themselves can be calculated synthetically from observable market (stock price) data.[26]

Improving Monte Carlo–Importance Sampling

When applying a standard Monte Carlo simulation run, we can ask whether the drawn set of samples (the X_j) could be improved. The areas of

---

[24] See Frey and McNeil (2001).

[25] It is generally possible to generate latent variable models with a Gaussian copula whose marginal distributions are not univariate normal but, e.g., exponential, or it is possible to generate default times with exponential dependency structure but arbitrary marginals.

[26] See Schmidt (2003).

interest should be more finely sampled but this oversampling needs to be compensated by attaching smaller probability weights to the samples of the overrepresented regions. This is especially advisable if sampling is to take place from the tails of a distribution. If we are dealing with rare events, then importance sampling or comparable methods are needed to obtain an acceptably accurate approximation. In terms of credit risk, default is indeed a rare event and applying a noncustomized Monte Carlo simulation (in other words, simply "throw the dice") would be suboptimal since a lot of computational time is wasted. Speaking more generally, the variance reduction technique of importance sampling requires the probability measure to be changed and the value function f in $E(f(X))$ to be multiplied by the Radon–Nikodym derivative,[27] and payout according to Girsanov's theorem (change of measure) has to be appropriately reduced to compensate for the oversampling. A detailed treatment of this special topic, however, would be beyond the scope of this article.[28]

A first insight into the technique is provided by the following case. Let us assume we have just one risky underlying whose survival probability $P(\tau \geq T)$ for an arbitrary but fixed time T is to be simulated with a Monte Carlo simulation run, provided τ is exponentially distributed with parameter λ and density f. The standard Monte Carlo estimator in this case is

$$P(\tau \geq T) \approx \frac{1}{n}\sum_{j=1}^{n} 1_{\{\tau_j \geq T\}}$$

We now introduce a new importance sampling density $g \sim \exp(\mu)$ and modify our estimator via a Girsanov density transformation via[29]

$$E_f 1_{\{\tau \geq T\}} = E_g 1_{\{\tau \geq T\}} \frac{f(\tau)}{g(\tau)}$$

Hence,

$$P(\tau \geq T) \approx \frac{1}{n}\sum_{j=1}^{n} 1_{\{\tau_j \geq T\}} \frac{f(\tau_j)}{g(\tau_j)}$$

---

[27] See Bauer (2000).
[28] See Schmidt (2003).
[29] E_f and E_g denote the expectation with respect to the densities f and g.

where τ_j now is sampled from g with a likelihood $(\lambda/\mu)e^{(\mu-\lambda)T}$. The target is now to determine g such that the variance of the estimator is minimized. Hence, we have to minimize

$$E(1_{\{\tau \geq T\}} \frac{f(\tau)}{g(\tau)})^2 = \int_0^\infty 1_{\{t \geq T\}}^2 \frac{\lambda^2 e^{-2\lambda t}}{\mu^2 e^{-2\mu t}} \mu e^{-\mu t} \, dt = \frac{\lambda^2}{\mu(2\lambda - \mu)} e^{(\mu - 2\lambda)T}$$

and obtain as a solution

$$\mu = \frac{1}{T}(1 + T\lambda) - \frac{1}{T}\sqrt{1 + (T\lambda)^2} < \frac{1}{T}$$

For the expectation $E_g\tau$ of the default time τ we acquire with the new sampling density g $E_g\tau = 1/\mu > T$, but also $E_g\tau > E_f\tau$. This result confirms our intuitive view that the resampling of this variance reduction method stems from a region generating higher expected values for τ than with the density f. Consequently, the indicator function above generates more often a positive contribution than without importance sampling, and we obtain an estimation of the default probability with acceptable accuracy much faster. This also is the most important building block of the Monte Carlo pricing of a CDS. One can extend this procedure with more technical effort onto two or more credits to valuate BDS. Therefore, if we deal with rare events, importance sampling or comparable methods are extremely useful to achieve an approximation of adequate accuracy. A default indeed is a rare event, and blind application of standard Monte Carlo in any case turns out to be suboptimal.

POSSIBLE APPLICATION AND MARKET OUTLOOK

We have already observed that CDS and other credit derivatives enable us to trade financial standing or creditworthiness in form of future transactions and hence give the market participants an efficient means to hedge themselves favorably against rating changes. We are also dealing with a standardized and transparent way for market participants to deal with their risk management, contrary to the over-the-counter (OTC) contracts for credit derivatives between banks and brokers.

Another burst of liquidity for the market is expected by introducing the future contract on the CDS-Index DJ I-Traxx Europe. This important credit index was constructed in 2004 from the merger of the European and Asian market barometers of the two index providers TRAC-X and DJ iBoxx representing the credit risk of 125 liquid European enterprises and, hence, is a benchmark for the current creditworthiness assessment of the market as well as the risk appetite of the investors. The index is rebalanced every half year.

One more reason to assume high growth for the credit derivatives market is the new Basel II regulation enforcing new rules for company capital. This new regulation only affects counterparty default risk, and it is advisable to transfer credit risks to counterparties with high creditworthiness and to use the thus freed regulatory company capital to safeguard other risks. Given that CDS are typically traded for any large company, the price of such a contract provides an additional assessment of the market and the pricing of new fixed income products. Empirical investigations have shown that the CDS markets process new market information more quickly than the traditional bond markets and thus provide a price leadership as well as an early indication of credit downgrades by rating agencies. The newly created CDS market contributes to an early discovery of financial market risks. With the help of CDS it is possible to exploit arbitrage possibilities in bond markets since a riskless bond and the respective CDS contract may duplicate a credit risky bond.[30]

CONCLUSION

We have gained valuable insight into the increasingly popular world of credit risk derivatives and have seen why CDS and BDS play an important role as financial instruments and risk management tools. Techniques for pricing these derivatives heavily depend on the reliance of the underlying credits (credit default times, respectively) and, in general, are only possible in the form of Monte Carlo simulation methods. Most difficult in this case turns out to be the modeling and evaluation of the joint distribution of dependent credit default times—this is when sophisticated concepts like

---

[30] See Deutsche Bundesbank (2004).

copula functions and importance sampling techniques enter the scene and save the day. Provided that you have the right mathematical toolbox at hand, CDS & Co. can be a powerful instrument in every investor's portfolio.

REFERENCES

Arvanitis, A. and Gregory, J. (1999) A Credit Risk Toolbox. In *Credit Risk — Models and Management*. London: Risk Books.

Bauer, H. (2000): *Maß- und Integrationstheorie*, de Gruyter.

Boyle P., Broadie M., and Glasserman, P. (2003): Monte Carlo Methods for Security Pricing. Working paper, School of Accountancy, University of Waterloo, Canada.

Deutsche Bundesbank (2004): CDS—Funktionen, Bedeutung und Informationsgehalt. *Deutsche Bundesbank Monatsbericht*, Dezember.

Frey, R. and McNeil, A. (2001) Modelling Dependent Defaults. Working paper, *ETH Zürich*, Zürich.

Frey, R., McNeil, A., and Nyfeler, M. (2001) Copulas and Credit Models. Working paper, *ETH Zürich*, Zürich.

Giesecke, K. (2001) Successive Correlated Defaults: Compensators and Simulation. Working paper, Cornell University, Ithaca, NY.

Giesecke, K. (2002) An Exponential Model for Dependent Defaults. Working paper, Department of Economics, Humboldt Universität, Berlin.

Hull, J. and White, A. (2000) Valuing CDS I: No Counterparty Default Risk. University of Toronto, Toronto, ON.

Jäckel, P. (2002) *Monte Carlo Methods in Finance*. Chichester, UK: John Wiley & Sons.

Karels, R. (2003) Valuing Credit Risk—Variance Reduction Techniques for MC Methods, *HfB* — Business School of Banking and Finance, Frankfurt, Germany.

Li, D.X. (1999): Constructing a Credit Curve. In *Credit Risk — Models and Management*, London: Risk Books.

Robert, C. and Casalla, G. (1999) *Monte Carlo Statistical Methods.* New York: Springer.

Schmidt, W. (2001) Credit Default Swaps: Analyse und Bewertung. Working paper, Deutsche Bank, Global Markets, Research and Analytics, Frankfurt, Germany.

Schmidt, W. (2003) First-to-Default Baskets und synthetische CDOs: Theorie und Bewertung, Working paper, Advanced Credit Derivatives, HfB, Frankfurt, Germany.

Schmidt, W. (2004) Kreditderivate und Defaultmodelle. HfB, Frankfurt, Germany.

Schmidt, W. and Ward, I. (2002) Pricing Default Baskets. *Risk Magazine*, January, 15(1): 111–114.

CHAPTER 15

Loan-Only Credit Default Swaps[1]

Moorad Choudhry

ABSTRACT

Credit default swaps have developed into a flexible and widely used tool for the management of credit risk and may be viewed as synthetic credit assets in their own right. A development in the credit default swap market from 2006 is the loan-only credit default swap. This is a credit default swap that references specifically a syndicated secured loan and not any other type of asset. The main motive for the creation of a specific loan-only credit default swap is that syndicated loans rank above bonds in a corporate winding-up (where loans are secured), so they are slightly different assets compared to bonds. As such, there are times when only this specific asset class, as opposed to loans and bonds together, needs to be hedged or accessed by investors. Hence, the loan-only credit default swap has potential to be a very popular hedging tool for commercial banks. In this chapter we describe the structure and characteristics of loan-only credit default swaps, and how it differs from vanilla credit default swaps.

---

[1] This article is an extract from Chapter 16 of *Bank Asset and Liability Management: Strategy, Trading, Analysis* by Moorad Choudhry, published by John Wiley & Sons (Asia), 2007. Reproduced with permission.

INTRODUCTION

Credit default swaps (CDSs) are synthetic credit instruments that can be used to mitigate credit risk exposure. A CDS is sometimes described as analogous to an insurance contract, but actually this is not quite correct. The risk protection buyer does not need to own an asset in the name on which the CDS is written or to have suffered a loss on occurrence of a credit event. Also different from conventional insurance is that a CDS contract has a payoff amount that is pre-determined by a set formula.

A development in the CDS market from 2006 is the loan-only credit default swap (LCDS). This is a CDS that references specifically a syndicated secured loan and not any other type of asset.[2] The main motive for the creation of a specific LCDS is that syndicated loans rank above bonds in a corporate winding-up (where loans are secured), so they are slightly different assets compared to bonds. As such, there are times when only this specific asset class, as opposed to loans and bonds together, needs to be hedged or accessed by investors. Written on the same reference name an LCDS would, all else being equal, trade tighter than a CDS, because there is a higher expected recovery rate on the former. Loan-only credit default swaps has potential to be a very popular hedging tool for banks.

At the time of writing, LCDS contract documentation had not been standardized, although the International Swaps and Derivatives Association (ISDA) published template forms for LCDS documentation in May 2006 and June 2006 for the European and U.S. markets, respectively. This highlights how the instruments differ in some respects in the two markets. The main difference is a U.S. LCDS does not automatically expire following the maturity or repayment of the underlying reference loan. This is not the case with European LCDS. In effect the U.S. instrument is more of an investment product, while the European LCDS is more of a hedging product. It is possible that ultimately both forms of product will be available in either market.

---

[2] A vanilla CDS would reference bonds and unsecured loans, ABS-CDS would reference asset-backed securities.

GROWTH OF LCDS

The motives behind the inception of the LCDS are essentially the same as those behind the rise of the original credit derivative market. The instrument is used for the same reasons as vanilla CDS, including credit risk management, as an alternative to the cash market; its principal use in the European market is as a risk management tool by banks that originate syndicated secured loans. The implementation of Basel II has also been a trade driver, as the new regulatory regime will result in higher capital charges for certain types of syndicated loans. The growth in collateralized loan obligation (CLO) business has also lead to the demand for LCDS, in two ways: as a hedging tool and also as an investment tool for synthetic CLOs that source their assets in the LCDS market. The advantages of LCDS to a synthetic CLO manager mirror those of CDS with regard to synthetic CDOs: They provide access to assets that might not otherwise be available in the cash loan market.

Loan-only credit default swaps have the same flexibility as vanilla CDSs and have the same application for bank asset and liability management (ALM) purposes. These include

- Credit risk management: Managing exposure of syndicated loan books, without having to impact on client relationships
- Regulatory capital management: Reducing the Basel regulatory capital charge (connected with the above)

For investors, LCDS enable access to the syndicated loan market, which might not otherwise be available; other advantages include

- Ability to transact tax-efficient deals that might not be possible in the cash market, where loans are subject to withholding tax and other tax consequences
- Capital structure arbitrage: Relative-value-type trades involving loans spread against bonds, senior loans against mezzanine or junior loans, etc.

At the time of writing, in the European market LCDS were trading at a negative basis to cash loans, making them unattractive for investment purposes when compared to cash.[3] The negative basis appeared to be

---

[3] See Choudhry (2004) for details on the CDS-cash basis.

driven by an excess of demand over supply, driving spreads down; this demand was driven by banks hedging their syndicated loan books.

CHARACTERISTICS OF LCDS

The loan-only credit default swap features the following characteristics, which are worth considering when making a comparison to vanilla CDS contracts:

- **Reference obligation:** In the European market the reference obligation for an LCDS is all the tranches of a syndicated loan in the name of the obligor, including any undrawn tranches or an undrawn credit facility. It can be a second-lien or third-lien tranche as well as a first-lien tranche. In a U.S. LCDS the reference obligation is similar except it must be specifically designated as a reference obligation. In theory this is more restrictive. The deliverable obligation on occurrence of credit event is (1) for European LCDS, the reference obligation and (2) for U.S. LCDS a loan as defined in the contract definitions.

- **Cancelability:** In the cash market in Europe, syndicated loans may be paid off ahead of the stated maturity date (in some cases there is a period of one year after the start of the loan when they cannot be repaid). Consequently, European LCDSs terminate on paydown of the underlying reference loan. However there is no feature for adjusting notional on the LCDS, which one might have expected given that many syndicated loans are amortizing. United States LCDSs are not cancelable upon repayment of the reference asset and instead allow for substitution of the reference asset with an equivalent one.

- **Restructuring:** European LCDSs include loan restructuring as a credit event. Such occurrences are fairly frequent in the syndicated loan market, and hence banks would wish to be able to buy protection on the loans that covered for this risk. Restructuring is not a credit event for U.S. LCDS.

- ○ Note that under Basel II, full regulatory capital relief on a syndicated loan asset is granted only if credit derivative protection written on that asset includes restructuring as a credit event. Otherwise, only partial capital relief can be obtained, to a maximum of 60 percent of the LCDS notional value.
- **Pricing:** LCDS premiums, like vanilla CDS, are fixed. This contrasts with the underlying syndicated loan, which is invariably floating rate. In addition, there will be a basis difference between the swap and loan, arising from a number of different factors.
- **Settlement:** the settlement mechanism for both European and U.S. LCDS is predominantly physical settlement. This has the potential to create delivery issues in the future if there is a shortage of deliverable assets. A notice of physical settlement (NOPS) must be delivered within 30 days of the credit event determination date, upon which the protection seller must pay over the protection payment to the protection buyer.
  - ○ For physical settlement, an amount equal to the notional amount multiplied by the reference price. The protection buyer delivers the deliverable obligation in return.
  - ○ For cash settlement, an amount equal to the reference price minus the recovery rate on the reference obligation, multiplied by the notional amount.

Note how the protection payment formulas for settlement of LCDS differ from those of vanilla CDS.

Partly as a means to avoid such problems, in a European LCDS the protection seller can request cash settlement. If no market price is available for any of the deliverable obligations, the physical settlement will have to apply.

The protection buyer cannot select cash settlement.

SUMMARY

It is unlikely that the differences between European and U.S. LCDS will remain in place, and we would expect some convergence between the two forms. Possibly both versions may be available in either market at some stage, but market demand will ultimately determine which structure is most popular and thus retained.

REFERENCE

Choudhry, M. (2004) *Structured Credit Products: Credit Derivatives and Synthetic Securitisation.* Singapore: John Wiley & Sons.

CHAPTER 16

Definition and Evaluation of Basket Credit Derivatives and Single-Tranche Collateralized Debt Obligation Swaps

Marcus R. W. Martin, Stefan Reitz, and Carsten S. Wehn[1]

ABSTRACT

In this chapter, the authors introduce methods for the evaluation of basket credit derivatives as well as for standardized single-tranche collateralized debt obligation swaps. Therefore, first, we provide an in-depth definition and introduction of credit derivatives on baskets of reference assets including indexes and single-tranche collateralized debt obligation swaps. Then, the model by Li with a Gaussian copula acts as an indicator for valuation models of basket credit derivatives. We also present the general single-factor model and methods for an industry standard quotation incorporating the Vasiczek model and recursive determination of the loss distribution. We complete our article with a presentation of the latest developments including models with local and stochastic correlation. Finally, we provide a résumé and draw some conclusions from the presented definition and methods for evaluating basket credit derivatives.

---

[1]All opinions given within this text are those of the authors and should not be assumed to be those of their respective employers. None of the methods described herein is claimed to be in actual use.

INTRODUCTION

When modeling a portfolio of reference assets, one has to take into account elements that may complicate the issue, which is why industrial models are still not fully developed. As a starting-point, we introduce credit derivatives on baskets of reference asset of increasing complexity, describing first-to-default baskets, collateralized debt obligations, and single-tranche collateralized debt obligations. We propose the Gaussian copula model as an established evaluation tool for basket default swaps and collateralized debt obligations in the third section of this article. The fourth section extends the multifactor model by incorporation of the Gauss–Vasicek model and recursive determination of the loss distribution, and discusses related issues. The last section discusses recent developments and extensions to be considered in the future.

CREDIT DERIVATIVES ON BASKETS OF REFERENCE ASSETS

First-to-Default Basket

We can consider a first-to-default (FTD) basket as an extension of a standard credit default swap (CDS), where the reference now consists of a basket of single reference assets. The single reference assets themselves are very often corporate bonds or loans. The construction is very similar to a CDS (cf. Figure 16.1); thus, the protection buyer regularly pays a premium to the protection seller. Once the first credit event occurs in the basket of M reference assets, the protection seller has to pay compensation to the protection buyer, and the contract expires.

At first glance, the premium for the protection seller should be higher for a basket of different reference assets compared with a single reference asset because the probability of a first arbitrary default is higher than the probability of a special default. This reflects the motivation of the protection seller to sell protection on a basket that typically consists of 3 to 10 reference assets. The maximum loss is per construction restricted to a single reference asset.

Heuristically, the level of diversification plays an important role in the valuation of the basket credit derivative in contrast with a single-name credit derivative. The higher the diversification is between the reference

Scheme of a first-to-default basket

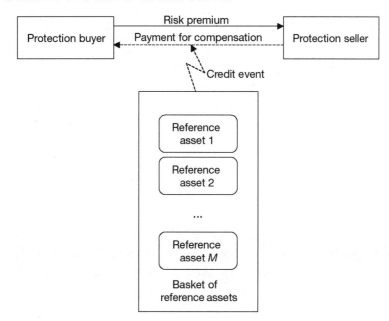

assets in the basket, the higher the premium should be, because the probability of an arbitrary default increases. The fair risk premium is between the maximum of the single CDS spreads and the sum of the single CDS spreads. The protection buyer has to pay a lower premium to receive protection for the basket of reference assets than with single-name CDS. A further derivative from the FTD basket is the mth-to-default basket, where the protection seller gives protection not on the first default but on the mth default that occurs in the basket. Owing to the fact that the FTD already takes a large proportion of credit risk from the basket of reference assets, mth-to-default baskets are rather rare.

Collateralized Debt Obligations

In addition other credit derivatives, collateralized debt obligations (CDOs) are a way to securitize credit risks. Here, the basket of reference assets consists of a relatively high number M of single names, e.g., more than 100 to several hundreds. A basket or portfolio of reference assets is securitized via a special purpose vehicle, a corporation only existing for this task, into several tranches of different seniority. Losses coming from the portfolio strike the different tranches very differently. The more senior tranches are preferred to the tranches with lower seniority. Hence, the first losses will strike the equity piece (sometimes also called *first loss tranche* or *junior piece*), which is thus subordinated to the other tranches.

Figure 16.2 depicts the mode of operation of a securitization by a CDO. Whenever a credit event (e.g., a default) of a certain reference asset occurs, the respective losses are accumulated in the equity piece. The premiums of the basket of reference assets are first served to the most senior tranches, and this principle is known as *waterfall structure* [see, e.g., Fabozzi et al. (2004)]. If for the equity piece the nominal value is exhausted, the next losses are given to the least senior mezzanine piece. Historically, CDOs served as a tool to restructure junk bonds and illiquid instruments [thus being very close to the asset class of asset-backed securities (ABS)], but now they are most commonly created synthetically, implying that the basket of reference assets is created by CDS. Within a synthetic CDO, the investor is in a much better position to deploy his own models rather than within ABS, where the basket is also larger.

F I G U R E   16.2

Securitization via a CDO and tranching, accumulation of premiums and losses

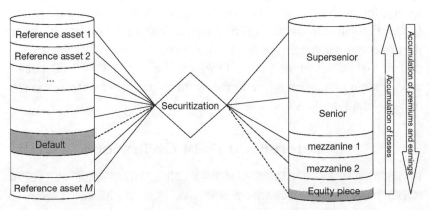

The mathematical treatment of a CDO requires a credit risk model as mentioned above. In addition, the correlated behavior of the different reference assets plays an important role within this context. For a basket of reference assets consisting of loans, the denomination as collateralized loan obligation (CLO) is quite common as well as for collateralized bond obligations (CBOs).

Standardized Single-Tranche CDO Swaps

For each tranche of a CDO, one has to define an attachment point and a detachment point. These values (given as a percentage of the CDO's nominal value) determine the beginning and ending value for an investor in a respective tranche, where losses occurring in the whole basket of reference assets will strike the investor. The equity tranche has an attachment point of 0 percent, whereby the most senior tranche has a detachment point of 100 percent. The investment resembles the investment in a bull call spread in the losses of the portfolio, i.e., a long call position with a strike of the attachment point and a short call with the strike equaling the detachment point (see Figure 16.3, where the accompanying payment function is shown).

F I G U R E   16.3

Interpretation of a tranche investment in a CDO as a bull call spread

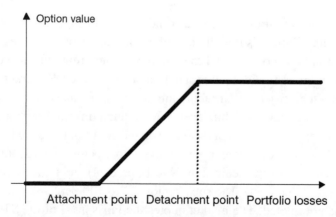

Attachment point   Detachment point   Portfolio losses

We use the following example to illustrate this relationship. Having a basket of 100 equally weighted reference assets with an attachment point of 3 percent and a detachment point of 6 percent and assuming a loss given default of 60 percent, the investor in the tranche will not be strike by the first five credit events (having a total loss of $5/100 \cdot 60\% = 3\%$ of the nominal value): starting from the sixth credit event and ending with the 10th event. The investor participates in the losses with one-fifth of the invested nominal value, respectively [see, e.g., Schlögl (2005)]. Thus, subordinated tranches exhibit a higher risk than the more senior ones. The thinner the tranche (i.e., the closer are the attachment and detachment points), the higher is the leverage. With regards to the effect of diversification, it is clear at first sight that (if we simplify "correlation" to a single figure) the higher the correlation, the higher the probability, so that at least one arbitrary default occurs. Hence, the value of the equity tranche is higher, and the value of the supersenior tranche becomes lower [see, e.g., Amato and Gyntelburg (2005)].

Since the merger of the companies iBoxx Ltd and TRAC-X LLC to the International Index Company (IIC), derivatives on standardized products like the so-called single-tranche standardized collateralized debt obligation (STCDO) swaps are becoming more popular. The STCDO is very similar to a CDO owing to construction as a CDS on a tranche of a portfolio. The protection seller receives a regular premium and has to pay for eventual defaults in the underlying basket. The credit derivatives indexes iTraxx and CDX are very popular portfolios. Owing to their standardization, credit indexes and derivatives on them are very liquid products. Nowadays also futures on the iTraxx index are exchange traded. The main index iTraxx Europe is liquidly traded in four different maturities, 3, 5, 7, and 10 years and consists of 125 equally weighted reference names comprising the most liquid single-traded names on the CDS market. A new series is issued twice a year taking into account the latest and most liquid CDS as well as several subindexes that are quoted from different sectors.

The tranching points of STCDOs on the credit indexes are fixed with equity (0 to 3 percent), junior mezzanine (3 to 6 percent), mezzanine (6 to 9 percent), junior supersenior low (9 to 12 percent) and junior supersenior high (12 to 22 percent). The supersenior (22 to 100 percent) is not traded and thus not quoted. The market quotes the fair spread of the STCDO in basis points (bps). Exceptionally, for the equity piece with a fixed premium of 500 bps, the up-front payment is quoted as a percentage of the nominal value.

As correlation is the main parameter that determines the premium or the value of the STCDO, the market nowadays is quoting the implicit correlation of a tranche (see the Introduction to this chapter). The Gaussian model that only needs a single correlation value as input yields as a market standard, although as for the implicit volatility within the market standard model of Black–Scholes, the parameter implicit correlation is not constant for different tranches as the model would assume (see the Introduction to this chapter). Empirically, higher tranches show a higher implicit correlation, reflecting that for senior tranches the spread is relatively high. The correlation crisis of 2005 first demonstrated the different beliefs of the market in the correlation and led to high losses by several investors.

EVALUATION OF BASKET DEFAULT SWAPS AND CDOs

For the evaluation of basket default swaps or CDOs we assume that the reader is familiar with the concepts of pricing single-name credit derivatives using simple (deterministic) intensity-based approaches [see, e.g., Schönbucher (2003) for an excellent introduction and discussion of this approach, or Martin et al. (2006)]. In the following section, we provide the classical copula modeling approach of Li (2000) to come up with the standard approach to default basket pricing, which also provides the basis for pricing STCDO swaps and more recent pricing techniques.

Quick Reminder Pricing of Single-Name Credit Default Swap

The basic idea is that all information needed to price single-name credit default swaps (CDSs) can be derived exogenously from the market quotations on fair CDS spreads. In this model a default occurs resulting from the first jump of the exponentially distributed default time τ having deterministic intensity λ. Following market practices for quotation of plain vanilla CDS, we assume that (1) the recovery rate is constant, (2) the intensity rate is continuous from the right, and (3) the intensity rate has limits from the left.

A CDS can be decomposed into two legs of cash flows, which are called *premium leg* and *protection leg*, respectively. They describe the cash flows to be exchanged by the counterparties at the settlement days $t_j \in [0, T], j \in \{1, \ldots, v\}$, over the whole lifetime T of the contract or at (and, in this case only, until) time of default τ, respectively. The present value of a CDS for a protection seller is now given by

$$\text{PV}_{sell} = N \left\{ s \sum_{j=1}^{v} df(t_j)\left(t_j - t_{j-1}\right) G(t_j) - (1-R) \sum_{j=1}^{v} df\left(\tfrac{t_{j-1}+t_j}{2}\right)\left[G(t_{j-1}) - G(t_j) \right] \right\}$$

with notional amount N, credit spread s, discount factor function $df(\cdot)$, and recovery rate R wherein for calculating the survival probabilities G we have $G\,(0) = 1$ and

$$G(t_j) = \exp\left(-\sum_{k=1}^{j} \lambda_k \left(t_j - t_{j-1}\right) \right) = G(t_{j-1}) \exp\left(-\lambda_j \left(t_j - t_{j-1}\right) \right)$$

For deriving the survival probabilities we assume the default intensity to be a piecewise constant function of time, $\lambda(t) := \Sigma \lambda_k \, 1_{[t_{j-1}; t_j]}(t)$ that can be derived by market data via bootstrapping.

Under the rather restrictive assumptions of flat risk-free yield curves, flat intensity curves, and flat credit spread curves, one can easily derive a rule of thumb, well-known as *credit triangle*, which is given by $\lambda \approx s/(1 - R)$. This formula illustrates that, even in this rather simplistic situation, fair credit spreads, intensity rates, and recovery rates (as well as interest rates) directly influence one another. Hence, the formula already implies the need for a thorough modeling approach recognizing these dependencies.

The Li Gaussian Copula Model

Li's (2000) approach to model multiname (basket) credit derivatives [cf. Li's original paper and Schmidt and Ward (2002)] is to derive correlated default times of the single underlyings using a Gaussian copula. This is achieved by a two-step approach.

Step 1: Prepare the Simulation of Possible Default Times for Each Single Asset

Taking the cumulated distribution function (CDF) $F_j(t) = Q(\tau_j < t)$ of the default time τ_j of a single asset $j \in \{1, \ldots, n\}$ as a starting point, we have $F_j(\tau_j) \sim U[0, 1]$, i.e., $F_j(\tau_j)$ is a uniformly distributed random variable (RV) on $[0, 1]$. Consequently, the RV $\tau_j := F_j^{-1}(U_j)$ has the CDF $F_j(\cdot)$ for every uniformly distributed random number $U_j \sim U[0, 1]$. Therefore, using any random number generator, we can easily simulate default times of asset number $j \in \{1, \ldots, n\}$ in our basket.

Step 2: Use the Gaussian Copula to Model Dependence of Default Times

The cash flows of the CDO depend on the defaulting times of the single assets in the pool, i.e., on the default time vector $\tau := (\tau_1, \tau_2, \ldots, \tau_n)$. Hence, for the pricing of the respective credit derivative we need the joint default time distribution of this vector of single default times. In other words, we are looking for a multivariate CDF $F(t) = F(t_1, t_2, \ldots, t_n) = Q$ $(\tau_1 < t_1, \tau_2 < t_2, \ldots, \tau_n < t_n)$ of $\tau := (\tau_1, \tau_2, \ldots, \tau_n)$ that has the marginal CDFs $F_j(\cdot)$ for $j \in \{1, \ldots, n\}$. According to Sklar's classical theorem, we know that there always exists a (continuous) copula that fulfils all these requirements. Unfortunately, the theorem only states the pure existence of such a copula but gives no clue how to derive it explicitly.

Li (2000) was the first to model the dependence structure of the default times by using the Gaussian copula as a first guess to incorporate the dependencies between the single underlyings starting from the marginal distributions. Clearly, this choice includes a fairly high model risk such that one has to keep an eye on any circumstances indicating a better choice of the model or even copula [cf. Frey et al. (2001)].

Therefore, to facilitate the two-step approach described above, we use the multivariate CDF derived from the Gaussian copula $F(t_1, \ldots, t_n)$: $= \Phi_n (\Phi^{-1}(F_1(t_1)), \ldots, \Phi^{-1}(F_n(t_n)), \Sigma)$ where $\Phi_n (\ldots, \Sigma)$ denotes the CDF of the n-dimensional normal distribution with zero mean and correlation matrix Σ. Note that $F_j^{-1}(\Phi(x_j)) < t_j \Leftrightarrow x_j < \Phi^{-1}(F_j(t_j))$ holds for all assets $j \in \{1, \ldots, n\}$. Hence, we can start with a random realization $(x_1, \ldots, x_n)$ drawn from an n-dimensional normal distribution with zero mean and correlation matrix Σ to simulate the correlated default times of the assets as follows:

1. Use the market-quoted CDS spreads to derive the piecewise constant intensity functions $\lambda_j (\cdot) = \Sigma^v_{k=1} \lambda_{j,k} 1_{[t_{k-1},\, t_k)}$ by bootstrapping, which yield the marginal default distributions $F_j (\cdot) = 1 - G_j (\cdot)$ for $j \in \{1, \ldots, n\}$ (cf paragraph 3).

2. To generate a sample of random realizations $(x_1, \ldots, x_n)$ drawn from an n-dimensional normal distribution with zero mean and correlation matrix Σ, we proceed as follows:

   a. Generate n independent standard normal distributed RVs r_j forming a random vector $r := (r_1, \ldots, r_n)^T$.

   b. Find a lower triangular matrix Γ (the Cholesky matrix), such that $\Sigma = \Gamma \cdot \Gamma^T$.

   c. Defining $x = (x_1, \ldots, x_1)^T := \Gamma \cdot (r_1, \ldots, r_1)^T = \Gamma \cdot r$, we obtain a vector of normally distributed RVs x_j with zero mean that are correlated according to Σ.

3. Finally, we derive from this drawing the default times $\tau_j := F^{-1}_j (\Phi(x_j))$ for $j \in \{1, \ldots, n\}$. Observe that existence and uniqueness of these default times are ensured by the strict monotonicity of $F_j (\cdot)$ and $\lim_{t \to \infty} F_j (t) = 1$.

This procedure has to be repeated in a Monte Carlo simulation for the appropriate number of times.

Evaluation of CDO and STCDO Swaps

For the evaluation of a CDO or STCDO swap on a given pool of assets with total notional $N := \Sigma_{j=1}^n N_j$, where each asset $j \in \{1, \ldots, n\}$ has notional N_j and deterministic recovery rate R_j, respectively, we need to model the cumulated loss on that pool. Therefore, let us denote by

$$L_t := \frac{1}{N} \sum_{j=1}^n N_j \left(1 - R_j\right) 1_{\{\tau_j \leq t\}}$$

the RV that gives cumulated percentage loss of our collateral pool up to time t. Now, for any STCDO swap with given attachment point $A \in [0\%, 100\%]$ and detachment point $B \in [A, 100\%]$ [with respect to (w.r.t.)

the total notional of the pool] the cumulated percentage loss of tranche $\langle A, B \rangle$ is calculated as

$$L_{\langle A;B \rangle}(t) := \frac{1}{B-A}\left[\left(L_t - A\right)^+ - \left(L_t - B\right)^+\right] = \frac{-A}{B-A}L_{\langle 0;A \rangle}(t) + \frac{B}{B-A}L_{\langle 0;B \rangle}(t)$$

Hence, the cumulated percentage loss $L_{\langle A; B \rangle}(t)$ of tranche $\langle A; B \rangle$ can be interpreted in terms of a call spread option on the total cumulative percentage loss L_t. Alternatively, it can also be interpreted as a simple linear combination of the percentage cumulative losses of the equity tranches $\langle 0; A \rangle$ and $\langle 0 ; B \rangle$. Every STCDO swap consists of two legs, the premium leg and the protection leg. They describe the cash flows to be exchanged by the counterparties entering a STCDO swap on a tranche $\langle A; B \rangle$ at the settlement days $t_j \in [0; T]$, $j \in \{1, ..., v\}$, over the whole lifetime T of the contract:

- *Protection leg cash flows*: The protection seller provides the incremental percentage loss of the tranche $\langle A; B \rangle$ between any two settlement days given any default that took place in the respective time period $[t_{j-1}; t_j]$ of length $\Delta_j : = (t_j - t_{j-1})_{DCC}$ [according to the chosen day count convention (DCC)].

- *Premium leg cash flows*: The protection buyer has to pay the premium $s_{A; B}$ on the last day $t_j \in [0; T], j \in \{1, ..., v\}$, of each settlement period $[t_{j-1}; t_j]$ and is given as a percentage of the outstanding notional at the point in time. This is equal to $N \cdot [1 - L_{\langle A; B \rangle}(t_j)]$; thus the protection seller will receive an amount of on $\Delta_j N [1 - L_{\langle A; B \rangle}(t_j)]$ on this settlement date for selling protection to the protection buyer over the settlement period $[t_{j-1}; t_j]$.

In mathematical terms, this means today's present value of the protection leg equals

$$PV_{\langle A; B \rangle}^{Prot.} = N \cdot E\left(\sum_{j=1}^{v} df\left(\tau_j\right) \cdot \left[L_{\langle A;B \rangle}\left(t_{j-1}\right) - L_{\langle A; B \rangle}\left(t_j\right)\right] 1_{\left\{\tau_j \in [t_{j-1}; t_j]\right\}} \right)$$

$$\approx N \sum_{j=1}^{v} df\left(t_j\right) \cdot \left[E\left(L_{\langle A;B \rangle}\left(t_{j-1}\right)\right) - E\left(L_{\langle A;B \rangle}\left(t_j\right)\right)\right]$$

while today's present value of the premium leg of the STCDO swap is given by

$$
PV_{\langle A;B \rangle}^{Prem.} = s_{\langle A;B \rangle} N \cdot E\left(\sum_{j=1}^{v} \Delta_j \cdot df\left(t_j\right)\left[1 - L_{\langle A;B \rangle}\left(t_j\right)\right] \right) =: s_{\langle A;B \rangle} \cdot CBPV_{\langle A;B \rangle}
$$

wherein

$$
CBPV_{<A;B>} := N \cdot E\left(\sum_{j=1}^{v} \Delta_j\, df\left(t_j\right)\left[1 - L_{\langle A;B \rangle}\left(t_j\right)\right] \right)
$$

is called the *credit risky basis point value* (bpv) of the tranche $\langle A; B \rangle$ and is similar to the bpv typically used for interest rate swaps. It measures the loss on a STCDO swap position in case the traded fair tranche spread $s_{\langle A;\,B \rangle}$ increases by 1 bp—according to the market practice in all liquidly traded derivatives markets, the STCDO swap is entered at no costs for both counterparties, i.e., today's present values of the premium and protection leg have to cancel out. This is achieved by choice of the premium equal to

$$
s_{\langle A;B \rangle} = \frac{\sum_{j=1}^{v} df\left(t_j\right)\left[E\left(L_{\langle A;B \rangle}\left(t_{j-1}\right)\right) - E\left(L_{\langle A;B \rangle}\left(t_j\right)\right)\right]}{E\left(\sum_{j=1}^{v} \Delta_j\, df\left(t_j\right)\left[1 - L_{\langle A;B \rangle}\left(t_j\right)\right] \right)} = \frac{PV_{\langle A;B \rangle}^{Prot.}}{CBPV_{\langle A;B \rangle}}
$$

Since the loss on a tranche can be directly derived from the portfolio loss as described above, the risk premium quoted in the markets (as, e.g., on iTraxx or CDX tranches) can be used to infer information on those parameters needed to model the cumulative percentage loss of the underlying portfolio.

QUOTATION BY A SINGLE-FACTOR MODEL

General Framework and Incorporation of the Gauss–Vasicek Model

A multifactor model is defined by a M-dimensional real RV $Y := Y_t$ with time-dependent density function $\psi : [0, \infty] \times IR^m \to [0, 1]$ and conditional default probabilities $f_j\,(t, y): [0, \infty) \times IR^m \to [0, 1]$, $f_j\,(t, y) := Q$

$(\tau_j > t \mid Y = y)$, where the variables τ_j represent random default time for $j \in \{1, ..., n\}$ (conditionally independent with respect to $Y = y$) and Q is the risk-neutral measure (which is assumed to exist and be uniquely determined). Unconditional default probabilities can be obtained by integration

$$\int_{y \in IR^m} f_j(t, y) \cdot \psi(t, y)\, dy = Q(\tau_j > t)$$

Within this general framework, factor models for pricing standardized STCDO swaps can be formulated, e.g., the one-factor model with Gaussian copula (Gauss–Vasicek model). We now choose $M: = 1$ and $Y \sim N(0, 1)$ with non-time-dependent density function

$$\psi(t, y): = \varphi(y) : = (1/\sqrt{2\pi})\exp(-y^2/2)$$

Our calculation shows that in this case we have

$$f_j(t, y) = 1 - \Phi\left(\frac{c_j(t) - \sqrt{\rho}y}{\sqrt{1-\rho}}\right)$$

where Φ is the CDF of a standardized normal distribution and ρ as well as $c_j(t)$ can be interpreted as parameters of a one-factor Gauss–Vasicek model. For each asset, a variable $B_j : = \sqrt{\rho} \cdot Y + \sqrt{1-\rho} \cdot \varepsilon_j$ with $\rho \in (0, 1)$ and $\varepsilon_j \sim^{iid.} N(0, 1)$ is introduced, indicating the creditworthiness of asset j, where the default event is defined by $B_j < c_j(t)$. Assuming an intensity-based model for individual defaults, i.e., $Q(\tau_j > t) = \exp(-\int_0^t \lambda_j(u)\, du)$ with time-dependent intensity $\lambda_j(\cdot)$, we finally obtain

$$Q(\tau_j \leq t) = Q(B_j \leq c_j(t)) = \Phi(c_j(t)) \iff c_j(t) = \Phi^{-1}\left(1 - \exp\left(-\int_0^t \lambda_j(u)\, du\right)\right)$$

This describes the single-factor model used by markets to quote CDO and STCDO tranches.

Determination of the Loss Distribution with Factor Models

In order to determine the conditional loss distribution of a portfolio of n assets (notional N_j, recovery rate R_j), we define a two-step recursive algorithm.

In the first step, potential losses within the time interval $[0, T]$ for asset j are expressed in the form $l_j(T) = k_j \cdot E\ (k_j \in IN_0)$, where E is a predefined loss unit (the smaller E is chosen, the better is the approximation, but the more calculation steps have also to be performed). The random portfolio loss (in multiples of E) resulting form the first j assets is given by

$$L_j := \sum_{i=1}^{j} \frac{l_i}{E} = \sum_{i=1}^{j} \frac{(1-R_i)\cdot N_i}{E} \cdot 1_{\{\tau_i \le T\}}$$

for $j \in \{1, \ldots, n\}$ and with $L_0 := 0$.
We set

$$p_j(Y) := Q(\tau_j \le T \mid Y) = 1 - f_j(T \mid Y) = \Phi\left(\frac{c_j(t) - \sqrt{\rho}Y}{\sqrt{1-\rho}}\right)$$

In the second step, the conditional distribution of L_j (in multiples of E) is computed according to the recursion formula

$$Q(L_{k+1} = K \mid Y) = \begin{cases} p_{j+1}(Y)\cdot Q(L_j = K - k_{j+1} \mid Y) + \\ (1 - p_{j+1}(Y))\cdot Q(L_j = K \mid Y), & \text{if } K \ge k_{j+1}, \\ (1 - p_{j+1}(Y))\cdot Q(L_j = K \mid Y), & \text{if } K < k_{j+1} \end{cases}$$

Here, we have $K \in IN_0$, and the first line describes the case of a loss amount of $K - K_{k+1}$ from the assets $1, \ldots, j$, whereas the second line handles the case of a loss of K from the assets $1, \ldots, j$, so that a loss of 0 has to occur for asset $j + 1$.

The above-mentioned steps define a recursive algorithm for calculating the conditional loss distribution where we have the initial condition $Q(L_0 = K \mid Y) = 1_{\{0\}}(K)$. Therefore, the unconditional loss distribution of a portfolio consisting of n assets is given by $Q\ (L \ge x) = \int_{I\!R} Q(L \ge x \mid Y = y) \cdot \varphi(y)\ dy$. When the conditional loss distribution has been determined by the recursion algorithm described in the previous section, it can be used to compute the above-mentioned integral numerically. For pricing CDO or STCDO tranches, we calculate the expected values of the type $E^Q(h(L))$, where h is a (piecewise) continuous real-valued function. Furthermore, it is important to quantify the sensitivity of these expected values with respect to the (unconditional) default probabilities p_j of the assets:

$$\frac{\partial E^Q(h(L))}{\partial p_j} = \int_{I\!R} \frac{\partial E^Q(h(L)\,|\,y)}{\partial p_j} \cdot \varphi(y)\,dy = \int_{I\!R} \frac{\partial p_j(y)}{\partial p_j} \cdot \frac{\partial E^Q(h(L)\,|\,y)}{\partial p_j(y)} \cdot \varphi(y)\,dy$$

$$= \int_{I\!R} \frac{\partial p_j(y)}{\partial c_j} \cdot \left(\frac{\partial p_j}{\partial c_j}\right)^{-1} \cdot \frac{\partial E^Q(h(L)\,|\,y)}{\partial p_j(y)} \cdot \varphi(y)\,dy$$

The first two factors of the integrand function can be computed as follows:

$$\frac{\partial p_j(y)}{\partial c_j} = \frac{\partial}{\partial c_j} \; \Phi\!\left(\frac{c_j - \sqrt{\rho}\cdot y}{\sqrt{1-\rho}}\right) = \frac{1}{\sqrt{1-\rho}} \varphi\!\left(\frac{c_j - \sqrt{\rho}\cdot y}{\sqrt{1-\rho}}\right)$$

and $\partial p_j/\partial c_j = \partial/\partial c_j \; \Phi\,(c_j)/ = \varphi(c_j)$. The third factor can be obtained by using the recursion:

$$\frac{\partial E^Q(h(L)\,|\,y)}{\partial p_j(y)} = \sum_K h(K) \cdot \frac{\partial Q(L_n = K\,|\,y)}{\partial p_j(y)}$$

$$= \sum_K h(K) \cdot \left[Q(L_{n-1}^{(j)} = K - k_j\,|\,y) - Q(L_{n-1}^{(j)} = K\,|\,y) \right]$$

Here, $L_{n-1}^{(j)}$ denotes the loss of the portfolio excluding asset j. By our explanations it has been demonstrated that factor models allow an effective computation of loss distributions as well as sensitivities, which are important tools for pricing and hedging credit derivatives.

Asymptotic Analytical Approximations and STCDO Swaps

We now focus on homogeneous, perfectly diversified portfolios, i.e., the following conditions are assumed to be fulfilled:

1. All default probabilities are equal to a value $p \in (0, 1)$,
2. All *EAD* numbers are set to 1 for each asset.

It can be shown that on these assumptions within the one-factor model, we have

$$Q(L \leq x) = \Phi\left(\frac{\sqrt{1-\rho} \cdot \Phi^{-1}(x) - c}{\sqrt{\rho}}\right)$$

where $c: = \Phi^{-1}(p)$ and $x \in [0, 1 - R]$ and where $R : = 1 - LGD$ is the recovery rate. Moreover, we have the following valuation formula for CDO or STCDO tranches:

Theorem: *In the above situation we have for* $A \in [0, 1)$

$$E^Q((L - A)^+) = (1 - R) \cdot \Phi_2\left(-\Phi^{-1}\left(\frac{A}{1-R}\right), c; -\sqrt{1-\rho}\right)$$

where $\Phi_2(x, y, z)$ *denotes the CDF of a bivariate Gaussian distribution with expectation vector* $(x, y)^t$, *variances equal to 1, and correlation* z. *The expected loss for a tranche with attachment point A and detachment point* $B \in [A, 1]$ *is given by*

$$E^Q(L_{<A;\ B>}) = E^Q\left(\frac{1}{B-A} \cdot \left[(L - A)^+ - (L - B)^+\right]\right)$$

$$= \frac{1-R}{B-A} \cdot \left(\begin{array}{l} \Phi_2\left(-\Phi^{-1}\left(\dfrac{A}{1-R}\right), c; -\sqrt{1-\rho}\right) - \Phi_2 \\[4mm] \left(-\Phi^{-1}\left(\dfrac{B}{1-R}\right), c; -\sqrt{1-\rho}\right) \end{array}\right)$$

The proof of this theorem is a straightforward computation of the expectation values in the one-factor model, and we will demonstrate the application of our results to STCDO swaps.

Consider a five-year STCDO swap on the iTraxx Europe index with a current average CDS spread of $s = 37.5$ bp for all 125 names in the underlying portfolio. We presume a flat interest rate curve with constant rate $r = 2$ percent for all maturities. Furthermore, we assume a homogeneous perfectly diversified portfolio with constant recovery rate $R = 40$

percent. The credit triangle as introduced above delivers an intensity rate of $\lambda = s/(1 - R) = 62.5$ bp for each name in the portfolio. If payments occur quarterly, then we can write $c_j(t) = \Phi^{-1}(1 - \exp(-\lambda(0.25)j)) = \Phi^{-1}(1 - \exp(-0.00625(0.25)j))$. With a correlation of ρ, the expected loss of a tranche with attachment point A and detachment point B at time $t_j = 0.25 \cdot j$ is given by

$$E^Q(L_{<A;B>}(t_j)) = \frac{0.6}{B-A} \cdot \left(\begin{array}{c} \Phi_2\left(-\Phi^{-1}\left(\dfrac{A}{0.6}\right),\, c_j(t); -\sqrt{1-\rho}\right) \\[2mm] -\Phi_2\left(-\Phi^{-1}\left(\dfrac{B}{0.6}\right),\, c_j(t); -\sqrt{1-\rho}\right) \end{array} \right)$$

Now the fair spread of this tranche is

$$S_{<A;B>} = \frac{PV_{<A;B>}^{Prot.}}{CBPV_{<A;B>}} = \frac{\sum_{j=1}^{20} e^{-2\% \cdot t_j} \cdot [q_j(\rho) - q_{j-1}(\rho)]}{\sum_{j=1}^{20} 0.25 \cdot e^{-2\% \cdot t_j} \cdot [1 - q_j(\rho)]}$$

where $q_j(\rho) := E^Q(L_{<A;B>}(t_j))$ The equity tranche $<0\%; 3\%>$ of the iTraxx Europe is quoted by a fixed spread of $s = 500$ bp plus an upfront payment. Observing a market quote for the up-front payment of e.g., 24.7 percent for the principal amount, we have $24.7\% = -\,CBPV_{<0\%;3\%>}(\rho) \cdot 500$ bp $+ PV_{<0\%;3\%>}^{Pot.}(\rho)$, which is a nonlinear equation for the unknown correlation ρ in the one-factor model. Solving the last equation yields $\rho = 21.0625$ percent, and this implied correlation can be used for pricing the other tranches. Alternatively, we could calibrate the correlation ρ such that the deviation between market quotes and model prices for all tranches are minimal. In both cases we observe that market quotes cannot be perfectly reproduced by means of the one-factor model, as there are always differences between market quotes and model prices.

Correlation, Smile Effect, and Skew

If the one-factor model for calculating values of STCDO tranches is used, then which correlation $\rho_{<A;B>}$ has to be used in order to produce the actual market quote of a tranche using our pricing model? This so-called implicit correlation can be observed by equating market prices with the theoretical pricing formula. We can determine implicit correlations for all tranches by solving nonlinear equations as per the example in the last section. If the fair spread $s_{<A;B>}$ for a tranche is observable in the market and no up-front payment has to be made, then we can write $s_{<A;B>} \cdot CBPV_{<A;B>} (\rho_{<A;B>})$ $= PV_{<A;B>}^{Prot.} (\rho_{<A;B>})$ and subsequently calculate $\rho_{<A;B>}$ from this relationship. This produces a set of implied correlations for all liquid tranches with observable spreads, e.g., the iTraxx tranches. Typically, we do not obtain a flat curve if we plot the tranches versus the accordingly implied correlations—although a flat curve should be expected if the assumptions of the one-factor model describe the behavior of the market correctly. Instead, we obtain a smile structure (the so-called correlation smile) similar to the volatility smiles observed in option markets (see Figure 16.4).

As an alternative to implicit correlations the so-called base correlations can be used. A base correlation is formally defined as an implicit correlation ρ_B belonging to a (synthetic) equity tranche with attachment point 0 and detachment point $B \in [0; 1]$, such that all market prices and implicit correlations for subordinated tranches can be reproduced by means of ρ_B.

Base correlations can be obtained by a bootstrapping procedure in the following way by considering the STCDO swap from the last section. First, we calculate the base correlation $\rho_{3\%}$ for the $<0\%; 3\%>$ equity

FIGURE 16.4

Implicit correlation smile for the different tranches of a STCDO

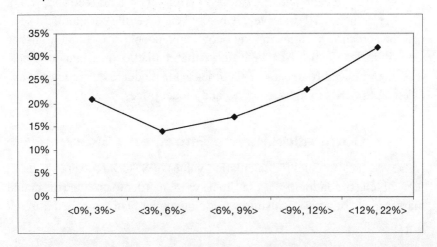

tranche, which we have previously obtained as $\rho_{3\%} = 21.0625$ percent. Second, we would to find the base correlation $\rho_{6\%}$ for the synthetic equity tranche $<0\%; 6\%>$. For this purpose we assume that the $<0\%; 3\%>$ tranche is priced with the observable market spread $s_{<3\%; 6\%>}$ of the $<3\%; 6\%>$ tranche using the base correlation $\rho_{3\%}$:

$$-\mathrm{CBPV}_{<0\%; 3\%>} \ (\rho_{3\%}) \ s_{<0\%; 3\%>} + \mathrm{PV}_{<0\%; 3\%>}^{\mathrm{Prot.}} \ (\rho_{3\%}).$$

All quantities in this formula can be calculated, and we obtain 0.1751 by calibration. The crucial point is a $<0\%; 6\%>$ tranche with spread $s_{<0\%; 6\%>}$ can be considered as a portfolio consisting of a $<0\%; 3\%>$ tranche with spread $s_{<0\%; 3\%>}$ and a $<3\%; 6\%>$ tranche with spread $s_{<3\%; 6\%>}$. As the fair market price of a $<3\%; 6\%>$ tranche with spread $s_{<3\%; 6\%>}$ will be 0, we can formally write for the $<0\%; 6\%>$ tranche $\mathrm{PV}_{<0\%; 6\%>} \ (s_{<0\%; 6\%>}, \rho_{6\%} = 0.1751 + 0 = 0.1751$, and solving for $\rho_{6\%}$ delivers the desired base correlation. It should be clear now that this algorithm can be applied to obtain base correlations for all "standard" detachment points $B \in \{3\%, 6\%, 9\%, 12\%, 22\%\}$. Plotting base correlations versus the corresponding detachment points reveals the so-called base correlation skew, which corresponds to an increase of implied correlations in more senior tranches (see Figure 16.5).

F I G U R E   16.5

Base correlations against detachment points

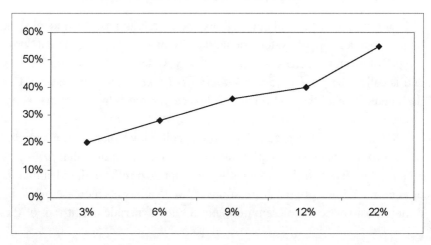

A monotony argument shows that base correlations are always uniquely determined, if they exist. They offer certain advantages compared with the implied correlations investigated in the last section and can be shown that the sum of all expected losses for all tranches is always equal to the expected loss of the entire portfolio when base correlations are used for pricing. When implied correlations are used, every tranche has "its own" correlation parameter, and it is not possible to compare different tranches using a consistent correlation structure. This problem does not exist with base correlations as they provide a consistent correlation structure over all tranches.

RECENT DEVELOPMENTS AND MODELS FOR EVALUATING STCDO AND BASKET CREDIT DERIVATIVES

The simple factor models described above are not able to capture the correlation skew adequately, as became evident during the so-called correlation crisis, which started in May 2005. Analogous with extensions of the classical Black–Scholes model for equity options to incorporate volatility smiles and skews, the classical one-factor correlation model has also been extended recently in various ways to cope with the correlation skew. Most strikingly, this has been done by the introduction of local correlations, stochastic correlations, or even jump processes [for further references as well as some comparison of these modeling approaches, please refer to Martin et al. (2006)].

Factor Models with Local Correlations

In factor models with local correlations, the correlation itself is modeled as being dependent on the systematic market factor $Y: = Y_t$. A prominent "prototype" of this model class was introduced by Andersen and Sidenius (2004) and is called the *random factor-loading (RFL) model*, which we intend to draft here. By slightly modifying the classical approach to the credit quality of each single asset j to $B_j: = a_j(Y) \cdot Y + v_j \cdot \varepsilon_j + m_j$ with ε_j iid., Andersen and Sidenius (2005) introduced an asset-specific idiosyncratic β weighting of the driving systematic market factor $Y: = Y_t$, which they call *firm-specific loading function*. Economically, this approach reflects the idea that in an economic downturn the correlations between all assets increase, while in a more positive economic environment the idiosyncratic credit risk of the underlyings is dominant. In order to normalize the RVs B_j with a mean of 0 and a variance of 1, we choose the parameters

$$m_j := -E^Q (a_j (Y) \cdot Y) = - \int_{y \in R^m} a_j (y) y \, dF^y (y)$$

and

$$v_j := \sqrt{1 - \mathrm{Var}^Q (a_j (Y) \cdot Y}} = \sqrt{1 - \int_{y \in R^m} (a_j (y) \cdot y)^2 \, dF^Y (y) + m_j^2}$$

where F^Y denotes the CDF of the systematic market factor. However, note that in the RFL model the variables B_j are in general *not* standard normally distributed any more. Nonetheless, following the same lines as for the Gauss–Vasicek one-factor model, we can easily derive the conditional loss distribution (conditional on the systematic market factor) based on the simple recursion described above. For this reason, we use the conditional probability

$$p_j(Y) = F_j^\varepsilon \left(\frac{c_j(t) - a_j(Y)Y - m_j}{v_j} \right) = 1 - f_j(t, Y)$$

where F_j^ε denotes the CDF of the independent identically idiosyncratic risk factors ε_j. Since the unconditional default probabilities are now available, by integration of the systematic market risk factor we obtain

$$p_j = Q(\tau_j \le T) = Q(B_j \le c_j) = E^Q \left(Q \left(\varepsilon_j \le \frac{c_j - a_j(Y)Y - m_j}{v_j} \middle| Y \right) \right)$$

This equation can now be used to derive the default thresholds c_j from market-quoted CDS prices as already described above. For some simple parametric forms of the firm-specific loading function, it is now straightforward to derive simple closed formulas that can be used to calibrate the RFL model [cf. Martin et al. (2006)]. Using a piecewise-constant step function, e.g., $a_j (Y) = \alpha_j \cdot 1_{Y \le \theta j} + \beta_j \cdot 1_{Y > \theta} j$, one can easily derive the model parameters to fit the market-quoted base correlation skew.

Another important example of local correlation models is given by Turc et al. (2005a; 2005b). Relatively similar approaches model the systematic or idiosyncratic factors using distributions other than the standard normal distribution [cf., among others, Burtschell et al. (2005a; 2005b), Kalemanova et al. (2005), and Moosbrucker (2006)].

A Brief Survey of Other Models

Despite having a correlation that is dependent on the systematic market factor in a deterministic way, the correlation itself can be modeled stochastically. The canonical way of stochastic correlation modeling is based on modeling the credit quality RV given by $B_j: = X_j \cdot Y + \sqrt{1 - X_j^2} \cdot \varepsilon_j$ with ε_j *iid.*, where the "correlation" RVs X_j are assumed to be stochastically independent of the systematic market risk factor $Y: = Y_t$ and all idiosyncratic factors ε_j. Note that in this special setting the RVs B_j are standard-normally distributed again, given that the systematic market risk factor as well as the idiosyncratic risk factors is standard normally distributed as well. This property considerably simplifies the calibration of stochastic correlation models (as compared to local correlation models) since default times $\tau_j = F_j^{-1}$ $(\Phi(B_j))$ can now easily be modeled by means of a Monte Carlo simulation.

In practice, the stochastic correlation X_j is modeled on the assumption that that it follows a discrete distribution in order to keep the number of model parameters treatable. This model class has the disadvantage that the resulting skews are in most cases not steep enough to reflect the actual skew observed in the markets and can lead to significant mispricings of mezzanine tranches, as reported by Andersen (2005).

Furthermore, some researchers and practitioners proposed the incorporation of systemic shock elements into the pricing models as a result of the correlation crisis 2005 [cf. Trinh et al. (2005) and Trinh Devarajan 2005), Turc et al. (2005), Tavares et al. (2004), or Burtschell et al. (2005a; 2005b)]. Since several questions concerning the actual applicability of these kinds of models arise, it remains an open question whether they will gain broad acceptance among practitioners [cf. Burtschell et al. (2005a; 2005b)].

Résumé and Prospects

We have discussed the evaluation of basket credit derivatives and STCDOs with various models and illustrated recent developments in the markets and

in the models used in the markets to quote STCDO swaps. We described
the relevant basket products as FTD and CDOs, starting with Li's (2000)
model, then introducing factor models similar to the Gauss–Vasicek model,
accompanied by some explanatory examples, pointing out the complexity
and dynamics in the models as well as the recent developments. From this
last section, it is clear that models are still evolving and that current market
developments are even faster than theoretical models.

REFERENCES

Amato, J.D. and Gyntelburg, J. (2005) Indextranchen von Credit Default
    Swaps und die Bewertung von Kreditrisikokorrelationen (in
    German). *BIZ quarterly report*, March.

Andersen, L. (2005) Portfolio Credit Derivatives—The State of Affairs.
    Working paper, Bank of America Securities, October.

Andersen, L. and Sidenius, J. (2004) Extensions to the Gaussian Copula:
    Random Recovery and Random Factor Loadings. *Journal of Credit
    Risk*, 1(1): 29–69.

Andersen, L. and Sidenius, J. (2005) Factor Models for CDO Pricing:
    Survey and Comments. *Journal of Credit Risk*, 1(3): 71–88.

Burtschell, X., Gregory, J., and Laurent, J.-P. (2005a) A Comparative
    Analysis of CDO Pricing Models. Working paper, BNP Paribas.

Burtschell, X., Gregory, J., and Laurent, J.-P. (2005b) Beyond the
    Gaussian Copula: Stochastic and Local Correlation. Working
    paper, BNP Paribas, October.

Fabozzi, F.J, Anson, M.J.P., Choudry, M., and Chen, R.R. (2004) *Credit
    Derivatives — Instruments, Applications and Pricing*. Hoboken,
    NJ: John Wiley & Sons.

Frey, R., McNeil, A.J., and Nyfeler, M. (2001) Copulas and Credit
    Models. *Risk*, (10): 111–114.

Kalemanova, A., Schmid, B., and Werner, R. (2005) The normal inverse
    Gaussian distribution for synthetic CDO pricing. Working Paper,
    RiskLab Germany, Algorithmics & Allianz.

Li, D.X. (2000) On Default Correlation—A Copula Approach. *Journal of Fixed Income*, 9: 43–54.

Martin, M.R.W., Reitz, S., and Wehn, C.S. (2006) Kreditderivate und Kreditrisikomodelle—Eine mathematische Einführung (in German). Wiesbaden: Vieweg Verlag.

Moosbrucker, Th. (2006) Pricing CDOs with Correlated Variance Gamma Distributions. Working paper, Cologne: University of Cologne.

Schlögl, L. (2005) Eine Einführung in die Bewertung von CDO Tranchen (in German). In J. Gruber, W. Gruber, and H. Braun (eds), *Praktikerhandbuch ABS und Kreditderivate, Stuttgart: Verlag Schäffer-Poeschel*.

Schmidt, W.M. and Ward, I. (2002) Pricing Default Baskets. *Risk*, (1): 111–114.

Schönbucher, P.J. (2003) Credit Derivatives Pricing Models: Models, Pricing and Implementation. Hoboken, NJ: John Wiley & Sons.

Tavares, P.A.C., Nguyen, T.-U., Chapovsky, A., and Vaysburd, I. (2004) Composite Basket Model. Working paper, Merrill Lynch.

Trinh, M. and Devarajan, M. (2005) Base Correlation in the Large Homogeneous Portfolio with Jumps (LHPJ) Model. *Lehman Bros. Fixed Income Quantitative Credit Research Quarterly*, Q–3.

Trinh, M., Thompson, R., and Devarajan, M. (2005) Relative Value in CDO Tranches: A View through ASTERION. *Lehman Bros. Fixed Income Quantitative Credit Research Quarterly*, Q–1.

Turc, J., Very, P., and Benhamou, D. (2005a) Pricing CDO with a Smile. Quantitative strategy paper. Société Générale Credit Research, February.

Turc, J., Very, P., and Benhamou, D (2005b) A Note on the Distribution of Asset Value in the Local Correlation Model. Quantitative strategy paper, Société Générale Credit Research, June.

CHAPTER 17

Contingent Credit Portfolio Management: Converting Derivatives Credit Risk into Market Risk

Kai Pohl

ABSTRACT

Credit default swaps have been used as a means for hedging credit exposures arising from either bonds or loans for several years. More recently, over the past five years or so, the focus has been extended to the credit exposure arising from derivatives transactions. The result of this is the establishment of a contingent credit portfolio management function at the leading financial institutions. They are generally driven by the "fair value" approach required by accounting standards (IAS 39) and are centered on the concept of a credit valuation adjustment to the mark-to-market valuation of the derivatives book of a bank, which essentially converts the credit risk of a derivatives book into a market risk.

This chapter on contingent credit portfolio management should enable the reader to get a good understanding of how the conversion of credit risk of derivatives into market risk is carried out at the top-tier investment banks.

INTRODUCTION

Credit default swaps (CDS) have been used as a means for hedging credit exposures arising from either bonds or loans for several years. More recently, over the past five years or so, the focus has been extended to the credit exposure arising from derivatives transactions. We observe varying degrees of implementation of a contingent credit portfolio management (CCPM) function at the leading financial institutions.

They are generally driven by the "fair value" approach required by accounting standards (IAS 39) and are centered on the concept of a credit valuation adjustment (CVA) to the mark-to-market valuation of the derivatives book of a bank. The assumptions behind the calculation of the CVA at different financial institutions are typically based on a comparable methodology, but the accuracy of this methodology ranges from the classic credit risk management approach using historical input parameters to true risk-neutral pricing concepts.

More advanced CCPM departments view the conversion of the credit risk into market risk as a profit opportunity that will enable a bank to develop new products mainly around the correlation between credit and non-credit risk factors that drive the risk-adjusted value of derivatives transactions. Before we discuss the finer points of advanced CCPM, we will look at the common methodology shared by both approaches to derive the credit risk-adjusted value of a derivative.

This chapter on CCPM should enable the reader to get a good understanding of how the conversion of credit risk of derivatives into market risk is carried out at the top-tier investment banks. It cannot cover all the slight variations of the theme as practiced by different market players. The author would be very interested in reader's comments on the topic because this function is still an emerging product for the banking industry and the industry as a whole will benefit from this function becoming more efficient.

DETERMINING THE CREDIT VALUATION ADJUSTMENT
Definition of the CVA

The CVA can loosely be described as the difference between risk free and the "risky" mark to market of a derivatives book. In other words, the CVA is the net present value of the derivatives book discounted with risky yield curves, whereby a risky yield curve would be defined as the risk-free yield curve as observed in the interbank market plus the spreads quoted on CDS for the various counterparties of the trades in the derivatives book.

Another definition is to view the CVA as the expected loss of the derivatives book. We have $CVA = \Sigma_{cp} \, EL_{cp}$, where EL_{cp} is the expected loss for counterparty cp.

The expected loss is derived from the future expected exposure (FEE) of the derivatives portfolio for a given counterparty and a vector of default probabilities that get applied to the FEE. We now define the expected loss of a derivatives portfolio with a given counterparty as

$$EL_{cp} = (1 - R_{cp}) \int \mathrm{FEE}_{cp}(t) p_{cp}(t) \, d(0, \ t) \, dt$$

where R_{cp} is the recovery assumption for counterparty cp, i.e., the price (as percentage) the derivatives portfolio could be sold at in the event of a default. FEE_{cp} is the FEE of the derivatives portfolio of counterparty (cp) expressed as a function of time; p_{cp} is the instantaneous default probability for counterparty cp, also expressed as a function of time; and $d(0, \ t)$ is the discount factor in the accounting currency between the base date and the valuation date t.

While there is no disagreement about the parameters used to calculate the mark to market (MTM) of a derivatives portfolio, the same cannot be said for the default probabilities used. Here it is where the varying degrees show how the CCPM function is implemented. An institution that follows the classic credit risk management approach will typically use historical default probabilities, while a risk-neutral pricing requires market implied default probabilities. These can be derived from quotes on CDS contracts (please refer to the standard literature on default swaps). Problems arise under this approach if there is no quoted CDS contract for a derivatives counterparty. We need to find proxies for market implied default probabilities, which we will discuss in a subsequent section.

In addition, please note that while we used the integral in the above formula for the calculation of the expected loss, in practice we would use a discreet version of that formula to reduce the number of time points for which we need to calculate both the FEE and the default probabilities.

Simulation of Future Expected Market Values

Option-based Approach

The profile of the FEE can be obtained by using an option-based approach in which we work with the fact that the present value of an option is the discounted expected future intrinsic value of the option. If the underlying of the option, e.g., is a swap, then the price of the swaption is the discounted expected mark to market of the underlying swap. Therefore, we can determine the FEE of a swap at any point over its life by pricing a series of swaptions, where the underlying swaps show the same parameters as the original swap (i.e., strikes are the same as the fixed rate, same payment frequencies, etc.), but the tenor of these swaps declines, while the FEE moves forward in time. More precisely,

$$FEM_{S(T.d,f,N,\Sigma)}(t) = O(t, T - t, d, f, N^*, \Sigma^*) / d(0, t)$$

where $S(T, d, f, N, \Sigma)$ stands for a swap with a tenor T, a direction (payer or receiver) d, a fixed rate f, notional schedule N, and payment schedule Σ. $O(t, T - t, d, N^*, \Sigma^*)$ is the swaption with expiry t on a swap with tenor $T - t$, direction d, a strike f equal to the fixed rate of the swap, adjusted notional schedule N^* (to account for roll down of cash flows in swap S), and adjusted payment schedule Σ^*. $d(0, t)$ is the discount factor between the base date and the value date t.

This closed-form approach only works easily for simple derivatives. Already for cross-currency swaps it poses significant mathematical challenges, and even interest rate swaps with payment mismatches require adjustments to the options price to account for the accrual generated by the timing difference of the coupon payments. While the attraction of the options-based approach is its calculation speed, it is generally too complicated to be used in the context of a portfolio of transactions. We will therefore not explore this approach further.

Monte Carlo Simulation

The more general and more widely used method to determine the FEE is Monte Carlo simulation (MCS). Monte Carlo simulation is insofar much more flexible and powerful as it can use any type of pricing formula for any type of derivative and wrap a simulation framework around it to generate future market values of the underlying transaction. It is also necessary if we want to determine the FEE of a portfolio of derivatives transactions. The downside of a MCS is that it requires a powerful information technology (IT) infrastructure to simulate large portfolios of complicated exotic derivatives.

The MCS uses a vector of valuation points that cover the life of the portfolio to be simulated. Ideally they cover all the payment dates of all the transactions in the portfolio to not miss out on any potential spikes in FEE. The MCS generates a distribution of future market values for those time points. This distribution is then used to determine the FEE at each of these time points. Please note that, in general, the FEE for a specific time points is not simply the average of the simulated future market values, but since credit losses only occur if the mark to market is positive, all negative mark to markets are set to zero and then the average is applied. We determine, $FEM(t) = \Sigma_n \max(0, MtM(n, t))$, where n is the number of MCS paths generated. For a more detailed description and discussion of MCS please refer to the relevant literature.

Correlation

Correlation is an important input parameter in determining the CVA. We have to distinguish two types of correlation that are applied differently. There is the correlation between the points on the yield curves and the foreign exchange rates. Every standard MCS engine will include correlation matrices to address these. Even in a risk-neutral pricing framework these will typically be historical correlation that requires periodic recalibration.

The more interesting and more hotly debated correlation is the correlation between the default probability and/or credit spreads and the FEE. This correlation is not typically part of the MCS framework, and not every CCPM desk applies it in its CVA calculation. It is necessary because obviously credit spreads and thus default probabilities are not stationary by nature. We therefore would like to make credits spreads stochastic for which we require a correlation assumption between them and other market variables.

This correlation is much more challenging to model and to determine. We will not go into the modeling details but will discuss some implications of this correlation in a following section.

Example

Consider a portfolio of derivatives transactions with the FEE profile shown in Figure 17.1. The dotted line shows the future expected mark to market as a result of purely averaging the paths of the MCS without setting negative mark to markets to zero. The solid line shows the profile with that correction as typically used for the expected loss calculation.

Further assume the following CDS curve for a AA-rated client in Table 17.1, which will be used to determine the default probabilities.

Assuming a recovery of 40 percent, we arrive at a CVA of €394,967. This number may appear surprisingly low given the approximately 10-year horizon of the exposure and a peak FEE of about €50 million, but due to the significant negative mark to market as at the base date and the low

F I G U R E   17.1

Future Expected Exposure profiles for AA client portfolio

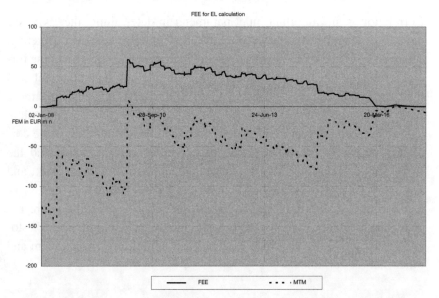

T A B L E   17.1

Credit default swap curve in
basis points for AA client

6 m	5
1 y	14
2 y	15
3 y	16
4 y	18
5 y	23
7 y	25
10 y	27
12 y	30
15 y	30
20 y	30
30 y	30

credit spreads, the expected exposure is greatly reduced, and the default probability is low.

APPLICATION OF THE CVA

Hedging and Pricing

Hedging Credit Sensitivities

The impact of using the concept of a CVA to value a fixed income derivatives book is that an additional degree of volatility is added to a bank's profit and loss (P&L) calculation. Before the introduction of the CVA banks would only hedge noncredit sensitivities such as interest rate and foreign exchange rate volatility. The CVA adds to this the sensitivity to changes in the credit quality, which we measure and observe by looking at changes in the credit spreads.

The logical consequence is to hedge the additional P&L volatility using instruments whose market values are sensitive to changes in credit spreads. These instruments will typically be credit default swaps. It would also be possible to use bonds, but that is less straightforward because bonds are not only sensitive to credit but also interest rates.

Similar to instruments with interest rate sensitivity, we determine the credit sensitivity or credit delta by individually shifting the points on the CDS curve. Let us label the credit sensitivity CV01. The individual shift of the CDS curve results in a vector of CV01s for the maturities on the CDS curve. These will be nonzero if there is exposure at the corresponding maturity. We now delta hedge these CV01s by buying or selling a CDS contract with the same maturity as the CV01 and a notional that results in the same CV01 for the CDS contract than for the FEE that generated the CV01.

The construction of CDS curves generally works with inter- and extrapolation to generate more points than there are tradable CDS contracts. Therefore, even perfectly CV01 hedged portfolios will still be exposed to curve risk due to flattening or steepening of the CDS curve. Flattening or steepening denotes a situation where segments or individual points on the CDS curve move more or less relative to others. Flattening implies that a segment or point of the curve with a longer maturity tightens more than a segment or point with a shorter maturity. Steepening denotes the opposite scenario. This risk is particularly prominent for portfolios that have a maturity longer than 10 years since liquid CDS contracts are rarely available beyond 10 years. This is a risk that an experienced CVA trader will factor into their hedging decisions and will always lead to a degree of position taking even if the overall goal is only to minimize any positions by hedging as completely as possible.

As an example we consider a BBB+ client with the following exposure profile (Figure 17.2) and credit curve (Table 17.2).

The CV01s of the portfolio are shown in Table 17.3.

Ideally we would enter into CDS contracts for all the maturities shown in Table 17.3, but it will be more efficient to concentrate on the more liquid points and to add the CV01s of the less liquid points to the CV01s of the points that we chose to use as hedges. One possible hedge could be to sell five years of protection with a notional of €3.3 million (CV01 €−1,449) and to buy 10 years of protection with a notional of €8.1 million (CV01 €5,806). That would almost completely neutralize the CV01 of the position; however, due to only using 5- and 10-year CDS contracts, there remains unhedged curve risk. If the three-year point on the CDS curve declines by 10 bps, then that would lead to a €8,330 P&L loss

F I G U R E   17.2

Exposure profile for BBB+ client

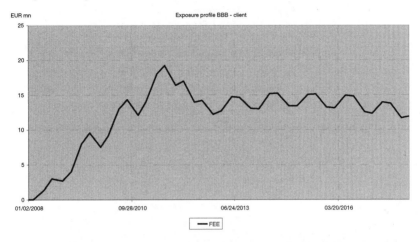

T A B L E   17.2

Credit default swap curve in
basis points for BBB+ client

6 m	47
1 y	167
2 y	167
3 y	167
4 y	173
5 y	196
7 y	201
10 y	203

despite the hedges put in place. From that perspective we could argue that
we should just sell five years of protection equal to the amount indicated
by the 5-year CV01, but since large moves in credit spreads never happen
on individual points on the curve alone, it is better to cover the majority
of the total CV01. Figure 17.3 illustrates the matching process achieved
by the hedges.

T A B L E   17.3

CV01s in euro for
BBB+ client

Maturity	CV01
3 m	30
6 m	22
1 y	316
2 y	646
3 y	833
4 y	−929
5 y	516
7 y	148
10 y	−5,982

F I G U R E   17.3

CV01s of exposure and hedges

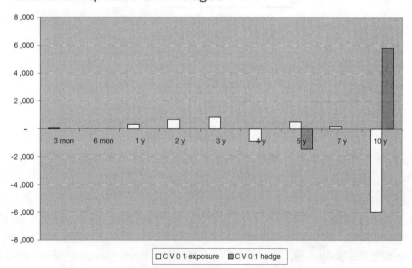

Hedging Noncredit Sensitivities

Delta hedging the CV01s does not complete the task of hedging the CVA.
The CVA is sensitive to both credit spreads changing as well as to changes
in other noncredit variables and the volatilities thereof because they are

input parameters to the MCS. Any changes to these parameters will lead to a different FEE profile and thus a different CVA even if credit spreads stay unchanged. This leads us to conclude that in addition to hedging the credit deltas, we also need to hedge the noncredit deltas (e.g., interest rates and foreign exchange) and the vegas[1] of these noncredit sensitivities.

The instruments typically used would be spot transactions in the underlying market variable for asset classes like foreign exchange or equities. Interest rate risk would be hedged with vanilla interest rate swaps. The process for hedging the interest rate risk is more elaborate since the underlying has a term structure. The same is true for commodities where we would use the relevant futures contract.

The noncredit hedges are put in place at the book level and not at an individual counterparty level. This way if exposure increases overall due to changes in noncredit market variables, leading to a net increase in the CVA and thus to a P&L hit—the profit from the noncredit hedges put on earlier offsets that P&L loss.

Let us look at an example of a book of derivatives portfolios with a total CVA of € 38,212,285.79. The portfolios consist of plain vanilla fixed-income transactions, that is mainly interest rate and cross-currency swaps. The main noncredit sensitivities of that book are shown in Table 17.4. We only show a subset of the most significant sensitivities and also ignore vegas and second-order sensitivities. The base currency for all foreign exchange sensitivities is U.S. dollars. This implies that for foreign exchange the shift to determine the sensitivity is applied to the exchange rate that we would need to multiply the amount of foreign currency by to convert it into U.S. dollars. Again, a positive number means a P&L profit (CVA declines) due to the shift, and a negative number, a loss.

The numbers also indicate which direction the sensitivity takes. For foreign exchange a positive number means that the book makes a profit if the currency in the table appreciates against U.S. dollars and a loss if it depreciates. For the interest rate sensitivity a positive number means that the book makes a profit if the interest rates go up (in parallel) and a loss if they go down. Looking at Table 17.4 we see that the book needs to be

---

[1] The sensitivity to changes in the volatility that drives pricing formulas and Monte Carlo simulation.

T A B L E   17.4

Main noncredit sensitivities of a derivatives book

Sensitivities in EUR			
Currency	Type	Shift	Value
EUR	Foreign exchange	1%	−83,248.64
GBP	Foreign exchange	1%	226,536.82
JPY	Foreign exchange	1%	28,085.61
EUR	Interest rates	10 bps parallel	55,264.09
GBP	Interest rates	10 bps parallel	−33,581.11

hedged against EUR strengthening and GBP as well as JPY weakening against USD. For interest rates the book needs to be hedged against EUR interest rates falling and GBP rates rising.

As mentioned above, interest rate deltas should be hedged bucketwise, but to keep the example simple, we only assume a parallel shift of the whole yield curve. Based on the deltas in Table 17.4, we arrive at the following noncredit hedges, which are shown in Table 17.5. Foreign exchange hedges are spot transactions against USD dealt at current sport (1.4750 against EUR, 1.9711 against GBP, and 109.32 against JPY). Since we only performed a parallel shift on the whole yield curve, we chose a 5-year tenor for

T A B L E   17.5

Required noncredit hedges for a derivatives book

Hedges			
Currency	Type	Notional	Direction
EUR	Foreign exchange	8,408,112.64	Buy
GBP	Foreign exchange	16,952,047.56	Sell
JPY	Foreign exchange	452,872,035.57	Sell
EUR	Interest rates	12,491,035.87	Receive fixed
GBP	Interest rates	5,836,326.71	Pay fixed

the interest rate swap hedges used to hedge the interest rate risk. These would be at the money swaps with a fixed rate equal to the 5-year swap rate. The direction column in Table 17.5 indicates whether we buy or sell the .corresponding currency against USD and whether we pay or receive fixed, which has to offset the sensitivity displayed in Table 17.4.

Cross Gamma

We have now covered hedging the deltas of both credit and noncredit sensitivities. Hedging the vegas of the market variables that drive the exposure profile in the MCS is similarly straightforward and will be done using options on these market variables.

There is another type of risk sensitivity that was mentioned briefly in the section about correlation. It is a second-order gamma-type risk. While the gammas of both the noncredit and credit deltas in isolation are not significant, there is another quite significant gamma sensitivity, which in the CCPM world is called *cross gamma*. It is defined as the sensitivity of the CVA toward a simultaneous change in the credit spreads and the noncredit market variables. The delta hedges mentioned above will mitigate some of this risk but not all of it as they assume that one market variable moves in isolation and all others remain static. The sum of the impacts of the individual moves is not equal to the impact of all moves together.

Unfortunately hedging the cross gamma is very difficult as it requires an instrument that is sensitive both to changes in credit and noncredit. Foreign exchange-based cross gamma can be hedged by doing a cross-currency basis default swap trade whereby protection is bought in one currency and protection is sold on the same reference entity in the other currency of the currency pair to be hedged. This trade will change in value if the exchange rate varies, which gets magnified if credit spreads change at the same time. Another instrument that is sensitive to cross gamma is a credit hybrid product like contingent credit default swaps. The pros and cons of these will be discussed in a following section.

Pricing

Changing the portfolio composition by adding, removing, or in any way restructuring one or more trades will lead to a requirement to rebalance the CVA hedge for the portfolio. In the case of additional risk this will lead to additional hedging costs; in the case of a reduction of risk this will lead to a freefall of hedging costs. Both scenarios need to be priced in correctly when quoting the new trade (which can mean any of the activities mentioned above) to the client. The price of the new trade will therefore typically comprise a component to cover the cost for hedging the traditional market risk (levied, e.g., by the swap desk and usually part of the bid—offer spread), a component to cover the cost of hedging the CVA (levied by the CCPM desk), and any additional markup the derivatives marketer feels appropriate to add. We get, $P = Mid + Cost_{MarketHedge} + Cost_{CVAHedge} + Markup$, where Mid is the fair, risk-free market value of the trade and the other components are as described above.

The cost of the CVA hedge has to encompass the cost of all the individual hedges put on as described in the section Hedging and Pricing. Given the difficulty of hedging the cross gamma, this element is often only factored in as an approximation. A more precise calculation requires credit spreads to be stochastic and the correlation between credit and noncredit to be modeled.

Another important consideration is whether the cost of the CVA hedge is priced as an up-front premium, in which case it is simply the marginal expected loss, or whether it is priced as a running, deferred premium that is paid in installments as, for example, an adjustment to the fixed rate in a swap transaction. In the latter case a default of the client would mean that not all premium has been received. The premium itself becomes credit contingent and needs to be weighted by the survival probability in the same fashion as the premium of a CDS is treated in its pricing formula. The expected loss needs to be equal to the deferred premia weighted by the survival probability and a discount factor. To determine a constant premium to be paid on specific payment dates, we need to solve the equation for the premium P, where $marEL_{cp,S} = P_{cp,S} \sum_{i=1}^{n} s_{cp}(0, t_i) \cdot d(0, t_i)$ and $marEL_{cp,S}$ is the marginal expected loss for counterparty cp when adding transaction S to its portfolio, $P_{cp,S}$ is the constant premium for counterparty cp specific to transaction S, $s_{cp}(0, t_i)$ is the survival probability between the base date and the premium payment date $t_i \in \{t_1, \ldots, t_n\}$, and $d(0, t_i)$ is the discount factor between the base date and the premium payment date in the base currency.

This premium would be an absolute amount to be paid at each payment date, which typically gets converted into whichever method of quoting prices

T A B L E   17.6

Credit default swap curve for
pricing example

6 m	10
1 y	15
2 y	31
3 y	51
4 y	63
5 y	78
7 y	89
10 y	100
12 y	114

the underlying new transaction uses (e.g., number of basis points per annum for interest rate swap transactions).

As an example, consider a portfolio of fixed-income derivatives with a CVA of €292,690 and a CDS curve as shown in Table 17.6.

The portfolio consists of four cross-currency swaps in three of which the client receives GBP and pays USD and one where he or she pays GBP and receives EUR. Adding another cross-currency swap where the client also receives GBP and pays USD with a notional of GBP 30 millions and a tenor of 5 years increases the CVA to €362,802. The premium to be charged to the client is 3.9 bps per annum on the new transactions.

That premium is, however, different if the direction of the new trade is the other way round. That is the client pays GBP and receives USD, which is offsetting to the major foreign exchange sensitivity of the portfolio. Adding the offsetting trade actually reduces the CVA to €273,090, meaning that theoretically the client could ask for the premium to be paid to her as she provides an offsetting, risk-reducing trade. Since the cost of the CVA hedge is not the only component that goes into the pricing, this will in practice, however, only reduce the overall price paid by the client.

Illiquid Credits

To this point in the chapter, we always assumed that there is a CDS curve available for the obligors in the derivatives book for which the CVA is to be calculated and managed. This will of course not be the case if a financial institution wants to include all counterparties it has booked a derivative transaction with. Most likely the majority of the counterparties will not exhibit any tradable CDS contracts and thus no credit curve.

Including these counterparties into the CVA calculation requires a proxy for a CDS curve to be found. Most of these obligors will for the least have an internal credit rating. Therefore, a common approach is to assign a credit curve to a specific rating. This could be sampled from the total universe of available credit curves. If the data offers enough depth then further partitioning into regional and industry categories can be considered.

Another possibility would be to use CDS indexes (e.g., iTraxx or CDX) that are available for various groupings of reference credits. They will, however, not provide the same granularity as a ratings-based approach. The benefit is that while the default risk itself cannot directly be mitigated, the sensitivity to changes in credit spreads, and thus a change in the CVA can be hedged by using those indexes.

Credit Hybrids and Contingent Credit Default Swaps

Almost every major financial institution has made an attempt at establishing a book for credit hybrid products with varying degrees of success. While often this was purely motivated by the effort to find another source of revenue, credit hybrids need to be considered when talking about CCPM, since they are a means of generating an instrument that has a sensitivity to more than one market variable, and one of them is credit. Relatively successful products in the past have been transactions that link credit and commodities because there is often a relatively clear correlation between the creditworthiness of the reference credit and this reference credit's profitability dependency on the noncredit market variable that is included into the hybrid transaction.

For other asset classes the correlation may not be so clear. We did however observe the emergence of contingent credit default swaps (CCDSs), which are similar to vanilla CDS only that the notional of the CCDs is not fixed but usually linked to the mark to market of an underlying transaction. This transaction can be any transaction that is of a contingent nature; it could even be a portfolio of derivatives transactions. However, the more complex the underlying transaction, the more difficult the pricing model and, in particular, the correlation assumptions between the credit and noncredit variables that has to go into the model. For this reason the majority of transactions that have taken place have referenced actual existing derivatives transactions of mostly simple, vanilla nature.

The beauty of a CCDS transaction is that it addresses the whole credit-hedging requirement for a derivatives trade with only that one transaction. This even includes the cross gamma and also implies that the way a protection seller of a CCDS would hedge himself or herself is exactly the same as hedging the CVA. Given that this is quite complex and hardly ever possible to perfection, leaving a residual risk, the protection seller will ask for a premium above the cost that would be determined for hedging the CVA. Thus the CCDS is often described as too expensive, and many CCPM desks will not consider hedging themselves that way as they feel that they have got enough expertise to carry out the hedging with simpler instruments and manage the cross gamma themselves. Typically, they are, however, very happy to sell CCDS because they are keen to earn that pickup in premium. Selling a CCDS is not a lot different than entering into the derivatives transaction from a risk perspective but with added revenue potential (even if that ignores other positive aspects of doing a transaction directly with a client instead of synthetically via CCDS).

CONTINGENT CREDIT PORTFOLIO MANAGEMENT

Typical Department Structure

CCPM generally provides a set of the following core functions (see Figure 17.4):

1. *Trading:* This function is responsible for hedging the CVA and protecting the P&L of the desk. It differs from other classic trading desk in that the process of hedging is of the highest complexity out of all of trading desks, but typically the amount of risk taking and running of positions is smaller. The work of a CVA trader usually consists of 70 percent hedging and 30 percent active position taking, whereas this ratio is expected to be reversed for other trading desks. The activity of this group will be controlled by a set of market risk limits that outline the

F I G U R E   17.4

Typical setup of a CCPM desk

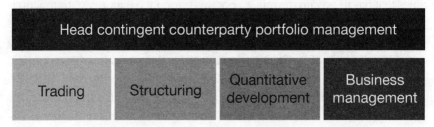

boundaries for any position taking and ensure that the book is tightly hedged.

There is usually a degree of specialization among CVA traders in that there may be individuals focusing on CDS transactions (potentially grouped into industry sector specialists) and others on noncredit hedging. There may also be the more quantitatively oriented credit hybrid trader that would deal with the more complex hedging requirements.

2. *Structuring:* The responsibility of this function encompasses all inception pricing for any changes to the derivatives book of the institution that have an impact on the CVA. The structuring function plays an important part in the derivatives deal facilitation for a financial institution overall as they help to structure new transactions competitively by keeping the cost of hedging the CVA to a minimum and by helping to overcome potential credit constraints. Another important aspect of the structuring team is the redistribution of the credit risk in the CVA book. They will try to find investors or other market counterparties that are interested in acquiring some of the credit risk the CCPM has in its book. Finally, they may also originate new credit risk that complements and diversifies the CCPM book. The contact to the institutions client base may either be direct or via the derivatives sales force of a bank.

3. *Quantitative development:* Contingent credit portfolio management relies heavily on advanced pricing models and is computationally very intense. It is therefore mandatory to have a strong quantitative development team that will deal in

particular with the more complex aspects of the business and provides ad hoc pricing models for all types of new derivatives trades. The quant team will be augmented by a state-of-the-art IT group. Since there are very few vendors that provide IT solutions for CCPM trading infrastructure, it will often be built in-house.

4. *Business management:* Contingent credit portfolio management is a function that combines many aspects of the classic derivatives business of a bank. Establishing and maintaining the processes for a successful implementation of a CCPM desk requires a significant amount of attention on a daily basis. Thus, a dedicated business management function is invaluable.

Varying Degrees of Development

The way the typical setup described earlier is implemented varies across the banks that have an active CCPM desk. On the one hand, it varies due to the institution's philosophy in terms of whether CCPM is seen as service function or a profit center. On the other hand, it is also dependent on the size of the CVA book.

Institutions that run the CCPM desk as a profit center are more aggressive in the redistribution of the credit risk on their books. Setting up the infrastructure for a CCPM desk means a significant investment and it appears only logical to demand a monetary return from the activity. There is after all significant value to be released by finding intelligent means of hedging the risk and by increasing capital velocity through frequent turnover of the position instead of a buy and hold attitude.

Organizations have a clear separation between the functions mentioned above. These would typically be the more advanced players in the market who cover a large variety of derivatives products. Smaller players that only manage a subset of their institution's derivatives book may be set up in a less specialized fashion. The degree of specialization often goes hand in hand with the decision whether to treat CCPM as a profit or a service center. For a profit center the importance of the P&L statement is much more pronounced and likely to be a significant part of the group's objectives. For service center groups this will be less so, and their objectives tend to be dominated by more qualitative objectives.

While there is commonly a separation of the illiquid transactions in the CVA book from the liquid ones, the treatment of the illiquid book varies. At some banks the expected loss is calculated using historical default probabilities, and the credit risk is just warehoused. The more advanced CCPM desks will try to find proxies in the credit market and use macro hedges that, for example, use CDS indexes to manage the CVA for those obligors.

Another point is the recognition of the hedging activity in the bank's risk systems. The ability to realize the impact of the hedging activity of the CCPM desk in terms of reduced credit limit utilization and thus reduced capital requirements is a sign of an organization that possesses a good understanding of the concepts behind CCPM. However, that is not a given for all financial institutions that are active in the CCPM space.

Future Challenges

Future challenges and areas for development are abundant for CCPM. As outlined in an earlier section, there are varying degrees of implementation of this function at different financial institutions. While the basics of the topics like the pricing methodology are very similar, there is some inconsistency in the treatment of more detailed aspects.

An interesting question is whether there is an opportunity to relax the assumption that to determine the expected exposure, we should only look at the expectation of the positive mark to markets. Is there anything that can be done to unlock the hidden value in the negative market value of a portfolio of derivatives from a bank's perspective? One possible idea is to hold bond positions with the same reference credit with a notional smaller or equal to the negative mark to market. That would enable the CCPM function to earn the credit spread of the derivatives counterparty when the mark to market of the portfolio is negative. The motivation behind this idea is that in the event of default it will be possible to offset the liability on the derivatives portfolio with the asset held in from of the bonds of the defaulted counterparty. The extra income would enable a bank to earn some of the monies spent on hedging in this fashion and thus allow it to price its derivatives transactions more aggressively. The challenge here is the legal risk of whether the offset will work. This mainly depends on the jurisdiction that will be applicable in the default event and is not a question that can be answered with any certainty yet.

Another interesting point is the recovery assumption used in the pricing methodology. The straightforward answer is to use the same recovery assumption as used in the CDS market, which is geared toward the bond market. It is, however, doubtful if recovery for bonds will be the same as for derivatives, in particular as derivatives often benefit from various forms of collateralization and other credit covenants like ratings triggers that terminate a derivatives transaction once the credit quality of the counterparty falls below a predefined threshold. Again this is a somewhat difficult call to make but has the potential to reduce the amount of hedge required and thus can make the pricing more competitive.

The future of CCPM depends on the willingness of derivatives market players to recognize the fact that these instruments generate a considerable amount of credit risk and that their valuation should reflect that by using a concept like the CVA. The institutions that will be successful in CCPM will be those that can make the step to a profit center or for the least are willing to realize that the CVA not only poses additional risk but also a profit opportunity in redistributing the credit risk of a derivatives book.

The difficult start of the CCDS market is a good example for the future challenges for CCPM. We mentioned in a previous section that typically there are more sellers than buyers because the product is not yet recognized as a hedge tool by derivatives end users like corporates, nonbank financial institutions, or even smaller, regional banks. This imbalance in perception by market participants is most likely one of the main reasons why the CCDS market has not developed in the form that was expected. This may change in the near future given the increasing pressure to more accurately value derivatives transactions, which could prompt other market players that are heavy users of derivatives transactions to recognize the credit risk inherent in them. They might then feel it necessary to hedge that credit risk. This is an opportunity for an experienced CCPM desk that can then offer this service to the bank's clients.

PART FOUR

Credit Portfolio Transactions

Chapter 18

Strategies of Hedge Funds and Robust Bayesian Portfolio Allocation in Fixed-Income Markets

Roland Füss, Dieter G. Kaiser, and Michael Stein

ABSTRACT

This chapter evaluates whether investors can diversify their traditional bond portfolios with fixed-income hedge fund styles. In doing so, we first introduce the main strategies: convertible arbitrage, fixed-income arbitrage, and distressed securities. Thereby, we also provide statistics about fund characteristics on an aggregated strategy level. Following this, we determine the efficient prior and posterior frontiers and the optimal allocations using a robust Bayesian mean-variance approach. We thus contrast the allocation results of a traditional fixed-income portfolio against portfolio compositions including explicit fixed-income hedge fund strategies. The robust portfolio allocations considering hedge fund strategies include distressed securities and convertible arbitrage, as well as the Lehman Mortgage Backed Securities Index in large amounts. Lower risk–return profiles are achieved with allocations to the 10-year Treasury for the long-term and posterior portfolio, while the short-term portfolio includes the

10-year Bund. In aggregate, we find that incorporating fixed-income hedge fund strategies into a traditional bond portfolio can result in higher risk-adjusted returns due to the diversification benefits.

INTRODUCTION

The importance of diversification was highlighted once again by the credit crisis of 2007, which was triggered by the meltdown of the U.S. subprime mortgage market and influenced investor portfolios worldwide. There are several options even for institutional investor portfolios, which are still dominated by fixed-income securities. These options outside fixed income (e.g., duration, currencies, regional, and corporate versus sovereign) include equities, commodities, real estate, private equity, or even hedge funds.

While today's investors are usually familiar with most of these types of investments, hedge funds are rarely their first choice. This is true even though numerous academic papers have highlighted the diversification benefits of including hedge funds in traditional investor portfolios. One reason is that hedge funds have a certain aura of opaqueness because of the complexity of their strategies and techniques. In this context, we could argue that fixed-income portfolio managers may find it easier to understand hedge fund strategies within the fixed-income market than those focused, e.g., on the commodity markets.

Our first step is therefore to illustrate the basic strategies used by hedge funds within the fixed-income space. Our second step is to illustrate the effect these fixed-income hedge fund strategies have on a traditional bond portfolio.

This chapter is structured as follows: In the first section, we discuss the main fixed-income hedge fund styles (convertible arbitrage, fixed-income arbitrage, and distressed securities) and give some descriptive statistics. Then, in the next section, we introduce the theoretical foundation of a robust Bayesian portfolio optimization approach. The fourth section presents the efficient prior and posterior frontiers and our optimal portfolio allocation results. The final section summarizes our main findings, points out the shortcomings of the Bayesian portfolio optimization approach when applied to hedge funds, and draws some conclusions.

FIXED-INCOME HEDGE FUND STRATEGIES
Convertible Arbitrage

The goal of convertible arbitrage strategies is to identify valuation errors in convertible bonds and use them to generate profits. This is usually done with specialized computer programs, which are an effective tool to analyze the bonds and reveal potential price inefficiencies. The convertible bonds are then reverse engineered into their constituents, which are valued one by one.

Convertible bonds, which are normally built by a corporate bond and an option, enable the owner to turn the notional of the bond into equity of the bond issuing company, according to strict regulations defined in advance [see, e.g., Calamos (2003)]. Due to the legal complexity of the optional components in the contract framework, it is possible that the sum of the individually valued components will not match the market price of the convertible bond.

Interest rate risk and credit risk are especially heavy influences on corporate bonds. The credit risk comes from the development of the spreads between the interest paid by a corporate and a risk-free government bond. The spreads themselves are heavily influenced by the general economic situation and the creditworthiness of the company. The interest rate risk is defined by the development of capital market interest rates, or by changes in the interest rate term structure curve.

According to Agarwal et al. (2004), equity, volatility, creditworthiness, and interest rate risk are the main risk factors driving convertible arbitrage strategies. When convertible bonds are analyzed for risk, the different implied risks may be hedged individually, or distinct risk positions may be taken on purpose. The rights contained in the option are mainly defined by the contract conditions (such as strike price or maturity) and may differ legally from those of a plain vanilla option. Hence, the option rights are greatly influenced by the price of the underlying equity and its volatility.

The assessment of the latter may lead to the initiation of a convertible arbitrage position. If the implied volatility of the convertible bond differs from the market volatility or from the volatility assessment of the hedge fund manager, there is profit potential. According to Tran (2006), there are two methods of alpha generation in convertible arbitrage: Valuation errors may occur on the creditworthiness side or as a result of wrongly priced convertible ratios.

In convertible arbitrage, fund managers try to determine which convertible bonds will decrease more slowly during market downturns than the underlying equities and which will more closely mirror the equities' prices during upward-trending markets. Managers will thus go long in convertible bonds and hedge these positions by shorting equities of the same company [see, e.g., Nicholas (2000) and Tomlinson (1998)].

Fifteen years ago, convertible bond arbitrage was just a niche strategy implemented primarily by brokers and hedge funds. Today, according to HFR (2007), it is an established trading strategy, with 3.32 percent market share of total invested volume in hedge funds. Convertible arbitrage transactions actually determine secondary markets of convertible bonds. According to Capocci (2003), investors can optimize their total portfolio return by adding convertible arbitrage hedge funds. However, it is important to consider the negative influence of skewness and kurtosis of the portfolio return distribution.

Table 18.1 gives descriptive characteristics for 176 convertible arbitrage hedge funds. These funds, on average, have a higher total volume (a median of US$120 million) than the sample average (US$83.5 million) (see Table 18.1). Fund size ranges from US$580,000 to US$3 billion.

Regarding hedge fund life span, the convertible arbitrage strategy, with an average of 55 months, just outlives the average hedge fund in the database. The average minimum investment of $1 million is twice that of other strategies. The level of dispersion we start to observe here is interesting. The minimum investment in convertible arbitrage hedge funds ranges from US$130 to US$10 million. The management fees range from 0.5 to 3 percent. The average management fee of 1.5 percent is exactly the database average. The performance fee also matches the database average, with a median of 20 percent (in a range of 10 to 35 percent).

Fixed-Income Arbitrage

Hedge fund managers using fixed-income arbitrage try to take advantage of the relative valuation inefficiencies between bonds with similar payment

T A B L E   18.1

Description of convertible arbitrage database (as of May 2006)

Characteristics	Minimum	Maximum	Range	Standard Deviation	Median	Mean
Assets under management (in USD millions)	0.58	3,044.00	3,043.42	494.55	120.00	284.04
Fund age (in months)	12.00	246.00	234.00	42.43	55.00	64.77
Minimum investment (in TUSD)	0.13	10,000.00	9,999.88	1,270.71	1,000.00	955.65
Management fee (p.a.)	0.50%	3.00%	2.50%	0.44%	1.50%	1.55%
Performance fee	10.00%	35.00%	25.00%	1.98%	20.00%	20.41%

Source: Hedge Fund Intelligence

characteristics or creditworthiness. It is assumed that these valuation differences will narrow or even vanish over time. Fixed-income arbitrage managers take long and short positions in interest rate-sensitive assets in order to eliminate interest rate change risk (Jaeger, 2002).

The typical fixed-income arbitrage portfolio is comprised of long and short positions of related or similar interest rate assets and their derivatives, which neutralize each other. Hence, parallel shifts in the interest rate term structure curve do not affect the portfolio. Decisions within fixed-income arbitrage strategies are based primarily on mathematical and statistical valuation models. Thus managers try to locate and profit from valuation anomalies that originate from changes in interest rate curves, creditworthiness ratings, or volatility curves (Lhabitant, 2002).

These managers aim to identify interest rate assets that display a high level of mathematical, fundamental, or historical correlation, and which are also characterized by a present or future price inefficiency.[1] Price inefficiencies within interest rate assets may occur, for example, because of structural changes in the interest rate market, shifts in investor preferences, or exogenous shocks that impact supply and demand. The

---

[1] However, identifying market price anomalies between similar interest rate securities is very difficult. Fixed-income arbitrageurs typically use complex analytical computer models to detect these potential anomalies.

fund manager profits if the current price ratio of these interest rate assets converges toward a historical "standard ratio." In the field of interest rate arbitrage, a high leverage level of 10 or more is common due to the very small price differences.[2]

A typical strategy within fixed-income arbitrage is to use interest rate changes among government and corporate bonds of high creditworthiness, bonds with differing creditworthiness, bonds of a debtor with different guarantees, or bonds of the same issuer with different maturities to generate profits. For investors, the advantage of fixed-income arbitrage is its low volatility and constant performance, which shows very little correlation to interest rate changes. According to Duarte et al. (2006), almost all excess returns generated by fixed-income arbitrage stem from interest rate risk and market risk. As a result, the risk-adjusted alphas generated by these strategies are significant, even after deducting the usual hedge fund fees.

Fung and Hsieh (2002) and Jaeger and Wagner (2005) have found, however, that heavy losses can occur with this strategy under certain conditions, such as investors choosing flight over quality, a sudden expansion in credit spreads, a lack of liquidity, or an emerging market downturn. Nevertheless, the events of summer 1998 remind us that fixed-income arbitrage can resemble a short option, incorporating the risk of significant losses during times of constant positive performance (Jaeger and Wagner, 2005).

Table 18.2 gives descriptive characteristics for 116 fixed-income arbitrage hedge funds. Fund size ranges from US$990,000 to $3.22 billion. Regarding fund life span, the average is over four years old, and thus somewhat older than the average fund in our database. The average minimum investment is US$1 million, which is again twice the database average of $500,000.

Note again the observed dispersion. The minimum investment in convertible arbitrage hedge funds ranges from US$630 to US$5 million. The management fee of hedge funds within this strategy ranges from 0.25 to 3 percent. The average management fee and the average performance fee

---

[2] Due to the heavy use of outside capital, risk control is of the utmost importance when using this strategy. If interest rate differences do not develop as expected, investors must have sufficient market liquidity to close the position. Hence, it is critical to maintain a permanent comparison between position sizes, using average historical and current traded volume.

T A B L E   18.2

Description of fixed-income arbitrage database (as of May 2006)

Characteristics	Minimum	Maximum	Range	Standard Deviation	Median	Mean
Assets under management (in USD millions)	0.99	3,220.00	3,219.01	596.42	140.08	377.78
Fund age (in months)	12.00	203.00	191.00	43.97	50.00	63.89
Minimum investment (in TUSD)	0.63	5,000.00	4,999.37	1,453.03	1,000.00	1,213.97
Management fee (p.a.)	0.25%	3.00%	2.75%	0.48%	1.50%	1.43%
Performance fee	2.00%	50.00%	48.00%	4.88%	20.00%	20.10%

Source: Hedge Fund Intelligence

again exactly match the database average, at 1.5 percent and a median of 20 percent, respectively. Note further that the hedge fund with the highest performance fee (50 percent) belongs to this strategy.

Distressed Securities

Funds using the distressed securities strategy invest in securities of companies that are economically, financially, or organizationally distressed (Füss et al., 2007). This strategy is thus referred to as a *results-oriented trading strategy*.[3]

A distressed situation may arise if (1) the financial situation of a company significantly deteriorates, (2) a company is unable to meet its financial obligations and/or its debt obligations, or (3) insolvency has occurred due to other factors. Distressed securities are normally traded at prices far below the notional or former prices. The goal is thus to buy these assets at a deep discount and to hold them until the company has

---

[3] We can further classify the distressed securities strategy into two components, active and passive, depending on the level of influence of the investor. In the active strategy class, investors may try to assume control of the company; the passive class is characterized by a non-control-oriented trading position. Hedge funds that follow an active strategy closely resemble private equity. We note correlations between hedge funds and private equity particularly within event-oriented strategies.

overcome its difficulties. According to HFR (2007), 4.70 percent of worldwide capital invested in hedge funds belongs to distressed securities.

Distressed securities managers attempt to invest only in companies they expect will recover. Hence, the return potential neutralizes the obvious risk. A typical company of interest might have temporary financial problems, but excellent potential future prospects due to, e.g., a specific area of expertise. Thus, managers may believe that restructuring, obtaining a new financing partner, or obtaining new management will turn around the situation and allow the company to become profitable again.

Owners of distressed securities are often willing to close these positions even with significant losses. Large price cuts may result from false valuations of the distressed securities by market participants. Selling pressure may also result from the fact that some investor groups (e.g., insurance companies) are unable to invest in distressed securities.[4] Hedge funds, however, have no restrictions on allocation, whether from insolvency (e.g., chapter 11 of the U.S. insolvency law), liquidation (e.g., chapter 7 of the U.S. insolvency law), or ratings downgrades.

However, doubts about company restructurings represent a significant disadvantage. This risk must be valued as closely as possible. Hedge fund managers must have excellent sector knowledge as well as close management contacts within the companies in question. Distressed securities investments are mostly long-term and are thus quite sensitive to liquidity pressure (this is why most require a long capital lockup period).

Table 18.3 gives descriptive characteristics for 42 distressed securities hedge funds. Funds within this strategy are on average relatively large, with a median of US$205.1 million under management. Note, however, that the largest fund in this category has only US$2.2 billion under management, which is considered small compared to other strategies.

The average life span of distressed securities hedge funds matches the database average of about four years old. However, note the high level of dispersion: The average minimum investment in fixed-income arbitrage

---

[4] Distressed securities hedge funds have a particularly large exposure to default risk. This risk can be most efficiently hedged by credit default swaps (CDS). However, it can be very difficult to find counterparties for a CDS on distressed securities. Hence, these funds perform very well if credit spreads narrow, and vice versa (Stefanini, 2006).

T A B L E   18.3

Description of distressed securities database (as of May 2006)

Characteristics	Minimum	Maximum	Range	Standard Deviation	Median	Mean
Assets under management (in USD millions)	10.10	2,200.00	2,189.90	454.84	205.10	363.81
Fund age (in months)	15.00	200.00	185.00	44.06	50.00	63.69
Minimum investment (in TUSD)	100.00	5,000.00	4,900.00	1,191.79	1,000.00	1,150.00
Management fee (p.a.)	1.00%	2.00%	1.00%	0.32%	1.50%	1.49%
Performance fee	10.00%	20.00%	10.00%	1.54%	20.00%	19.76%

Data Source: Hedge Fund Intelligence.

hedge funds is US$1 million, and thus quite high. We do not observe high dispersion for the management fee, however (between 1 and 2 percent), or the performance fee (between 10 and 20 percent). The median and arithmetic means are 1.5 and 20 percent, respectively, and represent the database average.

A ROBUST BAYESIAN PORTFOLIO OPTIMIZATION APPROACH

When constructing portfolios of financial assets or strategies, it is critical to consider both the nature of any single asset or strategy, as well as the interdependence among them. Diversification benefits stemming from low or even negative relationships among assets are important for the expected risk and return structure of the resulting portfolio.

Since Markowitz's (1959) seminal portfolio optimization work, this topic has been among the most researched and discussed by both academics and practitioners. Of special interest has been the problem of estimation risk, the distrust that experienced investors sometimes have toward historical data from assets, funds, or strategies being considered. Klein and Bawa (1976), Best and Grauer (1991), and Chopra and Ziemba (1993) discuss the sensitivity of portfolio weights to inputs. Michaud (1998), in a rigorous critique, labels mean-variance optimization as estimation-error maximizing.

Bayesian methods are among the most effective to account for such estimation risks. Klein and Bawa (1976), Jorion (1986), and, of course, Black and Litterman (1990; 1992) have used Bayesian methods in portfolio optimization. It is worth revisiting the classical approach before discussing the robust Bayesian method introduced by Meucci (2005; 2006). The remainder of this section borrows from Meucci (2005; 2006), with only marginal notational adjustments.

In the classical mean-variance portfolio optimization setting, we obtain the optimal weights of the respective assets by maximizing the weighted mean of the respective returns, as follows:

$$w^{(i)} = \arg\max_{w} w'\mu \tag{18.1}$$

subject to

$$w \in C \tag{18.2}$$

$$w'\Sigma w \le va^{(i)} \tag{18.3}$$

where w denotes the weight of any asset in the portfolio, C represents the set of investment constraints, Σ is the variance—covariance matrix of asset returns, $va^{(i)}$ incorporates the target variances, and μ is the vector of the respective expected asset returns. Note that, as Meucci (2001) states, the classical mean-variance portfolio optimization approach considers only linear returns, not logarithmic returns.

Equations (18.1) through (18.3) refer to the true values of μ and Σ. In practice, however, we generally do not know the true values of the parameters for the means and (co)variances of assets. It is thus necessary to use (point) estimates of the respective parameters. We can thus restate Equations (18.1) to (18.3) as follows:

$$w^{(i)} = \arg\max_{w} w'\hat{\mu} \tag{18.4}$$

subject to

$$w \in C \tag{18.5}$$

$$w'\hat{\Sigma}w \le va^{(i)} \tag{18.6}$$

Of course, $\hat{\mu}$ and $\hat{\Sigma}$ are the (point) estimates of the parameters mean and covariance. We are therefore exposed to estimation risk, which is ultimately a threat to the reliability of our results.

Meucci (2005; 2006) provides a Bayesian approach to the specification of the problem in a robust setting. He replaces the point estimates with uncertainty regions of the mean and variance–covariance matrix. Equations (18.4) through (18.6) thus become

$$w_{RB}^{(i)} = \arg\max_{w} \left\{ \min_{\mu \in \hat{\Theta}_{\mu}} \{w'\mu\} \right\} \qquad (18.7)$$

subject to

$$w \in C \qquad (18.8)$$

$$\max_{\Sigma \in \hat{\Theta}_{\Sigma}} \{w'\Sigma w\} \le va^{(i)} \qquad (18.9)$$

Here, the expressions $\hat{\Theta}_{\mu}$ and $\hat{\Theta}_{\Sigma}$ represent the location dispersion ellipsoids for the expected return and variance–covariance matrix, respectively. They are obtained from the Bayesian posterior distribution. When deriving this distribution, as per Meucci (2005; 2006), we assume that the returns are market invariant.[5] The estimation interval and the investment horizon are of equal length, and the linear returns are normally distributed:

$$R_{t,\tau} | \mu, \Sigma \sim N(\mu, \Sigma) \qquad (18.10)$$

We can model the prior, or the investor's view of the mean and covariance, by a normal inverse-Wishart distribution. This results from factoring the joint distribution of μ and Σ into μ given Σ and into the marginal distribution of Σ. With μ assumed to be normally distributed, and Σ modeled as an inverse-Wishart distribution,[6] we obtain the normal inverse-Wishart nature of the investor's prior.

---

[5] For a discussion of the attributes defining a market invariant (such as independent and identically distributed and time homogenous), see Meucci (2005).

[6] The inverse-Wishart distribution is symmetric, with v degrees of freedom. See Meucci (2006).

$$\mu|\Sigma \sim N\left(\mu_0, \frac{\Sigma}{T_0}\right) \tag{18.11}$$

$$\Sigma^{-1} \sim W\left(v_0, \frac{\Sigma_0^{-1}}{v_0}\right) \tag{18.12}$$

With v_0 degrees of freedom, the positive scalar T_0, and the experience of the investor with mean and covariance (μ_0, Σ_0), we obtain the experience set of the investor as follows:

$$e_C = \{\mu_0, \Sigma_0, T_0, v_0\} \tag{18.13}$$

Meucci (2006) uses the following specification of the sample parameters that define the information set $i_T = \{\hat{\mu}, \hat{\Sigma}, T\}$ on the market, where T is the sample length:

$$\hat{\mu} = \frac{1}{T}\sum_{t=1}^{T} r_{t,\tau} \tag{18.14}$$

$$\hat{\Sigma} = \frac{1}{T}\sum_{t=1}^{T}\left(r_{t,\tau} - \hat{\mu}\right)\left(r_{t,\tau} - \hat{\mu}\right) \tag{18.15}$$

From the prior experience set and the market information set, we can obtain the posterior distribution, which is again a normal inverse-Wishart distribution:

$$T_1[i_T, e_C] = T_0 + T \tag{18.16}$$

$$\mu_1[i_T, e_C] = \frac{1}{T_1}[T_0\mu_0 + T\hat{\mu}] \tag{18.17}$$

$$v_1[i_T, e_C] = v_0 + T \tag{18.18}$$

$$\Sigma_1[i_T, e_C] = \frac{1}{v_1}\left[v_0\Sigma_0 + T\hat{\Sigma} + \frac{(\mu_0 - \hat{\mu})(\mu_0 - \hat{\mu})'}{\frac{1}{T} + \frac{1}{T_0}}\right] \tag{18.19}$$

The expressions in Equations (18.16) to (18.19), therefore, incorporate all the available information from the market sample estimation and investor experience. We thus obtain a posterior distribution in which the market shrinks toward the investor's prior. Depending on the level of investor confidence, the posterior distribution will be more or less close to the market parameters or the experience parameters. The uncertainty sets concerning mean and (co)variance, $\hat{\Theta}_\mu$ and $\hat{\Theta}_\Sigma$, are now defined as follows:

$$\hat{\Theta}_\mu = \left\{ \mu : \left(\mu - \hat{\mu}_{ce} \right)' S_\mu^{-1} \left(\mu - \hat{\mu}_{ce} \right) \le q_\mu^2 \right\} \qquad (18.20)$$

$$\hat{\Theta}_\Sigma = \left\{ \Sigma : vech\left(\Sigma - \hat{\Sigma}_{ce} \right)' S_\Sigma^{-1} vech\left(\Sigma - \hat{\Sigma}_{ce} \right) \le q_\Sigma^2 \right\} \qquad (18.21)$$

The subscript ce indicates that a variable is the classical equivalent estimator for μ and Σ [see Meucci (2006)]:

$$\hat{\mu}_{ce}\left[i_T, e_C \right] = \mu_1 \qquad (18.22)$$

$$\hat{\Sigma}_{ce}\left[i_T, e_C \right] = \frac{v_1}{v_1 + N + 1} \Sigma_1 \qquad (18.23)$$

The respective scatter matrices for μ and Σ ($vech|\Sigma|$, respectively) are related to these classical equivalent estimators:

$$S_\mu\left[i_T, e_C \right] = \frac{1}{T_1} \frac{v_1}{v_1 - 2} \Sigma_1 \qquad (18.24)$$

$$S_\Sigma\left[i_T, e_C \right] = \frac{2v_1^2}{\left(v_1 + N + 1 \right)^3} \left(D_N' \left(\Sigma_1^{-1} \otimes \Sigma_1^{-1} \right) D_N \right)^{-1} \qquad (18.25)$$

Here D_N, represents the duplication matrix, and $\otimes$ is the Kronecker product [see Meucci (2006)].

Aversion to estimation risk is represented by the radius factors q_μ and q_Σ, which depend on the confidence and the number of observations for the prior and the market sample, respectively. Note that the robust Bayesian optimization problem outlined in Equations (18.7) to

(18.9) is generically of the form below and includes the radius factors q_μ and q_Σ:

$$w_{q_\mu, q_\Sigma}^{(i)} = \arg\max_w \left\{ \min_{\mu \in \hat{\Theta}_\mu^{q_\mu}} \{w'\mu\} \right\} \qquad (18.26)$$

subject to

$$w \in C \qquad (18.27)$$

$$\max_{\Sigma \in \hat{\Theta}_\Sigma^{q_\Sigma}} \{w'\Sigma w\} \leq va^{(i)} \qquad (18.28)$$

The higher is the investor aversion to poor μ and Σ estimates, the larger are the ellipsoids and thus the radius factors. The shape of the ellipsoids representing the uncertainty sets expresses this aversion. As outlined above, the degrees of freedom and the number of observations for the prior and data sample parameterize this shape, respectively.

As shown in Meucci (2005), one result from the setup of the robust Bayesian allocation is the three-dimensional representation of the optimal allocation weights. The weights are parameterized by the uncertainty sets $\hat{\Theta}_\mu$ and $\hat{\Theta}_\Sigma$ (dropping the radius factors from the notation) and the target variance grid $va^{(i)}$. With the assumptions and representations from above, this surface collapses to a line, and we obtain a two-dimensional frontier representing overall exposure to risk (consisting of market risk, estimation risk for μ, and estimation risk for Σ). From the optimization problem as outlined in Equations (18.7) to (18.9) or from the equivalent representations (18.26) to (18.28), we obtain several simplified representations for the robust Bayesian optimization [see Meucci (2005; 2006)].

FIXED-INCOME PORTFOLIO ALLOCATION INCLUDING HEDGE FUND STRATEGIES

In this section, we use the robust Bayesian optimization approach in a very intuitive way. Investor experience must be expressed in the classical expected mean and covariance structure and in the data sample that updates this prior view. We model investor experience by using historical observations for 12 assets or strategies by using a long-term sample spanning February 1996 through August 2007. Truncating the history of this sample, we take January 2006 to August 2007 as the updating market data sample. We thus have information about both the long-term structure and the interdependence between the assets and strategies and the actual short-term behavior of the portfolio constituents.

Using monthly linear returns, our long-term sample (the "prior," or "experience") has 139 observations; our short-term sample (the "market sample" in the model's setup) has 20 observations. Descriptive statistics for the respective assets and strategies for the long-term (prior) are reported in Table 18.4.

Unfortunately, the null hypothesis of normality is rejected for 9 of the 12 assets or strategies and especially for all hedge fund strategies at the 5 percent level. This shortcoming of the portfolio optimization is due to the violation of the normal assumption concerning the returns (see, e.g., Füss and Kaiser, 2007).[7]

Asset Allocation without Fixed-Income Hedge Fund Strategies

We conducted the first portfolio optimization using only fixed-income assets, with no fixed-income hedge fund strategies. The ratio for the number of observations is 139/20 for long term/short term, implying relatively high confidence. Thus it should come as no surprise that the posterior is nearer to the long-term structure representing the prior. As we see from Figures 18.1 and 18.2, the similarity between the long term and the posterior is obvious in both the pattern of the efficient frontier and the relative portfolio weights.

The results are striking: In all three portfolios, the Exane Europe Convertible Bond receives almost exactly the same allocation weights over the respective risk ranges. Except for a partial substitution of the Lehman High Yield Credit Bond Index in the short-term portfolio, the

---

[7] See www.hedgeindex.com for the construction methodology of the Credit Suisse/Tremont hedge fund indexes. For an overview of the problems and biases that can arise from using hedge fund indexes as proxies for hedge fund performance, see Heidorn et al. (2006).

T A B L E 18.4

Descriptive statistics

Asset/Strategy	Mean	Minimum	Maximum	Standard Deviation	Skewness	Kurtosis	Jarque-Bera
10-y Bund yield	−0.14%	−4.78%	5.90%	0.65%	0.41	2.77	4.02*
10-y Gilts yield	−0.21%	−7.44%	6.96%	0.72%	0.22	3.03	1.21
10-y Japan yield	−0.14%	−6.24%	13.56%	0.63%	1.79	13.59	790.32†
10-y Treasury yield	−0.09%	−6.48%	10.87%	0.89%	0.46	3.55	7.29‡
Lehman Aggregate Bond Index	5.81%	−40.32%	32.40%	3.58%	−0.55	3.75	11.48‡
Lehman high-yield credit bond index	6.60%	−88.44%	89.88%	7.00%	−0.68	6.51	91.20†
Lehman mortgage-backed securities index	5.84%	−22.44%	25.68%	2.65%	−0.35	3.04	3.16
Exane Europe convertible bond	10.21%	−118.38%	103.24%	9.59%	0.13	5.08	29.07†
CS/Tremont HFI convertible arbitrage	9.32%	−56.11%	42.82%	4.54%	−1.53	7.22	169.41†
CS/Tremont HFI Event Driven-Distressed	12.74%	−149.46%	46.88%	6.09%	−3.55	27.15	3,971.28†
CS/Tremont HFI fixed-income arbitrage	6.02%	−83.58%	24.63%	3.72%	−3.22	20.07	2,048.09†
CS/Tremont hedge fund composite	10.65%	−90.59%	102.34%	7.27%	0.02	6.16	64.99†

Source: Thomson Financial Datastream

Notes: Annualized (linear) returns and standard deviation:

† Significance at the 1 percent level (rejection of the normal distribution).

‡ Significance at the 5 percent level (rejection of the normal distribution).

* Significance at the 10 percent level (rejection of the normal distribution).

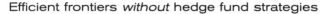

F I G U R E   18.1

Efficient frontiers *without* hedge fund strategies

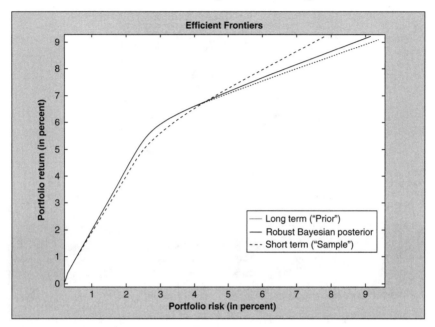

same is true for the Lehman Mortgage Backed Securities Index. Lower risk profiles see a high allocation of the 10-year Treasury for the long-term and posterior portfolios; the short-term portfolio also includes the 10-year Bund.

All three portfolios consist of largely the same assets, which illustrates the robustness of the efficient portfolio weights. This result, however, is unexpected. The periods differ greatly in nature, although the short-term sample is part of the long-term period.

Asset Allocation with Fixed-Income Hedge Fund Strategies

We conducted the second portfolio optimization using both fixed-income assets and fixed-income hedge fund strategies. Again, it is no surprise that the posterior more closely resembles the long-term structure representing the prior.

F I G U R E   18.2

Asset allocation without hedge fund strategies

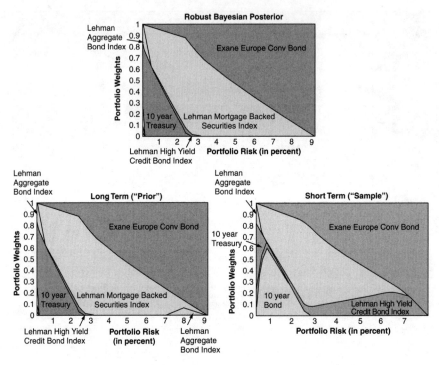

As in the optimization without the fixed-income hedge fund strategies, the three portfolios again show very similar allocation structures. All include the distressed securities and convertible arbitrage hedge fund strategies, as well as the Lehman Mortgage Backed Securities Index in large amounts. The lower risk—return profiles are again achieved with allocations to the 10-year Treasury for the long-term and posterior portfolios; the short-term portfolio again includes the 10-year Bund.

Note that the risk—return profiles are more favorable for the portfolios that include fixed-income hedge fund strategies (see Figures 18.3 and 18.4). In other words, higher risk-adjusted returns may be expected because of the diversification benefits.

F I G U R E   18.3

Efficient frontiers with hedge fund strategies

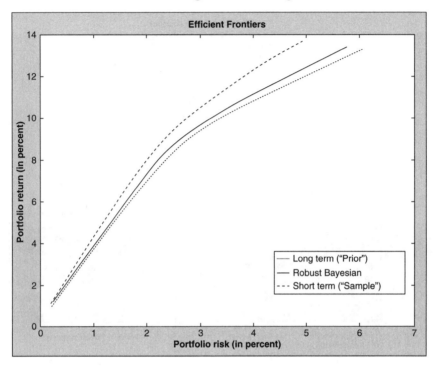

CONCLUSION

This chapter provides an overview of the investment techniques used by hedge funds in fixed-income markets. We evaluated whether investors can diversify their traditional bond portfolios with fixed-income hedge fund styles. The second section described the primary strategies of hedge funds in fixed-income markets: convertible arbitrage, fixed-income arbitrage, and distressed securities. The third section introduced the theoretical and mathematical framework of the robust Bayesian portfolio optimization approach that we used empirically in the fourth section.

Because the robust Bayesian approach is based on normally distributed returns, we expect it to have the same disadvantages as the original Markowitz (1959) mean-variance optimization. Thus, in light of

F I G U R E   18.4

Asset allocation with hedge fund strategies

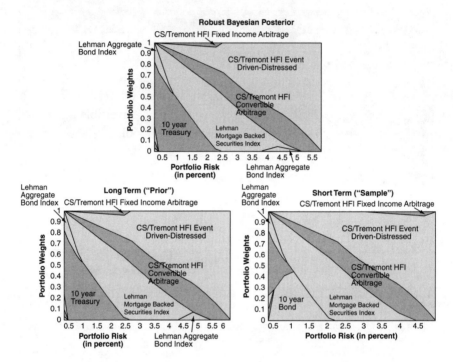

non-normally distributed hedge fund returns, our empirical results should be interpreted with caution.

In the fourth section, we determined the most efficient prior and posterior frontiers and the optimal allocations using the robust Bayesian mean-variance approach for eight traditional bond and four hedge fund indexes. We were thus able to contrast the allocation results of a traditional fixed-income portfolio with a portfolio that explicitly includes fixed-income hedge fund strategies.

The robust portfolio allocations that include hedge fund strategies show that all three portfolio sets exhibit similar allocation structures. In addition, all include the distressed securities and convertible arbitrage hedge fund strategies, as well as the Lehman Mortgage Backed Securities Index in large amounts. Lower risk—return profiles are achieved with allocations to the 10-year Treasury for the long-term and posterior portfolios; the short-term portfolio includes the 10-year Bund.

In conclusion, because of the diversification benefits that fixed-income hedge fund strategies can bring to a traditional bond portfolio, we expect higher risk-adjusted returns. However, the problem of non-normally distributed hedge fund returns continues to exist.

REFERENCES

Agarwal, V., Fung, W., Loon, Y., and Naik, N.Y. (2004) Risk and Return in Convertible Arbitrage: Evidence from the Convertible Bond Market. Working paper, London Business School.

Best, M.J. and Grauer, R.R. (1991) On the Sensitivity of Mean-Variance Efficient Portfolios to Changes in Asset Means: Some Analytical and Computational Results. *Review of Financial Studies*, 4(2), 315–342.

Black, F. and Litterman, R. (1990) Asset Allocation: Combining Investor Views with Market Equilibrium. Goldman Sachs fixed-income research.

Black, F. and Litterman, R. (1992) Global Portfolio Optimization. *Financial Analysts Journal*, 48(5), 28–43.

Calamos, N.P. (2003) *Convertible Arbitrage—Insights and Techniques for Successful Hedging*. Hoboken, NJ: Wiley.

Capocci, D. (2003) Convertible Arbitrage Funds in a Classical Portfolio. In G.N. Gregoriou, V.N. Karavas and F. Rouah, eds., *Hedge Funds: Strategies, Risk Assessment, and Returns*. Washington: Beard Books, pp. 71–98.

Chopra, V. and Ziemba, W.T. (1993) The Effect of Errors in Mean and Covariance Estimates on Optimal Portfolio Choice. *Journal of Portfolio Management*, 20: 6–11.

Duarte, J., Longstaff, F.A., and Yu, F. (2006) Risk and Return in Fixed Income Arbitrage: Nickels in Front of a Steamroller? Working paper, University of Washington.

Fung, W. and Hsieh, D.A. (2002) Risk in Fixed Income Hedge Fund Styles. *Journal of Fixed Income*, September, 12(1): 6–27.

Füss, R. and Kaiser, D.G. (2007) The Tactical and Strategic Value
of Hedge Fund Strategies: A Cointegration Approach.
Financial Markets and Portfolio Management, 21(4):
425–444.

Füss, R., Kaiser, D.G., and Adams, Z. (2007) Value at Risk, GARCH
Modelling and the Forecasting of Hedge Fund Return Volatility.
Journal of Derivatives and Hedge Funds, 13(1): 2–25.

Heidorn, T., Hoppe, C., and Kaiser, D.G. (2006) Construction Methods,
Heterogeneity and Information Ratios of Hedge Fund Indices. In
G.N. Gregoriou and D.G. Kaiser (eds.), *Hedge Funds and
Managed Futures–A Handbook for Institutional Investors*. London:
Risk Books, pp. 3–30.

HFR (2007) HFR Industry Report Year End 2006, Hedge Fund
Research, Inc., Chicago.

Jaeger, L. (2002) *Managing Risk in Alternative Investment Strategies—
Successful Investing in Hedge Funds and Managed Futures*.
London: Financial Times Prentice Hall.

Jaeger, L. and Wagner, C. (2005) "Factor Modelling and Benchmarking of
Hedge Funds: Can Passive Investments in Hedge Fund Strategies
Deliver?" *Journal of Alternative Investments*, Vol. 8, No. 3, pp. 9–36.

Jorion, P. (1986) Bayes-Stein Estimation for Portfolio Analysis, *Journal
of Financial and Quantitative Analysis*, 21: 279–292.

Klein, R. and Bawa, V. (1976) The Effect of Estimation Risk on Optimal
Portfolio Choice. *Journal of Financial Economics*, 3: 215–231.

Lhabitant, F.-S. (2002) *Hedge Funds—Myths and Limits*. Chichester:
Wiley.

Markowitz (1959) *Portfolio Selection,* Second edition. Oxford: Blackwell.

Meucci, A. (2001) Common Pitfalls in Mean-Variance Asset Allocation.
Wilmott technical article.

Meucci, A. (2005) Robust Bayesian Asset Allocation. Working paper,
ssrn.com.

Meucci, A. (2006) *Risk and Asset Allocation*. Springer Finance, Berlin.

Michaud (1998) *Efficient Asset Management*. Boston: Harvard Business School Press.

Nicholas, J.G. (2000) *Market Neutral Investing—Long/Short Hedge Fund Strategies*. Princeton: Bloomberg Press.

Stefanini, F. (2006) *Investment Strategies of Hedge Funds*. Chichester, UK: Wiley.

Tomlinson, B. (1998) Market-Neutral Investing. In S. Jaffer (ed.), *Alternative Investment Strategies*. London: Euromoney, pp. 47–59.

Tran, V.Q. (2006) *Evaluating Hedge Fund Performance*. Hoboken, NJ: Wiley.

CHAPTER 19

Characterization of the iTraxx Indexes and the Role of Credit Index-Linked Constant Proportion Portfolio Insurances

Greg N. Gregoriou and Christian Hoppe

ABSTRACT

Credit derivative index swaps are used for pricing purposes, for benchmarking reasons, and as underlyings for structured credit derivatives. This chapter describes the iTraxx indexes existing currently and analyzes their specific characteristics in order to explain how they react in different market environments. In the second half of the chapter we determine the role of credit index-linked constant proportion portfolio insurance as an alternative to investing in the iTraxx index family.

INTRODUCTION

The rather short history of credit indexes can be divided into three phases. In an initial phase that lasted until 2004, large, internationally active investment banks calculated proprietary credit indexes that had a low degree of standardization and transparency. This first trend was based on the rapid growth of credit derivatives used to transfer credit risk—in particular, credit default swaps (CDSs)—in the mid- to late 1990s.[1] The second phase began with the creation of the iTraxx and CDX indexes, which went along with increased transparency and efficiency, partly due to standardization efforts by the International Swaps and Derivatives Association (ISDA) and the introduction of a master agreement in 1999.[2,3] The iTraxx indexes are concerned with European and Asian markets for credit derivatives, whereas the CDX indexes cover North America and emerging markets. The most recent phase was initiated on November 14, 2007, when Markit Group Limited announced that it had acquired both index providers and was going to integrate their index families into its product portfolio. Markit is considered a leading provider of market prices and information in the areas of fixed income, credit derivatives, and commodities. In the past, the company already calculated and published market prices of both index families. The merger is supposed to further advance efficiency as well as product innovation.

A credit derivative index swap (CDIS) or credit index represents a combination of a number of single-name CDSs, which implies that a CDIS offers protection against the default risk of all (mostly equally weighted) names included in the index. The protection seller in a CDIS receives a quarterly premium as compensation for potential losses in case of credit events, just like the issuer of a single-name CDS. In contrast to single-name CDS, credit index products are not terminated upon default of an index component, but continue to exist with a premium that is adjusted for the reduced notional amount. The value of an index CDS solely depends upon the credit risk of the reference obligors or reference obligations representing the index, i.e.,

---

[1] Compare to Fabozzi et al. (2004), pp. 58ff.

[2] This original master agreement was amended and adapted to changes in the market in 2001 and 2003, respectively. It provides a high level of legal certainty to the involved counterparties by fixing essential components of the contract. Individual contracts may, however, contain specific provisions that deviate from this master agreement.

[3] According to a survey by the Bank for International Settlements (BIS), the outstanding notional amount of CDS based on credit indexes accounted for 34.5 percent of the entire CDS market in December 2006 (Compare www.bis.org). Markit, a database provider, even attributes a share of 40 percent of trading volume in the credit derivatives market to credit indexes (Compare www.markit.com).

the likelihood of a credit event occurring.[4] This way, credit risk can be isolated from other risks such as market and interest rate risk and be traded more efficiently relative to risk subparticipations or default insurance contracts.[5] Furthermore, the two index families have established themselves as global benchmarks, as underlyings for a multitude of financial instruments, as a basis for pricing methods, and as early warning indicators of the constituents' creditworthiness as well as that of constituent regions and sectors.[6]

This chapter provides an analysis of the iTraxx index family with respect to its construction, methodology, index constituents, and historical performance. It is intended to shed light on the behavior of the respective indexes and clarify the characteristics of this specific asset class to potential investors. The second section illustrates various design options for credit index-linked constant proportion portfolio insurance (CI-CPPI) as an alternative to direct iTraxx investments, which, in addition, includes a capital guarantee.

THE ITRAXX INDEX FAMILY

In June 2004, iBoxx Ltd. and TRAC-X LLC merged into the International Index Company (IIC),[7] including 23 market makers, resulting in several less significant credit indexes being combined into the iTraxx index family and its respective subindexes. The number of licensed market makers has risen to more than 35 banks within three years. In selecting index constituents, highest priority is placed on focusing on the most liquid CDS in order to reflect respective markets as efficiently as possible and to assure a high degree of replicability. In the process, the index provider fixes index constituents based on a survey of licensed markets makers on March 20th and September 20th of each year. Market makers quote the names they deem most liquid based on trading volumes over the six months prior to selection.[8] These semiannual editions of the index are called *Series X* and

---

[4] Compare to Fabozzi et al. (2004), pp. 58ff.
[5] Compare to Amato and Gyntelberg (2005), pp. 75–77.
[6] Compare to Choudhry (2006), pp. 2–10.
[7] Up until November 2007, IIC was owned by ABN AMRO, Barclays Capital, BNP Paribas, Deutsche Bank, Deutsche Börse, Dresdner Kleinwort, Goldman Sachs, HSBC, JPMorgan, Morgan Stanley, and UBS.
[8] Internal trading volume (e.g., from proprietary trading desks) are excluded from the observation.

reflect the most current market environment. Series terminate after 3, 5, 7, or 10 years, on June 20th or December 20th, respectively.[9] By contrast, rollover periods for single-name CDS are only three months: March 20th, June 20th, September 20th, and December 20th. The iTraxx protects against the three credit events commonly covered by the ISDA documentation, i.e., bankruptcy, failure to pay, and (modified-modified) restructuring.[10] Given any of these credit events, the affected loan is subject to physical settlement, with cash settlement an optional feature. The IIC divides its indexes into the following groups: iTraxx Europe, iTraxx Asia, and LevX.[11] European indexes including LevX are denominated in EUR, while iTraxx Australia is quoted in AUD, Japanese indexes in JPY, and Asia ex-Japan indexes in USD. Table 19.1 provides an overview of indexes available for the current series of the iTraxx index family, including their respective inception dates, the number of index constituents, and the consequent index weights.

A short explanation of the trading mechanics is provided in the paragraphs that follow. Three situations need to be distinguished. After a potential investor has decided upon a specific CDS index series and the amount of their investment, the purchase of an index exposure (protection seller) is executed at the premium as set forth by IIC at the time of inception of a series. The market maker makes quarterly payments to the investor of this premium with respect to the nondefaulted index volume. If the spread currently traded in the market is below the fixed premium, then the investor has to make an up-front payment to the market maker amounting to the difference plus future interest, i.e., the present value of the CDIS, within three days of entering into the transaction. In case of a market spread that is above the fixed premium, the market maker is obliged to pay to the investor the difference less future interest, within the same time frame. If both spreads are equal, then no upfrontup-front payment is exchanged. The exact present value of the iTraxx investment in

---

[9] Newly established series cause investors to roll over their positions into the current series from the prior one. This behavior implies that liquidity for a given series will diminish with its age [ompare Martin et al. (2006) pp. 49–52].

[10] Compare to www.isda.org.

[11] With respect to published index spreads, one may choose between 12.00 noon and end of day fixing.

T A B L E   19.1

iTraxx indexes overview

	Inception of Maturities					
	3y	5y	7y	10y	Constituents	Weighting (%)
iTraxx Europe Indexes						
Europe (overall)	03/2005	06/2004	03/2005	06/2004	125	0.80
Europe HiVol	03/2005	06/2004	03/2005	06/2004	30	3.33
Europe e Crossover*12	11/2007	06/2004	11/2007	06/2004	50	2.00
iTraxx Europe Sector Indexes						
Non-Financials		06/2004		06/2004	100	1.00
Senior Financials		06/2004		06/2004	25	4.00
Subordinated Financials		06/2004		06/2004	25	4.00
iTraxx Europe Total Return Indexes						
Europe long		09/2006			NA	NA
Europe short		03/2007			NA	NA
Crossover long		09/2006			NA	NA
Crossover short		03/2007			NA	NA
HiVol long		09/2006				
HiVol short		03/2007				
iTraxx LevX Indexes						
LevX Senior		10/2006			35	2.86
LevX Subordinated		11/2006			35	2.86
iTraxx Asia Indexes						
Australia		07/2004		03/2007	25	4.00
Japan	03/2006	07/2004		09/2004	50	2.00
Japan 80		03/2007			80	1.25
Japan HiVol		09/2004			25	4.00
Asia ex-Japan (overall)		07/2004			70	1.43
Asia ex-Japan HY		09/2007			20	5.00
Asia Japan IG		09/2007			50	2.00

NA = not available, HY = only composed of companies rated below investment grade, and IG = only contains companies rated investment grade.

* Subject to market conditions at the rollover date, the number of index constituents may be increased.

---

[12] Subject to market conditions at the rollover date, the number of index constituents may be increased.

question is calculated using the CDSW (credit default swap) function in Bloomberg in most cases.[13] The sale of an index exposure (i.e., buying protection) works conversely.

iTraxx Europe

The iTraxx Europe exists for all four maturities and consists of 125 equally weighted (at 0.8 percent each) CDSs in the most liquid European companies that have an investment grade rating by Fitch, Moody's, or Standard & Poor's (S&P). Companies with a rating of BBB−/Baa3/BBB− or a negative outlook are disregarded. If a company is rated by more than one rating fulfil the selection criteria. Furthermore, companies have to belong to the following sectors: autos (10), consumers (30), energy (20), industrials (20), technology, media, and telecommunications (TMT) (20), and financials (25). The subindexes belonging to the nonfinancial sector index (autos, consumer, energy, industrials, TMT) were only published for series 1 through 5. Of all sector indexes, only the following three are still administered currently: iTraxx Non-Financials, iTraxx Senior Financials, as well as iTraxx Subordinated Financials.

The iTraxx HiVol is created by extracting from the iTraxx Europe the 30 companies with the highest spreads. These companies are exclusively Non-Financials. The relevant selection criterion is the companies' average five-year spread as observed on the last business day of the month preceding rollover. This way, the more risky names within the investment grade-rated iTraxx Europe companies are considered (as measured by their spreads), which implies a high potential yield coupled with high volatility and a high beta versus the iTraxx Europe.

The iTraxx Crossover, on the other hand, focuses solely on European nonfinancials with a rating of BBB−/Baa3/BBB− (Fitch/Moody's/S&P) with a negative outlook, or worse. For any potentially relevant company, at least € 100 million of debt must be publicly traded. In addition, a minimum spread is stipulated, which takes into account the average iTraxx

---

[13] Information and data used below regarding iTraxx indexes are taken from the free download section of www.markit.com.

Non-Financials index spread prevalent at the next roll date. Hence, only companies are considered whose spread is at least twice the iTraxx Non-Financials index spread, but no more than 1,250 bps or 35 percent up-front payment.

iTraxx Total Return indexes reflect a long credit position, i.e., that of a protection seller in an iTraxx index. The remaining capital is invested in the money market, whereas quarterly premium payments are immediately reinvested into the respective index. By contrast to the remaining iTraxx indexes, which only show spread changes of a specific series, total return indexes constitute an on-the-run index, i.e., a permanently current index. This is because CDS index contracts are simultaneously rolled over on a new series' day of inception. The iTraxx Short Total Return indexes resemble the Total Return indexes in terms of methodology, the difference being their reflection of a short credit position in the respective on-the-run iTraxx index, i.e., that of a protection buyer. The remaining notional is invested in the money market here as well. With the exception of the iTraxx Subordinated Financials, which is quoted at a recovery rate of 20 percent, all Series 8 iTraxx Europe indexes imply a fixed recovery rate of 40 percent.

iTraxx LevX

The iTraxx LevX indexes are composed of European corporates whose leveraged loan exposures are traded in the single-name loan only CDS (LCDS) market and whose rating is lower than BB+/Ba1/BB+ (Fitch/Moody's/S&P). The index constituents are subject to further selection criteria that determine whether they belong to the iTraxx LevX Senior (first lien) or the iTraxx LevX Subordinated (second/third lien). These criteria include a minimum outstanding loan notional of €750 million (LevX Senior) or €100 million (LevX Subordinated), respectively. In addition, the respective single-name LCDS must be quoted at an average spread of more than 75 bps (LevX Senior) and more than 225bps (LevX Subordinated). Furthermore, there may not be any overlap between second and third lien index constituents in the LevX Subordinated, and the share of the total index consisting of second lien index constituents must be between 40 and 60 percent at all times.

iTraxx Asia

The iTraxx Asia index group is divided geographically into three index segments: Japan, Australia, Asia ex-Japan. By contrast to the European iTraxx indexes, liquidity in Asia is measured in terms of the average trading volume over the past 12 months. The 50 companies that make up the iTraxx Japan are selected from the 75 most liquid names with an investment grade rating. For companies domiciled in Japan, ratings by Japan Rating and Investments (R&I), founded in 1985, are relevant as an additional measure of credit quality. Out of the target companies, however, only 10 (i.e., 20 percent) may be constituents of the Nikkei Industry. This restriction does not apply to the iTraxx Japan 80, which selects the most appropriate 80 companies from the 100 most liquid investment grade-rated Japanese companies. The iTraxx Japan HiVol focuses on the 25 Japanese companies with the highest average five-year spread, selecting them from the 100 most liquid companies, irrespective of their rating. Japanese sector indexes were discontinued starting with Series 5.

The iTraxx Australia encompasses the 25 most liquid investment grade-rated companies (or their parent or subsidiary companies) listed on the Australian Stock Exchange. Furthermore, no more than five banks (20 percent) may be part of the index.

The iTraxx Asia ex-Japan is a combination of the iTraxx Asia ex-Japan HY, which is only composed of companies rated below investment grade, and the iTraxx Asia ex-Japan IG, which only contains companies rated investment grade. Hence, it is the only main index which also considers inferior credit qualities. The iTraxx Korea, iTraxx Greater China, and iTraxx Rest of Asia indexes were discontinued starting with Series 7. At inception, the recovery rate for all Asian iTraxx indexes was fixed at 35 percent, the only exception being the iTraxx Australia indexes with a recovery rate of 40 percent.

PERFORMANCE MEASUREMENT

For the performance analysis, as well as description of yields, only those iTraxx indexes are examined that are administered under the current Series 8 and whose historical time series dates back to 2005 or earlier. In the process, freely available iTraxx end-of-day mid spreads were instantly rolled over into newly established series in order to create on-the-run CDS indexes. The relevant time series begin at the initial inception date of the index and end November 22, 2007. In analyzing index developments, only month-end data were considered. This is because credit asset managers and fund managers usually make investment decisions on a monthly or even quarterly basis. Finally, it should be noted that using mid spreads neglects transaction costs during rollover. For Series 8, they were 1 percent of the old series and 1 percent of the new series. The series can be adjusted by IIC subject to significant market changes. Next, spread changes are evaluated from the point of view of a protection buyer, i.e., that of a seller of the CDS index. Implications for the counterparty (protection seller) hold vice versa.

Using the iTraxx Europe as an example, Figure 19.1 illustrates a rising risk appetite as evidenced by tightening spreads between April 2005 and June 2007. From the onset of the credit crisis and the resulting liquidity crisis, spreads widened significantly until August 2007, before returning to more normal levels.

The iTraxx indexes' annualized rates of return present a rather mixed picture (Table 19.2). The sustained drop in index spreads mentioned above could not be halted by the significant spread increases during the credit crisis for all indexes. For instance, this means that investors' risk

F I G U R E   19.1

Development of the iTraxx Europe indexes (on the run)

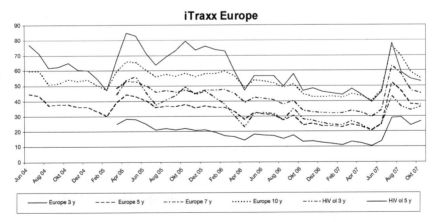

T A B L E   19.2

Rate of return (annualized) and standard deviation

	Rate of Return (Annualized) (%)				Standard Deviation (%)			
	3y	5y	7y	10y	3y	5y	7y	10y
iTraxx Europe Indexes								
Europe (overall)	2.3	−5.1	−3.0	−2.6	24.2	20.7	17.4	13.0
Europe HiVol	−7.6	−10.6	−8.0	−6.3	20.1	17.4	13.8	12.2
Europe crossover		1.7		5.5		18.3		12.9
iTraxx Europe Sector Indexes								
Non-Financials		−7.7		−3.5		18.7		12.5
Senior Financials		17.2		12.3		37.4		24.2
Subordinated Financials		11.6		6.7		32.4		18.7
iTraxx Asia Indexes								
Australia		2.9				14.4		
Japan		6.3		12.3		18.7		15.2
Japan HiVol		3.5				20.1		
Asia ex-Japan (overall)		12.2				20.9		

aversion as measured by widening spreads was more noticeable in the Asian indexes and the iTraxx Financials. Comparing index maturities, rates of return increase with higher maturities, with the exception of the iTraxx Subordinated Financials. At the same time, standard deviations decrease with higher maturities, i.e., indexes show less volatility and lower sensitivity toward market changes for longer maturities.

A parameter value above zero for the relative skewness measure used in the analysis indicates a higher probability of increasing index spreads, relative to a normal distribution. This characteristic, which is observed for all indexes, works in favor of the protection buyer, whereas it signifies losses to a protection seller. Furthermore, a relative kurtosis parameter of 3 indicates monthly spreads being concentrated around a mean, as in a normal distribution. Values above this threshold point to a higher probability of greater deviations from the mean, which implies

T A B L E   19.3

Distribution of monthly spreads

	Skewness				Kurtosis			
	3y	5y	7y	10y	3y	5y	7y	10y
iTraxx Europe Indexes								
Europe (overall)	3.42	4.17	4.11	3.14	14.98	21.70	20.41	13.80
Europe HiVol	1.79	2.02	1.76	1.48	4.69	5.99	5.68	3.36
Europe Crossover		2.69		2.14		8.97		5.51
iTraxx Europe Sector Indexes								
Non Financials		3.92		3.28		19.97		15.00
Senior Financials		4.84		4.24		27.35		22.91
Subordinated Financials		4.61		3.08		25.49		14.02
iTraxx Asia Indexes								
Australia		3.19				14.88		
Japan		2.69		2.80		10.28		11.73
Japan HiVol		1.51				6.72		
Asia ex-Japan (overall)		3.45				15.31		

higher risk for the investor. All indexes analyzed here display this risk, the exception being the iTraxx Europe HiVol 10-year on-the-run index. The Jarque-Bera test can be used to jointly test skewness and kurtosis. Its results indicate whether monthly spreads are normally distributed. For the indexes considered here (Table 19.3), a normal distribution of spreads can be ruled out.

The two-dimensional Sharpe performance measure developed by William F. Sharpe (1966) relates index performance minus a minimum risk-free yield (assumed here to be 4 percent per annum) to the risk inherent in an investment, as measured by the standard deviation of index yields. Thus analyzed, most iTraxx indexes offer a negative risk-adjusted yield to protection buyers, the most significant examples being the iTraxx Europe, iTraxx Europe HiVol, and iTraxx Europe Non-Financials. If only negative deviations from the minimum yield are considered risky, then

T A B L E   19.4

Sharpe and Sortino ratio

	Sharpe Ratio				Sortino Ratio			
	3y	5y	7y	10y	3y	5y	7y	10y
iTraxx Europe Indexes								
Europe (overall)	−0.02	−0.13	−0.12	−0.15	−0.05	−0.35	−0.32	−0.32
Europe HiVol	−0.17	−0.24	−0.25	−0.24	−0.32	−0.47	−0.44	−0.42
Europe Crossover		−0.04		0.03		−0.09		0.07
iTraxx Europe Sector Indexes								
Non Financials		−0.18		−0.17		−0.45		−0.39
Senior Financials		0.10		0.10		0.39		0.30
Subordinated Financials		0.07		0.04		0.24		0.10
iTraxx Asia Indexes								
Australia		−0.02				−0.05		
Japan		0.04		0.16		0.08		0.38
Japan HiVol		−0.01				−0.01		
Asia ex-Japan (overall)		0.11				0.32		

downside deviation can be measured, which is equivalent to a semistandard deviation. Relating excess returns to downside deviation yields the Sortino Ratio (Table 19.4). If the latter is lower compared to the Sharpe ratio, the distribution of index changes is skewed to the left. A protection buyer, however, would prefer to have Sortino ratio greater than the Sharpe ratio, with each being greater than zero. This property is displayed by the iTraxx Financial indexes, whose CDS index changes are driven by the recent liquidity crisis.

The analysis of index changes shows that spreads have behaved in a very volatile manner since inception. For the most part, only neutral or negative Sharpe ratios could be achieved. Thus, buying an iTraxx index CDS is a rather risky and hardly worthwhile investment for a protection buyer. In a portfolio context, however, adding index CDS may provide a sensible opportunity for diversification. For a protection seller, an investment is just as volatile and hence risky. The second section of this chapter illustrates an alternative investment, a dynamic portfolio hedge that reduces downside risk while allowing the investor to participate in any upside development.

CREDIT INDEX-LINKED CONSTANT PROPORTION PORTFOLIO INSURANCE

The most recent developments in the markets for credit and credit derivatives are reflected in the performance measures for the iTraxx indexes analyzed here, in that they display a higher range of deviations and hence higher risk to investors. First presented by Black and Jones in 1987, constant proportion portfolio insurance (CPPI) provides an opportunity to reduce the inherent downside risk, while offering partial participation in times of rising markets.[14] Papers by Perold (1986; 1988), Black and Rouhani (1987), Roman et al. (1989), and Black and Perold (1992) rank first in terms of relevance as pertains to the hedging of fixed-income portfolios. Next, an illustration of how CI-CPPIs work is followed by individual potential strategies based on these instruments.

The Concept of CI-CPPI

At the time of investment in a CI-CPPI or that of implementation, the investment notional N is discounted at the currently valid risk-free rate of interest. The value of the investment may never fall short of the present value (PV) thus derived over the life of the investment, so that a payoff of the initial notional is guaranteed at maturity. By reducing the initial investment amount by the present value and by fees payable (C, e.g., 1.5 percent), the so-called reserve R is calculated. The exposure in credit indexes E results from multiplying the reserve with the multiplier m (e.g., 15), which is set at inception and determines the riskiness of the structure. The exposure is adjusted at preset rebalancing dates, e.g. quarterly. For instance, if the reserve increases as a result of mark to market (MTM) gains and a premium payment within a given rebalancing period, the exposure in the credit index is increased as follows: $E = m \times (N - \mathrm{PV} - C)/N$.

---

[14] Compare to Black and Jones (1987), p. 49.

For practical reasons, a corridor from m^- to m^+ is set, such that the exposure need only be adjusted if the upper or lower threshold is exceeded. To present a more illustrative example, a five-year, €10 million iTraxx Europe investment via CI-CPPI at inception of a new series is considered. The €10 million N have to be reduced by €0.15 million costs C. As there is no up-front payment at inception of a new index series and hence the sale of protection on the iTraxx is unfunded, i.e., by means of a synthetic risk transfer, €9.85 million is invested in the money market for a five-year maturity. Assuming a PV of €8 million and $m = 15$, the iTraxx Europe exposure is equal to €27.75 million. In case the investor needs to make an up-front payment, the reserve R and hence the exposure in the CDS index are reduced. If, on the other hand, the investor receives an up-front payment from the market maker, then this amount weighted with the multiplier m is added to the investor's iTraxx Europe exposure. A schematic CI-CPPI structure (without any up-front payment) is illustrated in Figure 19.2. In the given example, the initial leverage of the risky investment is approximately 2.8 (€27.75 million/€10 million).

F I G U R E   19.2

Credit index-linked CPPI mechanics

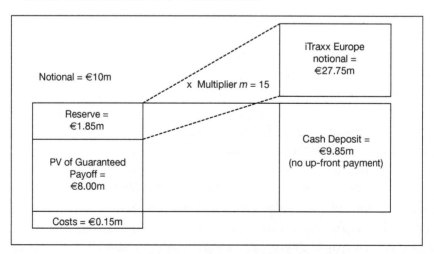

In case the iTraxx Europe spread has tightened by the next rebalancing date, the value of the risky investment is augmented by unrealized gains. In order to reestablish the initial leverage, a respective volume of additional protection on the iTraxx Europe needs to be sold.

To better illustrate a scenario in which losses are incurred, we assume the extreme case of all iTraxx Europe constituents defaulting overnight, with a zero recovery rate each. In this case, obligations of €29.6 million (the protection buyer is owed notional of €27.75 million plus the reserve of €1.85 million as collateral for the iTraxx notional) outweigh assets of €10 million (CI-CPPI notional without interest), resulting in a loss of €19.6 million. For an effective capital guarantee to be achieved, the reserve may never become negative. This can be assured by setting a so-called trigger at inception of the CI-CPPI. As soon as reserves fall short of this trigger, capital is shifted from the risky investments to money market products. If a trigger is implemented and geared toward the market risk of the underlying, then it should prevent reserves from being fully consumed. However, there remains a residual loss risk for the issuer of a CI-CPPI structure; called *gap risk*.[15] Gap risk may be reduced, e.g., by reducing rebalancing intervals, placing an upper limit on leverage, dynamically adjusting reserves (ratchet effect), or limiting the leverage effect of the multiplier.[16]

Credit Index-Linked CPPI Strategies

There are a number of variations of credit-linked CPPI structures that reference single-name CDS, basket CDS, loans, and CDS swaptions In the following, however, a brief depiction of CI-CPPI strategies is provided.

A basic credit index CPPI consists of simply investing the notional into an iTraxx or CDX index. This method of tracking the respective index unlevered ensures a high degree of transparency and plausibility with respect to the structure's behavior and valuation. Risks are limited to default risk and spread volatility risk. The investment yield is made up of premium payments, MTM gains and losses, and principal losses due to defaults.

---

[15] Compare to Balder et al. (2006), pp. 4–12.
[16] Compare to Bertrand, Prigent (2001), pp. 12–18.

The risk–return profile of the structure can be aligned more individually to an investor's requirements by investing into either of the five tranches of the iTraxx Europe (0 to 3 percent, 3 to 6 percent, 6 to 9 percent, 9 to 12 percent, 12 to 22 percent) or of the CDX (0 to 3 percent, 3 to 7 percent, 7 to 10 percent, 10 to 15 percent, 15 to 30 percent). Using index tranches allows investors to lever their credit index exposure, changing MTM behavior and increasing sensitivity to spread changes relative to an unlevered index investment.[17]

Combining various credit indexes or credit index tranches increases a structure's complexity, which may reduce transparency. For instance, several indexes or iTraxx index tranches may be combined that have identical or different maturities, are from identical or different series, or differ with respect to recovery rates or geographical focus. In addition, indexes from the CDX family may be used, e.g., in order to create a global credit index or to reduce an investment's inherent risk by means of higher diversification.

As a next step, short and long positions in the indexes or index tranches may be combined. Dependent upon relevant correlations, one could, for example, sell protection on the iTraxx HiVol 10 year while purchasing protection on the iTraxx Europe Senior Financials five year (see Table 19.5). Alternatively, one might sell protection on the equity tranche (0 to 3 percent) of the iTraxx Europe while buying protection on the mezzanine tranche (3 to 6 percent).[18]

A delta hedge, i.e., an effective immunization against spread changes in the iTraxx Europe, may be constructed by combining equity and mezzanine tranches. In order for the delta hedge to have the greatest effect, the ratios of the individual tranches would have to be adjusted continually. These kinds of CI-CPPI strategies typically include correlation (skew) risk and do not take into account spread heterogeneity within an index, which increases with deviation around the average spread.[19] The risky portion of a CI-CPPI structure may also be allocated by means of credit index-based derivatives such as iTraxx options, futures, or first-to-default baskets. However, this further changes the risk–return profile so that other risk types would have to be considered.

---

[17] Compare to Wang et al. (2007), pp. 4–9.
[18] Compare to Garcia et al. (2007), pp. 9–11.
[19] Compare to Acharya and Schäfer (2006).

T A B L E   19.5

Correlation matrix (iTraxx Europe: 03/2005 to 10/2007)

	a	b	c	d	e	f	g	h	i	j	k
Europe 5 y	.987	.836	.824	.931	.820	.976	.933	.822	.871	.854	.916
Europe 10 y (a)		.829	.844	.905	.805	.981	.955	.781	.832	.813	.879
HiVol 5 y (b)			.979	.731	.555	.883	.838	.436	.525	.494	.633
HiVol 10 y (c)				.705	.563	.878	.854	.413	.495	.465	.596
Crossover 5y (d)					.948	.908	.865	.825	.866	.853	.892
Crossover 10y (e)						.784	.760	.791	.807	.804	.795
Non-Financials 5y (f)							.972	.714	.778	.756	.847
Non-Financials 10 y (g)								.659	.725	.696	.792
Senior Financials 5 y (h)									.991	.995	.959
Senior Financials 10 y (i)										.995	.985
Subordinate Financials 5 y (j)											.975
Subordinate Financials 10 y (k)											

CONCLUSION

Our analysis of the iTraxx indexes yields a rather mixed picture. For example, rates of return range from −10.6 to +17.2 percent, standard deviations from 12.2 to 37.4 percent, and Sharpe ratios from −0.25 to +0.16. The performance of an index investment also strongly depends on timing. A buy-and-hold strategy as simulated by using on-the-run indexes does not yield any excess risk-adjusted returns (as measured by the Sharpe ratio) for the period considered, i.e., the years following the indexes' inception.

Therefore, using an investment structure that includes a dynamic capital guarantee, such as CI-CPPI, provides an opportunity apt to minimize downside risk and at the same time participate in upside developments. Credit index-linked constant proportion portfolio insurances have the advantage of being extremely variable in that they may reference nearly any underlying related to credit indexes. Following the credit crisis, investors will turn away from underlyings that are too complex and intransparent. As a disadvantage of this portfolio hedge relative to using embedded options, short-term losses may not simply be endured. Once the trigger level is reached, capital is immediately shifted into the risk-free investment to remain there until maturity. Hence, it becomes very difficult, if not impossible, to recover losses, and this has to be interpreted as the price of the capital guarantee.

REFERENCES

Acharya, V. and Schäfer, S. (2006) Liquidity Risk and Correlation Risk: Implications for Risk Management, London Business School.

Amato, J. and Gyntelberg, J. (2005) CDS Index Tranches and the Pricing of Credit Risk Correlations, *BIS Quarterly Review*, March: 73–87.

Balder, S., Brandl, M., and Mahayni, A. (2006) Effectiveness of CPPI Strategies under Discrete-Time Trading. *SSRN,* Working paper.

Bertrand, P. and Prigent, J.L. (2001) Portfolio Insurance Strategies: The Extreme Value of the CPPI Method. University of Cergy, Working paper.

Black, F. and Jones, R. (1987) Simplifying Portfolio Insurance. *Journal of Portfolio Management*, 14 (1): 48–51.

Black, F. and Perold, A.R. (1992) Theory of Constant Proportion Portfolio Insurance. *Journal of Economic Dynamics Control*, 16: 403–426.

Black, F. and Rouhani, R. (1987) Constant Proportion Portfolio Insurance and the Synthetic Put Option: A Comparision. *Portfolio Strategy*.

Choudhry, Moorad (2006) *The Credit Default Swap Basis*. New York: Bloomberg Press.

Fabozzi, F.J., Anson, M.J.P., Choudhry, M., and Chen, R.R. (2004) *Credit Derivatives—Instruments, Applications and Pricing*, New York: John Wiley & Sons.

Garcia, J., Goossens, S., and Schoutens, W. (2007) Let's Jump Together—Pricing of Credit Derivatives: From Index Swaptions to CPPIs, *Dexia Group,* Working paper.

Martin, M.R.W., Reitz, S., and When, C.S. (2006) *Kreditderivate und Kreditrisikomodelle*. Wiesbaden: Vieweg.

Perold, A.R. (1986) Constant Proportion Portfolio Insurance, Harvard Business School, Working paper.

Perold, A.R., Sharpe, W. (1988) Dynamic Strategies for Asset Allocations, *Financial Analysts Journal*, 16–27.

Roman, E., Kopprash, R., and Hakanoglu, E. (1989) Constant Proportion Portfolio Insurance for Fixed Income Investments. *Journal of Portfolio Management*.

Sharpe, W. (1966) Mutual Fund Performance. *Journal of Business*, 39(1): 119–138.

Wang, D., Rachev, S.T., and Fabozzi, F.J. (2007) Pricing of Credit Default Index Swap Tranches with One-Factor Heavy-Tailed Copula Models. Yale School of Management, Working paper.

CHAPTER 20

Trading the Credit Default Swap Basis: Illustrating Positive and Negative Basis Arbitrage Trades[1]

Moorad Choudhry

ABSTRACT

The development of a liquid market in credit derivatives has provided a new asset class for investors in credit risky assets. Given that the derivative represents the cash asset in synthetic form, there is a close relationship between the two types of credit market instrument, which manifests itself in the credit default swap basis. The existence of a non-zero basis, either positive or negative, can act as a powerful indicator of relative value in credit markets. Fluctuations in the basis give rise to arbitrage trading opportunities between the two forms of the asset, through which investors can exploit mis-pricing in cash and synthetic markets. We define two types of basis trade: the negative basis trade, where one is buying the bond and buying protection on the same reference name, and the positive basis trade, where the arbitrager will sell the bond and sell credit default swap protection on the same name.

---

[1] This chapter previously was published in *The Credit Default Swap Basis,* © 2006 by Moorad
    Choudhry. Reprinted by permission of Bloomberg Press. All rights reserved. Visit
    www.bloomberg.com.

INTRODUCTION

A basis exists in any market where cash and derivative forms of the same asset are traded. Given that a derivative instrument such as a credit default swap (CDS) represents the cash asset in synthetic underlying form, there is a close relationship between the two asset types, which manifests itself in the basis and its magnitude. Fluctuations in the basis give rise to arbitrage trading opportunities between the two forms of the asset. This has proved the case in the more recent market of credit derivatives.[2]

In Choudhry (2001) we summarized the logic behind the no-arbitrage theory of pricing credit default swaps (CDS), which suggests that the premium of a CDS should be equal to an asset-swap (ASW) spread for the same reference name. There are a number of reasons why this is not the case however,[3] and in practice a non-zero basis exists for all reference names in the credit markets. The existence of a non-zero basis implies potential arbitrage gains that can be made if trading in both the cash and derivatives markets simultaneously. In this chapter we describe trading the basis, with real-world examples given of such trades, illustrating the positive basis trade and the negative basis trade.

RELATIVE VALUE AND TRADING THE BASIS

The introduction of credit derivatives into the financial markets has provided a new asset class for investors in credit risky assets. That credit derivatives, particularly CDSs, can be traded in a liquid market in a wide range of names provides investors and other market participants with an additional measure of relative value across the cash and synthetic markets. The existence of a non-zero basis, either positive or negative, can act as a powerful indicator of value in either or both markets. In addition, during an economic boom period or time of general business confidence when corporate credit spreads are tight, investors look to new opportunities to meet target rates of return or realize value. Exploiting mis-pricing in cash and synthetic markets, through basis arbitrage trading, is one such opportunity.

---

[2] The trades described here are not pure arbitrage trades, because they are not completely risk free. This is discussed in the section on hedging and risk.

[3] Described in Choudhry (2001).

There are two types of basis trade:

1. *Negative basis* trade: This position is defined as buying the bond and buying protection on the same reference name. It is generally put on if the CDS spread[4] is relatively low compared to where it has been hitherto, and if the cash bond spread is relatively high. The objective of a negative basis trade is to earn a credit-risk-free return by buying the cash and buying protection in the synthetic. In a negative basis trade, the cash bond is viewed as cheap and the CDS as dear.

2. *Positive basis* trade: This is where the arbitrager will sell the bond and sell CDS protection on the same name to exploit a price differential that is brought about by a relatively high CDS price and a relatively low cash bond spread.

There is more than one way to measure the basis. Whichever approach we employ, in essence we are comparing a CDS premium to a spread over the London Interbank Offered Rate (LIBOR), so all analysis is undertaken relative to LIBOR. Put simply, we wish to earn a spread pickup on our trade, so the largest possible spread gain will generate the largest profit. There are other considerations as well, which can include the following:

- Extent of credit risk premium received and/or earned
- Any impact of the "cheapest-to-deliver" option for the protection buyer
- Impact of funding cost of the cash asset
- The effect of basis trades in reference names that trade at sub-LIBOR in the cash market[5]
- The relative levels of liquidity in the cash and synthetic market
- The effectiveness of the trade hedge

---

[4] Throughout this book we have referred to the CDS *spread* when a more accurate term would be *premium* or *fee*. The CDS spread is not a spread over anything, but more simply a fixed price quoted in basis points. However market common practice is to refer to the CDS *spread* in the same way as we refer to an *asset-swap spread,* which is a spread over LIBOR; so we continue the practice here.

[5] Names such as the World Bank or U.S. Agency securities trade at sub-LIBOR in the cash market; so additional analysis is required to determine basis trade profit potential.

T A B L E   20.1

Average CDS and ASW spreads for selected industrial
names during 2005

Credit Rating	Average CDS Premium	Average ASW Spread	Difference (CDS-ASW)
AAA	22	12	10
AA	26	17	9
A	39	36	3
BBB	88	87	1
BB	256	247	9
Average	86.2	79.8	6.4

Spread source: Bloomberg L.P.

The last point we mention is very important. To be a pure arbitrage, the basis package must hedge both credit risk and interest rate risk. For large-size trades, spread risk may also need to be hedged.[6] Otherwise the trade will not be a pure risk-free one, and the final return on it will be influenced by (at the time of inception) unknown factors.

The various factors that drive the basis tend to drive it to positive territory. In other words, a positive basis is the norm. Table 20.1 shows the average CDS premium and asset-swap (ASW) spread across the ratings categories for selected industrial names during 2005. For no set of names was a negative basis the average value. In other words, we should expect the CDS to trade higher than the cash. On average, CDS spreads are 6 to 7 basis points (bps) above ASW spreads. Overall, a negative basis is a good initial indicator that special factors are at work.

FACTORS INFLUENCING THE BASIS PACKAGE

When constructing the basis trade, it is important that we compare like for like and that we hedge the trade as effectively as possible. That is, we need

---

[6] This is the risk that the relative spread of cash assets to LIBOR or the swap rate changes. One instrument that can be used to hedge spread risk is the LIFFE SwapNote contract. For details of this derivative, see Choudhry (2004a; 2004b).

to consider the most appropriate cash market spread against which to measure the CDS spread, and we need to also construct the hedge with care.

Measuring the Basis

The question of which cash market spread to use when measuring the basis is an important one. The different measures for the cash spread, such as interpolated swap spread or ASW spread, produce different values for the basis. The answer to this problem is not clear-cut; credit default swaps and cash bonds trade in different markets, with different market drivers, and a pure comparison may not actually be possible. We know that we need to select a LIBOR-based spread; the question is which spread? The CDS "spread" is not a spread at all but rather a fixed premium received quarterly by the protection seller. While in theory the CDS spread and the ASW spread measure the credit risk of the reference name, other more specific factors drive each of them, such that, in effect, they are actually measuring slightly different things. The CDS premium can be viewed as a pure credit risk price; that is, it is the credit premium for the name. Although other factors will drive this premium, including supply and demand, at least as an unfunded instrument and par product we know these considerations do not apply. We want to compare it therefore to the cash measure that is the most accurate measure of the reference entity's credit risk.

A cash bond spread can be measured in a number of ways. Figure 20.1 shows the Bloomberg YAS page for a ThyssenKrupp AG issue, the 4.375 percent March 2015 bond. This shows the different bond spread measures that can be calculated. In a basis trade, it is the spread that is the best indicator of the reference name's credit risk premium to which we should, ideally, be comparing the CDS spread. The CDS price is 93.7 (bps), which is an interpolated spread based on the CDS curve. The CDS curve is shown on screen CRVD for this name, given at Figure 20.2.

We see from Figure 20.1 that for this name, we have

- I-spread (ISPRD) of 103.2 basis points (bps)
- Asset-swap (ASW) spread of 98.3 bps
- Z-spread (ZSPR) of 103.7 bps

F I G U R E   20.1

Bloomberg page YAS for Thyssenkrupp AG 4.375 percent March 2015, as at March 13, 2006

```
YAS                                                              P174 Corp   YAS
Enter 11<GO> for Historical Z-spreads
YIELD & SPREAD ANALYSIS                        CUSIPED842146  PCS BGN
THYSSENKRUPP AG  TKAGR 4 ³₈ 03/15   96.0769/96.4459   (4.92/4.87) BGN @ 3/10
SETTLE 3/16/06   FACE AMT        1000 M  or PROCEEDS        1,007,969.00
1) YA          YIELDS        2) YASD  RISK &   TKAGR 4 ³₈ 03/18
PRICE  96.445873 No Rounding      N  HEDGE       workout        HEDGE BOND
YIELD     4.872 Lst                 RATIOS    3/18/15  OAS        OAS
SPRD    121.00 bp  yld-decimals 3/3 Mod Dur  6.94    7.02       7.39
      versus           Consensus   Risk    6.993   7.077      7.491
   DBR 3 ³₄ 01/04/15    BENCHMARK  Convexity 0.62   0.64       0.67
   PRICE  100.640000   Save  Delete  Workout HEDGE Amount:939 M
   YIELD    3.662 %    sd:  3/16/06    OAS HEDGE Amount:945 M
  Yields are: Annual
3) OAS        SPREADS       4) ASW  5) FPA      FINANCING
OAS:   118.6 CRV# 960  VOL     Opt  Repo% 2.701  (360/365)360  Days   1
OAS:   102.0 CRV# I53  TED:         Int Income   119.86   Carry P&L
ASW (A/A)   98.3 ZSPR  103.7 11) History Fin Cost  -75.63         44.24
CRV#  I53  EURO SWAP ANNUAL         Amortiz     11.51<->       55.75
ISPRD  103.2 DSPRD  106.8          Forward Prc 96.441449
 Yield Curve: 113  EURO BENCHMARK CURVE  Prc Drop  0.004424
+ 120  v  9.0yr ( 3.667 %) INTERPOLATED  Drop (bp)   0.08
+ 165  v 3yr ( 3.22) OBL 3 ¹₂ 10/10/08 # Accrued Interest  /100  4.351027
+ 151  v 4yr ( 3.36) OBL 3 ¹₂ 10/09/09 # Number Of Days Accrued  363
+ 142  v 5yr ( 3.45) OBL 2 ¹₂ 10/08/10 #
Australia 61 2 9777 8600      Brazil 5511 3048 4500    Europe 44 20 7330 7500    Germany 49 69 920410
Hong Kong 852 2977 6000 Japan 81 3 3201 8900 Singapore 65 6212 1000 U.S. 1 212 318 2000 Copyright 2006 Bloomberg L.P.
                                                                  2 13-Mar-06 16:08:19
```

In other words the LIBOR spread for this bond ranges from 98.3 bps to 103.7 bps. The spread to the government bond benchmark is 121 bps, based on the price of the bond at €96.445. In other words,

- The interpolated spread of 103.2 bps is the straight difference between the bond gross redemption yield and LIBOR rate for the same term.

- In an ASW package, the investor would receive LIBOR + 98.3 bps and an implied receipt of €3.555 up-front (as the bond is priced below par) while paying the coupon of 4.375 percent over the term of the deal.

- The z-spread of 103.7 bps represents the spread over and above the interbank interest rate swap curve that would equal the bond's present value with its coupon and principal payments over the term to maturity.

F I G U R E   20.2

Bloomberg page CRVD for Thyssenkrupp AG reference
name, as at March 13, 2006

<HELP> for explanation, <MENU> for similar functions.   P174 **Corp   CRVD**

Credit Relative Value		

Currency: EUR - CBBT   Edit   Option   ThyssenKrupp AG

TKAGR Sr EUR CDS

			TKAGR Sr CDS Curve vs. Z-Spread	TKA GR Equity
1Yr	24.00	CBGN		Last 22.070
2Yr	30.06	Interp		Change N.A.
3Yr	36.06	CBGN		% Chg N.A.
4Yr	50.51	Interp		52 Wk Hi 22.60
5Yr	65.00	CBGN		52 Wk Lo 13.83
7Yr	80.75	CBGN		Div Yield N.A.
10Yr	100.08	CBGN		30D Vol 27.477
ICUR		Yr		60D Vol 28.316
				90D Vol 23.858
				BETA 1.159

Security (CBBT)	Time	Price	Sprd	Bench	Z-Sprd	Basis
1) TKAGR 7 03/19/09	16:59:31	108.562	62.3	DBR 3 ¾ 01/04/09	42.2	-5.9
2) TKAGR 5 03/29/11	17:02:14	102.841	86.8	DBR 5 ¼ 01/04/11	70.2	-4.9
3) TKAGR 4 ⅜ 03/18/15	17:02:18	96.081	124.1	DBR 3 ¾ 01/04/15	107.3	-13.6

BN 16:28 Salzgitter's 4th-Qtr Profit Doubles on Share Sale (Update3)
BN 11:39 Salzgitter's 4th-Qtr Profit Doubles on Share Sale (Update2)
BN 9:24 Salzgitter's 4th-Qtr Profit Doubles on Share Sale (Update1)
BN 9:09 Salzgitter's 4th-Quarter Profit More Than Doubles (Correct)

Australia 61 2 9777 8600   Brazil 5511 3048 4500   Europe 44 20 7330 7500   Germany 49 69 920410
Hong Kong 852 2977 6000 Japan 81 3 3201 8900 Singapore 65 6212 1000 U.S. 1 212 318 2000 Copyright 2006 Bloomberg L.P.
2 13-Mar-06 17:03:08

As we noted, for basis trading purposes ideally we should use the bond spread that best represents the credit premium payable for taking on the issuer's credit risk. There is no real "true" answer although in practice the ASW spread and the Z-spread are the most commonly used. Note however, as in this case, for bonds that trade close to par the various spread measures are actually quite close.

As part of the analysis in a real-world situation we should also consider the actual return generated by a basis trade package. This takes into account market factors such as bid–offer spread and funding costs. Table 20.2 shows how we would undertake this analysis at the close-out of the trade, be it after one month, three months, one year, or other target horizon. In this analysis the total return of the trade is, unsurprisingly, a function of the actual price of the bond at close-out. The actual result is not known, as we do not know the price of the bond in the future, at the time we put on the trade, hence the blank fields in Table 20.2. We show this table to suggest how we should

T A B L E   20.2

Suggested return analysis for negative basis trade for
six-month trade horizon, Thyssenkrupp bond

	Cash-Flow Position vs. Par	1.00795	
	Price Today March 13, 2006	Price at Closeout	Cost/Gain
Bond mechanics			
Clean	96,445	x	$x - 96.445$
Accrued	4,35	ai	$ai - 4.35$
Dirty	100,795	$x + ai$	$(x + ai) - 100.795$
Fund bond position in repo (pay 1.00795%)			
Six-month EUR LIBOR 2.847%			$-1,434$
Interest rate swap hedge: cash flow			
Pay fixed at 3.843%			$-1,936$
Receive 6–mo LIBOR 2.847%			$1,434$
Total bond cash flows			
CDS mechanics			
Buy 9–y CDS protection at 93.7 bps			$-0,4685$
Total return			

look to perform the analysis. Later on in this chapter we show some real-
world trade results.

The Hedge Construction

It is intuitively easy to view a basis package as a straight par-for-par trade
of notionals. That is, we would buy (or sell) US$10 million nominal of a
bond against buying (or selling) US$10 million of notional in the CDS.
This type of notional comparison in a basis trade is still quite common
due to its simplicity. However, unless the cash bond in question is priced
at par, this approach is not correct, and the analysis will not be accurate.

The biggest errors will arise when the bond is trading significantly away from par.

As part of the analysis into the trade then, we need to assess how much nominal of bond to buy or sell against a set amount of CDS notional, or conversely, how much CDS protection to put on against a set amount of the bond. There is no one way to approach this; the key is the assumption made about the recovery rate in the event of default. In practice traders will adopt one of the following methods:

- Par/par: This is a common approach. In such a trade, identical par amounts of the bond and the CDS are traded. The advantage of this method is that the position is straightforward to maintain. The disadvantage is that the trader is not accurately credit risk hedged if the bond is priced away from par. The CDS pays our par (minus the deliverable asset or cash value on default) on default, but if the bond is priced above par, greater cash value is at risk in a negative basis trade. Therefore, this approach is recommended for bonds priced near par or for trades with a long-term horizon. It is not recommended for use with bonds at higher risk of default (for instance, sub-investment grade bonds) as default events expose this trade to potentially the highest loss; it is also more at risk for anything other than small changes in spread;

- Delta neutral: This is a similar approach used to duration-weighted bond spread trades such as butterfly and/or barbell trades [see Choudhry (2004a)]. It is appropriate when the maturity of the bond does not match precisely the maturity of the CDS;

- DV01: This approach sets the CDS notional relative to the actual price of the bond. For example, in a negative basis trade if the bond is trading at €120, then we would buy 120 percent notional of the CDS. This is a logical approach and recommended if the bond is trading away from par.

An assumption of the recovery rate will influence the choice of hedging approach and the notional amount of CDS protection to buy. This is discussed in the next section.

Hedging and Risk

Basis trades are termed *arbitrage* trades but are not pure arbitrage because they are not risk free. More accurately, they should be called *relative value* trades. Here we discuss some issues in unhedged risk.

For instance, the coupon on the bond is not hedged: to do this, we would need to put on a series of coupon strips synthetically to hedge each coupon payable during the life of the bond. In the event of default, the timing of default is crucial; if this occurs just prior to a coupon payment, the actual loss on the trade will be higher than if default occurred just after a coupon payment. In either case, the CDS position does not protect against coupon risk, so remains unhedged.

Another risk factor is the recovery rate assumed for the bond. The rate of recovery cannot be hedged, and the actual recovery after event of default will impact the final profit and/or loss position. The impact is greatest for bonds that are priced significantly away from par. To illustrate this, consider a bond priced at $110.00. To hedge a long position of $10 million of this bond, assume we buy protection in $11 million notional of the CDS. We do not use a par–par approach because otherwise we would be underhedged. Now consider, in the event of default, the following recovery rates:

- Zero percent recovery: We receive $11 million on the CDS and lose $11 million ($1.10 \times 10{,}000{,}000$) on the bond; so net we are flat.
- Fifty percent recovery: We receive $5.5 million on the CDS and lose $6 million on the bond (the bond loss is $5million nominal, and so we receive back $5 million, having paid out $11 million); so net we are down $500,000.

In other words, under a 50 percent recovery rate scenario, we are still underhedged and would need more notional of CDS to cover the loss on the bond. If the recovery rate is 30 percent, we will still lose on the position; while the higher over 50 percent it is, we will start to gain progressively more. Note that the reverse analysis applies when the bond is priced below par. Overall then we conclude that the assumption of the recovery rate must influence the notional size of the CDS position.

Generally, the market assumes the following recovery rates:

- Investment-grade 40 percent
- Insurance companies and corporates 30 percent
- Sub-investment grade 20 percent.

Some banks assume a 50 percent recovery rate in their pricing models. While one more robust approach might be to take historical data of actual defaults and ultimate recovery rates; however, at the current time some markets, notably those in Europe and Asia, suffer from a paucity of data, and so for the time being market participants use assumed recovery rates. However, the issue of recovery rate remains problematic in both CDS and synthetic collateralized debt obligation (CDO) note pricing, because the assumed value can be far away from the actual realized recovery value in practice.

TRADE EXAMPLES

Here we illustrate the concept of basis trading with hypothetical trade ideas. For the purposes of this hypothetical illustration, we determine at the outset to run the trade for a one-month time horizon; so after one month we unwind the trade and see how the trade idea has performed, by checking market prices at the time of the unwind (that is, one month later). In reality we may have a longer horizon or keep running a trade that is offside because our view is a longer term one.

Positive Basis Trade

In a positive basis trade the CDS trades above the cash spread, which can be measured using the ASW spread or the Z-spread.[7] The potential arbitrage trade is to sell the basis; that is, sell the cash bond and sell protection on the same reference name. We would do this if we expect the basis to converge or narrow.

---

[7] See Chapter 2 of Choudhry (2006) for a description of the different ways to measure the basis and an example of a Z-spread calculation.

To illustrate this we describe an example of a basis trade in France Telecom. The cash side of the trade is a EUR-denominated bond issued by France Telecom, the 3.625 percent 2015, rated A3/A− and which is trading on December 8, 2005 as follows:[8]

Bond	France Telecom 3.625 2015
ISIN	FR0010245555
Maturity	October 14, 2015
Price	97.52 to 97.62 clean
ASW	42.9 bps
z-spread	45.2 bps
CDS price	77 to 87 bps (10-year CDS)
Repo rate	2.06 to 2.02 (LIBOR minus 35 bps)

The asset swap spreads can be seen in Figure 20.3 (they are slightly different from the levels quoted above because the screens were printed the next day and the market had moved). This is Bloomberg screen ASW for the bond. The basis for this bond is positive, as shown in Figure 20.4, which is Bloomberg screen CRVD.

From the above we see that the basis is $77 - 45.2 = +31.8$ bps If we have the view that the bond will underperfom or the basis will otherwise narrow and go toward zero and/or negative, we will sell the basis. We consider historical data on the basis during our analysis, as shown in Figure 20.5, which is from screen BQ and shows the one-year historical ASW spread against the five-year CDS spread.[9]

The trade is put on in the following terms:

- Sell €6 million nominal of the bond at 97.52 clean price, 98.1158 "dirty" price.
- Sell protection €5.85 million CDS at 77 bps.

---

[8] Prices are taken from Bloomberg L.P. (bond and repo) and market makers (CDS).

[9] Our view on where the basis is going may be based on any combination of factors. These can include speculation about future direction based on historical trade patterns, specific company intelligence such as expectations of a takeover or other buyout, views on credit quality, and so on. We do not discuss the rationale behind the trades in this chapter, merely the trade mechanics!

F I G U R E   20.3

Asset-swap spread on screen ASW, France Telecom 3.625%
2015 bond, December 9, 2005

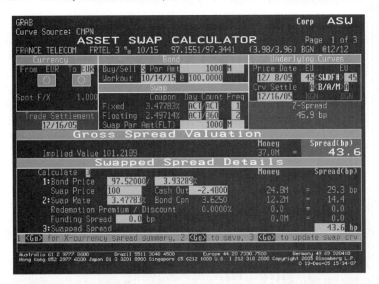

F I G U R E   20.4

Cash-CDS basis for France Telecom, December 9, 2005

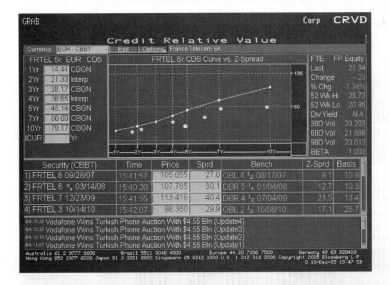

F I G U R E   20.5

One-year historical CDS-ASW spread, France Telecom, December 2005

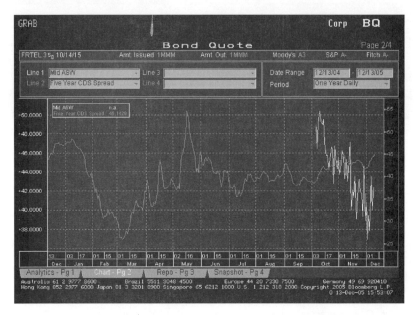

As we are shorting the bond, we fund it in reverse repo, which is done at 2.02 bps, or LIBOR minus 35 bps.

The credit risk on the bond position is hedged using the CDS. The interest rate risk (PVBP or "DV01") is hedged using Bund futures contracts. The hedge calculation is a straightforward one and uses the ratio of the respective DV01 of the bond and futures contract [see Choudhry (2005) for the hedge calculation mechanics].[10] From this we determine that we need to buy 52 lots of the Bund future to hedge the bond position.

For readers' reference we show the DV01 hedge calculation at Table 20.3, which is the Excel spreadsheet used to determine the futures hedge.[11] Note that the example shown is for an hypothetical hedge, not

---

[10] The hedge calculation is based on a ratio of basis point values (DV01) of the bond to be hedged and the futures contract. See Tables 20.3 and 20.4 for the calculation spreadsheet.

[11] The hedge spreadsheet was written by Stuart Turner and is reproduced with permission.

T A B L E   20.3

Futures hedge calculation spreadsheet

A1	B	C	D
2	**Hedging bonds with futures**		
3			
4			
5	$Number\ of\ contracts = \dfrac{Mbond}{Mfut} \times \dfrac{BPVbond}{BPVfut}$		
6			
7			
8			
9			
10	**Inputs**		
11			
12	**Nominal value of the bond (Mbond)**	10.000.000,00	
13			
14	**Nominal value of futures contract (Mfut)**	100.000,00	
15			
16	**BPV of the futures CTD bond**	7,484	
17			
18	**Conversion factor of CTD**	0,852	
19			
20	**BPV of the bond (BPVbond)**	7,558	
21			
22	BPV of the Future (BPVfut)	8,780	
23			
24			
25	**Number of contracts to hedge**	**86,083**	
26			

our example—we show it here for instructional purposes. Table 20.4 shows the Excel formulas.

The analysis is undertaken with reference to LIBOR, not absolute levels such as the yield to maturity. The cash flows are

Sell bond: pay 42.9 bps

Sell protection: receive 62 bps

TABLE 20.4

Showing Microsoft Excel formulas

A1	B	C
2	**Hedging bonds with futures**	
3		
4		
5	$Number\ of\ contracts = \dfrac{Mbond}{Mfut} \times \dfrac{BPVbond}{BPVfut}$	
6		
7		
8		
9		
10	**Inputs**	
11		
12	**Nominal value of the bond (Mbond)**	10.000.000,00
13		
14	**Nominal value of futures contract (Mfut)**	100.000,00
15		
16	**BPV of the futures CTD bond**	7,484
17		
18	**Conversion factor of CTD**	0,852
19		
20	**BPV of the bond (BPVbond)**	7,558
21		
22	BPV of the future (BPVfut)	= C16/C18
23		
24		
25	**Number of contracts to hedge**	= ((C12/C14)*(C20/C22))
26		

In addition the reverse repo position is 35 bps below LIBOR; as it represents interest income, we consider this spread a funding loss, so we incorporate this into the funding calculation, that is, we also pay 35 bps. We ignore the futures position for funding purposes. This is a net carry of

$$62 - (42.9 + 35) = -15.9 \text{ bps}$$

In other words the net carry for this position is negative. Funding cost must form part of the trade analysis. Funding has a greater impact on the trade net profit and loss (P&L) the longer it is kept on. If the trade is maintained over one month, the funding impact will not be significant if we generated, say, 5 bps gain in the basis, because that is 5 bps over a 10-year horizon (the maturity of the bond and CDS), the present value of which will exceed the 15.9 bps loss on one month's funding. If the position is maintained over a year, the impact of the funding cost will be greater.

Position after One Month

On January 10, 2006 we record the following prices for the France Tel bond and reference name:

Bond	France Telecom 3.625 percent 2015
Price	98.35 – 98.45
ASW	42.0 bps
z-spread	43.8 bps
CDS price	76 – 80 bps

Spreads are shown at Figure 20.6.

To unwind this position we would take the other side of the CDS quote; so the basis is now at $80 - 43.8 = 36.2$ bps. In other words, it has not gone the way we expected but has widened. As we sold the basis, the position has lost money if we unwind it now. The decision to unwind would be based on the original trade strategy: If the trader's time horizon was six months or longer, then the decision may be made to continue holding the position. If the trader's time horizon was shorter, it is probably sensible to cut one's losses now. Note that this trade is running at negative net carry, so it incurs a carry loss if maintained irrespective of where the basis is going.

Negative Basis Trade

In general, it is more common to observe a positive basis than a negative basis, for most market sectors. That said, negative basis observations are not uncommon. In the event of a negative basis condition, the potential arbitrage is to buy the basis, that is, to buy the bond and buy protection on the same reference name. A negative basis trade represents more straightforward trade

F I G U R E   20.6

France Telecom bond YAS page for ASW and Z-spreads, January 10, 2006

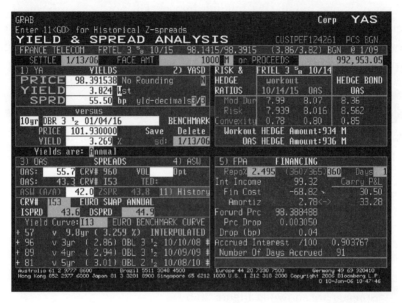

mechanics than a positive basis position, because there is no cash market short-covering issue to consider. We illustrate such a trade here.

The bond identified here was observed as trading at a negative basis on December 8, 2005. It is the Degussa AG 5.125 percent of December 2013, which is a EUR-denominated bond rated Baa1/ BBB+. Its terms are as follows:

Bond	Degussa AG 5.125 percent 12/2013
ISIN	XS0181557454
Maturity	December 10, 2013
Price	103.68
ASW	121.6
z-spread	122.7
CDS price	5-year: 75–80
	7-year: 95–105
	10-year: 113–123
	Interpolated 8-year offer price: 111 bps
Repo rate	2.44 (LIBOR + 2)

F I G U R E   20.7

Degussa 5.125 percent 2013 bond, ASW page,
December 9, 2005

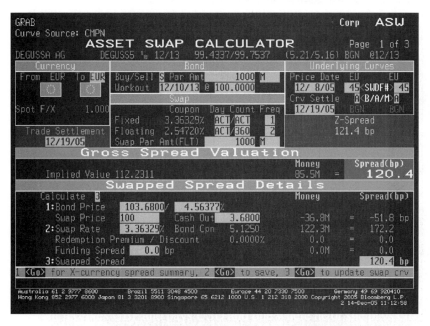

These rates are seen in Figure 20.7, the ASW page for this bond,
while the basis and basis history are seen at Figures 20.8 and 20.9, respectively. The basis is $111 - 122.7 = -11.7$ bps. We expect the basis to
widen, that is, move from negative toward zero and then into positive territory. We therefore buy the bond and buy protection on the Degussa
name. The interest rate hedge is put on in the same way as before; again,
we weight the CDS notional amount to match the risk of the bond because
the bond is trading away from par and so a greater amount of CDS
notional is required.

The trade cash flows are as follows:

Buy bond	Receive 121.6 bps
Buy protection	Pay 111 bps
Repo	Pay 2 bps

F I G U R E   20.8

Cash-CDS basis, Degussa AG, December 9, 2005

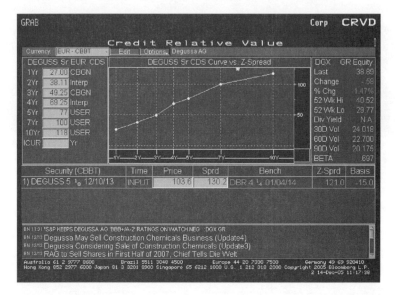

F I G U R E   20.9

One-year CDS-ASW spread, Degussa AG, December 9, 2005

This is a net carry of $+8.6$ bps; so this trade runs at a funding gain each day. We expect the basis to widen, at which point we will unwind the trade to extract our profit.

Position after One Month

On January 10, 2006 we record the following prices for the Degussa bond and reference name:

Bond	Degussa AG 5.125 percent 12/2013
Price	101.75
ASW	153.2 bps
z-spread	155.8 bps
CDS price	152 – 162

Spreads are shown at Figure 20.10.

F I G U R E   20.10

Asset-Swap and Z-spreads for Degussa bond, January 10, 2006

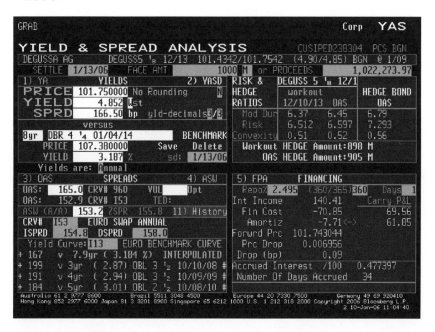

The basis is $152 - 155.8 = -3.8$ bps. The basis has tightened, as we expected, and is now in profit. The P&L is positive and is $-11.7 - (-3.8) = 7.9$ bps, together with the funding gain accrued each day. We can unwind the trade to take profit now or continue to run it at a net positive carry if we expect the basis to move further in the same direction and then into positive territory.

Notice how the gain itself is small, just a few basis points. Arbitrage basis trading in government bonds is often undertaken in very large size for precisely this reason, because the small potential gain means to make the trade worthwhile, we have to deal in size. This is not always possible in corporate markets because of lower liquidity levels in the cash market.

B O X   20.1

Example 1: Negative Basis Trade: British Airways

In this example we illustrate an unusual example of a reference name trading at large negative basis. The reference name is British Airways, which was experiencing credit downgrade issues during 2005, both general issues relevant to its (airline) sector and specific issues associated with its passenger performance and industrial relations. An observation of the negative basis spread, which widened considerably in a short time, suggested that the spread would narrow again (heading towards positive territory) over the next three to six months.

Accordingly a negative basis trade was considered an appropriate trade. Details of the bond being purchased, the 7.25 percent of August 2016, are shown at Figure 20.11. The performance of the basis in the three months preceding the trade start date is given at Figure 20.12, which is screen BQ from Bloomberg and shows the CDS-ASW spread during this time. Note how the basis, already negative, moves into greater negative territory quite quickly in early May 2005.

The trade is put on May 18, 2005 at the following terms:

- Buy GBP 5 million BAB 7.25 percent 2016.
- Price is £106.41 (yield 7.878 percent).
- Buy CDS protection £5 million notional.

The CDS spread is 180 bps. At the ASW spread of 332.58 this represents a basis of -152 bps. On October 17, 2005 we unwind the trade. The price of the bond is now £110.43 (yield is 7.337 percent), and the CDS spread is CDS 152.6 bps. At an ASW spread of 278.8 bps this represents a basis of -126 bps. So the profit on this trade is 26 bps.[12]

---

[12] This is gross profit, before factors such as bid-offer spread and hedge costs are taken into account.

F I G U R E   20.11

Bloomberg page DES for British Airways 7.25 percent
2016 bond

DES   P174 Corp   **DES**

SECURITY DESCRIPTION   Page 1/ 2
BRITISH AIRWAYS   BAB7 ¹₄ 08/23/16   108.9200/109.3600   (7.50/7.44) BGN @17:00

ISSUER INFORMATION	IDENTIFIERS	1) Additional Sec Info
Name BRITISH AIRWAYS	Common 013358214	2) Multi Cpn Display
Type Airlines	ISIN XS0133582147	3) ALLQ
Market of Issue Euro Non-Dollar	BB number EC4290101	4) Corporate Actions
SECURITY INFORMATION	RATINGS	5) Par Cds Spreads
Country GB Currency GBP	Moody's Ba2	6) Ratings
Collateral Type Sr Unsub	S&P BB-	7) Custom Notes
Calc Typ(133)MULTI-COUPON	Composite BB-	8) Identifiers
Maturity 8/23/2016 Series		9) Fees/Restrictions
MAKE WHOLE	ISSUE SIZE	10) Additional Note Pg
Coupon 7 ¹₄ Fixed	Amt Issued/Outstanding	11) Sec. Specific News
S/A ACT/ACT	GBP 250,000.00 (M)/	12) Involved Parties
Announcement Dt 7/26/01	GBP 250,000.00 (M)	13) Issuer Information
Int. Accrual Dt 8/23/01	Min Piece/Increment	14) Pricing Sources
1st Settle Date 8/23/01	1,000.00/ 1,000.00	15) Related Securities
1st Coupon Date 2/23/02	Par Amount 1,000.00	16) Issuer Web Page
Iss Pr 99.8730Reoffer 99.873	BOOK RUNNER/EXCHANGE	
SPR @ FPR 215.00 vs UKT 8 12/15	BARCLY,UBS	65) Old DES
NO PROSPECTUS	Multiple	66) Send as Attachment

CPN STEPS UP/DOWN IF RATINGS DOWNGRD/UPGRD BY MOODY'S & S&P; PLEASE SEE ADD NOTE
PAGE. CALL @HIGHER OF UKT 8% 12/7/15 OR 100%. PROV CALL/PUT. UNSEC'D.
Australia 61 2 9777 8600   Brazil 5511 3048 4500   Europe 44 20 7330 7500   Germany 49 69 920410
Hong Kong 852 2977 6000 Japan 81 3 3201 8900 Singapore 65 6212 1000 U.S. 1 212 318 2000 Copyright 2006 Bloomberg L.P.
                                                                                        2 09-Mar-06 18:07:10

F I G U R E   20.12

BA bond CDS-ASW basis performance, March 2005 to
May 2005

BAB 7 ¹₄ 08/16 ↑   **108.91 -.07**   108.91/109P174 Corp   **BQ**

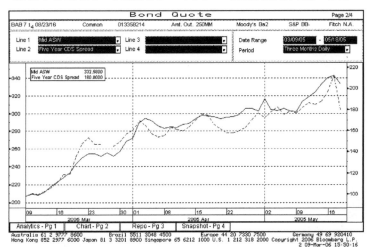

Australia 61 2 9777 8600   Brazil 5511 3048 4500   Europe 44 20 7330 7500   Germany 49 69 920410
Hong Kong 852 2977 6000 Japan 81 3 3201 8900 Singapore 65 6212 1000 U.S. 1 212 318 2000 Copyright 2006 Bloomberg L.P.
                                                                                        2 09-Mar-06 15:50:16

F I G U R E   20.13

BA bond CDS-ASW basis performance, March 2005 to October 2005

BAB 7 ¼ 08/16 ↓   **108.90** −.08   108.90/109P174 Corp   **BQ**

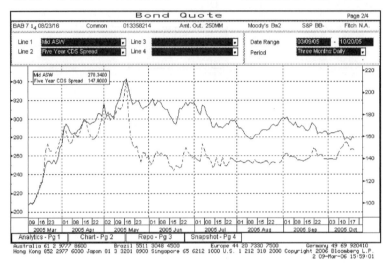

Figure 20.13 shows the basis performance from the trade start date to the trade unwind date. We note how the spread has narrowed – as predicted – during the trade term. Figure 20.14 shows the bond price performance, while Figure 20.15 shows how the basis has behaved since the trade was unwound: note how it widened out again up the March 2006, the time of writing.

The funding considerations followed those described earlier when we discussed the ThyssenKrupp bond. The bond was funded at LIBOR flat (L-flat) so there is no price impact either way on this side. This reflects that all analysis is conducted relative to (L-flat). Because in this case the funding is at L-flat there is no impact. The interest rate hedge can be carried out with futures contracts, the benchmark bond (in this case gilts) or with an interest rate swap. With a swap to matched maturity, we would pay fixed to receive floating, which would be LIBOR flat. If we hedge with futures, there are no funding issues. If we hedge with a gilt, we need to note the reverse repo rate applicable on the gilt, in case it goes special during the term of the trade. If it does not, then the gain on lending funds against gilts will be matched on the other side of what we pay out for shorting the gilt—both rates will be at sub-LIBOR and should have no impact. In the actual case of this bond, the hedge was undertaken with a matched-maturity interest rate swap.

Finally, Figure 20.16 shows the Bloomberg screen RRRA, used to calculate cash flows when we fund the BA bond in repo. The trade was funded at one-month intervals in repo.

F I G U R E   20.14

BA bond price performance, March 2005 to October 2005

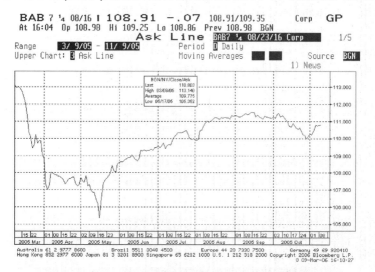

F I G U R E   20.15

BA bond CDS-ASW basis performance, March 2005 to March 2006

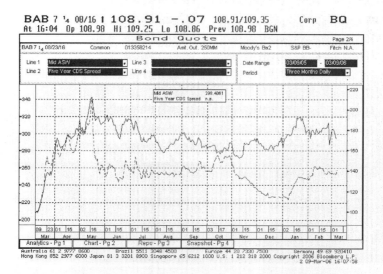

F I G U R E   20.16

Bloomberg screen RRRA, repo funding of BA bond at LIBOR flat

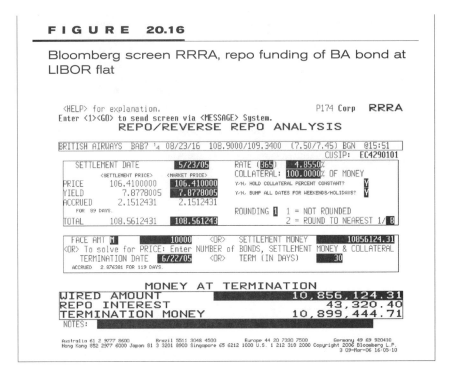

SUMMARY

The trades we have described illustrate the mechanics for CDS basis trades, both positive and negative basis. We saw how an arbitrage gain can be made, at theoretically zero credit risk, be buying or selling the basis, provided our initial view is correct. Opportunities for basis trading are rare and often require good market intelligence on specific corporate names, which can be used to formulate views on these names. Hence, an expertise in credit analysis is essential. In addition, liquidity levels in the cash Eurobond market can be low, depending on the name, and should therefore also be considered when formulating the trade idea.

REFERENCES

Choudhry, M. (2001) Some Issues in the Asset-Swap Pricing of Credit Default Swaps. *Derivatives Week,* Euromoney Publications, December 2.

Choudhry, M. (2004a) The Credit Default Swap Basis: Analysing the Relationship between Cash and Synthetic Markets. *Journal of Derivatives Use, Trading and Regulation,* June, pp. 9–26

Choudhry, M. (2004b) *Fixed Income Markets: Instruments, Applications, Mathematics.* Singapore: John Wiley & Sons

Choudhry, M. (2005) *Corporate Bond Markets: Instruments and Applications,* Singapore: John Wiley & Sons

Choudhry, M. (2006) *The Credit Default Swap Basis.* Princeton, NJ: Bloomberg Press

Securitization of Shipping Loans

Christian Kasten and Torsten Seil

ABSTRACT

This chapter deals with HSH Nordbank's Ocean Star securitizations of shipping loans originated by HSH Nordbank. Monte Carlo-based tools have been developed internally by specialists of the securitization team for the purpose of shipping loan transactions enabling HSH Nordbank to foresee credit enhancements demanded by rating agencies. A detailed overview of the transaction structure is presented.

INTRODUCTION

Securitization in general describes the practice of grouping assets or receivables and repackaging them for sale or for a synthetic risk transfer to investors. The first securitization transaction took place in the early 1980s in the United States, followed by the first European securitization in 1985. There has been a substantial increase in securitized volume in Europe from €90.4 billion in 2000 to €435.7 billion in 2006. However, in 2007 there was a decrease to €342.7 billion[1] caused by the 2007 market

---

[1] The Royal Bank of Scotland.

disruption. Compared to other asset classes there have not been many public shipping loan securitizations in the market. The shipping securitization market has seen a handful shipping transactions in the past, namely, the Latitude transaction for NIB Capital (NIBC), a merchant bank; two Ocean Star transactions for HSH Nordbank (one of which is the largest marine loan securitization by volume to date); and the 2006 Vega transaction for CMA-CGM (a worldwide leading container shipping group). Even though securitization is fairly new in shipping, it will likely be a growing feature of shipping finance in the future. The following chapter will only deal with HSH Nordbank's Ocean Star transactions.

HSH NORDBANK'S RATIONALE FOR SECURITIZING SHIPPING LOANS

Securitizations are used by HSH Nordbank to transfer credit risk of shipping loans to capital market investors, thus freeing economic capital and thereby increasing the bank's shipping lending capacity. In general, two possible securitization structures can be used to meet this objective, i.e., a "true sale" or a synthetic securitization. In a true sale securitization loans are sold directly to a special-purpose company (SPC) (i.e., a limited company or limited partnership). Proceeds are in cash, which can be used directly for new business. The selling bank may still act as servicer and have the loans under management. However, due to the nature of a true sale, the loans are removed from the bank's balance sheet reducing the balance sheet growth. By contrast, a synthetic securitization allows a bank to keep loans on the balance sheet and under management. This means that the entire servicing of securitized loans remains with the bank, and all rights and obligations under the shipping loan documentation between the bank and its customers remain unchanged, while credit risk is reduced. Hence, the client relationship, which is a core requirement of a customer-oriented bank, is not affected at all. This is the reason why HSH Nordbanks objectives were best met with a synthetic securitization, and the Ocean Star transactions were structured accordingly.

OCEAN STAR TRANSACTION STRUCTURE

Due to the nature of a synthetic securitization, only the credit risk associated with the assets is transferred to investors but not the legal ownership of the loans themselves. HSH Nordbank entered into a loss guarantee agreement with one SPC for each transaction, which was created for the purpose of the respective securitization. The SPC, named Ocean Star (Ocean Star 2004 or Ocean Star 2005), acts as a protection seller, selling credit default risk protection to HSH Nordbank as a protection buyer for the selected portfolio. In other words, under the loss guarantee agreement HSH Nordbank regularly pays protection premiums to Ocean Star. In return, HSH Nordbank will receive amounts equal to losses in the securitized loan portfolio caused by a bankruptcy or a failure to pay by the shipping loan borrowers. Failure to pay is defined as nonpayment of at least US$500,000 or 2 percent of the outstanding nominal amount after a period of 180 days.

Ocean Star is an unrated company without income and in order to finance its protection obligation to HSH Nordbank, Ocean Star issues rated securities, credit-linked notes, purchased by capital market investors. These credit-linked notes are linked to the performance of the protected portfolio of shipping loans and represent different rated tranches of the portfolio. Since losses in the portfolio of shipping loans are allocated to these tranches in a certain order such classes of credit-linked notes have achieved different ratings from the three large rating agencies according to their respective seniority. The nominal value of all tranches including the first loss tranche and the supersenior tranche equals the nominal value of Ocean Star's portfolio (see Cash Flows section). Figure 21.1 provides an overview of the synthetic structure of the transactions.

Ocean Star uses the proceeds of the credit-linked notes issue to purchase collateral with different ratings according to the rating of the different tranches. This collateral is used to repay investors at maturity and to fund any payments to HSH Nordbank under the protection obligation.

Tranches of Ocean Star's[2] portfolio received ratings on the credit-linked notes issued to investors range from BB to AAA. In addition, the issued credit-linked notes, HSH Nordbank kept a first loss tranche and the supersenior tranche of the portfolio of Ocean Star 2005. The first loss tranche is a self-retention of HSH Nordbank and serves as an important incentive to provide proper portfolio quality and servicing. In contrast to

[2] Ratings of Ocean Star 2005 [see prospectus, page 4].

FIGURE   21.1

Transaction structure

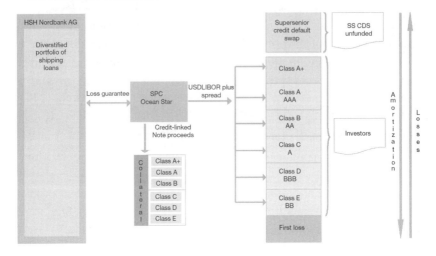

the first loss tranche, the supersenior tranche has a very low default probability. Therefore, it is an optional decision for HSH Nordbank to protect
itself against this default probability via a credit default swap or to keep
this minor risk on balance sheet if capital relief, according to Basel I is not
required. The first loss tranche and the supersenior swap tranche have not
received official ratings from the rating agencies since this was not essential for the issuance of credit-linked notes. Approximately 96 percent of the
portfolio achieved investment grade ratings (BBB and better). Investors
purchasing the credit-linked notes receive three months USD LIBOR, plus
a spread of 30 to 460 basis points (bps)[3] (see Table 21.1 for details).

The pricing depends on the tranche invested in, the higher the risk
the higher the spread, and pricing will vary from transaction to transaction. Superior portfolio quality coupled with investors becoming more
familiar with the underlying industry permits HSH Nordbank to achieve
lower spreads and better tranching—i.e., especially a smaller first loss
piece and a larger supersenior—for Ocean Star's 2005 transaction than for
the first securitization.

---

[3] Spreads of Ocean Star 2005 [see prospectus, page 3].

T A B L E   21.1

Tranching, ratings, and spreads of Ocean Star 2004 and
Ocean Star 2005

| | Ocean Star 2004 | | | Ocean Star 2005 | | |
Tranche	Size	Rating	Spread	Size	Rating	Tranche
Supersenior	70.46%	Nonrated		74.84%	Nonrated	
Class A+	0.02%	Aaa/AAA/AA+	0.30%	0.12%	Nonrated	0.20%
Class A	5.00%	Aaa/AAA/AA+	0.47%	5.02%	Aaa/AAA/AA+	0.30%
Class B	7.50%	Aa2/AA/AA	0.70%	4.51%	Aa2/AA/AA	0.45%
Class C	7.50%	A2/A/A	1.25%	7.51%	A2/A/A	0.75%
Class D	5.15%	Baa2/BBB−/BBB−	2.30%	4.10%	Baa2/BBB/BBB	1.50%
Class E	1.80%	Ba3/BB−/BB−	6.50%	1.70%	Ba3/BB/BB	4.60%
First loss	2.60%	Nonrated		2.20%	Nonrated	

CASH FLOWS

It is necessary to differentiate among the three forms of cash flow in the
structure: (1) payments of premium, (2) amortization of the credit-linked
notes, and (3) loss allocation. The premium Ocean Star as the issuer of the
credit-linked notes is required to pay its investors equals the amount of
interest received on the collateral and on the loss guarantee premium that
HSH Nordbank (as the protection buyer for the securitized pool) has to
pay Ocean Star under the loss guarantee.

Amortizations on the various tranches will be sequentially in order
of seniority (from the supersenior tranche downward to the first loss
tranche). This implies the supersenior tranche is amortized first, until no
supersenior amount is outstanding any longer, then the AAA tranche, followed by AA and so on, a so-called waterfall structure. In contrast to
amortizations, losses are allocated bottom up to the tranches—first to the
first loss tranche until it is used up, then to the BB tranche and so on. If
losses occur, then Ocean Star will pay HSH Nordbank the amount of loss
under the loss guarantee agreement, and it must sell collateral securing the
tranche to which losses have been allocated equal to the amount of the
loss. For example, if losses are allocated to tranche BB in an amount of

US$1 million, collateral in the same amount for tranche BB has to be sold. The funds received from the sale of the collateral are paid to HSH Nordbank thereby creating credit protection for HSH Nordbank.

LOSS DETERMINATION

In general, two different credit event scenarios are possible under Ocean Star: (1) bankruptcy or (2) failure to pay of the borrower. If a credit event occurs, then an appraised value of the mortgaged vessel securing the loan that is in default will be determined by at least two independent vessel appraisers. The loss is calculated by comparing this appraised value with the amount outstanding under the defaulted shipping loan. This loss (amount outstanding under the loan minus the appraised value of the vessel) is then allocated to the appropriate tranche and the appraised value concept protects investors from potential downside risks allowing HSH Nordbank to manage the enforcement of securities on the loans separately from the securitization.

OCEAN STAR PORTFOLIO RISK MODELING AND RATING PROCESS

A cross-sectional representation of shipping loans has been selected from HSH Nordbank's shipping loan portfolio for Ocean Star's 2004 and 2005 securitizations. The portfolios are well diversified in regard of segment (container vessels, tanker, and dry bulk carriers), subsegment, domicile, and age distribution. The modeling of this selection for securitization purposes was carried out using a state-of-the-art portfolio model, created by HSH Nordbank. Modeling a new asset class such as shipping loans requires industry-specific risk modeling know how and historic portfolio data in order to give input to the rating process. HSH Nordbank worked with a quantitative shipping rating tool for several years before the first Ocean Star transaction was structured. Hence, key experience and empirical data were available at the bank to develop a portfolio model for the securitization of shipping loans.

Cash-flow analysis and cash-flow-based Monte Carlo techniques are widely used for rating applications and portfolio risk modeling in shipping finance, because predominatly single-purpose vehicles (SPV) are financed having only cash inflows from chartering out vessels and cash outflows as operating expenses and for debt services. Moreover, the asset value of the company is the price of the vessel(s), which plays a central role as it is the collateral value of a loan. Hence, all key risk drivers for solvency and the recovery rate of a single-purpose shipping company are known, and any kind of risk analysis on a single loan level as well as on a portfolio level should be directly based on the charter income, the operational costs, the (floating) interest payments, loan redemption, and ship values. This straightforward approach is appealing because no additional theoretical framework is required to derive financial strength as in Merton-style models, where default probabilities are based on option price theory. Consequently, HSH Nordbank developed a cash-flow based Monte Carlo portfolio model and all rating agencies selected this type of simulation techniques when assessing the creditworthiness of the Ocean Star transactions.

All vessels collateralizing the loans in the Ocean Star transactions belong to standardized shipping segments. Vessels within one segment obtain the same changes in their short-term charter rates and operational costs as well as in their vessel values. Therefore, the core module of a shipping portfolio model is a vector time series model that draws industry scenarios in a quarterly periodicity over the lifetime of the respective transaction. Each of these scenarios comprises correlated cumulative changes of short-term charter income, operational costs, second-hand values for all included shipping subsegments, and simulation of interest rates.

Figure 21.2 provides an example for the simulation of one time series. The figure shows a set of scenarios for panamax bulker charter rates along with the mean of the sample (thick line) as well as the mean plus and minus one standard deviation (scattered lines). After the scenarios have been drawn, a cash-flow module analyzes each loan in each scenario. For this purpose, the industry scenarios are connected with each single loan, i.e., the segment specific changes in short-term charter rates and operational costs of a scenario are multiplied with the starting values of the ship(s) of a borrower. Starting values are charter rates (USD per quarter), which can be earned on the short-term charter market, as well as operational costs (USD per quarter) at the cut-off day.[4] Additionally,

---

[4] The cut-off date is used to collect all relevant information on the portfolio on debt and collateral
    side as of a specific date that will also serve as starting point for modeling the portfolio.

F I G U R E   21.2

Scenarios of panamax bulker charter rates

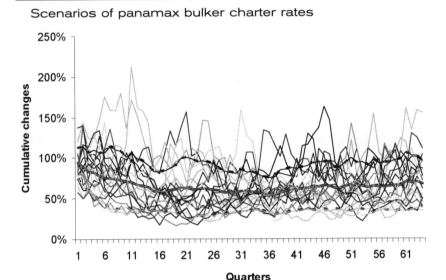

the scenario information regarding the interest rate movements is connected with the LIBOR rate plus loan margin at the cut-off day.
Therefore, a complete cash-flow analysis in terms of deducting operational costs, interest payment, and debt service from charter income is
possible on a quarterly basis.

Simulating changes of short-term charter income is preferred rather
than simulating the level of charter income in a segment directly, because
of the significant difference in size of the vessels in one segment. For
example, panamax bulker range from 55,000 dwt[5] to 100,000 dwt, and
even if their income changes are about 100 percent correlated, an absolute
difference in income will be in place. Moreover, the age and technical features like the sailing speed of a ship cause absolute differences as well.

If a credit event is observed in the cash-flow analysis, a loss under
Ocean Star transactions is calculated from the outstanding loan amount and
the collateral value of a loan. The outstanding loan amount takes possible

---

[5] Deadweight tons (dwt) is vessel's capacity to carry cargo.

F I G U R E   21.3

Loss distribution example

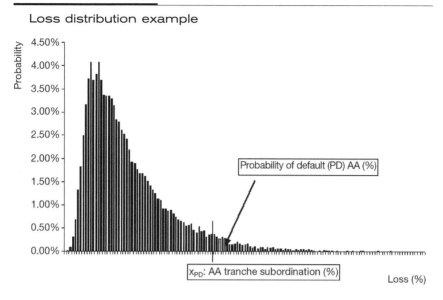

loan repayments (in the cash-flow analysis) into account rather than look-ing at the scheduled numbers in the loans' contract. The collateral value of a loan in the model is calculated from the appraised second-hand ship value at the cut-off day multiplied with the segment specific changes of the respective industry scenario. In addition, straight-line depreciation over the useful life of a vessel is assumed.

Cash-flow analysis results in individual loan losses in each of the sce-narios. These losses are aggregated at the portfolio level, so the model can compute a portfolio loss distribution across all scenarios (see Figure 21.2).

As shown in Figure 21.3, the loss distribution comprises the infor-mation required for the credit assessment of the tranches, i.e., the loss dis-tribution quartile of 1 minus default probability (1 − PD) is the credit enhancement of a certain tranche. If an expected loss rating is desired, then the mean of the simulated tranche losses must be in line with the crit-ical value of the respective rating table.

The cash-flow-based modeling approach suites the predominantly SPV financing in the shipping industry, and only short-term charter income has been taken into account above. However, the special aspects of shipping loans in the Ocean Star transactions make it necessary to introduce a more complicated analysis of the cash flows in certain cases.

The charter income of ships is oftentimes fixed by time charter contracts. These contracts may last until loan maturity or even longer. Time charter agreements stabilize the earnings and are therefore important risk mitigants. Hence, the modelling assumes that all vessels that have time charter agreements earn the contractual rate as long as the contract lasts. Additionally, the assumption is made that ships move to the short-term charter market thereafter. Time charter agreements do not necessarily last until the contracts' maturity, because a charterer can go into default. To capture this, charterer defaults are simulated according to their rating while performing cash-flow analysis. The same methodology is applied in cases were defaults of loans granted to substantial corporate entities rather than to an SPV have to be drawn (correlated).

We undertake also an econometric task when constructing a portfolio simulation model for shipping loans. Historical data are available from ship brokers or specialized industry consultants. One key question in time series analysis is, whether we deal with nonstationary data. Table 21.2 displays the results using the well-known augmented Dickey–Fuller unit root test (ADF test), where small p values (e.g., <0.05) reject the null hypothesis of analyzing a nonstationary time series. But even if the ADF tests indicate nonstationary data, practitioners usually favor mean reversion models because of the cycling nature of the shipping industry.

The type of model to choose remains model risk. In the rating process of Ocean Star transactions model risk is mitigated because rating agencies select different time series models [see Moody's Investors Service Structured Finance (2004, p. 9) and FitchRatings Structured Finance (2004, p. 10)]. This is not the only aspect where risk assessment explicitly differs and therefore reduces model risk further. Standard & Poor's uses a deterministic table of (stressed) collateral values for the vessels in a portfolio rather than relying on simulated ones [Standard & Poor's Corporate Securitization (2004, p. 8)]. Moreover, the application of stresses varies between rating agencies: S&P and Fitch both apply haircuts on the second-hand ship values and charter income. The haircuts are rating specific, which implies that they run the model for every tranch [Standard & Poor's Corporate Securitization (2004, p. 8) and FitchRatings Structured Finance (2004, p. 8)]. Moody's runs the model only

T A B L E   21.2

Augmented Dickey–Fuller unit root test

Time Series (log)	Level of Time Series		First Differences of Time Series	
	t statistic	p value	t statistic	p value
Charter rates subpanamax container vessels	−3.337	0.071	−4.521	0.003
Charter rates handymax container vessels	−2.647	0.262	−4.979	0.001
Charter rates panamax bulker	−3.012	0.133	−8.860	0.000
Charter rates handymax bulker	−2.006	0.590	−6.549	0.000
Charter rates suezmax tanker	−3.510	0.043	−7.756	0.000
Charter rates aframax tanker	−3.800	0.020	−8.649	0.000
Second hand ship values subpanamax container vessels	−2.616	0.276	−3.421	0.063
Second hand ship values handymax container vessels	−2.235	0.459	−3.683	0.035
Second hand ship values panamax bulker	−2.582	0.290	−6.655	0.000
Second hand ship values handymax bulker	−2.043	0.569	−6.042	0.000
Second hand ship values suezmax tanker	−2.303	0.429	−6.134	0.000
Second hand ship values aframax tanker	−3.323	0.067	−7.256	0.000

Null hypothesis: has a unit root. Exogenous: constant and trend. Calculation based on Clarkson's data.

once for deriving ratings for all tranches. Instead of haircuts, Moody's prefers to stress the volatility assumptions in their simulation model [Moody's Investors Service Structured Finance, (2004, p. 10)].

INVESTORS

Investors in Ocean Star transactions to date have been institutional investors from Europe, Asia, and the United States, namely, banks, insurance companies, or investment funds. Without actually granting direct shipping loans, Ocean Star investors have the opportunity to participate in the shipping debt asset class and diversify their portfolios. Hence, investors benefit from HSH Nordbank's shipping expertise, and a sophisticated rating process makes an expensive building up of industry specific know-how unnecessary. Therefore, the Ocean Star transactions open the shipping industry to new investors and make it more transparent for international capital markets. Simultaneously, an "illiquid" asset class such as shipping gets more liquid, and HSH Nordbank becomes more flexible in managing its shipping loan book. From its past experience with the two Ocean Star transactions, it is likely that frequent shipping loan securitizations will lead to a further tightening of spreads in this asset class and would also coincide with progression in more common asset classes.

CONCLUSION

Shipping loan securitizations are used by HSH Nordbank to transfer credit risk in order to free up economic capital and increase the bank's shipping lending capacity. Since the client relationship is not affected at all, a synthetic structure, which only transfers the risk associated with the assets, has been selected. HSH Nordbank entered into a loss guarantee agreement with the SPC Ocean Star for a portfolio of shipping loans. In addition, Ocean Star hedges itself against its obligation to HSH Nordbank by issuing credit-linked notes, which are purchased by capital market investors. Investors therefore bear the losses of the shipping loan portfolio except for the first loss piece, which is held by HSH Nordbank.

Cash-flow-based Monte Carlo techniques have been used to assess the risk of the credit-linked notes. Ratings of the main three rating agencies give comfort to capital market investors outside the shipping industry that take the chance to diversify their portfolio. Even though securitization is not to be seen as a replacement for loan syndication, it opens the industry to new investors. The broadened investor base makes the asset class shipping more liquid and hence provides more flexibility for HSH Nordbank to manage its shipping loan book.

REFERENCES

FitchRatings Structured Finance (2004) Ocean Star 2004 PLC.
    Presale Report.
Moody's Investors Service Structured Finance (2004) Ocean Star 2004
    PLC. *Presale Report.*
Prospectus Ocean Star (2005) PLC.
Standard & Poor's Corporate Securitization (2004) Ocean Star 2004
    PLC. *Presale Report.*

CHAPTER 22

How Cheap is "Zero" Cost Protection?

Panayiotis Teklos, Michael Sandigursky, Michael Hampden-Turner, and Matt King

ABSTRACT

Zero initial cost protection is a new credit derivatives contract that enables the buyer to hedge the risk of a portfolio or take an outright short position in a (potentially) cost-efficient way. The buyer of protection has the same level of default coverage as with an ordinary portfolio credit default swap, but if no defaults occur, no premium is paid. The premium steps up with the number of defaults and timing of defaults is crucial when considering the product. Low and late defaults will still make the product attractive relative to standard protection, whereas many and early defaults will make it more expensive. As such, we expect this product to be appealing to portfolio managers, with a low and late default view, that wish to hedge their portfolio risk and reduce their economic and/or regulatory capital while not paying excess premia in case of very few defaults. This article analyzes how zero initial cost protection is constructed, when it works well, and when it doesn't.

INTRODUCTION

Zero initial cost protection (ZICP) brings the concept of "no win, no fee" legal cases to the world of credit derivatives. Like ordinary credit default swap (CDS) protection, the product pays out in the event of defaults but, most unusually, does not require any premium unless and until defaults actually occur, at which point the premium steps up. As such, we see it appealing primarily to investors or lenders who have been put off from buying traditional credit protection because of the need to "waste" premium in the event that there are not many defaults. This chapter analyzes how it is constructed, when it works well, and when it doesn't. Naturally, it proves more efficient than traditional protection when defaults are low and occur later, but it is more expensive when defaults are numerous and occur soon.

CONTRACT MECHANICS

Zero initial cost protection is an over-the-counter (OTC) contract that aims to provide protection against defaults in a credit portfolio at zero initial cost. In a traditional portfolio CDS, the protection buyer pays the protection seller a contractually agreed fixed premium throughout the life of the contract. By contrast, with ZICP, the protection buyer obtains the same level of protection (all default losses are covered) but pays no premium at the outset. So, where is the catch? Well, there's no free lunch and it's certainly not magic. The catch is that the premium steps up should the portfolio experience any defaults. The product is typically structured so that it has a cap on the premium in case portfolio losses exceed a predetermined threshold. Table 22.1 is an example of ZICP written on iTraxx S7 with a cap at seven defaults.

At initiation of the contract no premium is paid. If we assume one name out of 125 in the iTraxx IG index goes into default, then the protection buyer becomes entitled to receive 0.48 percent of the contract notional (0.8% × 0.6; assuming 40 percent recovery), but a higher-than-standard protection premium going forward will have to be paid. This new premium is now payable at 29 bps (181.5 bps × 0.48%/3%). The table and graph in Figure 22.1 show how the premium increases with more defaults in the portfolio. After seven defaults, it gets capped at 181.5bps.

T A B L E   22.1

Example of ZICP term sheet

Protection seller	Citigroup
Format	Unfunded swap
Scheduled maturity date	June 20, 2012
Currency	EUR
Reference portfolio	iTraxx IG S7
Protection premium	182 bps × min(cumulative portfolio loss, 3%)/3%
Credit event settlement	Cash settlement
Calculation agent	Citigroup Global Markets Limited

F I G U R E   22.1

Step-up schedule of ZICP premium

Credit premium events	Portfolio loss	ZIC (bps)
0	0%	0
1	0.48%	29
2	0.96%	58
3	1.44%	87
4	1.92%	116.5
5	2.40%	145.5
6	2.88%	174.5

Source: Citi

CONSTRUCTING A REPLICATING STRATEGY

As with all derivative claims, one way of pricing a derivative is to construct a replicating portfolio. By decomposing the original claim into standard strategies, we are able to price each part separately and then sum them up to obtain the required price. The replicating portfolio strategy for ZICP is as follows (see also Figure 22.2):

   1. *Buy protection* on the underlying portfolio (index) paying all premiums up front. This is equal to the PV of expected loss of this portfolio and could be estimated as the DV01 of the index

F I G U R E   22.2

Zero initial cost protection cash-flows (000 for 10m notional)

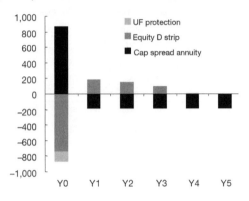

Source: Citi

times the index spread. This is equivalent to shorting the default risk and requires immediate cash outlay.

2. *Fund this position* by going long duration (timing of defaults):

   a. Sell an annuity promising to pay a fixed premium equal to the cap spread. The coupon of this annuity is independent of the credit loss experienced by the portfolio. The value of this stream of cash flows is therefore a "riskless" PV01 times the cap spread.

   b. Buy an interest-only (IO) strip referencing the 0 to 3 percent tranche of the underlying portfolio. Initially, the strip pays the cap spread on the contract notional, but will pay progressively less as defaults erode the equity tranche notional. Eventually, after seven defaults, the IO strip will terminate. The value of the IO strip is estimated as risky DV01 of the equity tranche times the cap spread.

Initially, the outflow of the cap-spread annuity is fully matched by the inflow from the IO strip. However, the balance breaks down after the first default occurs and the IO strip notional is reduced. The ZICP premium steps up to bridge the gap between the two. Clearly, the maximum premium is reached once the entire IO strip notional is eroded and the full cap spread is now payable (Figure 22.2). Hence, at the outset the cap spread is the value that makes the PV of ZICP equal to zero (Table 22.2).

T A B L E   22.2

ZICP replicating strategy

	DV01	Spread (bps)	PV
Buy up-front protection	4,740	25.56	−121,154
Sell cap spread annuity	4,774	181.5	866,481
Buy equity IO strip	4,106	181.5	−745,326
ZICP			0

Source: Citi

Alternatively, rearranging the equation of the PV of ZICP and solving for the cap spread will give us the following:

$$CapSpread = \frac{IndexSpread \times DV01_{INDEX}}{DV01_{RISKLESS} - DV01_{EQUITY}}$$

MAJOR RISKS AND SENSITIVITY ANALYSIS

Default Risk and Timing of Defaults

We have constructed three different scenarios, shown in Figures 22.3 to 22.5, to illustrate the performance of the ZICP product against buying standard index protection.

Scenario 1: One Default at the End of Year 1

Under the first scenario, we have a default at the end of year 1 and no subsequent defaults thereafter. Both ZICP and standard protection will pay out 48,000 for 10 million notional assuming 40 percent recovery. Furthermore, a standard protection buyer has already paid 25,560 by the end of year 1 and will now pay the same 25.56bps on the reduced notional of 124/125 × 10 million. With ZICP, up until the end of year 1, the protection buyer has paid nothing; from year 2, however, the premium will step up, resulting in 29,040 being payable. Comparing the PV of both strategies we can see that in this scenario ZICP is more efficient.

F I G U R E   22.3

Zero initial cost protection cash-flow profile vs. standard
protection (scenario 1)

	PV	Y1	Y2	Y3	Y4	Y5
Cumulative defaults		0	1	1	1	1
Discount factors		0.96	0.92	0.89	0.85	0.82
ZICP	101,358	0	29,040	29,040	29,040	29,040
Standard protection	113,075	25,560	25,356	25,356	25,356	25,356

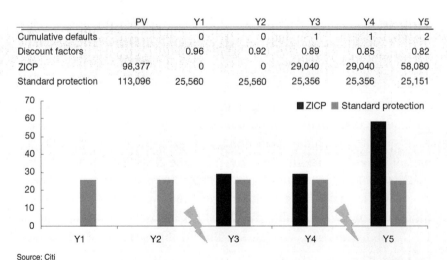

Source: Citi

F I G U R E   22.4

Zero initial cost protection cash-flow profile vs. standard
protection (scenario 2)

	PV	Y1	Y2	Y3	Y4	Y5
Cumulative defaults		0	0	1	1	2
Discount factors		0.96	0.92	0.89	0.85	0.82
ZICP	98,377	0	0	29,040	29,040	58,080
Standard protection	113,096	25,560	25,560	25,356	25,356	25,151

Source: Citi

F I G U R E   22.5

Zero initial cost protection cash-flow profile vs. standard
protection (scenario 3)

	PV	Y1	Y2	Y3	Y4	Y5
Cumulative Defaults		0	1	2	3	4
Discount Factors		0.96	0.92	0.89	0.85	0.82
ZICP	248,428	0	29,040	58,080	87,120	116,160
Standard Protection	112,039	25,560	25,356	25,151	24,947	24,742

Source: Citi

Scenario 2: Two Defaults—the End of Years 2 and 4

Although the portfolio experienced two defaults, the total cost of protection using the ZICP product turns out to be less than the cost under scenario 1. As a result, the defaults occur later in the structure and a higher premium is paid for a shorter period only thereby reducing the overall carry. This example illustrates the intuition behind the importance of timing of defaults for this product; more delayed defaults translate into lower total cost of ZICP protection. Consequently, ZICP protection under this scenario is cheaper than buying protection under the standard contract.

Scenario 3: One Default at the End of Years 1, 2, 3, and 4

This is a rather harsh scenario with one default occurring at the end of each year, thus causing the premium to step up four times to 116.5bps on 10 million notional, while standard protection remains fixed at 25.5bps. This results in making ZICP twice as expensive as the standard alternative.

Hedging with ZICP can be cost efficient provided the portfolio manager has a generally bearish view and expects defaults to be more back

FIGURE 22.6

Difference in PV of standard protection and ZICP (000) for number of defaults shown occurring from inception to end of year 4

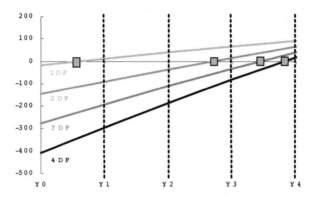

Source: Citi

loaded. While the default risk is fully hedged, early defaults can be rather damaging. The associated steep increase in the protection premium can make the structure very expensive. The breakeven analysis of time to default is provided in Figure 22.6. For instance, for one expected default ZICP will become more efficient should the structure experience no defaults for approximately six months.

Additionally, when defaults occur, the standard protection premium is only accrued on the reduced notional, i.e., nondefaulted part of the portfolio. In the case of ZICP, in contrast, not only is there a step up in premium, but also the premium is typically applied to the original notional fixed at inception. In other words, ZICP notional doesn't get reduced with defaults. This makes the "effective premium" slightly higher than the one quoted in Figure 22.1.

Spread Sensitivity

One of the major parameters that distinguish ZICP from standard protection is its peculiar spread sensitivity (Figure 22.7). Mark to market (MTM) of ZICP can be broadly defined as following: $\Delta MtM_{ZICP} = \Delta MtM_{INDEX} + \Delta MtM_{EQUITY}$. While the PV of the risk-free annuity remains the same, the MTM of both the index and equity IO parts move when

Mark to market of ZICP and standard protection (000) vs.
spread change (bps)

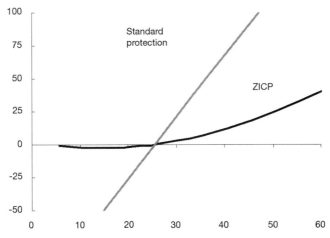

Source: Citi

there is a change in spreads. With spreads tightening, the value of index protection goes down (less risk) while the PV of the equity IO strip goes up (longer risky duration). As a result, the impact of spread change on the index is partially offset by the opposite effect it has on the IO strip.

The product works well as an outright short. Under certain default and spread scenarios ZICP is cheaper than standard protection, and more importantly has less MTM impact on the downside (when spreads tighten). Naturally, it will have less upside should spreads widen. Hence the overall MTM volatility of the product is significantly reduced when compared with standard protection. The comparison of MTM for ZICP and standard protection is presented in Figure 22.8.

Using ZICP as a spread hedge for an underlying portfolio, therefore, results in a mismatch with respect to default risk. As we have seen, hedging a portfolio with ZICP in a 1:1 proportion makes the portfolio default neutral. However, due to its lower spread sensitivity, the ZICP MTM will only partially cover MTM losses on the underlying portfolio. Fully hedging spread risk would imply overhedging default risk. Since most users of the product are likely to be focused on default risk, we do not think this should be a major concern.

F I G U R E   22.8

Mark to market of ZICP protection, UF index and equity IO strip (right panel in 000 vs. spreads in bps) under various curve-widening scenarios (left panel spreads in bps vs. maturity in years)

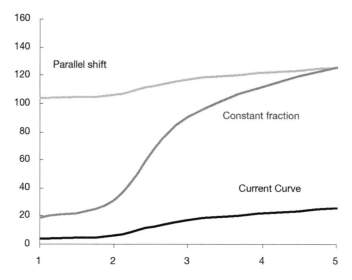

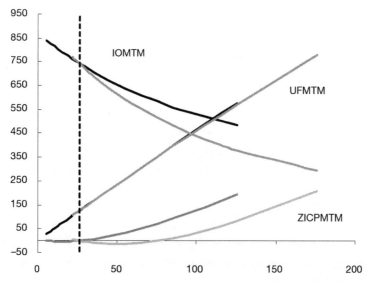

Source: Citi

Curve Impact

As shown in Figure 22.7, the MTM of ZICP is impacted by changes in value of both the index and the equity IO strip: When buying ZICP protection, the investor goes short the index and long the IO strip. Spread widening will have opposite and partially offsetting effects on both legs of ZICP MTM. Additionally, the IO strip has a significantly higher sensitivity to curve steepening than UF index position. Flatter curves for the same five-year level mean that the IO strip is shorter in risky duration (lower PV) and hence ZICP MTM will be lower as well.

In Figure 22.8 we show the impact of 100-bps spread widening on MTM ZICP and its components. The first scenario assumes spread widening and curve steepening, while the second demonstrates a pure parallel shift of the curve. Interestingly, one can construct a scenario (i.e., significant bear flattening) when losses on the IO strip will exceed gains on the UF index position. Under this relatively unusual scenario, ZICP protection would actually behave as a net long.

Correlation Risk

Zero initial cost protection could be replicated by buying protection on the portfolio (index), selling a risk-free annuity, and buying an equity IO strip on the same portfolio. While both the index and the risk-free annuity are correlation independent, ZICP is exposed to the correlation risk inherent in the equity IO strip. If correlation increases, the IO strip value increases, resulting in positive ZICP MTM. As such, ZICP is long correlation risk.

WHO MIGHT USE IT?

At the risk of stating the obvious, we believe that ZICP will clearly be of most use to investors who want protection against defaults today but do not fancy paying for it. These, though, fall into two categories. First, there are those primarily interested in the accounting benefit. These would typically be managers of non-MTM loan portfolios but conceivably could include other hold-to-maturity investors such as some insurers and pension funds.

They typically do not like buying protection, which digs into their profits, under macroeconomic circumstances when the protection proves to be of little use. While they can, of course, decide simply not to hedge, the advantage of ZICP is that—by construction—the hedge is paid for only when defaults pick up and hence when it is having some effect. For such investors, this benefit could serve to unblock what had previously been a major sticking point for many.

Unfortunately for loan portfolio managers, the current form of the product does not look efficient in terms of regulatory capital. Indeed, Basel II explicitly (if not particularly logically in this case) prohibits granting capital relief on products that feature a step up in premium. Basel II will not be a concern for all investors, but we still think this represents a significant hurdle in terms of ZICP gaining widespread acceptance. It would likely appear that there would be further innovations made in this space to try to solve the regulatory capital issues.

The second category of users is simply those who find the product attractive from their market point of view. Quite apart from the accounting benefit of "buying now, paying later," ZICP is a more efficient hedge than conventional protection when defaults remain low and are backloaded. Such a view seems quite widespread at the moment—in particular for managers who have selected the names in their portfolios explicitly in the hope of avoiding defaults and, hence, do not want to pay full whack for protection. With so many investors having been caught short over the past year, many would probably consider giving up some upside in the event of spread widening in return for dramatically curtailed downside in the event of spread tightening—which is of course exactly what ZICP offers.

CONCLUSION

Zero initial cost protection is a new way to short credit. The enticing proposition of no-initial-carry protection performs best when defaults are low and occur later in the life of the contract. The structure has speedy penalties, though, for early defaults. A moderate premium of 29 bps is payable after the first default, but steps up quickly to cap at 181.5 bps after seven defaults. Lower MTM volatility combined with zero initial carry makes ZICP an attractive alternative for taking outright shorts. However, its lower delta makes hedging spread risk relatively less efficient. We think the product will be popular both with those who value it from an accounting perspective (and who do not fall foul of Basel II regulatory capital rules) and among the majority of investors who seem to want protection against defaults but are still not really convinced that many defaults lie around the corner.

Managing Country Risk

Nandita Reisinger-Chowdhury

ABSTRACT

Country risk and country risk management have become major issues for the international financial community over the last two decades. This chapter provides an overview of the country rating practices and techniques used to evaluate country risk, the main factors affecting country risk, country risk indicators and early warning systems. Relevant information sources and country risk service providers are described. The author also gives insights into credit decision making involving country risk, country portfolio management and country risk mitigation techniques.

INTRODUCTION

Country risk and country risk management have become major issues for the international financial community over the last two decades. *Sovereign* or *country risk* is defined as the risk that occurrences in a foreign country may affect the willingness or ability of the sovereign or entities in that country to service their debt, and this risk introduces an additional aspect in the credit risk measurement of cross-border lending and investment—not only does the creditworthiness of the party need to be assessed but so does the stability of the country. Assessing and understanding country risk has increased significantly for bankers, regulators, and investors over recent years and will continue to do so both on a quantitative and qualitative basis.

Country risk can therefore be seen as the probability that developments in or affecting a country will harm your business or as the risk that a country is unable or unwilling to fulfil its external obligations. It is also the risk that an economic unit is unable to service its foreign obligations owing to developments within the country of domicile.

WHO NEEDS TO WORRY ABOUT SOVEREIGN RISK?

The moment one enters into dealings with another country one faces sovereign risk. Every cross-border transaction is subject to sovereign risk, regardless of whether one is dealing with the sovereign itself or with a quasi-sovereign organization, a corporate or financial institution. This is due to the fact that in order to fulfil its external obligations, a country has to earn the foreign exchange required to cover its debt service, and should the country face difficulties is doing so, it is likely to be unable to repay its foreign debt in an orderly fashion. This applies to all entities within a particular country.

WHY DO WE NEED COUNTRY RISK MANAGEMENT?

History has shown us that defaults and rescheduling are not infrequent occurrences. "The fiscal history of Latin America . . . is replete with instances of governmental defaults. Borrowing and default follow each other with almost perfect regularity. When payment is resumed, the past is easily forgotten and a new borrowing orgy ensues" (Max Winkler, 1933, p. 22). During the last 200 years, the world has experienced a number of payments crises, the most important being those in 1820, 1870, 1930, 1980, 1993, 1997, and 2001 (Suter, 1992). Since 1975 more than 75 countries have defaulted on their foreign debt. Creditworthiness is not a constant, with many countries that are considered highly creditworthy today having gone through periods of rescheduling and default in the past.

The shift in borrowing from purely government-to-government transactions and a limited issuance of bonds by governments to commercial

F I G U R E   23.1

Net capital flows to emerging markets, U.S.dollars billion

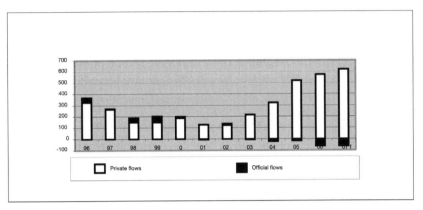

Source: Institute of International Finance

borrowing by governments and other entities in the emerging world have led to a sea change in the structure and distribution of emerging market risks in the financial markets (Figure 23.1).

During the 1970s, banks increased their exposure to emerging market sovereigns, thus filling the financing gap that could not be covered by funds from governments and the international financial institutions. The buildup of foreign debt by many of these governments led to the first major crises in the postwar period, with Poland and other Eastern European countries delaying payments in the early 1980s. This was followed by the debt moratoria announced by Brazil and Mexico in late 1982, which led to large write-offs by many of the major U.S. banks. During the late 1980s to early 1990s, Western banks began to lend considerable amounts to emerging markets, primarily in Latin America, thus fueling rising trade deficits in these countries. In 1994 Mexico was forced to devalue the peso in the wake of dwindling foreign exchange reserves, and the first major support package was put together by the International Monetary Fund (IMF), the Bank for International Settlements (BIS), and the U.S. government to help Mexico reschedule its debt over a longer tenor.

In spite of the Mexican "tequila" crisis, confidence recovered shortly and the focus began to shift to the booming "Tiger economies" in Eastern

Asia, which became the favored countries for Western banks. Capital flows to these countries fueled rapid growth and imbalances during the mid-nineties of the last century and led to a major crisis in this area that had massive repercussions in the whole world. Thailand was forced to devalue its currency in mid-1997, which resulted in contagious devaluations in South Korea, Indonesia, and Malaysia and which led to a major banking and financial crisis in the region. South Korea was forced to reschedule interbank lines, and Indonesia had to reschedule a large proportion of its foreign debt. The international community, the IMF, World Bank, and a large number of governments provided very large financing packages to these countries in order to support the rescheduling efforts. The financial crisis in Asia had further repercussions worldwide when in August 1998 Russia devalued its currency and defaulted on its local debt simultaneously, leaving investors with large losses.

In 2001 Argentina defaulted on US$130 billion of official foreign debt, the rescheduling of which continues today. In 2002, Argentina lifted its peg to the USD and introduced legislation that led to the default of more than US$30 billion of corporate debt owed to foreign creditors. Although the country has reached a settlement with some of its creditors, litigation in the international courts continues to this day.

History has proved that sovereign defaults and country risk are a very real part of international bank lending. In order to minimize losses that could arise out of country risk, banks must therefore have robust systems that allow them to assess country risk, limit their risks in relationship to their risk-taking capacity, and mitigate the risks involved when necessary (Basle Committee on Banking Supervision, 1982). Many banking regulators specifically require that banks must have appropriate, well-documented, and clearly defined "country risk management" policies in place. In many countries banks are required to provision for exposures in countries as per their ratings.

COUNTRY RISK ASSESSMENT

Banks will find that it is necessary to assess country risk related to cross-border transactions in order to minimize the risks involved. Country risk events generally involve either *repudiation* of official and commercial foreign debt by the government of the country concerned or a *rescheduling* of foreign obligations. These may be accompanied by a moratorium and/or foreign exchange restrictions.

Key Sources of Sovereign Risk

Sovereign or country risk depends to a large extent on the fundamentals of a country, i.e., the economic framework that a country is operating in, and to a certain extent on the political setup within a country. We therefore differentiate between two major sources of sovereign or country risk, namely,

- Political risk
- Economic risk

In addition to the fundamentals of a country, market sentiment can have a large impact on capital flows to and from a country and, therefore, can also have a serious impact on a country's liquidity position.

Sovereign risk analysis is therefore an ongoing process that involves the analysis of fundamental data, the political setup, and the constant monitoring of changes in market sentiment. In evaluating sovereign risk, a bank can use a number of approaches, varying from the highly quantitative, focusing on economic indicators, to the highly qualitative, focusing on a qualitative assessment of economic and political risks. Banks may decide to rely on external evaluation models to assess their country risks. Alternatively, they may decide to set up their own evaluation model based on key indicators for political and economic risks as outlined in the following paragraphs.

Political Risk

Political risk is the risk that changes within the political environment will affect one's business and relates to the question of a country's willingness to pay.

What Is Political Risk?

- War, riots, strikes, revolution
- Trade embargoes

- Political and economic sanctions
- Expropriation
- Nationalization

How Do We Evaluate Political Risk?

- Analyze the regime and its setup.
- Identify the regime's strategy for dealing with economic and political expectations.
- Identify the ideology behind a regime.
- Analyze the opposition framework.
- Evaluate the geopolitical importance of the country.
- Look at the history of the country.
- Analyze possible developments.

The evaluation of political risk is a qualitative analysis of the country's political setup and is generally evaluated by using a scoring system.

Economic Risk

Economic risk involves the risk that economic events within or outside a country will have an effect on flows from that country. These events can affect the ability of a country to honor its foreign debt and result in

- Total insolvency (default), repudiation
- Partial insolvency
- Temporary insolvency, moratorium
- Hidden insolvency

Repudiation is the outright cancellation of a borrower's foreign debt obligations and may also involve nationalization and expropriation of assets in the country. Repudiation per se has not occurred very often, some examples being China after the Maoist revolution in 1949 and Cuba after the takeover of power by Fidel Castro in 1961. Rescheduling of foreign debt obligations has been a feature of the most recent crises in financial markets. Large rescheduling operations took place in the wake of the Asian Crisis in 1997 (Korea in early 1998), the Russian Crisis in 1998, and the Argentina Crisis in 2001, which also led to Uruguay having to reschedule its foreign bonds. (See S&P and Moody's reports on recent rescheduling and defaults.) Most recently we have seen sovereign defaults in Belize in 2006 and in the Dominican Republic in 2006. (See for example Moody's "Sovereign Default and Recovery Rates, 1983–2007" for details.)

How Do We Evaluate Economic Risk?

We evaluate economic risk by analyzing economic data available on the country. Data must be taken from the most reliable sources available. These include the IMF, Organisation for Economic Co-operation and Development (OECD), World Bank, national statistics, and data provided by commercial data providers such as the Economist Intelligence Unit (EIU). A wide range of indicators can be used to assess an economy (Manasse et al., 2003).

There are two major areas that have to be addressed when analyzing a country's economic data:

1. *Potential:* How much wealth can an economy generate?
2. *Balance:* Internal and external balance.

Economic Potential

The amount of wealth an economy can generate is an important indicator for the future creditworthiness of a country. It is important to point out that countries differ vastly, depending on their level of economic development and their sectoral concentration, and as such the creditworthiness of a country will depend to a large extent on the fundamental economic setup of that particular country.

A number of indicators have been proven to be of significance when assessing country risk.

- *Population:* Countries with large populations will find their resources strained.
- *Level of education:* Countries with highly educated populations are likely to generate higher levels of income.
- *Resources:* Countries that are endowed with natural resources will obviously have more potential for wealth but will be more dependent on commodity prices, e.g., Gulf countries (oil), South Africa (gold and diamonds).

- *Economic structure*: Do we have a country with a large primary sector or more concentrated on manufacturing and services. In general, the concentration will point to different levels of development, with more developed countries having a larger manufacturing or services sector.
- *Economic growth*: Countries with sustainable and high growth rates will find it easier to reach higher levels of development and generate more wealth. In particular, high growth rates will allow for an increase in per capita income and wealth.
- *Inflation:* Low inflation rates point to a stable economy and a stable currency.
- *Unemployment*: Countries with high unemployment rates have large pools of unused resources, which can be a source of political unrest.
- *Investment*: The level of investment and its ratio to GDP show us whether a country is investing in new plant and thus increasing its capital base.
- Investment has to be viewed in close context with savings; i.e., is a country generating enough by way of savings to finance its investments or does it have to rely on foreign inflows to finance capital growth?

The most important economic indicators are the following:

- Gross domestic product (GDP), gross national product (GNP), industrial production: Both levels and growth rates are important, as also aggregate values and per capita. A large aggregate GDP in a country with a small population will point to a different level of development than a large GDP in a country with a very large population.
- Structure of GDP, i.e., the proportion that is generated in the primary, secondary, and tertiary sectors.
- Investment/GDP.
- Savings/GDP.
- Unemployment rates, underemployment.
- Inflation rate, annual average and month/month rates.

Internal and External Balance

Apart from the economic potential that a country has, it is important that the country has both a balanced budget and also a balance of payments that is not in deficit. In the ideal world, a country that has both a balanced budget as well as balance of payments is unlikely to face any kind of payments crisis. A sovereign that has a balanced budget is one that can finance its budgetary expenditures solely out of its domestic income. This refers to domestic expenditure that is incurred by the sovereign and includes the budget and all related expenditure. A country that is in external balance is able to finance its foreign payments out of its foreign income. This refers to all transactions that involve foreign currency (in particular imports of goods and services) and debt service. Both these areas are closely connected. For example, if a country is internally in imbalance, i.e., if it has a budget deficit, it will have to finance the budget deficit and may have to borrow overseas in order to finance the budget deficit, thus leading to an external imbalance.

Internal Balance

The main indicators that are of interest for country risk assessment are

- *Budget balance/GDP:* The budget deficit should not exceed 3 percent of GDP. The Maastricht Criteria explicitly call for a reduction of the budget deficit to below 3 percent.
- *Government debt/GDP:* Sustained budget deficits generally lead to an increase in government debt. This should not exceed 60 percent of GDP (Maastricht criteria and generally accepted norm). High levels of government debt are a burden for the fiscal position of a country and lead to crowding out.
- *Inflation:* Fiscal deficits can be financed in several ways. One is an increase in government debt; the other is an increase in the money supply, brought about by printing money. This leads to an increase in inflation. As a result, the inflation rate is considered a very important indicator — high rates of inflation are often brought about by high budget deficits, and point to a highly unstable situation within a country. For example, warning signs for internal imbalances are displayed in Box 23.1.

B O X   23.1

Warning signs for internal imbalances

- Sharp rises in the budget deficit; should not exceed 3 percent of GDP.
- Sharp rises in government debt; should not exceed 60 percent of GDP
- Sharp rise in inflation; points to inflationary forms of government financing

External Balance

The external balances of a country give us important information on the financial and liquidity position of a country in its international context. The external position of a country can be seen in its balance of payments. The balance of payments shows us the inflows and outflows in foreign exchange to and from a country. Countries with imbalances on their external accounts will find that they are creating a deficit on the external account, making the country's demand for foreign exchange greater than the amount the country can generate. Countries with external deficits will need to raise the necessary funds in foreign markets to cover their needs, thus resulting in an increase in foreign debt.

The main sources of information on external balances are therefore the country's balance of payments, data on foreign debt, and the exchange rate.

Indicators that have been proved to be relevant in the analysis of country risk analysis are the following:

- Trade balance: The trade balance tells us whether a country is exporting more (or less) than it imports.
- Exports/imports: This is the ratio of exports to imports and is an important indicator for whether a country is exporting more than it imports or vice versa.
- Current account balance/GDP: The balance on the current account shows us whether a country is generating enough foreign exchange from the export of goods and services and transfers to cover its imports of goods and services and expenditure on transfers. The current account position indicates to us the borrowing needs of a country. In general, developing countries that have large imports of capital goods tend to have

larger deficits on the current account than industrialised countries. The level of the deficit may vary considerably from year to year, depending on the volume of imports. Countries that have large current account deficits over a number of years may find that they are unsustainable. A current account deficit of between 4 and 6 percent of GDP is considered sustainable over the short term.

- International reserves: These are the reserves of foreign exchange, gold, and special drawing rights that are held by the national bank of a country and give us the liquidity position of a country.
- Import cover:

$$\frac{\text{International reserves}}{(\text{Imports of goods} + \text{imports of services})/12} = x \text{ months import cover}$$

The import cover gives us the ratio of foreign reserves to imports of goods and services, in months and indicates the number of months of imports that a country can finance if access to financing is cut off. The International Monetary Fund has stipulated that their member countries should hold reserves equivalent to an import cover of 3 months. Countries with low levels of import cover and low levels of reserves have weaker liquidity positions, and are likely to have difficulties servicing their debt. In general, import cover ranges from between below 1 month (Ukraine) to 12 months and more (India, Taiwan, and China).

- Total foreign debt (TFD): Total foreign debt shows us the total amount of foreign debt that all entities in a country have incurred. History has shown that large absolute amounts of foreign debt can pose a problem, even when the ratio of foreign debt to GDP is within acceptable levels. This is because, in the event of rescheduling, it is easier to come to terms with a small number of creditors over a smaller sum. Examples for countries with large absolute levels of debt that are small in comparison to GDP are Brazil and Russia. Countries with high debt-to-GDP ratios but low absolute levels of debt are Slovakia and Romania.

A reduction in foreign debt can be a result of an orderly repayment of foreign debt following surpluses in the current account; it can also be the result of rescheduling and debt forgiveness.

- Debt ratio:
  External debt/GDP:
  The debt ratio represents external debt as a proportion of GDP. Debt ratios range from 10 to 85 percent and become problematic beyond 50 percent, as this implies that a country is highly indebted. Low debt ratios do not, however, automatically imply that a country is creditworthy. They can also imply that the country has little or no access to international capital markets, thus keeping external debt low. The composition of foreign debt is an important factor when analyzing the debt situation of a country. In general, public debt will be of a longer term nature and cheaper to service than private debt, as the sovereign is likely to get better terms on the capital markets than its subjects. Long-term debt with a longer repayment profile is also considered easier to service than short-term debt that has to refinance at regular intervals. Bilateral debt is likely to be long-term government debt at concessionary terms, and multilateral debt is also likely to be long term but could come with any number of conditions

- Debt-to-exports ratio:
  TFD/XGS goods and services:
  This indicator can lie between 50 and 300 percent and shows us the relationship between foreign debt and exports.

- Short-term debt/foreign reserves: This is an important liquidity indicator and tells us whether short-term debt (maturity of less than 1 year) is covered by international reserves. This indicator shows us whether a country can repay its short-term lines out of its reserves if market sentiment changes and short-term lines are not extended, or whether we are likely to face a liquidity crisis. Short-term debt should never exceed reserves. During the Asian crisis, Korea was forced to reschedule its short-term debt since short-term debt exceeded its reserves by far.

- Debt-to-service ratio:
  Total debt service/exports of goods and services:
  The debt-to-service ratio indicates the proportion of income
  generated by exports of goods and services that has to be used to
  service debt payments (interest and principal repayments). If a
  country spends a large amount of its export revenues on its debt
  service, it obviously will have less foreign exchange for other
  necessities such as imports. This ratio should not exceed
  25 percent, especially if the country has no nondebt capital
  inflows to cover its deficits.

How Are External Deficits Financed?

A deficit on the current account, combined with debt service repayments,
gives one the financing requirement of a country. The financing requirement
can be covered in a number of ways. Deficits can be financed by inflows of
nondebt creating capital inflows or by external borrowing. Nondebt creating inflows on the capital account can be inflows of *portfolio investments*
and/or *foreign direct investment* (FDI). Hungary, for example, has managed
to finance its deficits via large inflows of foreign direct investments, as also
has Malaysia. Countries that have sustainable investment inflows can afford
to run up larger current account deficits, as they are able to generate their
own financing. In general, portfolio inflows are considered more problematic than FDI since portfolio investments can be withdrawn very quickly, as
was the case in the Asian countries during the Asian crisis of 1997. Foreign
direct investment is considered a more sustainable financing instrument, as
it is difficult to withdraw FDI from a country. Countries that attract large
amounts of investment will be able to build up their foreign reserves.

Countries that cannot finance their deficits via voluntary capital
inflows will resort to raising money on the international capital markets,
either by issuing bonds or by borrowing from banks or governments.
Countries with large financing requirements may also have other options
with regard to raising the necessary funds. Among these we have loans
from the IMF and the World Bank and bilateral government credits. These
avenues are in general open to the less-developed countries that have limited access to international capital markets. If this option is not open to
them, they may have to resort to drawing down their foreign reserves.

It is at this point, when market sentiment and fundamentals do not allow a country to borrow on the international markets and a draw down of reserves is the only way out, that a liquidity crisis comes about.

When studying the financing requirement of a particular country, one therefore has to differentiate between the different avenues open for financing, e.g., does the country have access to capital markets or is it eligible for concessionary loans from the IMF. Developing and emerging market economies may be able to draw on IMF loans, industrialized countries will probably only be able to issue bonds, as they are not eligible for multilateral lending. Should all possibilities fail and market sentiment deteriorate, the country is likely to face a payments crisis.

Evaluating Sovereign Risk

The sovereign risk analyst will therefore evaluate the sovereign or country risk of a country by analyzing the economic and political situation. The sovereign rating of a country, which is the product of a quantitative analysis of the data available and a qualitative analysis of the political situation, gives one an idea of the economic potential of a country, its liquidity and external financing position, and its political setup.

Economic data should be gathered from the best possible sources and analyzed at regular intervals. Trends should be evaluated and potential trouble spots identified. In particular, policy actions taken to rectify

T A B L E   23.1

Warning signs

Real GDP growth	<2% a year
Inflation	>10% a year
Unemployment	>10% a year
Fiscal deficit	>3% of GDP
Current account deficit	>4–6% of GDP
Reserves	<3 months import cover
Foreign debt	>50% of GDP
Debt service/exports	>25%
Investment and savings	<20% of GDP
Short-term debt/reserves	>60%

negative developments should be monitored closely. All these factors combine to give one a picture of the creditworthiness of a particular country (see Table 23.1).

SOVEREIGN RATINGS

Risk rating models attempt to capture country risk in quantitative models. Indicators are chosen and assigned a weighting within the model. The sum of weighted scores then leads to an index for country risk. Deterioration in risk variables will lead to deterioration in the rating score for economic risk. Banks may wish to set up their own internal models based on some of the indicators put forward above. Alternatively, banks may wish to draw on external assessments of country risk and a number of institutions provide external assessments of country risk. External evaluation models that are available to the general public are those published by *Euromoney* and the *Institutional Investor* twice a year.

The *Institutional Investor* index is published twice a year and is based on an index between 0 and 100, with 100 signifying the least chance of default. The index is based on information provided by leading international banks. The individual responses are weighted, giving greater importance to responses from banks with a wider country exposure and more sophisticated country analysis systems.

The *Euromoney* index is published twice a year and is a combination of an internal model based on a number of economic and political indicators and the information provided by international risk analysts and economists. The index lies between 0 and 100, with 100 being the best score. The OECD has developed a seven-grade rating model that is used by all national export credit agencies and is available on the Web sites of these agencies.

External credit rating agencies also provide ratings on a large number of sovereigns. However, the ratings published by these agencies are not public information ratings that are freely available. These ratings are produced at the wish of the entity to be rated, and ratings are available only to subscribers to the respective agencies. These include Moody's, Standard and Poor's, and Fitch as the major external credit rating agencies.

Banks may also wish to use market data on bonds and credit default swaps in order to assess the implied creditworthiness of a sovereign.

SETTING COUNTRY LIMITS

Banks will need to set limits on their country exposure in relation to their regulatory capital with sublimits, if considered necessary, for products, branches, maturity, etc., in order to manage their cross-border exposures. Banks may also set up regional exposure limits for country groups in order to capture contagion risks that may be inherent in particular regions and neighboring countries. Exposure should be monitored on an ongoing basis.

Although country risk per se will depend on the rating of a country, the quality of the portfolio will depend on the types of risks in the particular limit. Risk will vary with the maturity of the loan, the type of borrower, and the purpose of the loan. All other things being equal, the longer the maturity, the greater the uncertainty, and the higher is the risk involved. Governments are usually better risks than private banks and corporates. Trade finance and structured trade finance is usually more likely to be paid than commercial loans. Project finance has also proved to be less risky that straight loans.

In determining the size of a country limit, a bank will usually consider its business prospects in the country against the background of perceived country risk, constrained by its loss-taking capacity (see Box 23.2) (Ensor, 1981).

Only countries with an acceptable risk can be viewed as acceptable partners. It is obvious that countries with a better risk rating are less likely to fail, and therefore, the bank can afford to put at risk a larger proportion of its equity by exposure to such countries. Banks should decide which

B O X   23.2

Setting country limits

Limit proposals will determined by the following main criteria:
  Risk: Rating
  Market size:
  • GDP
  • Imports

  Diversification:
  • Consolidated capital
  • Market share (derived from BIS claims)

rating scale is to be taken as a basis for setting country limit, an internal scale or an external one. Market size is the second most important criterion. It appears clear that exposure can be greater in Germany than in Switzerland although both are first-class risks. The level of debt a country can safely carry depends not least on the size of its GDP and shows borrowing capacity. Banks may wish to limit their exposure to a country in terms of a percentage of that country's GDP. External borrowing requirements are, to some extent, related to imports, and thus, imports provide an idea of market size with respect to borrowing needs. Limits should therefore take a certain percentage of the imports of a country as a benchmark. Diversification is necessary to minimize potential losses.

Banks may wish and need to limit their exposure to a given percentage of the bank's capital, in order to minimize losses; however large the market and negligible the risk, capital acts as a constraint. Banks will have to decide how much capital is available to cover any losses and assign certain percentages of their capital to rating grades, with a higher percentage in lower risk categories and a lower percentage in higher risk categories. The choice of these percentages will depend on the bank's strategy and international focus.

Although a large market share may be desirable in some countries, risk is lower when market share is smaller as other banks will help in bailing out in case of debt-servicing problems. Banks should set a threshold beyond which they do not wish to have a share in the foreign commercial debt of a country. The result of such an exercise gives us benchmark figures that act as guidelines in setting limits. The *conservative* approach is to take the *lowest* figure; the *aggressive* approach is to take the *average* figure.

COUNTRY RISK MITIGATION

Banks might find it necessary to mitigate country risk, because either approved limits are full or transactions do not fit into the risk profile that is defined within the risk policy. Deterioration in country risk could lead to a reduction in limits, thus necessitating a reduction in risk.

Risk mitigation can take a number of forms. As in classic risk participations, banks can reduce their exposure to counterparties in a particular country by selling the risks to other financial investors.

Banks may wish to insure their risks with insurance companies. Insurable political risks include expropriation, currency inconvertibility, moratorium, and nationalization. Government export credit agencies will insure both political and economic risks in connection with export transactions from the home country. Multilateral organizations such as the Multilateral Investment Guarantee Agency, an arm of the World Bank, provide political risk coverage for a wide variety of transactions, including shareholder loans to subsidiaries and equity insurance.

Credit default swaps (CDSs) can also be used to reduce exposure in a particular country. A single-name CDS will give one protection against the default of the customer. Credit default swaps can be used on a single-name basis for corporate customers and as protection of exposure to the sovereign. Credit default swaps on a single-name basis, if tenor, amount, and currency are congruent with the original transaction, are accepted by the regulators as risk mitigants. Many banks also use CDS on the sovereign as a proxy for hedging country risks, assuming that even if the sovereign does not default, the CDS would cover some portion of losses incurred if a commercial counterparty defaulted as a result of a country risk event. Statistical tests show a fairly high correlation between the development of CDS spreads and country risk, but the basis risk continues to be high, implying that this particular form of protection is more suitable for those markets where the basis risk is low.

CONCLUSION

Country risk and country risk management have become major issues for the international financial community over the last two decades. Financial institutions and firms engaged globally will find it necessary to analyze the risks involved in their cross-border activities and set appropriate limits to their exposure. A wide range of analysis tools is available to estimate country risk. External agencies provide regular information on their assessment of sovereign risk. In addition, a wide range of tools can help mitigate country risk when necessary, thus making it easier to manage country risks in a given portfolio.

REFERENCES

Basle Committee on Banking Supervision (1982) Management of Banks International Lending (Country Risk Analysis and Country Exposure Measurement and Control). Basel, Switzerland.

Ensor, R. (1981) *Assessing Country Risk*. London: Euromoney Publications.

Manasse, P., Roubini, N., and Schimmelpfeng, A. (2003) Predicting Sovereign Debt Crises. IMF, Working paper, Washington, D.C.

Institute of International Finance (2007) *Capital Flows to Emerging Market Economies*. Washington, D.C.

Suter C. (1992) *Debt Cycles in the World Economy: Foreign Loans, Financial Crises and Debt Settlements, 1820–1990*. Boulder, CO: Westview Press.

Winkler, M. (1933) *Foreign Bonds, An Autopsy: A Study of Defaults and Repudiations of Government Obligations*. Philadelphia, PA: Roland Swain.

Distressed Credit Assets of German Lending Banks

Thomas C. Knecht and Michael Blatz

ABSTRACT

Distressed debt management for corporate bank customers has changed considerably in Germany in response to a changed legal framework and capital market conditions. Until 2003, the decision was whether to actively monitor the turnaround process or write off the loan. Since then, new asset classes have been established and distressed investors have emerged on the market. The key questions are the following: Do German banks have the organizational structures required for state-of-the-art workout management? Are German banks capable of using adequate turn-around financing tools?

This chapter focuses on the general framework and tools banks use to carry out turnaround and workout management. In doing so, the authors discuss the necessity and effectiveness of organizational structures and relevant turnaround tools. The chapter also examines the extent to which German banks have the skills and expertise required to successfully handle distressed debt in a new framework. In conclusion, the chapter presents the results of an empirical survey on workout management at German banks.

INTRODUCTION

As corporate bond markets become more important for banks' lending business, subperforming loans or nonperforming loans are becoming more important as true "credit assets." When corporate debtors can no longer meet all or part of their interest and repayment obligations, such debt is classified as *distressed*. Special distressed debt or workout departments at banks take charge. When the ratings go down, the banks' cost of capital goes up, and their financial position is negatively affected. To reduce the balance sheet effect and minimize their exposure at risk, banks are using more and more financial derivatives to shift their risk to the corporate bond market. As ties with their corporate customers loosen[1] and banks start diversifying their credit risk by means of syndicated loans, banks have a firm grip on their credit risks even when their loans turned bad. Capital market-based products make it possible for banks to shift their risks to the capital market, removing the risk-bearing items from their own balance sheets and still maintaining their dominant position in the corporate sector.

Simultaneously, the development of the corporate bond market highlights the correlation between syndicated loan volumes and the volume of distressed assets. In Germany, the volume of syndicated bank loans in 2006 was almost €246.7 billion, nearly twice the previous year's figure. At the same time, the volume of loans granted to domestic corporate customers leveled off at about €2.2 trillion, and the banks reduced their bad debt provisions by approximately 70 percent. Obviously, the capital market has become a major factor of corporate finance in Germany: By selling their loan risks to the corporate bond market, banks could offer their customers a financing option and without involving any write-downs even in the event of distressed debt. In mid-2007, however, the subprime crisis hit the United States, massively restricting the option of shifting risk to the capital markets. Trading in loan derivates has ground to a standstill as a result of the general insecurity on the financial markets. Syndicated loans can today be sold only at significant discounts. As shifting risk to the capital markets becomes more difficult, distressed debt is creeping

---

[1] In Germany, companies used to maintain close and long-term relationships with a local bank; this was referred to as the *house bank principle*.

back into bank balance sheets, sometimes causing massive write-downs. This implies that the requirements for banks' risk management are becoming stricter, and as a consequence, banks should be shifting their attention to their own workout units by creating rigorous credit risk management for their distressed loans. The key challenges for banks lie in the organizational structures and the tools for financing in workout situations.

The organizational setup is stipulated in general legislation such as MaRisk (the minimum requirements for risk management) in Germany. As long as a debtor services a loan according to the underlying loan agreement, it is usually managed by the bank's regular front office. When the debtor defaults on or delays interest payments or repayments or overdraws his or her credit line, this can trigger a lower bond rating. As a result, the loan may be transferred from regular front-office support to a back-office unit that specializes in distressed debt. Different banks deal very differently with this back-office function, and some distribute the loan according to the debtor's sales volume to the different organizational back-office units. Other banks base their decision on the strategy required in the circumstances. The support mechanisms, procedures, and competencies of this "distressed" asset category are key success factors and should be in line with regulatory requirements.

The tools and support approaches designed to help distressed corporate bank customers have drastically changed over the past few years. When a distressed loan is transferred to back-office functions, banks have four generic options for action: sell, wait, liquidate, or turn around. Although liquidating and selling the loan improve the creditor's risk position, it usually terminates the customer relationship, which can jeopardize sales of other financial products and harm the bank's reputation. To maintain the customer relationship and return the loan to regular support, banks must actively turn the debtor around. At this stage, management, owners, and creditors work together to nurse the distressed company back to good health. To do so, the banks have a wide range of financial and nonfinancial tools at their disposal. Nonfinancial contributions usually aim to support accounting and management. Financial turnaround tools include debt deferrals, waivers, turnaround loans, and debt-equity swaps. Taking a stake in the debtor's equity usually presents the banks with significant challenges in terms of structures and staff.

The changed economic and legal framework is affecting the importance, effectiveness, and procedures of established distressed debt management at German banks. How will the German banks' current and future workout business fit in with their current structures and financing options? A special focus should be on how organizational structures that are set up in response to MaRisk requirements will meet the changed workout requirements. At the same time, we need to look into how effectively banks are using existing turnaround tools.

To answer the questions raised, this chapter is organized as follows: The second section looks at the organizational requirements of workout management and presents selected turnaround tools. These will then be reflected in the third section, where we present the results of an empirical survey on distressed debt management. In conclusion, the fourth section provides a summary and highlights the implications.

CONCEPTUAL FOUNDATIONS OF WORKOUT MANAGEMENT

Basics

Definitions

Neither German nor international usage offers a clear-cut definition of nonperforming loans, i.e., distressed credit assets, or distressed debt for short (Knecht and Schoon, 2007). The differences are to be found in the legal, fiscal, accounting, and supervisory details. Most definitions, however, include a debtor defaulting on some or all of her obligations. Where bank loans are concerned, the loans in question have already been canceled or the banks have at least a reason to cancel their loans. The following question remains: How long or how often must a debtor be in default to qualify as distressed? If the debtor has filed for insolvency, their debt is always classified as distressed.

The basic definition was developed in the United States where a corporate bond with an interest rate 1,000 basis points or more over its respective Treasury benchmark meets the conventional definition of distressed debt. There are two reasons why this definition does not serve for the German market:

- The definition is based on the structure of the U.S. corporate bond market where secondary market liquidity is much higher and trading is much more active.
- History has shown that risk premiums can be very volatile — more and more often, the real threshold is below 1,000 basis points.

It does not help for definition purposes when rating agencies classify certain corporate bonds as "speculative grade" (rating of BB or lower). The ratings usually lag behind loan developments, and most distressed debt in Germany does not come as bonds with ratings but is traditionally financed through bank loans.

The distinction between subperforming loans (SPL) and nonperforming loans (NPL) is particularly difficult. Distressed debt covers both terms, and they both refer exclusively to debt. When people talk about distressed debt, it is difficult to know if they mean subperforming or nonperforming loans — regrettably, as the distinction is a useful one. Debt is usually referred to as *subperforming* when the debtor is not likely to repay the principal in full and pay interest and commissions and the underlying loan agreement has not (yet) been canceled. Debt is considered *nonperforming* when repayment in full and payment of interest and commissions is not to be expected and the loan agreement has already been canceled. According to this definition, NPL servicing usually focuses on processing loan commitments that have already been canceled.

MaRisk Sets the Regulatory Framework

MaRisk defines the minimum requirements for risk management in Germany and was issued by BaFin, the German Financial Supervisory Authority, to implement Articles 22 and 123 of EU Directive 2006/48/EC as of 2007. The regulations of Basel II and MaRisk are designed to guarantee the highest possible degree of stability in the banking sector, but this also limits the banks' room for maneuver in their management of loan risk.

MaRisk's stipulation that banks' front-office functions should be completely separated from their back-office functions is nothing new. Similar arrangements were already prescribed in MaH.[2] Front-office functions must be clearly separated from back-office functions in risk-relevant business all the way through the organization, right up to board level, and must be upheld even when managers take interdependent responsibility. This is designed to spread risk, ensure efficient self-control, and avoid sales units pursuing their own interests in loan commitments.

By inspecting audit reports, BaFin tries to make sure that credit institutions implement and maintain the minimum requirements. Where audit reports (e.g., year-end financial statements or special audits) show evidence that specific requirements have not been met, BaFin is obliged to take action.[3]

Although MaRisk limits the banks' room for maneuver, it does not provide detailed instructions for all the relevant structures and processes. Indeed, it includes many opt-out clauses that provide banks with the flexibility they require for their business while also providing specific structures.

Organizational Aspects of Distressed Debt Management

Separating Distressed Debt from Front-Office Functions

BaFin allows banks significant freedom in allocating distressed debt within their organization. When a bank's corporate debt meets the criteria for distressed debt defined by BaFin, it is only obliged to involve an employee who is familiar with workout situations. The bank is not required to set up a dedicated workout unit. This leniency is clearly designed to protect small banks. It is not even necessary to shift debt processing completely to the in-house workout specialist. The bank must simply make sure that the employee in charge takes all the necessary actions and manages the case in question. Therefore, it is not necessarily the back office that is in charge of workout management. BaFin stipulates that workout can stay with front-office functions, provided units that are separate from them supervise the workout process. In other words, where distressed debt is not handled

---

[2] "The minimum requirements for the trading business of credit institutions," dated October 23, 1995, especially No. 4 "Organization and trading activities."
[3] See § 6 Abs. 2 and 3 KWG (s. 6, par. 2 and 3, German Banking Act).

outside front-office functions, it must be the responsibility of units that are separate from them. In this context, *responsibility* refers to the power to make decisions in all risk-relevant issues, i.e., in particular in the distressed debt process (e.g., turnaround loan approvals), negotiations with third parties involved in restructuring efforts, and the continuous supervision of distressed debt handling based on validity checks. BaFin endeavors to maintain the advantages of workout management that is close to the front office where relevant expertise is required to handle corporate loans efficiently. Its aim is merely to ensure that a "workout master" acts as a decision-making unit that is independent of the front-office functions.

Exceptions for Less Risk-Relevant Business

Apart from these process-related reliefs, MaRisk allows for a number of risk-related simplifications. Each bank can, based on its own discretion and taking into account § 25a KWG (s. 25a, German Banking Act), define which businesses or segments are risk relevant and which ones are less risky. The basis for determining the risk relevance of loans usually is the borrower's total debt, while total risk capacity is to be checked at a portfolio level. Risk capacity is to be defined and monitored in line with the bank's specific requirements and must be separated from the front-office functions and backed up by in-house guidelines. Where loans fall below the defined threshold, a simple decision is required. For such loans, e.g., with corporate customers, a structural separation between front-office and back-office functions is therefore unnecessary.

Whether it makes sense to have skilled workout managers in both front-office and independent functions should be decided on a case-by-case basis. Generally speaking, the workout specialists should be in the back office, where decisions about risk-relevant business are made. A key account manager can always be involved in individual steps of the workout process.

Duties of Distressed Debt Managers

When a debtor's company encounters trouble, its loans must be taken care of by a workout manager. The workout manager must identify suitable financial action: suspend or reschedule repayments, extend deadlines, ask owners to inject fresh capital as well as discuss and decide on nonfinancial strategies. When the matter at hand is complex or when a comprehensive turnaround opinion is to be produced, in-house workout units often find themselves overstretched. They must identify the problem, determine if the debtor can and should be restructured, find out if the turnaround strategy is convincing, decide if a turnaround loan should be granted, and decide whether an interim manager is required. In such cases, not only is it advisable to involve an external specialist, but an obligation to fulfill the requirements of adequate risk management according to § 25a Abs. 1 KWG (s. 225a, par. 1, German Banking Act) may be needed. If a bank decides to provide financial support to a distressed company, then it should commission a specialized management consultancy or audit firm to examine whether the distressed company can and should be turned around and to draw up a turnaround strategy. This helps deal with the massive civil liability risks involved when banks audit their own commitments and avoids charges of delaying insolvency proceedings. Banks must examine suitable organizational structures for efficient and sustainable workout management while taking the regulatory options into account and map the business processes as well as invest these with the required powers and instruments.

Selected Turnaround Tools Used by Banks

Turnaround Loan, Deferral, Waiver, and Subordination

Banks have a large number of tools designed to turn distressed debtors around. Turnaround tools must help restore the debtor to good health and enable the company to continue operating. The tools available either inject fresh money into the business or relieve the debtor's balance sheets on the debt or equity side. They include the following:

- Turnaround loans: When a bank or bank pool (group of banks) grants another loan or extends existing credit lines, this is called a *turnaround loan* (Schiereck and Weigl, 2006). Banks grant such loans to distressed debtors when they are short of liquidity but not yet insolvent. The term of the loan is usually based on the turnaround strategy. The interest charged usually takes the liquidity bottleneck into account, which means that it is not in line with the risk involved (also known as *turnaround interest*). Therefore, providers of turnaround loans increasingly demand a share in the profits of the restructured debtor. By granting a turnaround loan, the banks hope to have their loans fully repaid once the debtor has been successfully restructured.

- Deferrals and subordination: To stabilize the debtor's cash position, banks can also defer repayment and suspend interest payments. Subordination is another effective tool for workout. Under such an arrangement, the creditor does not receive any payments in the event of insolvency before all other creditors have been completely satisfied. Comprehensive subordination can mean that obligations that fall under the arrangement do not have to be shown as liabilities in the event of negative equity.

- Waivers: Here, the creditor relieves the debtor of all or part of his or her clearly defined financial obligations (principal or interest). It should be noted, however, that waivers represent extraordinary income and a provision may have to be charged based on a debtor warrant (Strüber and von Donat, 2003).

The legal framework in Germany implies that traditional turnaround tools used by banks do not usually involve any equity investments for the creditors. Instead, they concentrate on different combinations of debt. Today's more global focus of distressed debt management and closer involvement of institutional investors imply that equity-related turnaround tools are becoming more and more important. The lending banks are called upon to face the challenge of using equity as a turnaround tool.

Debt–Equity Swaps

Perhaps the most widely discussed turnaround tool with an equity focus is debt–equity swap. Developed originally within the UK and U.S. legal framework, debt–equity swaps are now also gaining importance in Germany. The focus of such swaps is not on injecting fresh capital but on exchanging existing debt for equity. The creditor injects all or part of his accounts receivable from the distressed debtor into the debtor's equity by way of a capital increase from noncash contributions (Hass et al., 2006). The accounts receivable thus contributed become extinguished through what is called a *confusion of rights* (creditor and debtor being the same person). This raises the debtor's equity ratio, overcoming or relieving the previous negative equity position. At the same time, it lowers the debtor's financing costs as interest-bearing debt is reduced, pushing up the prospects of future profitability. It does not, however, mean that cash is injected. In accounting terms, debt-equity swaps take place on the liabilities side of the balance sheet.

By gaining shares in the debtor's equity, the former creditor can benefit from improvements in the debtor's position following successful restructuring. This makes the transaction very attractive to the creditor, who can now fully benefit from any future profits generated by the successfully restructured debtor. In the absence of a debt-equity swap, the creditor can only recover his receivables plus interest—despite the massive risks involved. By becoming an owner of the company, the former creditor can also make sure he or she has an impact on the management of the distressed debtor, while the relative share of the former owners decreases through the transaction. Today, distressed debt investors are making increasing use of debt-equity swaps to gain influence over the distressed debtor. They do this by buying doubtful debt and then swapping it for equity. Where debt is swapped for equity, the financier becomes an owner. For German banks in particular, this means significant personnel and structural complexity, especially in light of the opportunities enjoyed by active distressed investors.

AN EMPIRICAL INVESTIGATION OF WORKOUT MANAGEMENT

Background, Data, and Methodology

Despite its great importance, very few empirical studies have investigated the question of workout in German banks. Part of the reason is that getting hold of data can be tricky since banks are often unwilling to provide such information. However, Knecht and Dickopf (2007) successfully investigate the current situation with regard to workout in German banks by means of a series of expert interviews. The study describes the key details and structural aspects of distressed debt management in leading commercial banks (Geschäftsbanken), state banks (Landesbanken), and savings banks (Sparkassen) and identifies the main characteristics and trends in this area.

The data stems from five commercial banks, five state banks, and five savings banks, each of them key players in their sector. These are the largest types of bank in Germany in terms of credit volume, accounting for more than half the total volume of loans. The analysis reveals clear differences in how the banks handle distressed loans—partly due to the difference in the average size of the banks and partly owing to differences in policy, objectives, and the banks' self-perception.[4]

The data were collected by means of telephone interviews with the individuals responsible for distressed debt management or workout in the banks. A structured questionnaire was used to elicit key data on the issues examined in the study. Other comments and details relating to the sector mentioned during the interviews were also recorded.

Selected Findings on Workout in German Banks

Organizational Implications

The organizational implications outlined below do not represent a comprehensive or statistically significant investigation of how German banks implement the current legislation. However, they shed some useful light on certain structural differences between the three main types of institution: commercial banks, state banks and savings banks.

- Volume of workout cases: The commercial banks included in the study handle an average of 298 cases per year in their workout departments. This is the highest level of the three types of bank investigated. State banks are not far behind, with an average of 270 cases of workout, while savings banks handle a somewhat smaller number of cases—154 on average.[5] The study also investigated the number of employees in the workout department. This indicates the level of support per case offered by the bank. For savings banks, the case load per employee was around 11 cases, for state banks around six cases, and for commercial banks just three cases. This implies that the commercial banks show a greater awareness of distressed credit assets and so offer a greater

---

[4] In addition to leading banks, smaller banks and savings banks were also contacted on a random basis. However, the majority responded that the volume of their loans in workout and the size of the relevant departments were too small to be of interest to the current study.

[5] Commerical banks in particular usually have separate organizational units or subsidiaries that deal with smaller loans. This probably accounts for their larger total number of workout cases they handle.

F I G U R E   24.1

Split of workout volume by revenue of debtor in Germany

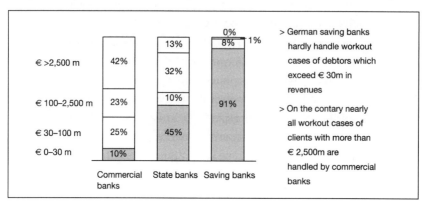

Source: Knecht and Dickopf (2007)

level of support per case. However, the size of the debt should also be taken into account (see Figure 24.1).

- Size of workout cases: Borrowers with larger balance sheets or loans have more complex financing structures and require greater coordination of creditors than is needed for smaller debts. They also require greater resources on the part of the banks. Grouping workout cases on the basis of the borrower's revenue class reveals that borrowers with revenues of over €2.5 billion represent 42 percent of workout cases in commercial banks. For state banks, these large customers account for just 3 percent of workout cases, while savings banks have no customers in this class. Instead, savings banks show a clear concentration of customers with up to €30 million in revenues, who account for 91 percent of cases. This class also forms the largest group of customers for state banks. Commercial banks have the largest average revenue size in their workout portfolio, followed by state banks and savings banks. Thus the average revenue size is in line with the distribution of the volume in the workout department or the size of the type of bank, measured on the basis of average total assets. This distribution of revenues supports our assumption regarding the level of support offered by the banks: Commercial banks, on average, have customers in workout with larger revenues. Such cases require greater employee capacity than for customers with smaller revenues, as they involve more complex financing structures and a larger number of stakeholders (including equity investors as well as banks).

- Turnaround strategies: The survey also examines the behavior of different types of bank in terms of their strategies for dealing with debts—sale, liquidation, or turnaround (including "wait and see"). Savings banks actively pursue turnaround in over half (56 percent) of the cases and liquidate the other 44 percent; they do not sell debts as a rule. The state banks examined in the survey sell an average of 25 percent of cases, the highest level of the three types of bank in the survey. They give turnaround and liquidation roughly the same weight—40 percent of cases undergo turnaround and 36 percent go for liquidation. Commercial banks liquidate 34 percent of cases, a somewhat smaller proportion than state banks, and carry out turnaround for 51 percent, almost as high a level as for savings banks. The low tendency of banks in general to sell distressed debt, especially in the case of savings banks, is worth noting. In the expert interviews, almost all the banks mentioned that the savings banks were highly committed to their customers, most of them are based locally. This is due to the strong local orientation of the savings banks business model, which means that on top of losing customers, they are also afraid of damaging their reputation in their local area. State banks and commercial banks are generally less involved in their local area. Moreover, they have a sufficient volume of workout cases to warrant separate departments specializing in distressed debt transactions. The banks in the survey considered selling debts only in the following situations:

1. The option of sale seems attractive in a cost-benefit calculation.
2. The bank's influence on possible turnaround is very low due to their low level of participation.
3. Internal disagreements mean that the chances of developing and implementing a turnaround concept in the immediate future are low.

Savings banks are the fastest at deciding how to deal with workout cases, while commercial banks on average take the longest amount of time to do so. As with the level of support, the average size and therefore complexity of commercial banks' cases are probably the key factors here—the more complex the case, the more time and effort needed to examine the debt in detail and hence the longer the decision process. The decision process at savings banks is also simpler, as the option of selling the debt can generally be dismissed from the outset, as it is incompatible with their business policy.

This general examination of the practice of workout in German banks reveals a clear tendency. Commercial banks deal with the biggest cases of restructuring and provide a relatively high level of support. However, it remains to be seen whether their current organizational setup can cope with the complexity of this greater level of support and is able to provide the expertise required.

Use of Turnaround Instruments

The survey shows that German banks still favor turnaround instruments involving the borrower's debt capital, whereby these tools range from bringing in fresh money to subordination. When asked about possible action in the area of debt, 92 percent of banks specifically mention reducing interest in the form of turnaround interest, deferrals, and waivers as well as injecting fresh money (turnaround loans). By contrast, subordination is mentioned as a frequently used turnaround instrument by just 25 percent of the banks surveyed. A detailed analysis of individual cases is necessary to determine clear preferences for different tools (Figure 24.2).

The study also examined specifically the use of equity-based turnaround instruments allowing us to analyze the impact of changes in the general environment. Participants stated that in the majority of cases when they used an equity-based turnaround instrument, it was a debt-equity swap—58 percent of respondents named this as the equity-based instrument that they used. Some 33 percent said that in cases of crisis, they actively requested new equity from the owners or required that they find new owners if necessary. Only around a quarter of respondents mentioned the use of mezzanine financing products as a common turnaround instrument in the area of equity.

Almost all the experts described actions focusing on the borrower's equity as the exception rather than the rule. Debt-equity swaps were used

Most frequently applied restructuring tools in Germany
(Number of nominations)

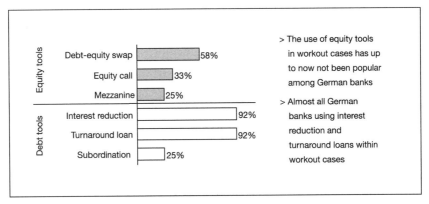

Source: Knecht and Dickopf (2007)

as a turnaround instrument by 58 percent of banks, but the number of
cases in which they were used was small. The types of debt-capital instruments used are highly consistent across all types of bank.

Future Development of Workout Departments

As well as investigating data on the structure and instruments used by
leading commercial banks, state banks and savings banks, the study also
aimed to find out how the experts expected their own departments to
develop in the coming years. The following issues were raised repeatedly:

- Give greater weight to the option of selling: Almost all the
  experts considered selling distressed debt to be an attractive
  option. It should be borne in mind that the price achieved by the
  sale is a key decision factor, and one that is determined by the
  capital market options.
- Expand the business model: Some experts are considering
  extending the business model used in their workout departments.
  This would include product-related developments such as
  supporting structured finance cases, as well as new customer-
  related ideas such as offering other banks full support for their
  distressed debt.

- Turn cost centers into profit centers: Nearly all banks investigated in the survey have been thinking for many years about changing their workout department from a cost center into a profit center. (As a cost center, the workout department receives a set budget and must account for its costs without making any profits; as a profit center, it would be responsible for both its own profits and costs, and it could draw up its own profit and loss accounts.) The added value of pursuing this option should be investigated separately.

As far as the future development of the sector is concerned, banks are generally well aware of the fact that foreign investors have an increasing influence on the German markets for distressed debts and companies. The general opinion is that this tendency is likely to increase over time.

CONCLUSION

This short review of the empirical findings on the state of workout in German banks and its conceptual foundations brings to light a certain discontinuity between the conceptual requirements and the challenges of the market.

The business of distressed debts is increasingly coming under the influence of international investors. Distressed investors have different objectives to those of German banks in their workout operations, and the tools they employ are different. Banks aim to manage the distressed debt and the corresponding risk as far as possible, with the aim of recovering the loan. Distressed investors, on the other hand, view the purchase, management, and sale of a distressed debt as an investment and speculate on the profit potential that can be generated over and above the repayment of the loan.

To date, few standard structures exist for the practice of workout in Germany. We have outlined the major differences between different types of banks, but there are also sometimes large deviations from the average values within one type of bank. The only clear similarities occur in the banks' choice of instruments for turnaround. Equity-based contributions are very rarely demanded, and the range of tools involving debt capital is by and large the same for all banks.

So where does that leave us? German banks show clear preferences as far as turnaround instruments are concerned. They are also relatively unwilling to actively buy and sell debt. By contrast, distressed investors have much greater options. They have a wide range of methods for supporting a distressed company and in so doing gaining control over it, realigning it, and directly participating in increasing its value. These include not just debt-capital actions but also equity-based actions. We should therefore continue to monitor whether traditional workout, in the form in which it is practiced today, is still truly competitive. Certain banks have already become aware of the need to adapt to the international market for distressed credit assets and are introducing appropriate professional methods.

REFERENCES

Hass, D., Schreiber, W., and Tschauner, H. (2006) Sanierungsinstrument Debt for Equity Swap. Hommel, U., Knecht, T.C., und Wohlenberg, H. (Hrsg.): *Handbuch Unternehmensrestrukturierung: Grundlagen, Konzepte, Maßnahmen*, pp. 841–874.

Knecht, T.C. and Dickopf, C. (2007). Kreditrisikomanagement und Workout 2007—Status Quo, Working paper, pp. 1–15.

Knecht, T.C. and Schoon, S. (2007). Distressed Assets—Risiko und Ertragsstruktur einer Investitionsklasse, Euroforum (Hrsg.): *Schriftlicher Management-Lehrgang Distressed Investments— Bewertung, Erwerb und Restrukturierung angeschlagener Assets*, Edition one, Lecture 1, Düsseldorf, pp. 1–113.

Schiereck, D. and Weigl, T. (2006). Prognose von Sanierungskreditvergaben in Deutschland. Hommel, U., Knecht, T.C., und Wohlenberg, H. (Hrsg.): *Handbuch Unternehmensrestrukturierung: Grundlagen, Konzepte, Maßnahmen*, pp. 934–959.

Strüber, M., and von Donat, C. (2003). Die ertragssteuerliche Freistellung von Sanierungsgewinnen durch das BMF-Schreiben vom 27.03.2003. *Betriebsberater*, 2003: 2036ff.

INDEX

ABCP. *See* Asset-backed commercial paper
ABS. *See* Asset-backed securities
Accelerated failure time (AFT) models, 223, 226, 235, 238
Acceptance credits, 106–107
Accounting, 21–36
    asymmetric, xiv, 28, 35, 36
    example of treatments, 33–35
    hedge, 28–31, 33–36
    introduction to, 22–23
    reporting, external *v.* internal management, 203, 205
Acerbi, C., 89
Active advisor, 14, 15, 17
Actual capital, 84–85
Ad hoc syndication, 112
Administrative cost, 6
Advance Payment Guarantee, 109
Advanced Internal Rating-Based Approach (AIRB), 43, 51, 87–88, 90
Adverse selection problems, 42, 228, 230, 240, 241
AFT. *See* Accelerated failure time models
Agarwal, V., 327
Agency problems, 225, 228–233, 241
AIRB. *See* Advanced Internal Rating-Based Approach
Akayke and Schwarz information criterions, 238
ALM. *See* Asset and liability management
Amortization, 113, 115, 116, 190–192, 193, 401
Andersen, L., 296, 298
Arbitrage
    capital structure, 273
    convertible, 325, 327–329
    fixed-income, 325, 328–331
    regulatory, 58, 63
    trades, 369–370, 372, 378, 379, 390
Archimedean copulas, 173, 176, 179
Arrangement fee, 229
ASRF. *See* Asymptotic single risk factor framework
Asset(s), xiii–xiv
    classes, 59
    CPM and, 10–11
    owner of, 12–13
    provisioning, 203
    transfer, 11, 101
Asset allocation
    within credit portfolios, responsibility for, 12
    with fixed-income hedge fund strategies, 341–344
    without fixed-income hedge fund strategies, 339–341
Asset and liability management (ALM), 273
Asset swap package, 27–28, 29
Asset value correlation, 132–133, 135
Asset value, terms for describing, 146

Asset-backed commercial paper (ABCP) program, 49
Asset-backed securities (ABS), 135, 137–138, 280
Asset-swap (ASW) spread, 251, 370, 371–375, 379
ASW. *See* Asset-swap spread
Asymmetric accounting, xiv, 28, 35, 36
Asymptotic single risk factor (ASRF) framework, 129
Available for sale assets, 25

Back testing algorithm, steps in, 192–193
Backhaus, J., 146
BaFin (German Supervisory Authority), 56, 447–449
Balance, internal and external, 431–435
Bank for International Settlements (BIS), 350, 425
Bankruptcy, 165, 166, 200, 203, 249, 399, 402
Banks, xiii, 121, 203, 443–459
Barro, D., 145–147, 149
Barth, J., 235
Base case scenario, 137–138
Base correlation, 294–296
Base correlation skew, 295, 297
Basel Committee on Banking Supervision, 39.
    See also Basel II
Basel II, xiv, 16, 273, 447
    amendments in, 43–56, 62, 64
    ASRF framework, 129
    Basel I *v.,* 40–41, 43, 45–46, 50–52, 54, 56–57, 61–63, 85
    capital relief and, 60, 63, 68, 275, 420
    credit derivatives and, 256, 267
    credit risk and, 40–43, 51–56
    diversification and, 6
    EL and, 67–78
    general principles of, 40–43, 59
    investment decisions impacted by, 39–64
    outstanding issues regarding, 60–62
    Pillar 1, 61
    Pillar 2, 43, 61
    Pillar 3, 43, 78
    regulatory treatment of shares in a fund according to, 56–60
    securitization transactions according to, 44–51
    Standardized Approach of, 41–42, 45–47, 50–52, 57–59, 62–64
Basis, measuring, 373–376
Basis package, factors influencing, 372–379
Basis trades, 369–394
    examples of, 379–394
    hedges and, 376–379
    negative, 369, 371, 376, 385–394
    positive, 369, 371, 379–386
    relative value and, 370–372
Basket credit derivatives, 277–299
    recent developments and models for evaluating, 296–299